Delicious
Healthy Eating

Delicious
Healthy Eating

Mouth-watering recipes for a low fat lifestyle

edited by Anne Sheasby

HERMES
HOUSE

This edition is published by Hermes House

Hermes House is an imprint of Anness Publishing Ltd
Hermes House, 88–89 Blackfriars Road, London SE1 8HA
tel. 020 7401 2077; fax 020 7633 9499; info@anness.com

A CIP catalogue record for this book is available from the British Library.

Publisher: Joanna Lorenz
Senior Editor: Linda Fraser
Designers: Sara Kidd and Bill Mason
Photographers: Karl Adamson, Edward Allwright, Steve Baxter,
James Duncan, Amanda Heywood, Don Last,
Michael Michaels, Patrick McLeavey, Thomas Odulate, Peter Reilly
Recipes: Carla Capalbo, Laura Washburn, Stephen Wheeler, Christine France,
Shirley Gill, Roz Denny, Annie Nichols, Catherine Atkinson, Maggie Pannell,
Kit Chan, Sue Maggs and Christine Ingram
Home Economists: Wendy Lee, Jane Stevenson, Elizabeth Wolf-Cohen, Kit Chan,
Kathryn Hawkins and Carla Capalbo
Stylists: Blake Minton, Kirsty Rawlings, Fiona Tillett, Hilary Guy, Thomas Odulate,
Madeleine Brehaut and Jo Harris

Previously published as *Low Fat Low Cholesterol*

1 3 5 7 9 10 8 6 4 2

CONTENTS

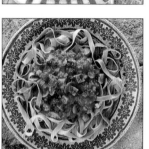

INTRODUCTION

Cooking and eating good food is one of life's greatest pleasures – and there's nothing wrong with enjoying good food, except that for too long good often meant fatty. Butter, oil, cheese and other fatty foods were considered essential for good cooking. We know now that all this fat – along with too much sugar and salt – has a huge impact on health.

Most of us eat fats in one form or another every day. In fact, we need to consume a small amount of fat to maintain a healthy and balanced diet, but almost everyone can afford to, and should, reduce their fat intake, particularly of saturated fats. Weight for weight, dietary fats supply far more energy than all the other nutrients in our diet. If you eat a diet that is high in fats and don't exercise enough to use up that energy, you will put on weight. By cutting down on fat, you can easily reduce your energy intake without affecting the other essential nutrients. And by choosing the right types of fat, using low fat and fat-free products whenever possible, and making small, simple changes to the way you cook and prepare food, you can reduce your overall fat intake quite dramatically and enjoy a much healthier diet without really noticing any difference.

As you will see, watching your fat intake doesn't have to mean dieting and deprivation. *The Ultimate Healthy Eating Cookbook* opens with an informative introduction about basic healthy eating guidelines – you'll find out about the five main food groups, and how, by simply choosing a variety of foods from these groups every

day, you can ensure that you are eating all the nutrients you need. One way to enjoy your favourite foods without guilt is to substitute lower fat ingredients for higher fat ones. This book will introduce you to these lower fat ingredients and show you how to use them. There are hints and tips on how to cook with fat-free and low fat ingredients; techniques for using healthy, fat-free fruit purée in place of butter or margarine in all your favourite baking recipes; suggestions for which foods to cut down on and what to try instead; easy ways to reduce fat and saturated fat in your foods; new no fat and low fat cooking techniques and information on the best cookware for fat-free cooking; along with a delicious section on low fat and very low fat snacks.

There are over 400 easy-to-follow recipes for delicious dishes that your whole family can enjoy. Every recipe has been developed to fit into modern nutritional guidelines, and each one has at-a-glance nutritional information so you can instantly check the calories and fat content. The recipes are very low in fat – all contain less than five grams of fat per serving and many contain less than one. The selection of foods included will surprise you: there are barbecues and bakes, pizza and pastas, tasty sautés and stews, vegetable dishes and vegetarian main courses, fish and seafood dishes galore and delicious breads, biscuits and cakes. All without as much fat as traditional recipes, of course, but packed with flavour and vitality.

Fresh vegetables and pulses (far left) and fresh fruit (left and above) make ideal choices for fat-free and low fat cooking.

HEALTHY EATING GUIDELINES

A healthy diet is one that provides the body with all the nutrients it needs to be able to grow and repair properly. By eating the right types, balance and proportions of foods, we are more likely to feel healthy, have plenty of energy and a higher resistance to illness that will help protect our body against developing diseases such as heart disease, cancers, bowel disorders and obesity.

By choosing a variety of foods every day, you will ensure that you are supplying your body with all the essential nutrients, including vitamins and minerals, it needs. To get the balance right, it is important to know just how much of each type of food you should be eating.

There are five main food groups (see right), and it is recommended that we should eat plenty of fruit, vegetables (at least five portions a day, not including potatoes) and foods such as cereals, pasta, rice and potatoes; moderate amounts of meat, fish, poultry and dairy products; and only small amounts of foods containing fat or sugar. By choosing a good balance of foods from these groups every day, and choosing lower fat or lower sugar alternatives wherever possible, we will be supplying our bodies with all the nutrients they need for optimum health.

THE ROLE AND IMPORTANCE OF FAT IN OUR DIET

Fats shouldn't be cut out of our diets completely. We need a small amount of fat for general health and well-being – fat is a valuable source of energy, and also helps to make foods more palatable to eat. However, if you lower the fats, especially saturated fats, in your diet, you will feel healthier; it will help you lose weight and reduce the risk of developing some diseases.

THE FIVE MAIN FOOD GROUPS

● Fruit and vegetables

● Rice, potatoes, bread, pasta and other cereals

● Meat, poultry, fish and alternative proteins

● Milk and other dairy foods

● Foods which contain fat and foods which contain sugar

Aim to limit your daily intake of fats to no more than 30% of total calories. In real terms, this means that for an average intake of 2,000 calories per day, 30% of energy would come from 600 calories. Since each gram of fat provides 9 calories, your total daily intake should be no more than 66.6g fat. Your total intake of saturated fats should be no more than 10% of the total calories.

TYPES OF FAT

All fats in our foods are made up of building blocks of fatty acids and glycerol and their properties vary according to each combination.

There are two types of fat – saturated and unsaturated. The unsaturated group is divided into two types – polyunsaturated and monounsaturated fats.

There is always a combination of each of the three types of fat (saturated, polyunsaturated and monounsaturated fats) in any food, but the amount of each type varies greatly from one food to another.

Left: By choosing a variety of foods from the five main food groups, you will ensure that you are supplying your body with all the nutrients it needs.

SATURATED FATS

All fatty acids are made up of chains of carbon atoms. Each atom has one or more free "bonds" to link with other atoms and by doing so the fatty acids transport nutrients to cells throughout the body. Without these free "bonds" the atom cannot form any links, that is to say it is completely "saturated". Because of this, the body finds it hard to process the fatty acid into energy, so it simply stores it as fat.

Saturated fats are the fats which you should reduce, as they can increase the level of cholesterol in the blood, which in turn can increase the risk of developing heart disease.

The main sources of saturated fats are animal products, such as meat, and fats, such as butter and lard that are solid at room temperature. However, there are also saturated fats of vegetable origin, notably coconut and palm oils, and some margarines and oils, which are processed by changing some of the unsaturated fatty acids to saturated ones – they are labelled "hydrogenated vegetable oil" and should be avoided.

POLYUNSATURATED FATS

There are two types of polyunsaturated fats, those of vegetable or plant origin (omega 6), such as sunflower oil, soft margarine and seeds, and those from oily fish (omega 3), such as herring, mackerel and sardines. Both fats are usually liquid at room temperature. Small quantities of polyunsaturated fats are essential for good health and are thought to help reduce the level of cholesterol in the blood.

MONOUNSATURATED FATS

Monounsaturated fats are also thought to have the beneficial effect of reducing the blood cholesterol level and this could explain why in some

Above: A selection of foods containing the three main types of fat found in foods.

Mediterranean countries there is such a low incidence of heart disease. Monounsaturated fats are found in foods such as olive oil, rapeseed oil, some nuts such as almonds and hazel-nuts, oily fish and avocado pears.

CUTTING DOWN ON FATS AND SATURATED FATS IN THE DIET

About one quarter of the fat we eat comes from meat and meat products, one-fifth from dairy products and margarine and the rest from cakes, biscuits, pastries and other foods. It is easy to cut down on obvious sources of fat in the diet, such as butter, oils, margarine, cream, whole milk and full fat cheese, but we also need to know

about – and watch out for – "hidden" fats. Hidden fats can be found in foods such as cakes, biscuits and nuts. Even lean, trimmed red meats may contain as much as 10% fat.

By being aware of foods which are high in fats and particularly saturated fats, and by making simple changes to your diet, you can reduce the total fat content of your diet quite considerably. Whenever possible, choose reduced fat or low fat alternatives to foods such as milk, cheese and salad dressings, and fill up on very low fat foods, such as fruit and vegetables, and foods that are high in carbohydrate such as pasta, rice, bread and potatoes.

EASY WAYS TO CUT DOWN FAT AND SATURATED FAT IN THE DAILY DIET

There are lots of simple no-fuss ways of reducing the fat in your diet. Just follow the simple "eat less – try instead" suggestions below to discover how easy it is.

● EAT LESS – Butter, margarine and hard fats.

● TRY INSTEAD – Low fat spread, very low fat spread or polyunsaturated margarine. If you must use butter or hard margarine, make sure they are softened at room temperature and spread them very thinly. Better still, use fat-free spreads such as low fat soft cheese, reduced sugar jams or marmalades for sandwiches and toast.

● EAT LESS – Fatty meats and high fat products such as meat pâtés, pies and sausages.

● TRY INSTEAD – Low fat meats, such as chicken, turkey and venison.

Use only the leanest cuts of such meats as lamb, beef and pork.

Always cut any visible fat and skin from meat before cooking.

Choose reduced fat sausages and meat products and eat fish more often.

Try using low fat protein products such as Quorn or tofu in place of meat in recipes.

Make gravies using vegetable water or fat-free stock rather than using meat juices.

● EAT LESS – Full fat dairy products such as whole milk, cream, butter, hard margarine, crème fraîche, whole milk yogurts and hard cheese.

● TRY INSTEAD – Semi-skimmed or skimmed milk and milk products, low fat yogurts, low fat fromage frais and low fat soft cheeses, reduced fat hard cheeses such as Cheddar, and reduced fat creams and crème fraîche.

● EAT LESS – Hard cooking fats, such as lard or hard margarine.

● TRY INSTEAD – Polyunsaturated or monounsaturated oils, such as olive, sunflower or corn for cooking.

● EAT LESS – Rich salad dressings like full-fat mayonnaise, salad cream or French dressing.

● TRY INSTEAD – Reduced fat or fat-free mayonnaise or dressings. Make salad dressings at home with low fat yogurt or fromage frais.

● EAT LESS – Fried foods.

● TRY INSTEAD – Fat-free cooking methods such as grilling, microwaving, steaming or baking whenever possible.

Try cooking in a non-stick wok with only a very small amount of oil.

Always roast or grill meat or poultry on a rack.

● EAT LESS – Deep-fried chips and sautéed potatoes.

● TRY INSTEAD – Fat-free starchy foods such as pasta, couscous and rice.

Choose baked or boiled potatoes.

● EAT LESS – Added fat in cooking.

● TRY INSTEAD – To cook with little or no fat. Use heavy-based or good quality non-stick pans, so that the food doesn't stick.

Try using a small amount of spray oil in cooking to control exactly how much fat you are using.

Use fat-free or low fat ingredients for cooking, such as fruit juice, low fat or fat-free stock, wine or even beer.

● EAT LESS – High fat snacks such as crisps, tortilla chips, fried snacks and pastries, chocolate cakes, muffins, doughnuts, sweet pastries and biscuits – especially chocolate ones!

● TRY INSTEAD – Low fat and fat-free fresh or dried fruits, breadsticks or vegetable sticks.

Make your own home-baked low fat cakes and bakes.

If you do buy ready-made cakes and biscuits, always choose low fat and reduced fat versions.

FAT-FREE COOKING METHODS

It's very easy to cook without fat – whenever possible, grill, bake, microwave or steam foods without the addition of fat, or try stir-frying without fat – use a little low fat or fat-free stock, wine or fruit juice instead.

● Choosing heavy-based or good quality cookware, you'll find that the amount of fat needed for cooking foods can be kept to an absolute minimum. When making casseroles or meat sauces such as bolognese, dry-fry the meat to brown it and then drain off all the excess fat before adding the other ingredients. If you do need a little fat for cooking, choose an oil which is high in unsaturates such as corn, sunflower, olive or rapeseed oil and always use as little as possible.

● When baking low fat cakes and bakes, use good quality bakeware which doesn't need greasing before use, or use non-stick baking paper and only lightly grease before lining.

● Look out for non-stick coated fabric sheet. This re-usable non-stick material is amazingly versatile, it can be cut to size and used to line cake tins, baking sheets or frying pans. Heat resistant up to 290°C/550°F and microwave safe, it will last for up to 5 years.

● When baking foods such as chicken or fish, rather than adding a knob of butter to the food, try baking the food in a loosely sealed parcel of foil or greaseproof paper and adding some wine or fruit juice and herbs or spices to the food before sealing the parcel.

● When grilling foods, the addition of fat is often unnecessary. If the food shows signs of drying, lightly brush with a small amount of unsaturated oil such as sunflower or corn oil.

Above: Invest in a few of these useful items of cookware for easy fat-free cooking: non-stick cookware and accurate measuring equipment are essential.

● Microwaved foods rarely need the addition of fat, so add herbs or spices for extra flavour and colour.

● Steaming or boiling are easy, fat-free ways of cooking many foods, especially vegetables, fish and chicken.

● Try poaching foods, such as chicken, fish and fruit, in stock or syrup – it is another easy, fat-free cooking method.

● Try braising vegetables in the oven in low fat or fat-free stock, wine or simply water with the addition of some herbs.

● Sauté vegetables in low fat or fat-free stock, wine or fruit juice instead of fat or oil.

● Cook vegetables in a covered saucepan over a low heat with a little water so they cook in their own juices.

● Marinate food such as meat or poultry in mixtures of alcohol, herbs or spices, and vinegar or fruit juice. This will help to tenderize the meat and add flavour and colour and, in addition, the marinade can be used to baste the food while it is cooking.

● When serving vegetables such as boiled potatoes, carrots or peas, resist the temptation to add a knob of butter or margarine. Instead, sprinkle with chopped fresh herbs or ground spices.

COOKING WITH LOW FAT OR NON-FAT INGREDIENTS

Nowadays many foods are available in full fat and reduced fat or very low fat forms. In every supermarket you'll find a huge array of low fat dairy products, such as milk, cream, yogurt, hard and soft cheeses and fromage frais; reduced fat sweet or chocolate biscuits; reduced fat or fat-free salad dressings and mayonnaise; reduced fat crisps and snacks; low fat, half-fat or very low fat spreads; as well as such reduced fat ready-made food products as desserts.

Other foods, such as fresh fruit and vegetables, pasta, rice, potatoes and bread, naturally contain very little fat. Some foods, such as soy sauce, wine, cider, sherry, sugar, honey, syrup and jam, contain no fat at all. By combining these and other low fat foods you can create delicious dishes which contain very little fat.

Some low fat or reduced fat ingredients and products work better than others in cooking but often a simple substitution of one for another will work. The addition of low fat or non-fat ingredients, such as herbs and spices, also add plenty of extra flavour and colour to recipes.

LOW FAT SPREADS IN COOKING

There is a huge variety of low fat, reduced fat and half-fat spreads available in our supermarkets, along with some spreads that are very low in fat. Some are suitable for cooking, while others are only suitable for spreading.

Generally speaking, the very low fat spreads with a fat content of around 20% or less have a high water content and so are all unsuitable for cooking and are only suitable for spreading.

Low fat or half-fat spreads with a fat content of around 40% are suitable for spreading and can be used for some cooking methods. They are suitable for recipes such as all-in-one cake and biscuit recipes, all-in-one sauce recipes, sautéing vegetables over a low heat, choux pastry and some cake icings.

When using these low fat spreads for cooking, the fat may behave slightly differently to full fat products such as butter or margarine.

With some recipes, the cooked result may be slightly different, but will still be very acceptable. Other recipes will be just as tasty and successful. For example, choux pastry made using half- or low fat spread is often slightly crisper and lighter in texture than traditional choux pastry, and a cheesecake biscuit base made with melted half- or

low fat spread combined with crushed biscuit crumbs, may be slightly softer in texture and less crispy than a biscuit base made using melted butter.

When heating half- or low fat spreads, never cook them over a high heat. Always use a heavy-based pan over a low heat to avoid the product burning, spitting or spoiling, and stir all the time. With all-in-one sauces, the mixture should be whisked continuously over a low heat.

Half-fat or low fat spreads are not suitable for shallow or deep-fat frying, pastry making, rich fruit cakes, some biscuits, shortbread, clarified butter and preserves such as lemon curd.

Remember that the keeping qualities of recipes made using half- or low fat spreads may be reduced slightly, due to the lower fat content.

Almost all dairy products now come in low fat or reduced fat versions.

Another way to reduce the fat content of recipes, particularly cake recipes is to use a fruit purée in place of all or some of the fat in a recipe.

Many cake recipes work well using this method but others may not be so successful. Pastry does not work well. Breads work very well, perhaps because the amount of fat is usually relatively small, as do some biscuits and bars, such as brownies and flapjacks.

To make the dried fruit purée to use in recipes, chop 115g/4oz ready-to-eat dried fruit and place in a blender or food processor with 75ml/5 tbsp water and blend to a roughly smooth purée. Then, simply substitute the same weight of this dried fruit purée for all or just some of the amount of fat in the recipe. The purée will keep in the fridge for up to three days.

You can use prunes, dried apricots, dried peaches, or dried apples, or substitute mashed fresh fruit, such as ripe bananas or lightly cooked apples, without the added water.

Above: A selection of cooking oils and low fat spreads. Always check the packaging of low fat spreads – for cooking, they must have a fat content of about 40%.

LOW FAT AND VERY LOW FAT SNACKS

Instead of reaching for a packet of crisps, a high fat biscuit or a chocolate bar when hunger strikes, choose one of these tasty low fat snacks to fill that hungry hole.

● A piece of fresh fruit or vegetable such as an apple, banana or carrot – keep chunks or sticks wrapped in a polythene bag in the fridge.

● Fresh fruit or vegetable chunks – skewer them on to cocktail sticks or short bamboo skewers to make them into mini kebabs.

● A handful of dried fruit such as raisins, apricots or sultanas. These also make a perfect addition to children's packed lunches or to school break snacks.

● A portion of canned fruit in natural fruit juice – serve with a spoonful or two of fat-free yogurt.

● One or two crisp rice cakes – delicious on their own, or topped with honey, or reduced fat cheese.

● Crackers, such as water biscuits or crisp breads, spread with reduced sugar jam or marmalade.

● A bowl of wholewheat breakfast cereal or no-added-sugar muesli served with a little skimmed milk.

● Very low fat plain or fruit yogurt or fromage frais.

● A toasted teacake spread with reduced sugar jam or marmalade.

● Toasted crumpet spread with yeast extract or beef extract.

THE FAT AND CALORIE CONTENTS OF FOOD

The following figures show the weight of fat (g) and the energy content per 100g/4oz of each food.

VEGETABLES

	FAT (g)	ENERGY		FAT (g)	ENERGY
Broccoli	0.9	33 Kcals/138 kJ	Onions	0.2	36 Kcals/151 kJ
Cabbage	0.4	26 Kcals/109 kJ	Peas	1.5	83 Kcals/344 kJ
Carrots	0.3	35 Kcals/146 kJ	Potatoes	0.2	75 Kcals/318 kJ
Cauliflower	0.9	34 Kcals/142 kJ	Chips, home-made	6.7	189 Kcals/796 kJ
Courgettes	0.4	18 Kcals/74 kJ	Chips, retail	12.4	239 Kcals/1001 kJ
Cucumber	0.1	10 Kcals/40 kJ	Oven-chips, frozen, baked	4.2	162 Kcals/687 kJ
Mushrooms	0.5	13 Kcals/55 kJ	Tomatoes	0.3	17 Kcals/73 kJ

BEANS AND PULSES

	FAT (g)	ENERGY		FAT (g)	ENERGY
Black-eyed beans, cooked	1.8	116 Kcals/494 kJ	Hummus	12.6	187 Kcals/781 kJ
Butter beans, canned	0.5	77 Kcals/327 kJ	Red kidney beans, canned	0.6	100 Kcals/424 kJ
Chick-peas, canned	2.9	115 Kcals/487 kJ	Red lentils, cooked	0.4	100 Kcals/424 kJ

FISH AND SEAFOOD

	FAT (g)	ENERGY		FAT (g)	ENERGY
Cod fillets, raw	0.7	80 Kcals/337 kJ	Prawns	0.9	99 Kcals/418 kJ
Crab, canned	0.5	77 Kcals/326 kJ	Trout, grilled	5.4	135 Kcals/565 kJ
Haddock, raw	0.6	81 Kcals/345 kJ	Tuna, canned in brine	0.6	99 Kcals/422 kJ
Lemon sole, raw	1.5	83 Kcals/351 kJ	Tuna, canned in oil	9.0	189 Kcals/794 kJ

MEAT PRODUCTS

	FAT (g)	ENERGY		FAT (g)	ENERGY
Bacon rasher, streaky	39.5	414 Kcals/1710 kJ	Chicken fillet, raw	1.1	106 Kcals/449 kJ
Turkey rasher	1.0	99 Kcals/414 kJ	Chicken, roasted	12.5	218 Kcals/910 kJ
Beef mince, raw	16.2	225 Kcals/934 kJ	Duck, meat only, raw	6.5	137 Kcals/575 kJ
Beef mince, extra lean, raw	9.6	174 Kcals/728 kJ	Duck, roasted, meat,		
Rump steak, lean and fat	10.1	174 Kcals/726 kJ	fat and skin	38.1	423 Kcals/1750 kJ
Rump steak, lean only	4.1	125 Kcals/526 kJ	Turkey, meat only, raw	1.6	105 Kcals/443 kJ
Lamb chops, loin, lean and fat	23.0	277 Kcals/1150 kJ	Liver, lamb, raw	6.2	137 Kcals/575 kJ
Lamb, average, lean, raw	8.3	156 Kcals/651 kJ	Pork pie	27.0	376 Kcals/1564 kJ
Pork chops, loin, lean and fat	21.7	270 Kcals/1119 kJ	Salami	45.2	491 Kcals/2031 kJ
Pork, average, lean, raw	4.0	123 Kcals/519 kJ	Sausage roll, flaky pastry	36.4	477 Kcals/1985 kJ

Information from *The Composition of Foods* (5th Edition 1991) is reproduced with the permission of the Royal Society of Chemistry and the Controller of Her Majesty's Stationery Office.

DAIRY, FATS AND OILS

	FAT (g)	ENERGY		FAT (g)	ENERGY
Cream, double	48.0	449 Kcals/1849 kJ	Low fat yogurt, plain	0.8	56 Kcals/236 kJ
Cream, single	19.1	198 Kcals/817 kJ	Greek yogurt	9.1	115 Kcals/477 kJ
Cream, whipping	39.3	373 Kcals/1539 kJ	Reduced fat Greek yogurt	5.0	80 Kcals/335 kJ
Crème fraîche	40.0	379 Kcals/156 kJ	Butter	81.7	737 Kcals/3031 kJ
Reduced fat crème fraîche	15.0	165 Kcals/683 kJ	Margarine	81.6	739 Kcals/3039 kJ
Reduced fat double cream	24.0	243 Kcals/1002 kJ	Low fat spread	40.5	390 Kcals/1605 kJ
Milk, skimmed	0.1	33 Kcals/130 kJ	Very low fat spread	25	273 Kcals/1128 kJ
Milk, whole	3.9	66 Kcals/275 kJ	Lard	99.0	891 Kcals/3663 kJ
Brie	26.9	319 Kcals/1323 kJ	Corn oil	99.9	899 Kcals/3696 kJ
Cheddar cheese	34.4	412 Kcals/1708 kJ	Olive oil	99.9	899 Kcals/3696 kJ
Cheddar-type, reduced fat	15.0	261 Kcals/1091 kJ	Safflower oil	99.9	899 Kcals/3696 kJ
Cream cheese	47.4	439 Kcals/1807 kJ	Eggs	10.8	147 Kcals/612 kJ
Fromage frais, plain	7.1	113 Kcals/469 kJ	Egg yolk	30.5	339 Kcals/1402 kJ
Fromage frais, very low fat	0.2	58 Kcals/247 kJ	Egg white	Trace	36 Kcals/153 kJ
Skimmed milk soft cheese	Trace	74 Kcals/313 kJ	Fat-free dressing	1.2	67 Kcals/282 kJ
Edam cheese	25.4	333 Kcals/1382 kJ	French dressing	49.4	462 Kcals/1902 kJ
Feta cheese	20.2	250 Kcals/1037 kJ	Mayonnaise	75.6	691 Kcals2843 kJ
Parmesan cheese	32.7	452 Kcals/1880 kJ	Mayonnaise, reduced calorie	28.1	288 Kcals/1188 kJ

CEREALS, BAKING AND PRESERVES

	FAT (g)	ENERGY		FAT (g)	ENERGY
Brown rice, uncooked	2.8	357 Kcals/1518 kJ	Digestive biscuit (plain)	20.9	471 Kcals/1978 kJ
White rice, uncooked	3.6	383 Kcals/1630 kJ	Reduced fat digestive biscuits	16.4	467 Kcals/1965 kJ
Pasta, white, uncooked	1.8	342 Kcals/1456 kJ	Shortbread	26.1	498 Kcals/2087 kJ
Pasta, wholemeal, uncooked	2.5	324 Kcal/1379 kJ	Madeira cake	16.9	393 Kcals/1652 kJ
Brown bread	2.0	218 Kcals/927 kJ	Fatless sponge cake	6.1	294 Kcals/1245 kJ
White bread	1.9	235 Kcals/1002 kJ	Doughnut, jam	14.5	336 Kcals/1414 kJ
Wholemeal bread	2.5	215 Kcals914 kJ	Sugar, white	0.3	94 Kcals/1680 kJ
Cornflakes	0.7	360 Kcals/1535 kJ	Chocolate, milk	30.7	520 Kcals/2177 kJ
Sultana bran	1.6	303 Kcals/1289 kJ	Chocolate, plain	28	510 Kcals/2157 kJ
Swiss-style muesli	5.9	363 Kcals/1540 kJ	Honey	0	288 Kcals/1229 kJ
Croissant	20.3	360 Kcals/1505 kJ	Lemon curd	5.0	283 Kcals/1198 kJ
Flapjack	26.6	484 Kcals/2028 kJ	Fruit jam	0.3	268 Kcals/1114 kJ

FRUIT AND NUTS

	FAT (g)	ENERGY		FAT (g)	ENERGY
Apples, eating	0.1	47 Kcals/199 kJ	Pears	0.1	40 Kcals/169 kJ
Avocados	19.5	190 Kcals/784 kJ	Almonds	55.8	612 Kcals/2534 kJ
Bananas	0.3	95 Kcals/403 kJ	Brazil nuts	68.2	682 Kcals/2813 kJ
Dried mixed fruit	0.4	268 Kcals/1114 kJ	Hazelnuts	63.5	650 Kcals/2685 kJ
Grapefruit	0.1	30 Kcals/126 kJ	Pine nuts	68.6	688 Kcals/2840 kJ
Oranges	0.1	37 Kcals/158 kJ	Walnuts	68.5	688 Kcals/2837kJ
Peaches	0.1	33 Kcals/142 kJ	Peanut butter, smooth	53.7	623 Kcals/2581 kJ

SOUPS

Home-made soups are ideal served as a starter, a snack or a light lunch. They are filling, nutritious and low in fat and are delicious served with a chunk of fresh crusty bread. The wide variety of fresh vegetables available nowadays ensures that the freshest ingredients can be used to create tempting and delicious home-made soups. We include a tasty selection, including vegetable soups, chowders and bean and pasta soups. Choose from temptations such as Italian Vegetable Soup, Spicy Tomato and Lentil Soup, and Creamy Cod Chowder.

Mediterranean Tomato Soup

Children will love this soup –
especially if you use fancy shapes
of pasta such as alphabet or
animal shapes.

INGREDIENTS

Serves 4

675g/1½ lb ripe plum tomatoes
1 medium onion, quartered
1 celery stick
1 garlic clove
15ml/1 tbsp olive oil
450ml/¾ pint/1⅞ cups chicken stock
15ml/2 tbsp tomato purée
50g/2oz/½ cup small pasta shapes
salt and black pepper
fresh coriander or parsley, to garnish

1 Place the tomatoes, onion, celery
and garlic in a pan with the oil.
Cover and cook over a low heat for
40–45 minutes, shaking the pan
occasionally, until very soft.

2 Spoon the vegetables into a food
processor or blender and process
until smooth. Press though a sieve, then
return to the pan.

3 Stir in the stock and tomato purée
and bring to the boil. Add the pasta
and simmer gently for about 8 minutes,
or until the pasta is tender. Add salt
and pepper, to taste, then sprinkle with
coriander or parsley and serve hot.

NUTRITION NOTES

Per portion:
Energy	112Kcals/474kJ
Fat	3.61g
Saturated fat	0.49g
Cholesterol	0
Fibre	2.68g

Mushroom, Celery and Garlic Soup

INGREDIENTS

Serves 4

350g/12oz/3 cups chopped mushrooms
4 celery sticks, chopped
3 garlic cloves
45ml/3 tbsp dry sherry or white wine
750ml/1¼ pints/3⅓cups chicken stock
30ml/2 tbsp Worcestershire sauce
5ml/1 tsp grated nutmeg
salt and black pepper
celery leaves, to garnish

NUTRITION NOTES

Per portion:
Energy	48Kcals/200kJ
Fat	1.09g
Saturated fat	0.11g
Cholesterol	0
Fibre	1.64g

1 Place the mushrooms, celery and
garlic in a pan and stir in the sherry
or wine. Cover and cook over a low
heat for 30–40 minutes, until tender.

2 Add half the stock and purée in a
food processor or blender until
smooth. Return to the pan and add the
remaining stock, the Worcestershire
sauce and nutmeg.

3 Bring to the boil, season and serve
hot, garnished with celery leaves.

ITALIAN VEGETABLE SOUP

The success of this clear soup depends on the quality of the stock, so for the best results, be sure you use home-made vegetable stock rather than stock cubes.

INGREDIENTS

Serves 4
1 small carrot
1 baby leek
1 celery stick
50g/2oz green cabbage
900ml/1½ pints/3¾ cups vegetable stock
1 bay leaf
115g/4oz/1 cup cooked cannellini or haricot beans
25g/1oz/⅓ cup soup pasta, such as tiny shells, bows, stars or elbows
salt and black pepper
snipped fresh chives, to garnish

1 Cut the carrot, leek and celery into 5cm/2in long julienne strips. Slice the cabbage very finely.

NUTRITION NOTES	
Per portion:	
Energy	69Kcals/288kJ
Protein	3.67g
Fat	0.71g
Saturated Fat	0.05g
Fibre	2.82g

2 Put the stock and bay leaf into a large saucepan and bring to the boil. Add the carrot, leek and celery, cover and simmer for 6 minutes.

3 Add the cabbage, beans and pasta shapes. Stir, then simmer uncovered for a further 4–5 minutes, or until the vegetables and pasta are tender.

4 Remove the bay leaf and season with salt and pepper to taste. Ladle into four soup bowls and garnish with snipped chives. Serve immediately.

CHICKEN AND PASTA SOUP

INGREDIENTS

Serves 4–6
900ml/1½ pints/3¾ cups chicken stock
1 bay leaf
4 spring onions, sliced
225g/8oz button mushrooms, sliced
115g/4oz cooked chicken breast
50g/2oz soup pasta
150ml/¼ pint/⅔ cup dry white wine
15ml/1 tbsp chopped fresh parsley
salt and black pepper

NUTRITION NOTES

Per portion:
Energy	126Kcals/529kJ
Fat	2.2g
Saturated Fat	0.6g
Cholesterol	19mg
Fibre	1.3g

1 Put the stock and bay leaf into a pan and bring to the boil.

2 Add the spring onions and mushrooms to the stock.

3 Remove the skin from the chicken and slice the meat thinly using a sharp knife. Add to the soup and season to taste. Heat through for about 2–3 minutes.

4 Add the pasta, cover and simmer for 7–8 minutes. Just before serving, add the wine and chopped parsley, heat through for 2–3 minutes, then season to taste.

BEETROOT SOUP WITH RAVIOLI

INGREDIENTS

Serves 4–6

1 quantity basic pasta dough (see page 116)
egg white, beaten, for brushing
flour, for dusting
1 small onion or shallot, finely chopped
2 garlic cloves, crushed
5ml/1 tsp fennel seeds
600ml/1 pint/2½ cups chicken stock
225g/8oz cooked beetroot
30ml/2 tbsp fresh orange juice
fennel or dill leaves, to garnish
crusty bread, to serve

For the filling

115g/4oz mushrooms, finely chopped
1 shallot or small onion, finely chopped
1–2 garlic cloves, crushed
5ml/1 tsp chopped fresh thyme
15ml/1 tbsp chopped fresh parsley
90ml/6 tbsp fresh white breadcrumbs
salt and black pepper
large pinch of ground nutmeg

1 Process all the filling ingredients and scoop into a bowl.

NUTRITION NOTES

Per portion:	
Energy	358Kcals/1504kJ
Fat	4.9g
Saturated Fat	1.0g
Cholesterol	110mg
Fibre	4.3g

2 Roll the pasta dough into thin sheets. Lay one piece over a ravioli tray and put a teaspoonful of the filling into each depression. Brush around the edges of each ravioli with egg white. Cover with another sheet of pasta, press the edges well together to seal and separate the individual shapes. Transfer to a floured dish towel and rest for 1 hour before cooking.

3 Cook the ravioli in a large pan of boiling, salted water for 2 minutes, in batches to stop them sticking together. Remove and drop into a bowl of cold water for 5 seconds before placing on a tray. (You can make these pasta shapes a day in advance. Cover with clear film and store in the fridge.)

4 Put the onion, garlic and fennel seeds into a pan with 150ml/ ¼ pint/⅔ cup of the stock. Bring to the boil, cover and simmer for 5 minutes until tender. Peel and finely dice the beetroot (reserve 60ml/4 tbsp for the garnish). Add the rest of the beetroot to the soup with the remaining stock and bring to the boil.

5 Add the orange juice and cooked ravioli and simmer for 2 minutes. Pour into shallow soup bowls and garnish with the reserved diced beetroot and fennel or dill leaves.

SPICY TOMATO AND LENTIL SOUP

INGREDIENTS

Serves 4

15ml/1 tbsp sunflower oil
1 onion, finely chopped
1–2 garlic cloves, crushed
2.5cm/1in piece fresh root ginger,
  peeled and finely chopped
5ml/1 tsp cumin seeds, crushed
450g/1lb ripe tomatoes, peeled, seeded
  and chopped
115g/4oz/½ cup red split lentils
1.2 litres/2 pints/5 cups vegetable or
  chicken stock
15ml/1 tbsp tomato purée
salt and black pepper
low fat natural yogurt and chopped
  fresh parsley, to garnish (optional)

1 Heat the sunflower oil in a large heavy-based saucepan and cook the chopped onion gently for 5 minutes until softened.

2 Stir in the garlic, ginger and cumin, followed by the tomatoes and lentils. Cook over a low heat for a further 3–4 minutes.

3 Stir in the stock and tomato purée. Bring to the boil, then lower the heat and simmer gently for about 30 minutes until the lentils are soft. Season to taste with salt and pepper.

4 Purée the soup in a blender or food processor. Return to the clean pan and reheat gently. Serve in heated bowls. If liked, garnish each portion with a swirl of yogurt and a little chopped parsley.

NUTRITION NOTES

Per portion:

Energy	165Kcals/695kJ
Fat	4g
Saturated Fat	0.5g
Cholesterol	0

CREAMY COD CHOWDER

A delicious light version of a classic, this chowder is a tasty combination of smoked fish, vegetables, fresh herbs and milk. To cut the calories and stock even more, use vegetable or fish stock in place of the milk. Serve as a substantial starter or snack, or as a light main meal accompanied by warm crusty wholemeal bread.

INGREDIENTS

Serves 4–6
350g/12oz smoked cod fillet
1 small onion, finely chopped
1 bay leaf
4 black peppercorns
900ml/1½ pints/3¾ cups skimmed milk
10ml/2 tsp cornflour
200g/7oz canned sweetcorn kernels
15ml/1 tbsp chopped fresh parsley

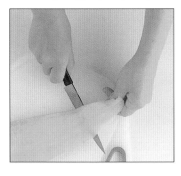

1 Skin the fish and put it into a large saucepan with the onion, bay leaf and peppercorns. Pour over the milk.

2 Bring to the boil, then reduce the heat and simmer very gently for 12–15 minutes, or until the fish is just cooked. Do not overcook.

3 Using a slotted spoon, lift out the fish and flake into large chunks. Remove the bay leaf and peppercorns and discard.

4 Blend the cornflour with 10ml/2 tsp cold water and add to the saucepan. Bring to the boil and simmer for about 1 minute or until slightly thickened.

5 Drain the sweetcorn kernels and add to the saucepan together with the flaked fish and parsley. Reheat gently and serve.

COOK'S TIP
The flavour of the chowder improves if it is made a day in advance. Leave to cool, then chill in the fridge until required. Reheat gently. Do not allow the soup to boil, or the fish will disintegrate.

NUTRITION NOTES

Per portion:
Energy	200Kcals/840kJ
Protein	24.71g
Fat	1.23g
Saturated Fat	0.32g

TOMATO AND CORIANDER SOUP

This delicious soup is an ideal solution when time is short but you still want to produce a very stylish starter.

—— INGREDIENTS ——

Serves 4

675g/1½lb small fresh tomatoes
30ml/2 tbsp vegetable oil
1 bay leaf
4 spring onions, cut into 2.5cm/1in
    pieces
5ml/1 tsp salt
5ml/1 tsp garlic pulp
5ml/1 tsp crushed black
    peppercorns
30ml/2 tbsp chopped fresh
    coriander
750ml/1¼ pints/3 cups water
15ml/1 tbsp cornflour
60ml/4 tbsp single cream, to garnish

1 To skin the tomatoes, plunge them into very hot water for 30 seconds, then transfer to a bowl of cold water. The skin should now peel off quickly and easily. Chop the tomatoes into large chunks.

2 Heat the oil in a large saucepan, add the bay leaf and spring onions, then stir in the tomatoes. Cook, stirring, for a few minutes more until the tomatoes are softened.

3 Add the salt, garlic, peppercorns, coriander and water, bring to the boil, then simmer for 15 minutes.

4 Dissolve the cornflour in a little water. Remove the soup from the heat and press through a sieve.

5 Return the soup to the pan, add the cornflour mixture and stir over a gentle heat until boiling and thickened.

6 Ladle the soup into shallow soup plates, then swirl a tablespoon of cream into each bowl before serving.

NUTRITION NOTES	
Per portion:	
Energy	113Kcals/474kJ
Fat	7.16g
Saturated fat	1.37g
Cholesterol	2.8mg

THAI-STYLE SWEETCORN SOUP

This is a very quick and easy soup, made in minutes. If you are using frozen prawns, then defrost them first before adding to the soup.

INGREDIENTS

Serves 4

2.5ml/½ tsp sesame or sunflower oil
2 spring onions, thinly sliced
1 garlic clove, crushed
600ml/1 pint/2½ cups chicken stock
425g/15oz can cream-style sweetcorn
225g/8oz/1¼ cups cooked, peeled
   prawns
5ml/1 tsp green chilli paste or chilli
   sauce (optional)
salt and black pepper
fresh coriander leaves, to garnish

1 Heat the oil in a large heavy-based saucepan and sauté the onions and garlic over a medium heat for 1 minute, until softened, but not browned.

2 Stir in the chicken stock, cream-style sweetcorn, prawns and chilli paste or sauce, if using.

3 Bring the soup to the boil, stirring occasionally. Season to taste, then serve at once, sprinkled with fresh coriander leaves to garnish.

COOK'S TIP
If cream-style corn is not available, use ordinary canned sweetcorn, puréed in a food processor for a few seconds, until creamy yet with some texture left.

NUTRITION NOTES	
Per portion:	
Energy	202Kcals/848kJ
Fat	3.01g
Saturated fat	0.43g
Cholesterol	45.56mg
Fibre	1.6g

SPINACH AND BEAN CURD SOUP

This appetizing clear soup has an extremely delicate and mild flavour that can be used as a perfect counterbalance to the intense heat of a hot Thai curry.

INGREDIENTS

Serves 6

30ml/2 tbsp dried shrimps
1 litre/1¾ pints/4 cups chicken stock
225g/8oz fresh bean curd, drained and
    cut into 2cm/¾in cubes
30ml/2 tbsp fish sauce
350g/12oz fresh spinach, washed
    thoroughly
black pepper
2 spring onions, finely sliced, to garnish

1 Rinse and drain the dried shrimps. Combine the shrimps with the chicken stock in a large saucepan and bring to the boil.

2 Add the bean curd and simmer for about 5 minutes. Season with fish sauce and black pepper to taste.

3 Tear the spinach leaves into bite-size pieces and add to the soup. Cook for another 1–2 minutes.

4 Remove from the heat and sprinkle with the finely sliced spring onions, to garnish.

NUTRITION NOTES

Per portion:

Energy	64Kcals/270kJ
Fat	225g
Saturated Fat	0.26g
Cholesterol	25mg
Fibre	1.28g

COOK'S TIP
Home-made chicken stock makes the world of difference to clear soups. Accumulate enough bones to make a big batch of stock, use what you need and keep the rest in the freezer.

Put 1.5kg/3–3½lb meaty chicken bones and 450g/1lb pork bones (optional) into a large saucepan. Add 3 litres/5 pints/12 cups water and slowly bring to the boil. Occasionally skim off and discard any scum that rises to the surface. Add 2 slices fresh root ginger, 2 garlic cloves (optional), 2 celery sticks, 4 spring onions, 2 bruised lemon grass stalks, a few sprigs of coriander and 10 crushed black peppercorns. Reduce the heat to low and simmer for about 2–2½ hours.

Remove from the heat and leave to cool, uncovered and undisturbed. Pour through a fine strainer, leaving the last dregs behind as they tend to cloud the soup. Leave to cool, then chill. Use as required, removing any fat that congeals on the surface.

VEGETABLE MINESTRONE

INGREDIENTS

Serves 6–8

large pinch of saffron strands
1 onion, chopped
1 leek, sliced
1 stick celery, sliced
2 carrots, diced
2–3 garlic cloves, crushed
600ml/1 pint/2½ cups chicken stock
2 x 400g/14oz cans chopped tomatoes
50g/2oz/½ cup frozen peas
50g/2oz soup pasta (anellini)
5ml/1 tsp caster sugar
15ml/1 tbsp chopped fresh parsley
15ml/1 tbsp chopped fresh basil
salt and black pepper

1 Soak the pinch of saffron strands in 15ml/1 tbsp boiling water. Leave to stand for 10 minutes.

2 Meanwhile, put the prepared onion, leek, celery, carrots and garlic into a large pan. Add the chicken stock, bring to the boil, cover and simmer for about 10 minutes.

3 Add the canned tomatoes, the saffron with its liquid and the frozen peas. Bring back to the boil and add the soup pasta. Simmer for 10 minutes until tender.

COOK'S TIP
Saffron strands aren't essential for this soup, but they give a wonderful delicate flavour, with the bonus of a lovely rich orange-yellow colour.

4 Season with sugar, salt and pepper to taste. Stir in the chopped herbs just before serving.

NUTRITION NOTES

Per portion:

Energy	87Kcals/367kJ
Fat	0.7g
Saturated Fat	0.1g
Cholesterol	0
Fibre	3.3g

SWEETCORN CHOWDER WITH PASTA SHELLS

Smoked turkey rashers provide a tasty, low fat alternative to bacon in this hearty dish. If you prefer, omit the meat altogether and serve the soup as is.

INGREDIENTS

Serves 4

1 small green pepper
450g/1lb potatoes, peeled and diced
350g/12oz/2 cups canned or frozen
  sweetcorn
1 onion, chopped
1 celery stick, chopped
a bouquet garni (bay leaf, parsley stalks
  and thyme)
600ml/1 pint/2½ cups chicken stock
300ml/½ pint/1¼ cups skimmed milk
50g/2oz small pasta shells
oil, for frying
150g/5oz smoked turkey rashers, diced
salt and black pepper
bread sticks, to serve

1 Halve the green pepper, then remove the stalk and seeds. Cut the flesh into small dice, cover with boiling water and stand for 2 minutes. Drain and rinse.

NUTRITION NOTES

Per portion:

Energy	215Kcals/904kJ
Fat	1.6g
Saturated Fat	0.3g
Cholesterol	13mg
Fibre	2.8g

2 Put the potatoes into a saucepan with the sweetcorn, onion, celery, green pepper, bouquet garni and stock. Bring to the boil, cover and simmer for 20 minutes until tender.

3 Add the milk and season with salt and pepper. Process half of the soup in a food processor or blender and return to the pan with the pasta shells. Simmer for 10 minutes.

4 Fry the turkey rashers in a non-stick frying pan for 2–3 minutes. Stir into the soup. Season to taste and serve with bread sticks.

RED PEPPER SOUP WITH LIME

The beautiful rich red colour of this soup makes it a very attractive starter or light lunch. For a special dinner, toast some tiny croutons and serve sprinkled into the soup.

INGREDIENTS

Serves 4–6
4 red peppers, seeded and chopped
1 large onion, chopped
5ml / 1 tsp olive oil
1 garlic clove, crushed
1 small red chilli, sliced
45ml / 3 tbsp tomato purée
900ml / 1½ pints / 3¾ cups chicken stock
finely grated rind and juice of 1 lime
salt and black pepper
shreds of lime rind, to garnish

1 Cook the onion and peppers gently in the oil in a covered saucepan for about 5 minutes, shaking the pan occasionally, until softened.

2 Stir in the garlic, then add the chilli with the tomato purée. Stir in half the stock, then bring to the boil. Cover the pan and simmer for 10 minutes.

3 Cool slightly, then purée in a food processor or blender. Return to the pan, then add the remaining stock, the lime rind and juice, and seasoning.

4 Bring the soup back to the boil, then serve at once with a few strips of lime rind, scattered into each bowl.

NUTRITION NOTES	
Per portion:	
Energy	87Kcals/366kJ
Fat	1.57g
Saturated fat	0.12g
Cholesterol	0
Fibre	3.40g

CHICKEN AND COCONUT SOUP

This aromatic soup is rich with coconut milk and intensely flavoured with galangal, lemon grass and kaffir lime leaves.

INGREDIENTS

Serves 4–6
750ml/1¼ pints/3 cups coconut milk
475ml/16fl oz/2 cups chicken stock
4 lemon grass stalks, bruised and
   chopped
2.5cm/1in section galangal, thinly sliced
10 black peppercorns, crushed
10 kaffir lime leaves, torn
300g/11oz boneless chicken, cut into
   thin strips
115g/4oz button mushrooms
50g/2oz baby sweetcorn
60ml/4 tbsp lime juice
about 45ml/3 tbsp fish sauce
2 fresh chillies, seeded and chopped,
   chopped spring onions, and coriander
   leaves, to garnish

1 Bring the coconut milk and chicken stock to the boil. Add the lemon grass, galangal, peppercorns and half the kaffir lime leaves. Reduce the heat and simmer gently for 10 minutes.

2 Strain the stock into a clean pan. Return to the heat, then add the chicken, button mushrooms and baby sweetcorn. Simmer for 5–7 minutes or until the chicken is cooked.

3 Stir in the lime juice, fish sauce to taste and the rest of the lime leaves. Serve hot, garnished with chillies, spring onions and coriander.

NUTRITION NOTES

Per portion:	
Energy	125Kcals/528kJ
Fat	3.03g
Saturated Fat	1.06g
Cholesterol	32.5mg
Fibre	0.4g

HOT AND SOUR PRAWN SOUP

This is a classic Thai seafood soup and is probably the most popular and well known soup from Thailand.

INGREDIENTS

Serves 4–6
450g/1lb king prawns
1 litre/1¾ pints/4 cups chicken stock
3 lemon grass stalks
10 kaffir lime leaves, torn in half
225g/8oz can straw mushrooms,
   drained
45ml/3 tbsp fish sauce
50ml/2fl oz/¼ cup lime juice
30ml/2 tbsp chopped spring onions
15ml/1 tbsp coriander leaves
4 fresh chillies, seeded and chopped
salt and black pepper

1 Shell and devein the prawns and set aside. Rinse the prawn shells, place them in a large saucepan with the stock and bring to the boil.

2 Bruise the lemon grass stalks with the blunt edge of a chopping knife and add them to the stock together with half the lime leaves. Simmer gently for 5–6 minutes, until the stalks change colour and the stock is fragrant.

NUTRITION NOTES

Per portion:	
Energy	49Kcals/209kJ
Fat	0.45g
Saturated Fat	0.07g
Cholesterol	78.8mg
Fibre	0.09g

3 Strain the stock, return to the saucepan and reheat. Add the mushrooms and prawns, then cook until the prawns turn pink. Stir in the fish sauce, lime juice, spring onions, coriander, chillies and the rest of the lime leaves. Taste the soup and adjust the seasoning – it should be sour, salty, spicy and hot.

RED ONION AND BEETROOT SOUP

This beautiful vivid ruby-red soup will look stunning at any dinner party.

INGREDIENTS

Serves 6
10ml/2 tsp olive oil
350g/12oz red onions, sliced
2 garlic cloves, crushed
275g/10oz cooked beetroot, cut into
  sticks
1.2 litres/2 pints/5 cups vegetable stock
  or water
50g/2oz/1 cup cooked soup pasta
30ml/2 tbsp raspberry vinegar
salt and black pepper
low fat yogurt and snipped chives,
  to garnish

COOK'S TIP
If you prefer, try substituting cooked barley for the pasta to give extra nuttiness.

1 Heat the olive oil and add the onions and garlic.

2 Cook gently for about 20 minutes or until soft and tender.

3 Add the beetroot, stock or water, cooked pasta shapes and vinegar and heat through.

4 Adjust the seasoning to taste. Ladle the soup into bowls. Top each one with a spoonful of yogurt and sprinkle with snipped chives. Serve piping hot.

NUTRITION NOTES

Per portion:
Energy	76Kcals/318kJ
Fat	2.01g
Saturated Fat	0.28g
Cholesterol	0.33mg
Fibre	1.83g

CAULIFLOWER AND BEAN SOUP

The sweet, liquorice flavour of the fennel seeds gives a delicious edge to this hearty soup.

INGREDIENTS

Serves 6
10ml/2 tsp olive oil
1 garlic clove, crushed
1 onion, chopped
10ml/2 tsp fennel seeds
1 cauliflower, cut into small florets
2 x 400g/14oz cans flageolet beans, drained and rinsed
1.2 litres/2 pints/5 cups vegetable stock or water
salt and black pepper
chopped fresh parsley, to garnish
toasted slices of French bread, to serve

1 Heat the olive oil. Add the garlic, onion and fennel seeds and cook gently for 5 minutes or until the onion is softened.

2 Add the cauliflower, half of the beans and all the stock or water.

3 Bring to the boil. Reduce the heat and simmer for 10 minutes or until the cauliflower is tender.

NUTRITION NOTES

Per portion:

Energy	194.3Kcals/822.5kJ
Fat	3.41g
Saturated Fat	0.53g
Cholesterol	0
Fibre	7.85g

4 Pour the soup into a blender and blend until smooth. Stir in the remaining beans and season to taste. Reheat and pour into bowls. Sprinkle with chopped parsley and serve with toasted slices of French bread.

MELON AND BASIL SOUP

A deliciously refreshing, chilled fruit soup, just right for a hot summer's day. It takes next to no time to prepare, leaving you free to enjoy the sunshine and, even better, it is almost totally fat-free.

INGREDIENTS

Serves 4–6
2 Charentais or rock melons
75g/3oz/6 tbsp caster sugar
175ml/6fl oz/³⁄4 cup water
finely grated rind and juice of 1 lime
45ml/3 tbsp shredded fresh basil
fresh basil leaves, to garnish

1 Cut the melons in half across the middle. Scrape out the seeds and discard. Using a melon baller, scoop out 20–24 balls and set aside for the garnish. Scoop out the remaining flesh and place in a blender or food processor. Set aside.

2 Place the sugar, water and lime zest in a small pan over a low heat. Stir until dissolved, bring to the boil and simmer for 2–3 minutes. Remove from the heat and leave to cool slightly. Pour half the mixture into the blender or food processor with the melon flesh. Blend until smooth, adding the remaining syrup and lime juice to taste.

3 Pour the mixture into a bowl, stir in the basil and chill. Serve garnished with basil leaves and melon balls.

NUTRITION NOTES

Per portion:
Energy	69Kcals/293.8kJ
Fat	0.14g
Saturated Fat	0
Cholesterol	0
Fibre	0.47g

COOK'S TIP
Add the syrup in two stages, as the amount of sugar needed will depend on the sweetness of the melon.

CHILLED FRESH TOMATO SOUP

This effortless uncooked soup can be made in minutes.

— INGREDIENTS —

Serves 6
1.5kg/3–3½lb ripe tomatoes, peeled and
  roughly chopped
4 garlic cloves, crushed
30ml/2 tbsp balsamic vinegar
4 thick slices wholemeal bread
black pepper
low fat fromage frais, to garnish

1 Place the tomatoes in a blender with the garlic. Blend until smooth.

2 Pass the mixture through a sieve to remove the seeds. Stir in balsamic vinegar and season to taste with pepper. Put in the fridge to chill.

3 Toast the bread lightly on both sides. While still hot, cut off the crusts and slice the toast in half horizontally. Place on a board with the uncooked sides facing down and, using a circular motion, rub to remove any doughy pieces of bread.

COOK'S TIP
For the best flavour, it is important to use only fully ripened, flavourful tomatoes in this soup.

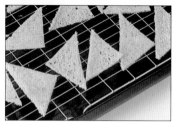

— NUTRITION NOTES —

Per portion:
Energy   111Kcals/475kJ
Fat   1.42g
Saturated Fat   0.39g
Cholesterol   0.16mg
Fibre   4.16g

4 Cut each slice into four triangles. Place on a grill pan and toast the uncooked sides until lightly golden. Garnish each bowl of soup with a spoonful of fromage frais and serve with the Melba toast.

Split Pea and Courgette Soup

Rich and satisfying, this tasty and nutritious soup will warm a chilly winter's day.

Ingredients

Serves 4

175g/6oz/1⅞ cups yellow split peas
1 medium onion, finely chopped
5ml/1 tsp sunflower oil
2 medium courgettes, finely diced
900ml/1½ pints/3¾ cups chicken stock
2.5ml/½ tsp ground turmeric
salt and black pepper

1 Place the split peas in a bowl, cover with cold water and leave to soak for several hours or overnight. Drain, rinse in cold water and drain again.

2 Cook the onion in the oil in a covered pan, shaking occasionally, until soft. Reserve a handful of diced courgettes and add the rest to the pan. Cook, stirring, for 2–3 minutes.

3 Add the stock and turmeric to the pan and bring to the boil. Reduce the heat, then cover and simmer for 30–40 minutes, or until the split peas are tender. Adjust the seasoning.

4 When the soup is almost ready, bring a large saucepan of water to the boil, add the reserved diced courgettes and cook for 1 minute, then drain and add to the soup before serving hot with warm crusty bread.

> **Cook's Tip**
> For a quicker alternative, use split red lentils for this soup – they need no presoaking and cook very quickly. Adjust the amount of stock, if necessary.

Nutrition Notes

Per portion:

Energy	174Kcals/730kJ
Fat	2.14g
Saturated fat	0.54g
Cholesterol	0
Fibre	3.43g

CARROT AND CORIANDER SOUP

Nearly all root vegetables make excellent soups as they purée well and have an earthy flavour which complements the sharper flavours of herbs and spices. Carrots are particularly versatile, and this simple soup is elegant in both flavour and appearance.

INGREDIENTS

Serves 6
10ml/2 tsp sunflower oil
1 onion, chopped
1 celery stick, sliced, plus 2–3 leafy celery tops
2 small potatoes, chopped
450g/1lb carrots, preferably young and tender, chopped
1 litre/1¾ pints/4 cups chicken stock
10–15ml/2–3 tsp ground coriander
15ml/1 tbsp chopped fresh coriander
200ml/7fl oz/1 cup semi-skimmed milk
salt and black pepper

1 Heat the oil in a large flameproof casserole or heavy-based saucepan and fry the onion over a gentle heat for 3–4 minutes until slightly softened but not browned. Add the celery and potato, cook for a few minutes, then add the carrot. Fry over a gentle heat for 3–4 minutes, stirring frequently, and then cover. Reduce the heat even further and cook for about 10 minutes. Shake the pan or stir occasionally so the vegetables do not stick to the base.

2 Add the stock, bring to the boil and then partially cover and simmer for a further 8–10 minutes until the carrot and potato are tender.

3 Remove 6–8 tiny celery leaves for a garnish and finely chop about 15ml/1 tbsp of the remaining celery tops. In a small saucepan, dry fry the ground coriander for about 1 minute, stirring constantly. Reduce the heat, add the chopped celery and fresh coriander and fry for about 1 minute. Set aside.

4 Process the soup in a food processor or blender and pour into a clean saucepan. Stir in the milk, coriander mixture and seasoning. Heat gently, taste and adjust the seasoning. Serve garnished with the reserved celery.

NUTRITION NOTES

Per portion:
Energy	76.5Kcals/320kJ
Fat	3.2g
Saturated fat	0.65g
Cholesterol	2.3mg
Fibre	2.2g

COOK'S TIP
For a more piquant flavour, add a little freshly squeezed lemon juice just before serving. The contrast between the orange-coloured soup and the green garnish is a feast for the eye as well as the tastebuds.

Cauliflower and Walnut Cream

Even though there's no cream added to this soup, the cauliflower gives it a delicious, rich, creamy texture.

— Ingredients —

Serves 4

1 medium cauliflower
1 medium onion, roughly chopped
450ml/¾ pint/1⅞ cups chicken or
*   vegetable stock*
450ml/¾ pint/1⅞ cups skimmed milk
45ml/3 tbsp walnut pieces
salt and black pepper
paprika and chopped walnuts, to
*   garnish*

1 Trim the cauliflower of outer leaves and break into small florets. Place the cauliflower, onion and stock in a large saucepan.

2 Bring to the boil, cover and simmer for about 15 minutes, or until soft. Add the milk and walnuts, then purée in a food processor until smooth.

3 Season the soup to taste, then bring to the boil. Serve sprinkled with paprika and chopped walnuts.

— Nutrition Notes —

Per portion:

Energy	166Kcals/699kJ
Fat	9.02g
Saturated fat	0.88g
Cholesterol	2.25mg
Fibre	2.73g

Curried Carrot and Apple Soup

— Ingredients —

Serves 4

10ml/2 tsp sunflower oil
15ml/1 tbsp mild Korma curry powder
500g/1¼ lb carrots, chopped
1 large onion, chopped
1 Bramley cooking apple, chopped
750ml/1¼ pints/3⅛ cups chicken stock
salt and black pepper
natural low fat yogurt and carrot curls,
*   to garnish*

— Nutrition Notes —

Per portion:

Energy	114Kcals/477kJ
Fat	3.57g
Saturated fat	0.43g
Cholesterol	0.4mg
Fibre	4.99g

1 Heat the oil and gently fry the curry powder for 2–3 minutes.

2 Add the carrots, onion and apple, stir well, then cover the pan.

3 Cook over a very low heat for about 15 minutes, shaking the pan occasionally until softened. Spoon the vegetable mixture into a food processor or blender, then add half the stock and process until smooth.

4 Return to the pan and pour in the remaining stock. Bring the soup to the boil and adjust the seasoning before serving in bowls, garnished with a swirl of yogurt and a few curls of carrot.

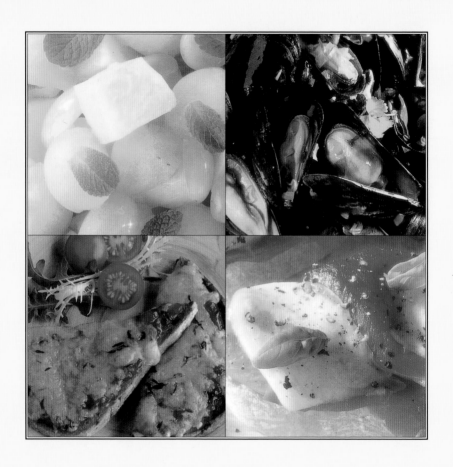

STARTERS AND SNACKS

Healthy low fat starters provide a delicious start to a meal and are quick and easy to make. Starters should not be too filling as they are simply setting the scene for the low fat main course to follow. Choose from a tempting selection of recipes, including light and refreshing fruit cocktails such as Minted Melon and Grapefruit and vegetable pâtés or dips such as Guacamole with Crudités. Quick and easy snacks and light dishes are ideal served with thick slices of warm, crusty bread for a low fat, nutritious lunch or supper. We include a selection of tasty snacks, such as Pasta with Herby Scallops, Cheese and Chutney Toasties and Parma Ham and Pepper Pizzas.

MELON, PINEAPPLE AND GRAPE COCKTAIL

A light, refreshing fruit salad, with no added sugar and virtually no fat, perfect for breakfast or brunch – or any time.

INGREDIENTS

Serves 4

½ melon
225g/8oz fresh pineapple or 225g/8oz
  can pineapple chunks in own juice
225g/8oz seedless white grapes, halved
120ml/4fl oz/½ cup white grape juice
fresh mint leaves, to decorate (optional)

1 Remove the seeds from the melon half and use a melon baller to scoop out even-size balls.

COOK'S TIP
A melon is ready to eat when it smells sweet even through its thick skin. Use a firm-fleshed fruit, such as a Galia or honeydew melon.

2 Using a sharp knife, cut the skin from the pineapple and discard. Cut the fruit into bite-size chunks.

3 Combine all the fruits in a glass serving dish and pour over the juice. If you are using canned pineapple, measure the drained juice and make it up to the required quantity with the grape juice.

4 If not serving immediately, cover and chill. Serve decorated with mint leaves, if liked.

NUTRITION NOTES

Per portion:

Energy	95Kcals/395kJ
Fat	0.5g
Saturated Fat	0
Cholesterol	0

GRAPEFRUIT SALAD WITH ORANGE

The bitter-sweet flavour of Campari combines especially well with citrus fruit. Because of its alcohol content, this dish is not suitable for young children.

INGREDIENTS

Serves 4
45ml/3 tbsp caster sugar
60ml/4 tbsp Campari
30ml/2 tbsp lemon juice
4 grapefruit
5 oranges
4 sprigs fresh mint

NUTRITION NOTES

Per portion:

Energy	196Kcals/822kJ
Fat	5.9g
Saturated Fat	2.21g
Cholesterol	66.37mg
Fibre	1.6g

1 Bring 150ml/5fl oz/²/₃ cup water to the boil in a small saucepan, add the sugar and simmer until dissolved. Leave to cool, then add the Campari and lemon juice. Chill until ready to serve.

COOK'S TIP
When buying citrus fruit, choose brightly coloured specimens that feel heavy for their size.

2 Cut the peel from the grapefruit and oranges with a serrated knife. Segment the fruit into a bowl by slipping a small paring knife between the flesh and the membranes. Combine the fruit with the Campari syrup and chill.

3 Spoon the salad into four dishes and garnish each dish with a sprig of fresh mint.

AUBERGINE, GARLIC AND PEPPER PÂTÉ

Serve this chunky, garlicky pâté of smoky baked aubergine and red peppers on a bed of salad, accompanied by crispbreads.

INGREDIENTS

Serves 4

3 aubergines
2 red peppers
5 garlic cloves
7.5ml/1½ tsp pink peppercorns in brine, drained and crushed
30ml/2 tbsp chopped fresh coriander

NUTRITION NOTES

Per portion:	
Energy	70Kcals/292kJ
Fat	1.32g
Saturated fat	0
Cholesterol	0
Fibre	5.96g

1 Preheat the oven to 200°C/400°F/ Gas 6. Arrange the whole aubergines, peppers and garlic cloves on a baking sheet and place in the oven. After 10 minutes remove the garlic cloves, and turn over the aubergines and peppers.

2 Carefully peel the garlic cloves and place in the bowl of a food processor or blender.

3 After a further 20 minutes remove the blistered and charred peppers from the oven and place in a plastic bag. Leave to cool.

4 After a further 10 minutes remove the aubergines from the oven. Split in half and scoop the flesh into a sieve placed over a bowl. Press the flesh with a spoon to remove the bitter juices.

5 Add the aubergine flesh to the garlic in the food processor or blender, and process until smooth. Place in a large mixing bowl.

6 Peel and chop the red peppers and stir into the aubergine mixture. Mix in the peppercorns and fresh coriander, and serve at once.

CUCUMBER AND ALFALFA TORTILLAS

Wheat tortillas are extremely simple to prepare at home. Served with a crisp, fresh salsa, they make a marvellous starter, light lunch or supper dish.

───── INGREDIENTS ─────

Serves 4
225g/8oz/2 cups plain flour, sifted
pinch of salt
45ml/3 tbsp olive oil
100–150ml/4–5fl oz/½–⅔ cup warm
   water
lime wedges, to garnish

For the salsa
1 red onion, finely chopped
1 red chilli, seeded and finely chopped
30ml/2 tbsp chopped fresh dill or
   coriander
½ cucumber, peeled and chopped
175g/6oz/2 cups alfalfa sprouts

For the sauce
1 large ripe avocado, peeled and stoned
juice of 1 lime
15ml/2 tbsp soft goat's cheese
pinch of paprika

1 Mix all the salsa ingredients together in a bowl and set aside.

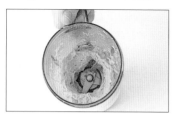

2 For the sauce, place the avocado, lime juice and goat's cheese in a food processor or blender and process until smooth. Place in a bowl and cover with clear film. Dust with paprika just before serving.

3 For the tortillas, place the flour and salt in a food processor or blender, add the oil and process. Gradually add the water until a stiff dough has formed. Turn out on to a floured board and knead until smooth.

4 Divide the mixture into eight pieces. Knead each piece for a couple of minutes and form into a ball. Flatten and roll out each ball to a 23cm/9 in circle.

NUTRITION NOTES	
Per portion:	
Energy	395Kcals/1659kJ
Fat	20.17g
Saturated fat	1.69g
Cholesterol	4.38mg
Fibre	4.15g

5 Heat a non-stick or ungreased heavy-based pan. Cook one tortilla at a time for about 30 seconds on each side. Place the cooked tortillas in a clean dish towel and repeat until you have made eight tortillas.

6 Spread each tortilla with a spoonful of avocado sauce, top with the salsa and roll up. Serve garnished with lime wedges and eat immediately.

COOK'S TIP
When peeling the avocado be sure to scrape off the bright green flesh from immediately under the skin as this gives the sauce its vivid green colour.

MINTED MELON AND GRAPEFRUIT

Melon is always a popular starter. Here the succulent flavour of the Galia melon is complemented by the refreshing taste of citrus fruit and a simple mustard and vinegar dressing. Fresh mint, used in the cocktail and as a garnish, enhances both its flavour and appearance.

INGREDIENTS

Serves 4

1 small Galia melon, weighing about
   1kg/2¼lb
2 pink grapefruit
1 yellow grapefruit
5ml/1 tsp Dijon mustard
5ml/1 tsp raspberry or sherry vinegar
5ml/1 tsp clear honey
15ml/1 tbsp chopped fresh mint
sprigs of fresh mint,
   to garnish

1 Halve the melon and remove the seeds with a teaspoon. With a melon baller, carefully scoop the flesh into balls.

NUTRITION NOTES

Per portion:

Energy	97Kcals/409kJ
Protein	2.22g
Fat	0.63g
Saturated Fat	0
Fibre	3.05g

2 With a small sharp knife, peel the grapefruit and remove all the white pith. Remove the segments by cutting between the membranes, holding the fruit over a small bowl to catch any juices.

3 Whisk the mustard, vinegar, honey, chopped mint and grapefruit juices together in a mixing bowl. Add the melon balls together with the grapefruit and mix well. Chill for 30 minutes.

4 Ladle the fruit into four glass dishes and serve garnished with sprigs of fresh mint.

GUACAMOLE WITH CRUDITÉS

This fresh-tasting spicy dip is made using peas instead of the avocado pears that are traditionally associated with this dish. This version saves on both fat and calories, without compromising on taste.

INGREDIENTS

Serves 4–6

350g/12oz/2¼ cups frozen peas,
  defrosted
1 garlic clove, crushed
2 spring onions, chopped
5ml/1 tsp finely grated rind and juice of
  1 lime
2.5ml/½ tsp ground cumin
dash of Tabasco sauce
15ml/1 tbsp reduced fat mayonnaise
30ml/2 tbsp chopped fresh coriander
  or parsley
salt and black pepper
pinch of paprika and lime slices,
  to garnish

For the crudités
6 baby carrots
2 celery sticks
1 red-skinned eating apple
1 pear
15ml/1 tbsp lemon or lime juice
6 baby sweetcorn

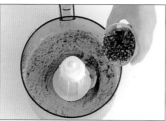

2 Add the chopped coriander or parsley and process for a few more seconds. Spoon into a serving bowl, cover with clear film and chill in the fridge for 30 minutes, to let the flavours develop fully.

3 For the crudités, trim and peel the carrots. Halve the celery sticks lengthways and trim into sticks, the same length as the carrots. Quarter, core and thickly slice the apple and pear, then dip into the lemon or lime juice. Arrange with the baby sweetcorn on a platter.

NUTRITION NOTES	
Per portion:	
Energy	110Kcals/460kJ
Protein	6.22g
Fat	2.29g
Saturated Fat	0.49g
Fibre	6.73g

1 Put the peas, garlic clove, spring onions, lime rind and juice, cumin, Tabasco sauce, mayonnaise and salt and black pepper into a food processor or a blender for a few minutes and process until smooth.

COOK'S TIP
Serve the guacamole dip with warmed wholemeal pitta bread.

4 Sprinkle the paprika over the guacamole and garnish with twisted lime slices.

TZATZIKI

Tzatziki is a Greek cucumber salad dressed with yogurt, mint and garlic. It is typically served with grilled lamb and chicken, but is also good served with crudités.

INGREDIENTS

Serves 4

1 cucumber
5ml/1 tsp salt
45ml/3 tbsp finely chopped fresh mint, plus a few sprigs to garnish
1 garlic clove, crushed
5ml/1 tsp caster sugar
200ml/7fl oz reduced fat Greek-style yogurt
cucumber flower, to garnish (optional)

1 Peel the cucumber. Reserve a little of the cucumber to use as a garnish if you wish and cut the rest in half lengthways. Remove the seeds with a teaspoon and discard. Slice the cucumber thinly and combine with salt. Leave for approximately 15–20 minutes. Salt will soften the cucumber and draw out any bitter juices.

COOK'S TIP
If you want to prepare Tzatziki in a hurry, then leave out the method for salting cucumber at the end of step 1. The cucumber will have a more crunchy texture, and will be slightly less sweet.

2 Combine the mint, garlic, sugar and yogurt in a bowl, reserving a few sprigs of mint as decoration.

3 Rinse the cucumber in a sieve under cold running water to flush away the salt. Drain well and combine with the yogurt. Decorate with cucumber flower and/or mint. Serve cold.

NUTRITION NOTES

Per portion:

Energy	41.5Kcals/174.5kJ
Fat	0.51g
Saturated Fat	0.25g
Cholesterol	2mg
Fibre	0.2g

CHILLI TOMATO SALSA

This universal dip is great served with absolutely anything and can be made up to 24 hours in advance.

INGREDIENTS

Serves 4
1 shallot, peeled and halved
2 garlic cloves, peeled
handful of fresh basil leaves
500g/1¼ lb ripe tomatoes
10ml/2 tsp olive oil
2 green chillies
salt and black pepper

1 Place the shallot and garlic in a food processor with the fresh basil. Whizz the shallot, garlic and basil until finely chopped.

2 Halve the tomatoes and add to the food processor. Pulse the machine until the mixture is well blended and coarsely chopped.

3 With the motor running, slowly pour in the olive oil. Add salt and pepper to taste.

NUTRITION NOTES

Per portion:
Energy	28Kcals/79kJ
Fat	0.47g
Saturated Fat	0.13g
Cholesterol	0
Fibre	1.45g

4 Halve the chillies lengthways and remove the seeds. Finely slice the chillies widthways into tiny strips and stir into the tomato salsa. Serve at room temperature.

COOK'S TIP
The salsa is best made in the summer when tomatoes are at their best. In winter, use a drained 400g/14oz can of plum tomatoes.

CHEESE AND SPINACH PUFFS

Serves 6

150g/5oz cooked, chopped spinach
175g/6oz/¾ cup cottage cheese
5ml/1 tsp grated nutmeg
2 egg whites
30ml/2 tbsp grated Parmesan cheese
salt and black pepper

1 Preheat the oven to 220°C/425°F/ Gas 7. Oil six ramekin dishes.

2 Mix together the spinach and cottage cheese in a small bowl, then add the nutmeg and seasoning to taste.

3 Whisk the egg whites in a separate bowl until stiff enough to hold soft peaks. Fold them evenly into the spinach mixture using a spatula or large metal spoon, then spoon the mixture into the oiled ramekins, dividing it evenly, and smooth the tops.

4 Sprinkle with the Parmesan and place on a baking sheet. Bake for 15–20 minutes, or until well risen and golden brown. Serve immediately.

NUTRITION NOTES

Per portion:	
Energy	47Kcals/195kJ
Fat	1.32g
Saturated fat	0.52g
Cholesterol	2.79mg
Fibre	0.53g

LEMONY STUFFED COURGETTES

Serves 4

4 courgettes, about 175g/6oz each
5ml/1 tsp sunflower oil
1 garlic clove, crushed
5ml/1 tsp ground lemon grass
finely grated rind and juice of ½ lemon
115g/4oz/1½ cups cooked long grain
  rice
175g/6oz cherry tomatoes, halved
30ml/2 tbsp toasted cashew nuts
salt and black pepper
sprigs of thyme, to garnish

NUTRITION NOTES

Per portion:	
Energy	126Kcals/530kJ
Fat	5.33g
Saturated fat	0.65g
Cholesterol	0
Fibre	2.31g

1 Preheat the oven to 200°C/400°F/ Gas 6. Halve the courgettes lengthways and use a teaspoon to scoop out the centres. Blanch the shells in boiling water for 1 minute, then drain well.

2 Chop the courgette flesh finely and place in a saucepan with the oil and garlic. Stir over a moderate heat until softened, but not browned.

3 Stir in the lemon grass, lemon rind and juice, rice, tomatoes and cashew nuts. Season well and spoon into the courgette shells. Place the shells in a baking tin and cover with foil.

4 Bake for 25–30 minutes or until the courgettes are tender, then serve hot, garnished with thyme sprigs.

TUNA CHILLI TACOS

Tacos are a useful, quick snack – but you will need to use both hands to eat them!

INGREDIENTS

Makes 8

8 taco shells
400g/14oz can red kidney beans, drained
120ml/4 fl oz/½ cup low fat fromage frais
2.5ml/½ tsp chilli sauce
2 spring onions, chopped
1 tsp/5 ml chopped fresh mint
½ small crisp lettuce, shredded
425g/15oz can tuna fish chunks in brine, drained
50g/2oz/¼ cup grated reduced fat Cheddar cheese
8 cherry tomatoes, quartered
mint sprigs, to garnish

1 Warm the taco shells in a hot oven for a few minutes until crisp.

2 Mash the beans lightly with a fork, then stir in the fromage frais with the chilli sauce, onions and mint.

3 Fill the taco shells with the shredded lettuce, the bean mixture and tuna. Top the filled shells with the cheese and serve at once with the tomatoes, garnished with sprigs of mint.

NUTRITION NOTES

Per portion:

Energy	147Kcals/615kJ
Fat	2.42g
Saturated fat	1.13g
Cholesterol	29.69mg
Fibre	2.41g

POTATO SKINS WITH CAJUN DIP

No need to deep fry potato skins for this treat – grilling crisps them up in no time.

INGREDIENTS

Serves 2

2 large baking potatoes
120g/4fl oz/½ cup natural yogurt
1 garlic clove, crushed
5ml/1 tsp tomato purée
2.5ml/½ tsp green chilli purée (or ½ small green chilli, chopped)
1.25ml/¼ tsp celery salt
salt and black pepper

1 Bake or microwave the potatoes until tender. Cut them in half and scoop out the flesh, leaving a thin layer on the skins. Keep the scooped out potato for another meal.

2 Cut each potato in half again then place the pieces skin-side down on a large baking sheet.

3 Grill for 4–5 minutes, or until crisp. Mix together the dip ingredients and serve with the potato skins.

NUTRITION NOTES

Per portion:

Energy	202Kcals/847kJ
Fat	0.93g
Saturated fat	0.34g
Cholesterol	2.3mg
Fibre	3.03g

MELON WITH WILD STRAWBERRIES

This fragrant, colourful starter is the perfect way to begin a rich meal as both melons and strawberries are virtually fat-free. Here several varieties are combined with strongly flavoured wild or woodland strawberries. If wild strawberries are not available, use ordinary strawberries or raspberries instead.

INGREDIENTS

Serves 4
1 cantaloupe or Charentais melon
1 Galia melon
900g/2lb watermelon
175g/6oz wild strawberries
4 sprigs fresh mint, to garnish

NUTRITION NOTES

Per portion:
Energy	42.5Kcals/178.6kJ
Fat	0.32g
Saturated Fat	0
Cholesterol	0
Fibre	1.09g

1 Using a large sharp knife, cut all three melons in half.

2 Scoop out the seeds from both the cantaloupe or Charentais and Galia melons with a spoon.

3 With a melon scoop, take out as many balls as you can from all three melons. Combine in a large bowl and chill for at least 1 hour.

4 Add the wild strawberries and mix together gently. Spoon out into four stemmed glass dishes.

5 Garnish each of the melon salads with a small sprig of mint and serve at once.

COOK'S TIP
Ripe melons should give slightly when pressed at the base, and should give off a sweet scent. Buy carefully if you plan to use the fruit on the day. If one or more varieties of melon aren't available, then substitute another, or buy two or three of the same variety – the salad might not be quite so colourful, but it will taste equally refreshing.

MUSSELS WITH THAI HERBS

Another simple dish to prepare. The lemon grass adds a refreshing tang to the mussels.

INGREDIENTS

Serves 6

1kg/2¼ lb mussels, cleaned and beards removed
2 lemon grass stalks, finely chopped
4 shallots, chopped
4 kaffir lime leaves, roughly torn
2 red chillies, sliced
15ml/1 tbsp fish sauce
30ml/2 tbsp lime juice
2 spring onions, chopped, and coriander leaves, to garnish

1 Put all the ingredients, except the spring onions and coriander, in a large saucepan and stir thoroughly.

2 Cover and cook for 5–7 minutes, shaking the saucepan occasionally, until the mussels open. Discard any mussels that do not open.

3 Transfer the cooked mussels to a serving platter.

4 Garnish the mussels with chopped spring onions and coriander leaves. Serve immediately.

NUTRITION NOTES	
Per portion:	
Energy	56Kcals/238kJ
Fat	1.22g
Saturated Fat	0.16g
Cholesterol	0.32g
Fibre	27g

PASTA WITH HERBY SCALLOPS

Low fat fromage frais, flavoured with mustard, garlic and herbs, makes a deceptively creamy sauce for pasta.

INGREDIENTS

Serves 4

120ml/4fl oz/½ cup low fat
  fromage frais
10ml/2 tsp wholegrain mustard
2 garlic cloves, crushed
30–45ml/2–3 tbsp fresh lime juice
60ml/4 tbsp chopped fresh parsley
30ml/2 tbsp snipped chives
350g/12oz black tagliatelle
12 large scallops
60ml/4 tbsp white wine
150ml/¼ pint/⅔ cup fish stock
salt and black pepper
lime wedges and parsley sprigs,
  to garnish

1 To make the sauce, mix the fromage frais, mustard, garlic, lime juice, parsley, chives and seasoning together in a mixing bowl.

2 Cook the pasta in a large pan of boiling salted water until *al dente*. Drain thoroughly.

3 Slice the scallops in half, horizontally. Keep any coral whole. Put the wine and fish stock into a saucepan and heat to simmering point. Add the scallops and cook very gently for 3–4 minutes. (Don't cook for any longer, or they will toughen.)

COOK'S TIP
Black tagliatelle, made with squid ink, is available from Italian delicatessens, but other colours can be used to make this dish – try a mixture of white and green.

4 Remove the scallops. Boil the wine and stock to reduce by half and add the green sauce to the pan. Heat gently to warm, then return the scallops to the pan and cook for 1 minute. Spoon over the pasta and garnish with lime wedges and parsley.

NUTRITION NOTES	
Per portion:	
Energy	368Kcals/1561kJ
Fat	4.01g
Saturated Fat	0.98g
Cholesterol	99mg
Fibre	1.91g

FRESH FIG, APPLE AND DATE SALAD

Sweet Mediterranean figs and dates combine especially well with crisp eating apples. A hint of almond serves to unite the flavours, but if you'd prefer to reduce the fat even more, omit the marzipan and add another 30ml/2 tbsp low fat natural yogurt or use low fat fromage frais instead.

INGREDIENTS

Serves 4

6 large eating apples
juice of ½ lemon
175g/6oz fresh dates
25g/1oz white marzipan
5ml/1 tsp orange flower water
60ml/4 tbsp low fat natural yogurt
4 green or purple figs
4 almonds, toasted

1 Core the apples. Slice thinly, then cut into fine matchsticks. Moisten with lemon juice to keep them white.

NUTRITION NOTES

Per portion:

Energy	255Kcals/876.5kJ
Fat	4.98g
Saturated Fat	1.05g
Cholesterol	2.25mg
Fibre	1.69g

2 Remove the stones from the dates and cut the flesh into fine strips, then combine with the apple slices.

3 Soften the marzipan with orange flower water and combine with the yogurt. Mix well.

COOK'S TIP
For a slightly stronger almond flavour, add a few drops of almond essence to the yogurt mixture. When buying fresh figs, choose firm, unblemished fruit which give slightly when lightly squeezed. Avoid damaged, bruised or very soft fruit.

4 Pile the apples and dates in the centre of four plates. Remove the stem from each of the figs and divide the fruit into quarters without cutting right through the base. Squeeze the base with the thumb and forefinger of each hand to open up the fruit.

5 Place a fig in the centre of each salad. Spoon the yogurt filling on to the figs and decorate each one with a toasted almond.

CHEESE AND CHUTNEY TOASTIES

Quick cheese on toast can be made quite memorable with a few tasty additions. Serve these scrumptious toasties with a simple lettuce and cherry tomato salad.

INGREDIENTS

Serves 4

4 slices wholemeal bread, thickly sliced
85g/3½oz Cheddar cheese, grated
5ml/1 tsp dried thyme
30ml/2 tbsp chutney or relish
black pepper
salad, to serve

1 Toast the bread slices lightly on each side.

2 Mix the cheese and thyme together and season to taste with pepper.

NUTRITION NOTES

Per portion:
Energy	157.25Kcals/664.25kJ
Fat	4.24g
Saturated Fat	1.99g
Cholesterol	9.25mg
Fibre	2.41g

3 Spread the chutney or relish on the toast and divide the cheese evenly between the four slices.

4 Return the toast to the grill and cook until the cheese is browned and bubbling. Cut each slice into halves, diagonally, and serve at once with salad.

COOK'S TIP
If you prefer, use a reduced fat hard cheese, such as mature Cheddar or Red Leicester, in place of the full fat Cheddar to cut both calories and fat.

PARMA HAM AND PEPPER PIZZAS

The delicious flavours of these
easy pizzas are hard to beat.

INGREDIENTS

Makes 4

½ loaf ciabatta bread
1 red pepper, roasted and peeled
1 yellow pepper, roasted and peeled
4 slices Parma ham, cut into
 thick strips
50g/2oz reduced fat mozzarella cheese
black pepper
tiny basil leaves, to garnish

NUTRITION NOTES

Per portion:	
Energy	93Kcals/395kJ
Fat	3.25g
Saturated Fat	1.49g
Cholesterol	14mg
Fibre	1g

1 Cut the bread into four thick slices
and toast until golden.

2 Cut the roasted peppers into thick
strips and arrange on the toasted
bread with the strips of Parma ham.
Preheat the grill.

3 Thinly slice the mozzarella and
arrange on top, then grind over
plenty of black pepper. Grill for 2–3
minutes until the cheese is bubbling.

4 Scatter the basil leaves on top and
serve immediately.

CHICKEN PITTAS WITH RED COLESLAW

Pittas are convenient for simple snacks and packed lunches and it's easy to pack in lots of fresh healthy ingredients.

INGREDIENTS

Serves 4

¼ red cabbage, finely shredded
1 small red onion, finely sliced
2 radishes, thinly sliced
1 red apple, peeled, cored and grated
15ml/1 tbsp lemon juice
45ml/3 tbsp low fat fromage frais
1 cooked chicken breast without skin, about 175g/6oz
4 large pittas or 8 small pittas
salt and black pepper
chopped fresh parsley, to garnish

1 Remove the tough central spine from the cabbage leaves, then finely shred the leaves using a large sharp knife. Place the shredded cabbage in a bowl and stir in the onion, radishes, apple and lemon juice.

2 Stir the fromage frais into the shredded cabbage mixture and season well with salt and pepper. Thinly slice the cooked chicken breast and stir into the shredded cabbage mixture until well coated in fromage frais.

3 Warm the pittas under a hot grill, then split them along one edge using a round-bladed knife. Spoon the filling into the pittas, then garnish with chopped fresh parsley.

> **COOK'S TIP**
> If the filled pittas need to be made more than an hour in advance, line the pitta breads with crisp lettuce leaves before adding the filling.

NUTRITION NOTES

Per portion:

Energy	232Kcals/976kJ
Fat	2.61g
Saturated fat	0.76g
Cholesterol	24.61mg
Fibre	2.97g

SMOKED TROUT SALAD

Salads are the easy answer to fast, healthy eating. When lettuce is sweet and crisp, partner it with fillets of smoked trout, warm new potatoes and a creamy horseradish dressing.

INGREDIENTS

Serves 4
675g/1½ lb new potatoes
4 smoked trout fillets
115g/4oz mixed lettuce leaves
4 slices dark rye bread, cut into fingers
salt and black pepper

For the dressing
60ml/4 tbsp creamed horseradish
60ml/4 tbsp groundnut oil
15ml/1 tbsp white wine vinegar
10ml/2 tsp caraway seeds

NUTRITION NOTES

Per portion:
Energy	487Kcals/2044kJ
Fat	22.22g
Saturated fat	4.1g
Cholesterol	52.1mg
Fibre	3.5g

2 Remove the skin from the trout, then pull out any little bones using your fingers or a pair of tweezers.

4 Flake the trout fillets and halve the potatoes. Scatter them together with the rye fingers over the salad leaves and toss to mix. Season to taste and serve.

1 Peel or scrub the potatoes. Place the potatoes in a large saucepan and cover with cold water. Bring to the boil and simmer for about 20 minutes.

3 To make the dressing, place all the ingredients in a screw-top jar and shake vigorously. Season the lettuce leaves and moisten them with the prepared dressing. Divide the dressed leaves among four plates.

COOK'S TIP
To save time washing lettuce leaves, buy them ready-prepared from your supermarket. It is better to season the leaves rather than the dressing when making a salad.

SALMON PARCELS

Serve these little savoury parcels just as they are for a snack, or with a pool of fresh tomato sauce for a special starter.

INGREDIENTS

Makes 12

90g/3½oz can red or pink salmon
15ml/1 tbsp chopped fresh coriander
4 spring onions, finely chopped
4 sheets filo pastry
sunflower oil, for brushing
spring onions and salad leaves, to
    serve

COOK'S TIP
When you are using filo pastry, it is important to prevent it drying out; cover any you are not using with a tea towel or cling film.

1 Preheat the oven to 200°C/400°F/ Gas 6. Lightly oil a baking sheet. Drain the salmon, discarding any skin and bones, then place in a bowl.

2 Flake the salmon with a fork and mix with the fresh coriander and spring onions.

3 Place a single sheet of filo pastry on a work surface and brush lightly with oil. Place another sheet on top. Cut into six squares, about 10cm/4in. Repeat with the remaining pastry, to make 12 squares.

4 Place a spoonful of the salmon mixture on to each square. Brush the edges of the pastry with oil, then draw together, pressing to seal. Place the pastries on a baking sheet and bake for 12–15 minutes, until golden. Serve warm, with spring onions and salad.

NUTRITION NOTES

Per portion:

Energy	25Kcals/107kJ
Fat	1.16g
Saturated fat	0.23g
Cholesterol	2.55mg
Fibre	0.05g

TOMATO CHEESE TARTS

These crisp little tartlets are easier to make than they look. Best eaten fresh from the oven.

INGREDIENTS

Serves 4

2 sheets filo pastry
1 egg white
115g/4oz/½ cup skimmed milk soft
    cheese
handful fresh basil leaves
3 small tomatoes, sliced
salt and black pepper

1 Preheat the oven to 200°C/400°F/ Gas 6. Brush the sheets of filo pastry lightly with egg white and cut into sixteen 10 cm/4 in squares.

2 Layer the squares in twos, in eight patty tins. Spoon the cheese into the pastry cases. Season with black pepper and top with basil leaves.

3 Arrange tomatoes on the tarts, add seasoning and bake for 10-12 minutes, until golden. Serve warm.

NUTRITION NOTES

Per portion:

Energy	50Kcals/210kJ
Fat	0.33g
Saturated fat	0.05g
Cholesterol	0.29mg
Fibre	0.25g

CHINESE GARLIC MUSHROOMS

Tofu is high in protein and very low in fat, so it is a very useful food to keep handy for quick meals and snacks like this one.

INGREDIENTS

Serves 4

8 large open mushrooms
3 spring onions, sliced
1 garlic clove, crushed
30ml/2 tbsp oyster sauce
285g/10 oz packet marinated tofu, cut into small dice
200g/7oz can sweetcorn, drained
10ml/2 tsp sesame oil
salt and black pepper

1 Preheat the oven to 200°C/400°F/ Gas 6. Finely chop the mushroom stalks and mix with the spring onions, garlic and oyster sauce.

2 Stir in the diced marinated tofu and sweetcorn, season well with salt and pepper, then spoon the filling into the mushrooms.

3 Brush the edges of the mushrooms with the sesame oil. Arrange the stuffed mushrooms in a baking dish and bake for 12–15 minutes, until the mushrooms are just tender, then serve at once.

COOK'S TIP
If you prefer, omit the oyster sauce and use light soy sauce instead.

NUTRITION NOTES

Per portion:	
Energy	137Kcals/575kJ
Fat	5.6g
Saturated fat	0.85g
Cholesterol	0
Fibre	1.96g

WILD RICE RÖSTI WITH CARROT PURÉE

Rösti is a traditional dish from Switzerland. This variation has the extra nuttiness of wild rice and a bright simple sauce as a fresh accompaniment.

INGREDIENTS

Serves 6

50g/2oz/½ cup wild rice
900g/2 lb large potatoes
45ml/3 tbsp walnut oil
5ml/1 tsp yellow mustard seeds
1 onion, coarsely grated and drained
30ml/2 tbsp fresh thyme leaves
salt and black pepper
vegetables, to serve

For the purée

350g/12oz carrots, peeled and roughly
    chopped
pared rind and juice of 1 large orange

NUTRITION NOTES

Per portion:
Energy	246Kcals/1035kJ
Fat	8.72g
Saturated fat	0.78g
Cholesterol	0
Fibre	3.8g

1 For the purée, place the carrots in a saucepan, cover with cold water and add two pieces of orange rind. Bring to the boil and cook for about 10 minutes or until tender. Drain well and discard the rind.

2 Purée the mixture in a food processor or blender with 60ml/4 tbsp of the orange juice. Return to the pan.

3 Place the wild rice in a clean pan and cover with water. Bring to the boil and cook for about 30–40 minutes, until the rice is just starting to split, but still crunchy. Drain the rice.

4 Scrub the potatoes, place in a large pan and cover with cold water. Bring to the boil and cook for about 10–15 minutes until just tender. Drain well and leave to cool slightly. When the potatoes are cool, peel and coarsely grate them into a large bowl. Add the cooked rice.

5 Heat 30ml/2 tbsp of the walnut oil in a non-stick frying pan and add the mustard seeds. When they start to pop, add the onion and cook gently for about 5 minutes until soft. Add to the bowl of potato and rice, together with the thyme, and mix thoroughly. Season.

6 Heat the remaining oil and add the potato mixture. Press down well and cook for about 10 minutes or until golden brown. Cover the pan with a plate and flip over, then slide the rösti back into the pan for another 10 minutes to cook the other side. Serve with the reheated carrot purée.

COOK'S TIP
Make individual rösti and serve topped with a mixed julienne of vegetables for an unusual starter.

AUBERGINE SUNFLOWER PÂTÉ

──────── INGREDIENTS ────────

Serves 4
1 large aubergine
1 garlic clove, crushed
15ml/1 tbsp lemon juice
30ml/2 tbsp sunflower seeds
45ml/3 tbsp natural low fat yogurt
handful fresh coriander or parsley
black pepper
black olives, to garnish

1 Cut the aubergine in half and place, cut side down, on a baking sheet. Place under a hot grill for 15–20 minutes, until the skin is blackened and the flesh is soft. Leave for a few minutes, to cool slightly.

2 Scoop the flesh of the aubergine into a food processor. Add the garlic, lemon juice, sunflower seeds and yogurt. Process until smooth.

3 Roughly chop the fresh coriander or parsley and mix in. Season, then spoon into a serving dish. Top with olives and serve with vegetable sticks.

──── NUTRITION NOTES ────

Per portion:	
Energy	71Kcals/298kJ
Fat	4.51g
Saturated fat	0.48g
Cholesterol	0.45mg
Fibre	2.62g

PEPPER DIPS WITH CRUDITÉS

Make one or both of these colourful vegetable dips – if you have time to make both they look spectacular together.

──────── INGREDIENTS ────────

Serves 4–6
2 medium red peppers, halved and
  seeded
2 medium yellow peppers, halved and
  seeded
2 garlic cloves
30ml/2 tbsp lemon juice
20ml/4 tsp olive oil
50g/2oz fresh white breadcrumbs
salt and black pepper
fresh vegetables, for dipping

1 Place the peppers in separate saucepans with a peeled clove of garlic. Add just enough water to cover.

2 Bring to the boil, then cover and simmer for 15 minutes until tender. Drain, cool, then purée separately in a food processor or blender, adding half the lemon juice and olive oil to each.

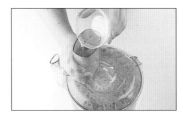

3 Stir half the breadcrumbs into each and season to taste with salt and pepper. Serve the dips with a selection of fresh vegetables for dipping.

──── NUTRITION NOTES ────

Per portion:	
Energy	103Kcals/432kJ
Fat	3.7g
Saturated fat	0.47g
Cholesterol	0
Fibre	2.77g

SMOKED SALMON PANCAKES WITH PESTO

These simple pancakes are quick to prepare and are perfect for a special occasion topped with smoked salmon, fresh basil and toasted pine nuts.

───── INGREDIENTS ─────

Makes 12–16
120ml/4fl oz/½ cup skimmed milk
115g/4oz/1 cup self-raising flour
1 egg
30ml/2 tbsp pesto sauce
vegetable oil, for frying
200ml/7fl oz/⅞ cup low fat crème fraîche
75g/3oz smoked salmon
15ml/1 tbsp pine nuts, toasted
salt and black pepper
12–16 basil sprigs, to garnish

───── NUTRITION NOTES ─────

Per portion:
Energy   116Kcals/485kJ
Fat   7.42g
Saturated fat   2.4g
Cholesterol   39.58mg
Fibre   0.34g

1 Pour half of the milk into a mixing bowl. Add the flour, egg, pesto sauce and seasoning, and mix to a smooth batter.

2 Add the remainder of the milk and stir until evenly blended.

3 Heat the vegetable oil in a large frying pan. Spoon the pancake mixture into the heated oil in small heaps. Allow about 30 seconds for the pancakes to rise, then turn and cook briefly on the other side. Continue cooking the pancakes in batches until all the batter is used up.

4 Arrange the pancakes on a serving plate and top each one with a spoonful of crème fraîche.

5 Cut the salmon into 1cm/½ in strips and place on top of each pancake.

6 Scatter each pancake with pine nuts and garnish with a sprig of fresh basil before serving.

COOK'S TIP
If not serving immediately, cover the pancakes with a dish towel and keep warm in an oven preheated to 140°C/275°F/Gas 1.

BUCKWHEAT BLINIS

INGREDIENTS

Serves 4

5ml/1 tsp easy-blend dried yeast
250ml/8fl oz/1 cup skimmed milk,
  warmed
40g/1½oz/⅓ cup buckwheat flour
40g/1½oz/⅓ cup plain flour
10ml/2 tsp caster sugar
pinch of salt
1 egg, separated
lamb's lettuce, to serve

For the avocado cream
1 large avocado
75g/3oz/⅓ cup low fat fromage blanc
juice of 1 lime
cracked black peppercorns, to garnish

For the pickled beetroot
225g/8oz beetroot, peeled
45ml/3 tbsp lime juice
snipped fresh chives, to garnish

1 Mix the dried yeast with the milk, then mix with the next 4 ingredients and the egg yolk. Cover with a dish towel and leave to prove for about 40 minutes. Then whisk the egg white until stiff but not dry and fold into the blini mixture.

2 Heat a little oil in a non-stick frying pan and add a ladleful of batter to make a 10cm/4 in pancake. Cook for about 2–3 minutes on each side. Repeat with the remaining batter mixture to make eight blinis.

3 For the avocado cream, cut the avocado in half and remove the stone. Peel and place the flesh in a food processor or blender with the fromage blanc and lime juice. Process until the mixture is very smooth.

4 For the pickle, shred the beetroot finely. Mix with the lime juice. To serve, top each blini with a spoonful of avocado cream, garnish with cracked peppercorns. Serve with lamb's lettuce and the pickled beetroot, garnished with chives.

NUTRITION NOTES

Per portion:

Energy	304Kcals/1277kJ
Fat	16.56g
Saturated fat	2.23g
Cholesterol	56.3mg
Fibre	3.3g

COOK'S TIP
Serve with a glass of chilled vodka for a special occasion.

SPINACH AND POTATO GALETTE

Creamy layers of potato, spinach and herbs make this a warming supper dish.

INGREDIENTS

Serves 6
900g/2 lb large potatoes
450g/1 lb fresh spinach
2 eggs
400g/14oz/ 1¾ cups low fat soft cheese
15ml/1 tbsp wholegrain mustard
50g/2oz/2 cups chopped fresh herbs
  (e.g. chives, parsley, chervil or sorrel)
salt and black pepper
mixed salad, to serve

1 Preheat the oven to 180°C/350°F/ Gas 4. Line a deep 23cm/9 in cake tin with non-stick baking paper. Place the potatoes in a large saucepan and cover with cold water. Bring to the boil and cook for about 10 minutes. Drain well and allow to cool slightly before slicing thinly.

2 Wash the spinach and place in a large pan with only the water that is clinging to the leaves. Cover and cook, stirring once, until the spinach has just wilted. Drain well in a sieve and squeeze out the excess moisture. Chop finely.

NUTRITION NOTES

Per portion:

Energy	255Kcals/1072kJ
Fat	9.13g
Saturated fat	4.28g
Cholesterol	81.82mg
Fibre	3.81g

3 Beat the eggs with the soft cheese and mustard then stir in the chopped spinach and fresh herbs.

4 Place a layer of the sliced potatoes in the lined tin, arranging them in concentric circles. Top with a spoonful of the soft cheese mixture and spread out. Continue layering, seasoning with salt and pepper as you go, until all the potatoes and the soft cheese mixture are used up.

5 Cover the tin with a piece of foil and place in a roasting tin.

6 Fill the roasting tin with enough boiling water to come halfway up the sides, and cook in the oven for about 45–50 minutes. Serve hot or cold with a mixed salad.

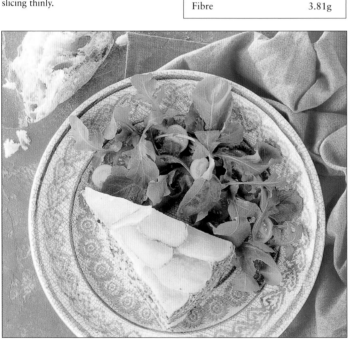

TOMATO PESTO TOASTIES

Ready-made pesto is high in fat but, as its flavour is so powerful, it can be used in very small amounts with good effect, as in these tasty toasties.

INGREDIENTS

Serves 2
2 thick slices crusty bread
45ml/3 tbsp skimmed milk soft cheese
    or low fat fromage frais
10ml/2 tsp red or green pesto
1 beef tomato
1 red onion
salt and black pepper

1 Toast the bread slices on a hot grill until golden brown on both sides turning once. Leave to cool.

2 Mix together the skimmed milk soft cheese and pesto in a small bowl until well blended, then spread thickly on to the toasted bread.

3 Cut the beef tomato and red onion, crossways, into thin slices using a large sharp knife.

4 Arrange the slices, overlapping, on top of the toast and season with salt and pepper. Transfer the toasties to a grill rack and cook under a hot grill until heated through, then serve immediately.

COOK'S TIP
Almost any type of crusty bread can be used for this recipe, but Italian olive oil bread and French bread will give the best flavour.

NUTRITION NOTES

Per portion:

Energy	177Kcals/741kJ
Fat	2.41g
Saturated fat	0.19g
Cholesterol	0.23mg
Fibre	2.2g

MUSHROOM CROUSTADES

The rich mushroom flavour of this filling is heightened by the addition of Worcestershire sauce.

INGREDIENTS

Serves 2–4
1 short French stick, about 25cm/10in
10ml/2 tsp olive oil
250g/9oz open cup mushrooms, quartered
10ml/2 tsp Worcestershire sauce
10ml/2 tsp lemon juice
30ml/2 tbsp skimmed milk
30ml/2 tbsp snipped fresh chives
salt and black pepper
snipped fresh chives, to garnish

1 Preheat the oven to 200°C/400°F/ Gas 6. Cut the French bread in half lengthways. Cut a scoop out of the soft middle of each, leaving a thick border all the way round.

2 Brush the bread with oil, place on a baking sheet and bake for about 6–8 minutes, until golden and crisp.

3 Place the mushrooms in a small saucepan with the Worcestershire sauce, lemon juice and milk. Simmer for about 5 minutes, or until most of the liquid is evaporated.

4 Remove from the heat, then add the chives and seasoning. Spoon into the bread croustades and serve hot, garnished with snipped chives.

NUTRITION NOTES

Per portion:

Energy	324Kcals/1361kJ
Fat	6.4g
Saturated fat	1.27g
Cholesterol	0.3mg
Fibre	3.07g

GRANARY SLTs

A quick, tasty snack or easy
packed lunch with a healthy
combination – sardines, lettuce
and tomatoes!

INGREDIENTS

Serves 2

2 small Granary bread rolls
120g/4¼oz can sardines in olive oil
4 crisp green lettuce leaves, such as
    Webbs
1 beef tomato, sliced
juice of ½ lemon
salt and black pepper

1 Slice the bread rolls in half crossways using a sharp knife. Drain off
the oil from the sardines into a small
bowl, then brush the cut surfaces of the
rolls with a small amount of the oil.

2 Cut or break the sardines into small
pieces, then fill each roll with a
lettuce leaf, some sliced tomato and
pieces of sardine, sprinkling the filling
with a little lemon juice, and salt and
pepper to taste.

3 Sandwich the rolls back together
and press the lids down lightly with
your hand. Serve at once.

NUTRITION NOTES

Per portion:

Energy	248Kcals/1042kJ
Fat	8.51g
Saturated fat	1.86g
Cholesterol	32.5mg
Fibre	3.01g

COOK'S TIP
If you prefer to use sardines in
tomato sauce, spread the bread
rolls thinly with low fat spread
before adding the filling.

SURPRISE SCOTCH 'EGGS'

This reduced fat version of Scotch eggs is great for packed lunches or picnics. If half fat sausagemeat isn't available, buy half fat sausages or turkey sausages and remove the skins.

INGREDIENTS

Makes 3

75ml/5 tbsp chopped parsley and snipped chives, mixed
115g/4oz/½ cup skimmed milk soft cheese
450g/1 lb half fat sausagemeat
50g/2oz /½ cup rolled oats
salt and black pepper
mixed leaf and tomato salad, to serve

1 Preheat the oven to 200°C/400°F/ Gas 6. Mix together the herbs, cheese and seasonings, then roll into three even-sized balls.

2 Divide the sausagemeat into three and press each piece out to a round, about 1cm/½ in thick.

3 Wrap each cheese ball in a piece of sausagemeat, smoothing over all the joins to enclose the cheese completely. Spread out the rolled oats on a plate and roll the balls in the oats, using your hands to coat them evenly.

4 Place the balls on a baking sheet and bake for 30–35 minutes or until golden. Serve hot or cold, with a mixed leaf and tomato salad.

NUTRITION NOTES

Per portion:

Energy	352Kcals/1476kJ
Fat	15.94g
Saturated fat	0.29g
Cholesterol	66.38mg
Fibre	3.82g

MIXED PEPPER PIPÉRADE

INGREDIENTS

Serves 4

30ml/2 tbsp olive oil
1 onion, chopped
1 red pepper
1 green pepper
4 tomatoes, peeled and chopped
1 garlic clove, crushed
4 size 2 eggs, beaten with
   15ml/1 tbsp water
ground black pepper
4 large, thick slices of wholemeal toast,
   to serve

1 Heat the oil in a large frying pan and sauté the onion gently until it becomes softened.

2 Remove the seeds from the red and green peppers and slice them thinly. Stir the pepper slices into the onion and cook together gently for 5 minutes. Add the tomatoes and garlic, season with black pepper, and cook for a further 5 minutes.

3 Pour the egg mixture over the vegetables in the frying pan and cook for 2–3 minutes, stirring until the pipérade has thickened to the consistency of lightly scrambled eggs. Serve immediately with wholemeal toast.

COOK'S TIP
Choose eggs that have been date-stamped for freshness. Do not stir the pipérade too much or the eggs may become rubbery.

NUTRITION NOTES

Per portion:

Energy	310Kcals/1300KJ
Fat	14.5g
Saturated Fat	3g
Cholesterol	231mg

CHICKEN NAAN POCKETS

INGREDIENTS

Serves 4

4 small naans
45ml/3 tbsp low fat natural yogurt
7.5ml/1½ tsp garam masala
5ml/1 tsp chilli powder
5ml/1 tsp salt
45ml/3 tbsp lemon juice
15ml/1 tbsp chopped fresh coriander
1 green chilli, chopped
450g/1 lb chicken without skin and
  bone, cubed
15ml/1 tbsp sunflower oil (optional)
8 onion rings
2 tomatoes, quartered
½ white cabbage, shredded

For the garnish
lemon wedges
2 small tomatoes, halved
mixed salad leaves
fresh coriander leaves

1 Cut into the middle of each naan to make a pocket, then set aside.

2 Mix together the yogurt, garam masala, chilli powder, salt, lemon juice, fresh coriander and chopped green chilli. Pour the marinade over the chopped chicken and leave to marinate for about 1 hour.

3 After 1 hour preheat the grill to very hot, then lower the heat to medium. Place the chicken in a flame-proof dish and grill for about 15–20 minutes until tender and cooked through, turning the chicken pieces at least twice. Baste with the oil while cooking if required.

> COOK'S TIP
> Use ready-made naans available in some supermarkets and Asian stores for speed.

4 Remove from the heat and fill each naan with the chicken and then with the onion rings, tomatoes and cabbage. Serve immediately with the garnish ingredients .

NUTRITION NOTES

Per portion:
Energy	364Kcals/1529kJ
Fat	10.85g
Saturated fat	3.01g
Cholesterol	65.64mg

CHICKEN TIKKA

INGREDIENTS

Serves 6

450g/1 lb chicken without skin and
  bone, chopped or cubed
5ml/1 tsp grated fresh root ginger
1 garlic clove, crushed
5ml/1 tsp chilli powder
1.5ml/¼ tsp turmeric
5ml/1 tsp salt
150ml/¼ pint/⅔ cup low fat
natural yogurt
60ml/4 tbsp lemon juice
15ml/1 tbsp chopped fresh coriander
15ml/1 tbsp sunflower oil

For the garnish
1 small onion, cut into rings
lime wedges
mixed salad
fresh coriander leaves

1 In a medium bowl, mix together the chicken pieces, ginger, garlic, chilli powder, turmeric, salt, yogurt, lemon juice and fresh coriander, and leave to marinate for at least 2 hours.

2 Place on a grill tray or in a flame-proof dish lined with foil and baste with the oil.

3 Preheat the grill to medium. Grill the chicken for about 15–20 minutes until cooked, turning and basting 2–3 times. Serve with the garnish ingredients.

> COOK'S TIP
> This is a quick and easy Indian starter. It can also be served as a main course for four.

NUTRITION NOTES

Per portion:
Energy	131Kcals/552kJ
Fat	5.5g
Saturated fat	1.47g
Cholesterol	44.07mg

COURGETTE AND POTATO TORTILLA

Serves 4

450g/1lb potatoes, peeled and diced
30ml/2 tbsp olive oil
1 onion, finely chopped
1 garlic clove, crushed
2 courgettes, thinly sliced
30ml/2 tbsp chopped fresh tarragon
4 size 2 eggs, beaten
salt and ground black pepper

NUTRITION NOTES

Per portion:

Energy	265Kcals/1100KJ
Fat	14.5g
Saturated Fat	3g
Cholesterol	231mg

1 Cook the potatoes in boiling, salted water for about 5 minutes.

2 Heat the oil in a large frying pan which can also be used under the grill. Add the onion and cook gently for 3–4 minutes until it is beginning to soften. Add the potatoes, garlic and courgettes to the pan. Cook for about 5 minutes more, shaking the pan occasionally to prevent the potatoes from sticking to the bottom, until the courgettes are softened and the potatoes are lightly browned.

3 Stir the tarragon into the eggs and season with salt and pepper. Pour the eggs over the vegetables in the pan and cook over a moderate heat until the underside of the tortilla is set. Meanwhile, preheat the grill.

4 Place the pan under the grill and cook for a few minutes more until the top of the tortilla has set. Cut into wedges and serve from the pan.

CHICKEN AND PESTO JACKETS

Although it is usually served with pasta, pesto also gives a wonderful lift to rice, bread and potato dishes – all good starchy carbohydrates. Here, it is combined with chicken and yogurt to make a low-fat topping for jacket potatoes.

Serves 4

4 baking potatoes, pricked
2 boned chicken breasts
250ml/8fl oz/1 cup low-fat
  natural yogurt
15ml/1 tbsp pesto sauce
fresh basil, to garnish

1 Preheat the oven to 200°C/400°F/ Gas 6. Bake the potatoes for about 1¼ hours, or until they are soft on the inside when tested with a knife.

2 About 20 minutes before the potatoes are ready, cook the chicken breasts, leaving the skin on, so that the flesh remains moist. Either bake the breasts in a dish alongside the potatoes in the oven, or cook them on a rack under a moderately hot grill.

3 Stir together the yogurt and pesto. When the potatoes are cooked through, cut them open. Skin the chicken breasts.

4 Slice the chicken, then fill the potatoes with the slices, top with the yogurt and garnish with basil.

NUTRITION NOTES

Per portion:

Energy	310Kcals/1295KJ
Fat	5.5g
Saturated Fat	1.5g
Cholesterol	35.5mg

PASTA, PIZZA, PULSES AND GRAINS

Pasta, pizza, pulses and grains on their own are low in fat and a good source of carbohydrate, but they are often prepared with high fat ingredients and sauces. However, recipes do not need to be high in fat to be appetizing. There are delicious low fat recipes for pasta, such as Fusilli with Smoked Trout and Spaghetti with Chilli Bean Sauce. Pulses and grains, too, are a popular choice at mealtimes, and these recipes offer delicious and nutritious options, from Cracked Wheat and Mint Salad, to Spicy Bean Hot Pot.

TAGLIATELLE WITH MUSHROOMS

INGREDIENTS

Serves 4

1 small onion, finely chopped
2 garlic cloves, crushed
150ml/¼ pint/⅔ cup vegetable stock
225g/8oz mixed fresh mushrooms, such
   as field, chestnut, oyster or
   chanterelles
60ml/4 tbsp white or red wine
10ml/2 tsp tomato purée
15ml/1 tbsp soy sauce
5ml/1 tsp chopped fresh thyme
30ml/2 tbsp chopped fresh parsley, plus
   extra to garnish
225g/8oz fresh sun-dried tomato and
   herb tagliatelle
salt and black pepper
shavings of Parmesan cheese, to serve
   (optional)

1 Put the onion and garlic into a pan with the stock, then cover and cook for 5 minutes or until tender.

NUTRITION NOTES

Per portion:
Energy	241Kcals/1010kJ
Fat	2.4g
Saturated Fat	0.7g
Carbohydrate	45g
Fibre	3g

2 Add the mushrooms (quartered or sliced if large or left whole if small), wine, tomato purée and soy sauce. Cover and cook for 5 minutes.

3 Remove the lid from the pan and boil until the liquid has reduced by half. Stir in the chopped fresh herbs and season to taste.

4 Cook the fresh pasta in a large pan of boiling, salted water for 2–5 minutes until *al dente*. Drain thoroughly and toss lightly with the mushrooms. Serve, garnished with parsley and shavings of Parmesan cheese, if you like.

PASTA PRIMAVERA

You can use any mixture of fresh, young spring vegetables to make this delicately flavoured pasta dish.

INGREDIENTS

Serves 4

225g/8oz thin asparagus spears,
  chopped in half
115g/4oz mange-tout, topped
  and tailed
115g/4oz baby sweetcorn
225g/8oz whole baby carrots, trimmed
1 small red pepper, seeded and chopped
8 spring onions, sliced
225g/8oz torchietti or other pasta shapes
150ml/¼ pint/⅔ cup low fat
  cottage cheese
150ml/¼ pint/⅔ cup low fat yogurt
15ml/1 tbsp lemon juice
15ml/1 tbsp chopped parsley
15ml/1 tbsp snipped chives
skimmed milk (optional)
salt and black pepper
sun-dried tomato bread, to serve

1 Cook the asparagus spears in a pan of boiling, salted water for 3–4 minutes. Add the mange-tout halfway through the cooking time. Drain and rinse both under cold water to stop further cooking.

2 Cook the baby corn, carrots, red pepper and spring onions in the same way until tender. Drain and rinse.

3 Cook the pasta in a large pan of boiling, salted water according to the packet instruction, until *al dente*. Drain thoroughly.

4 Put the cottage cheese, yogurt, lemon juice, parsley, chives and seasoning into a food processor or blender and process until smooth. Thin the sauce with skimmed milk, if necessary. Put into a large pan with the pasta and vegetables, heat gently and toss carefully. Serve at once with sun-dried tomato bread.

NUTRITION NOTES

Per portion:	
Energy	320Kcals/1344kJ
Fat	3.1g
Saturated Fat	0.4g
Cholesterol	3mg
Fibre	6.2g

Penne and Aubergine with Mint Pesto

This splendid variation on the classic Italian pesto uses fresh mint rather than basil.

──── Ingredients ────

Serves 4
2 large aubergines
pinch of salt
450g/1 lb/5 cups penne
50g/2oz/¹/₂ cup walnut halves

For the pesto
25g/1oz/1 cup fresh mint
15g/¹/₂oz/¹/₂ cup flat leaf parsley
40g/1¹/₂oz/¹/₂ cup walnuts
40g/1¹/₂oz/¹/₂ cup Parmesan cheese,
  finely grated
2 garlic cloves
45ml/3 tbsp olive oil
salt and black pepper

──── Nutrition Notes ────

Per portion:	
Energy	777Kcals/2364kJ
Fat	38.11g
Saturated fat	6.29g
Cholesterol	10mg
Fibre	8.57g

1 Cut the aubergines lengthways into 1cm/¹/₂ in slices.

2 Cut the slices again crossways to give short strips.

3 Layer the strips in a colander with salt and leave to stand for 30 minutes over a plate to catch any juices. Rinse well in cool water and drain.

4 For the pesto, place all the ingredients, except the oil, in a food processor or blender and blend until smooth, then gradually add the oil in a thin stream until the mixture amalgamates. Season to taste.

5 Bring a large saucepan of water to the boil, toss in the penne and cook for 8 minutes or until nearly cooked. Add the aubergine and cook for a further 3 minutes.

6 Drain well and mix in half of the mint pesto and walnut halves. Serve with the remaining pesto and walnut halves on top.

TAGLIATELLE WITH PEA AND BEAN SAUCE

A creamy pea sauce makes a wonderful combination with the crunchy young vegetables.

INGREDIENTS

Serves 4

15ml/1 tbsp olive oil
1 garlic clove, crushed
6 spring onions, sliced
115g/4oz/1 cup fresh or frozen baby
  peas, defrosted
350g/12oz fresh young asparagus
30ml/2 tbsp chopped fresh sage, plus
  extra leaves, to garnish
finely grated rind of 2 lemons
400ml/14fl oz/1⅔ cups vegetable stock
  or water
225g/8oz/1½ cups fresh or frozen
  broad beans, defrosted
450g/1 lb tagliatelle
60ml/4 tbsp low fat natural yogurt

NUTRITION NOTES

Per portion:

Energy	509 Kcals/2139kJ
Fat	6.75g
Saturated fat	0.95g
Cholesterol	0.6mg
Fibre	9.75g

1 Heat the oil in a pan. Add the garlic and spring onions, and cook gently for about 2–3 minutes until softened.

2 Add the peas and a third of the asparagus, together with the sage, lemon rind and stock or water. Simmer for about 10 minutes. Process in a food processor or blender until smooth.

3 Meanwhile remove the outer skins from the broad beans and discard.

4 Cut the remaining asparagus into 5cm/2 in lengths, trimming off any tough fibrous stems, and blanch in boiling water for about 2 minutes.

5 Cook the tagliatelle following the manufacturer's instructions until *al dente*. Drain well.

6 Add the cooked asparagus and shelled beans to the sauce, and reheat. Stir in the yogurt and toss into the tagliatelle. Garnish with a few extra sage leaves, and serve immediately.

COOK'S TIP
Frozen peas and beans have been suggested as an option here to cut down the preparation time, but the dish tastes even better if you use fresh young vegetables when in season.

TURKEY AND MACARONI CHEESE

A tasty low fat alternative to macaroni cheese, the addition of turkey rashers ensures this dish is a family favourite. Serve with warm ciabatta bread and a mixed leaf salad.

NUTRITION NOTES

Per portion:

Energy	152Kcals/637kJ
Fat	2.8g
Saturated Fat	0.7g
Cholesterol	12mg
Fibre	1.1g

INGREDIENTS

Serves 4

1 medium onion, chopped
150ml/¼ pint/⅔ cup vegetable or
    chicken stock
25g/1oz/2 tbsp low fat margarine
45ml/3 tbsp plain flour
300ml/½ pint/1¼ cup skimmed milk
50g/2oz reduced fat Cheddar
    cheese, grated
5ml/1 tsp dry mustard
225g/8oz quick-cook macaroni
4 smoked turkey rashers, cut in half
2–3 firm tomatoes, sliced
a few fresh basil leaves
15ml/1 tbsp grated Parmesan cheese
salt and black pepper

1 Put the chopped onion and stock into a non-stick frying pan. Bring to the boil, stirring occasionally and cook for 5–6 minutes or until the stock has reduced entirely and the onion is transparent.

2 Put the margarine, flour, milk and seasoning into a saucepan and whisk together over the heat until thickened and smooth. Draw aside and add the cheese, mustard and onion.

3 Cook the macaroni in a large pan of boiling, salted water according to the instructions on the packet. Preheat the grill. Drain thoroughly and stir into the sauce. Transfer to a shallow oven-proof dish.

4 Arrange the turkey rashers and tomatoes overlapping on top of the macaroni cheese. Tuck in the basil leaves, then sprinkle with Parmesan and grill to lightly brown the top.

PASTA WITH TOMATO AND TUNA

INGREDIENTS

Serves 6

1 medium onion, finely chopped
1 celery stick, finely chopped
1 red pepper, seeded and diced
1 garlic clove, crushed
150ml/¼ pint/⅔ cup chicken stock
400g/14oz can chopped tomatoes
15ml/1 tbsp tomato purée
10ml/2 tsp caster sugar
15ml/1 tbsp chopped fresh basil
15ml/1 tbsp chopped fresh parsley
450g/1lb pasta shells
400g/14oz canned tuna in
  brine, drained
30ml/2 tbsp capers in vinegar, drained
salt and black pepper

1 Put the chopped onion, celery, red pepper and garlic into a pan. Add the stock, bring to the boil and cook for 5 minutes or until the stock has reduced almost completely.

2 Add the tomatoes, tomato purée, sugar and herbs. Season to taste and bring to the boil. Simmer for about 30 minutes until thick, stirring occasionally.

3 Meanwhile, cook the pasta in a large pan of boiling, salted water according to the packet instructions, until *al dente*. Drain thoroughly and transfer to a warm serving dish.

COOK'S TIP
If fresh herbs are not available, use a 400g/14oz can of chopped tomatoes with herbs and add 5–10ml/1–2 tsp mixed dried herbs, in place of the fresh herbs.

4 Flake the tuna fish into large chunks and add to the sauce with the capers. Heat gently for 1–2 minutes, pour over the pasta, toss gently and serve immediately.

NUTRITION NOTES

Per portion:

Energy	369Kcals/1549kJ
Fat	2.1g
Saturated Fat	0.4g
Cholesterol	34mg
Fibre	4g

Spaghetti with Herb Sauce

Ingredients

Serves 4

50g/2oz/2 cups chopped fresh mixed
  herbs, such as parsley, basil and thyme
2 garlic cloves, crushed
60ml/4 tbsp pine nuts, toasted
60ml/4 tbsp olive oil
350g/12oz dried spaghetti
60ml/4 tbsp grated Parmesan cheese
salt and black pepper
basil leaves, to garnish

> Cook's Tip
>
> Spaghetti should be cooked until
> it is just firm to the bite, or *al
> dente*. If it is allowed to cook for
> too long, it will become soggy.

1 Put the herbs, garlic and half the pine nuts into a food processor or blender. With the machine running, gradually add the oil and process to form a thick purée.

2 Cook the spaghetti in plenty of boiling salted water for about 8 minutes until *al dente*. Drain.

Nutrition Notes	
Per portion:	
Energy	694Kcals/2915kJ
Fat	42.01g
Saturated fat	6.80g
Cholesterol	7.50mg
Fibre	3.18g

3 Transfer the herb purée to a large warm bowl, then add the spaghetti and Parmesan. Toss well to coat the pasta with the sauce. Sprinkle over the remaining pine nuts and the basil leaves, and serve immediately.

Chive Omelette Stir-fry

Ingredients

Serves 3–4

2 eggs
15–30ml/1–2 tbsp snipped fresh chives
30ml/2 tbsp groundnut oil
1 garlic clove, chopped
1cm/½ in piece fresh root ginger,
  chopped
2 celery sticks, cut into shreds
2 carrots, cut into shreds
2 small courgettes, cut into shreds
4 spring onions, cut into shreds
1 bunch radishes, sliced
115g/4oz/1⅓ cup beansprouts
¼ head of Chinese leaves, shredded
15ml/1 tbsp sesame oil
salt and black pepper

Nutrition Notes	
Per portion:	
Energy	188Kcals/788kJ
Fat	13.3g
Saturated fat	2.76g
Cholesterol	146.3mg
Fibre	3.85g

1 Whisk together the eggs, chives and seasoning in a bowl. Heat about 5ml/1 tsp of the groundnut oil in an omelette pan and pour in just enough of the egg mixture to cover the base of the pan. Cook for about 1 minute until set, then turn over the omelette and cook for a further minute.

2 Tip out the omelette on to a plate and cook the rest of the egg mixture in the same way to make several omelettes, adding extra oil to the pan, if neccessary. Roll up each omelette and slice thinly. Keep the omelettes warm in a low oven until required.

3 Heat the remaining oil in a wok or large frying pan, add the chopped garlic and ginger and stir-fry for a few seconds to flavour the oil.

4 Add the shredded celery, carrots and courgettes and stir-fry the vegetables for about 1 minute. Add the radishes, beansprouts, spring onions and Chinese leaves and stir-fry for a further 2–3 minutes, until all the vegetables are tender but still crunchy. Sprinkle a little sesame oil over the vegetables and toss gently.

5 Serve the stir-fried vegetables at once with the sliced chive omelettes scattered over the top.

Crab Pasta Salad

Low fat yogurt makes a piquant dressing for this salad.

Ingredients

Serves 6

350g/12oz pasta twists
1 small red pepper, seeded and
  finely chopped
2 x 175g/6oz cans white crab
  meat, drained
115g/4oz cherry tomatoes, halved
¼ cucumber, halved, seeded and sliced
  into crescents
15ml/1 tbsp lemon juice
300ml/½ pint/1¼ cups low fat yogurt
2 celery sticks, finely chopped
10ml/2 tsp horseradish cream
2.5ml/½ tsp paprika
2.5ml/½ tsp Dijon mustard
30ml/2 tbsp sweet tomato pickle
  or chutney
salt and black pepper
fresh basil, to garnish

1 Cook the pasta in a large pan of boiling, salted water, according to the instructions on the packet, until *al dente*. Drain and rinse thoroughly under cold water.

Nutrition Notes	
Per portion:	
Energy	305Kcals/1283kJ
Fat	2.5g
Saturated Fat	0.5g
Cholesterol	43mg
Fibre	2.9g

2 Cover the chopped red pepper with boiling water and leave to stand for 1 minute. Drain and rinse under cold water. Pat dry on kitchen paper.

3 Drain the crab meat and pick over carefully for pieces of shell. Put into a bowl with the halved tomatoes and sliced cucumber. Season with salt and pepper and sprinkle with lemon juice.

4 To make the dressing, add the red pepper to the yogurt, with the celery, horseradish cream, paprika, mustard and sweet tomato pickle or chutney. Mix the pasta with the dressing and transfer to a serving dish. Spoon the crab mixture on top and garnish with fresh basil.

FUSILLI WITH SMOKED TROUT

INGREDIENTS

Serves 4–6

2 carrots, cut in julienne sticks
1 leek, cut in julienne sticks
2 celery sticks, cut in julienne sticks
150ml/^{1}/4 pint/^{2}/3 cup vegetable or
  fish stock
225g/8oz smoked trout fillets, skinned
  and cut into strips
200g/7oz low fat cream cheese
150ml/^{1}/4 pint/^{2}/3 cup medium sweet
  white wine or fish stock
15ml/1 tbsp chopped fresh dill
  or fennel
225g/8oz fusilli (long, corkscrew pasta)
salt and black pepper
dill sprigs, to garnish

1 Put the carrots, leek and celery into a pan with the vegetable or fish stock. Bring to the boil and cook quickly for 4–5 minutes until the vegetables are tender and most of the stock has evaporated. Remove from the heat and add the smoked trout.

2 To make the sauce, put the cream cheese and wine or fish stock into a saucepan, heat and whisk until smooth. Season with salt and pepper. Add the chopped dill or fennel.

4 Return the pasta to the pan with the sauce, toss lightly and transfer to a serving bowl. Top with the cooked vegetables and trout. Serve at once garnished with dill sprigs.

NUTRITION NOTES

Per portion:

Energy	339Kcals/1422kJ
Fat	4.7g
Saturated Fat	0.8g
Cholesterol	57mg
Fibre	4.1g

3 Cook the pasta according to the packet instructions in a large pan of boiling, salted water until *al dente*. Drain thoroughly.

COOK'S TIP
When making the sauce, it is important to whisk it continuously while heating, to ensure a smooth result. Smoked salmon may be used in place of the trout, for a tasty change.

TABBOULEH WITH FENNEL

A fresh salad originating in the Middle East that is perfect for a summer lunch. Serve with lettuce and pitta bread.

INGREDIENTS

Serves 4

225g/8oz/1¼ cups bulgur wheat
2 fennel bulbs
1 small red chilli, seeded and chopped
1 celery stick, finely sliced
30ml/2 tbsp olive oil
finely grated rind and juice of
    2 lemons
6–8 spring onions, chopped
90ml/6 tbsp chopped fresh mint
90ml/6 tbsp chopped fresh parsley
1 pomegranate, seeded
salt and black pepper

NUTRITION NOTES

Per portion:
Energy	188Kcals/791kJ
Fat	4.67g
Saturated fat	0.62g
Cholesterol	0
Fibre	2.17g

1 Place the bulgur wheat in a bowl and pour over enough cold water to cover. Leave to stand for 30 minutes.

2 Drain the wheat through a sieve, pressing out any excess water using a spoon.

3 Halve the fennel bulbs and carefully cut into very fine slices with a sharp knife.

4 Mix all the remaining ingredients together, including the soaked bulgur wheat and fennel. Season well, cover, and set aside for 30 minutes before serving.

COOK'S TIP
Fennel has a very distinctive aniseed flavour. When you are buying fennel, choose well-rounded bulbs which are pale green to white in colour. Avoid any that are deep green. Fennel never goes out of season, it is available all year round.

SWEET VEGETABLE COUSCOUS

A wonderful combination of sweet vegetables and spices, this makes a substantial winter dish.

INGREDIENTS

Serves 4–6

generous pinch of saffron threads
45ml/3 tbsp boiling water
15ml/1 tbsp olive oil
1 red onion, sliced
2 garlic cloves
1–2 red chillies, seeded and finely chopped
2.5ml/½ tsp ground ginger
2.5ml/½ tsp ground cinnamon
400g/14oz can chopped tomatoes
300ml/½ pint/1¼ cups fresh vegetable stock or water
4 carrots, peeled and cut into 5mm/¼ in slices
2 turnips, peeled and cut into 2cm/¾ in cubes
450g/1 lb sweet potatoes, peeled and cut into 2cm/¾ in cubes
75g/3oz/½ cup raisins
2 courgettes, cut into 5mm/¼ in slices
400g/14oz can chick-peas, drained and rinsed
45ml/3 tbsp chopped fresh parsley
45ml/3 tbsp chopped fresh coriander
450g/1 lb/4 cups quick-cook couscous

1 Leave the saffron to infuse in the boiling water.

2 Heat the oil in a large saucepan or flameproof casserole. Add the onion, garlic and chillies, and cook gently for about 5 minutes.

3 Add the ground ginger and cinnamon, and gently cook for a further 1–2 minutes.

4 Add the tomatoes, stock or water, saffron and liquid, carrots, turnips, sweet potatoes and raisins, cover and simmer for a further 25 minutes.

5 Add the courgettes, chick-peas, parsley and coriander, and cook for a further 10 minutes.

6 Meanwhile prepare the couscous following the manufacturer's instructions, and then serve with the prepared vegetables.

NUTRITION NOTES

Per portion:

Energy	570Kcals/2393kJ
Fat	7.02g
Saturated fat	0.83g
Cholesterol	0
Fibre	10.04g

COOK'S TIP
Vegetable stock can be made from a variety of uncooked vegetables. These can include the outer leaves of cabbage, lettuce and other greens, carrot peelings, leeks and parsnips.

HOT SPICY PRAWNS WITH CAMPANELLE

This low fat prawn sauce tossed with hot pasta is an ideal supper-time dish. Add less or more chilli depending on how hot you like your food.

INGREDIENTS

Serves 4–6

225g/8oz tiger prawns, cooked
  and peeled
1–2 garlic cloves, crushed
finely grated rind of 1 lemon
15ml/1 tbsp lemon juice
1.5ml/¼ tsp red chilli paste or 1 large
  pinch of chilli powder
15ml/1 tbsp light soy sauce
150g/5oz smoked turkey rashers
1 shallot or small onion, finely chopped
60ml/4 tbsp dry white wine
225g/8oz campanelle or other
  pasta shapes
60ml/4 tbsp fish stock
4 firm ripe tomatoes, peeled, seeded
  and chopped
30ml/2 tbsp chopped fresh parsley
salt and black pepper

NUTRITION NOTES

Per portion:

Energy	331Kcals/1388kJ
Fat	2.9g
Saturated Fat	0.6g
Cholesterol	64mg
Fibre	3.2g

COOK'S TIP

To save time later, the prawns and marinade ingredients can be mixed together, covered and chilled in the fridge overnight, until ready to use.

1 In a glass bowl, mix the prawns with the garlic, lemon rind and juice, chilli paste or powder and soy sauce. Season with salt and pepper, cover and marinate for at least 1 hour.

2 Grill the turkey rashers, then cut them into 5mm/¼in dice.

3 Put the shallot or onion and white wine into a pan, bring to the boil, cover and cook for 2–3 minutes or until they are tender and the wine has reduced by half.

4 Cook the pasta according to the packet instructions in a large pan of boiling, salted water until al dente. Drain thoroughly.

5 Just before serving, put the prawns with their marinade into a large frying pan, bring to the boil quickly and add the smoked turkey and fish stock. Heat through for 1 minute.

6 Add to the pasta with the chopped tomatoes and parsley, toss quickly and serve at once.

SPAGHETTI WITH CHILLI BEAN SAUCE

A nutritious vegetarian option, ideal as a low fat main course.

INGREDIENTS

Serves 6

1 onion, finely chopped
1–2 garlic cloves, crushed
1 large green chilli, seeded
  and chopped
150ml/¼ pint/⅔ cup vegetable stock
400g/14oz can chopped tomatoes
30ml/2 tbsp tomato purée
120ml/4fl oz/½ cup red wine
5ml/1 tsp dried oregano
200g/7oz French beans, sliced
400g/14oz can red kidney
  beans, drained
400g/14oz can cannellini
  beans, drained
400g/14oz can chick-peas, drained
450g/1lb spaghetti
salt and black pepper

— NUTRITION NOTES —

Per portion:
Energy	431Kcals/1811kJ
Fat	3.6g
Saturated Fat	0.2g
Cholesterol	0
Fibre	9.9g

1 To make the sauce, put the chopped onion, garlic and chilli into a non-stick pan with the stock. Bring to the boil and cook for 5 minutes until tender.

2 Add the tomatoes, tomato purée, wine, seasoning and oregano. Bring to the boil, cover and simmer the sauce for 20 minutes.

3 Cook the French beans in boiling, salted water for about 5–6 minutes until tender. Drain thoroughly.

4 Add all the beans and the chick-peas to the sauce and simmer for a further 10 minutes. Meanwhile, cook the spaghetti in a large pan of boiling, salted water according to the individual packet instructions, until *al dente*. Drain thoroughly. Transfer the pasta to a serving dish or plates and top with the chilli bean sauce.

COOK'S TIP
Rinse canned beans thoroughly under cold, running water to remove as much salt as possible and drain well before use.

PINEAPPLE AND GINGER NOODLE SALAD

The tastes of the tropics are brought together in this appetizing noodle salad, ideal served as a lunch or suppertime dish.

INGREDIENTS

Serves 4

275g/10oz dried udon noodles
½ pineapple, peeled, cored and sliced into 4cm/1½in rings
45ml/3 tbsp soft light brown sugar
60ml/4 tbsp fresh lime juice
60ml/4 tbsp coconut milk
30ml/2 tbsp fish sauce
30ml/2 tbsp grated fresh root ginger
2 garlic cloves, finely chopped
1 ripe mango or 2 peaches, finely diced
black pepper
2 spring onions, finely sliced, 2 red chillies, seeded and finely shredded, plus mint leaves, to garnish

NUTRITION NOTES

Per portion:

Energy	350Kcals/1487kJ
Fat	4.49g
Saturated Fat	0.05g
Cholesterol	0
Fibre	3.13g

COOK'S TIP
Use 4–6 canned pineapple rings in fruit juice, if fresh pineapple is not available. If you haven't any fresh garlic, use 10ml/2 tsp ready-minced garlic instead. Choose ripe mangoes that have a smooth, unblemished skin and give slightly when you squeeze them gently.

1 Cook the noodles in a large saucepan of boiling water until tender, following the directions on the packet. Drain, then refresh under cold water and drain again.

2 Place the pineapple rings in a flameproof dish, sprinkle with 30ml/2 tbsp of the sugar and grill for about 5 minutes, or until golden. Cool slightly and cut into small dice.

3 Mix the lime juice, coconut milk and fish sauce in a salad bowl. Add the remaining brown sugar, with the ginger and garlic, and whisk well. Add the noodles and pineapple.

4 Add the mango or peaches to the bowl and toss well. Scatter over the spring onions, chillies and mint leaves before serving.

PASTA WITH PASSATA AND CHICK PEAS

──── INGREDIENTS ────

Serves 4
300g/10oz/2 cups pasta
5ml/1 tsp olive oil
1 small onion, finely chopped
1 garlic clove, crushed
1 celery stick, finely chopped
425g/15oz can chick-peas, drained
250ml/8 fl oz/1 cup passata
salt and black pepper
chopped fresh parsley, to garnish

1 Heat the olive oil in a non-stick pan and fry the onion, garlic and celery until softened but not browned. Stir in the chick-peas and passata, then cover and simmer for about 15 minutes.

2 Cook the pasta in a large pan of boiling, lightly salted water until just tender. Drain the pasta and toss into the sauce, then season to taste with salt and pepper. Sprinkle with chopped fresh parsley, then serve hot.

──── NUTRITION NOTES ────

Per portion:

Energy	374Kcals/1570kJ
Fat	4.44g
Saturated fat	0.32g
Cholesterol	0
Fibre	6.41g

PEPERONATA PIZZA

──── INGREDIENTS ────

Makes 2 large pizzas
450g/1 lb/4 cups plain flour
pinch of salt
1 sachet easy-blend yeast
about 350ml/12 fl oz/1½ cups warm water

For the topping
1 onion, sliced
10ml/2 tsp olive oil
2 large red and 2 yellow peppers, seeded and sliced
1 garlic clove, crushed
400g/14oz can tomatoes
8 pitted black olives, halved
salt and black pepper

──── NUTRITION NOTES ────

Per portion:

Energy	965Kcals/4052kJ
Fat	9.04g
Saturated fat	1.07g
Cholesterol	0
Fibre	14.51g

1 To make the dough, sift the flour and salt into a bowl and stir in the yeast. Stir in just enough warm water to mix to a soft dough.

2 Knead for 5 minutes until smooth. Cover and leave in a warm place for about 1 hour, or until doubled in size.

3 To make the topping, fry the onion in the oil until soft, then stir in the peppers, garlic and tomatoes. Cover and simmer for 30 minutes, until no free liquid remains. Season to taste.

4 Preheat the oven to 230°C/450°F/Gas 8. Divide the dough in half and press out each piece on a lightly oiled baking sheet to a 28cm/11in round, turning up the edges slightly.

5 Spread over the topping, dot with olives and bake for 15–20 minutes. Serve hot or cold with salad.

CAMPANELLE WITH YELLOW PEPPER SAUCE

Roasted yellow peppers make a deliciously sweet and creamy sauce to serve with pasta.

INGREDIENTS

Serves 4

2 yellow peppers, halved
50g/2oz/¼ cup low fat soft goat's cheese
115g/4oz/½ cup low fat fromage blanc
salt and black pepper
450g/1 lb/5 cups campanelle pasta
50g/2oz/¼ cup flaked almonds, toasted,
    to serve

NUTRITION NOTES

Per portion:	
Energy	529Kcals/2221kJ
Fat	11.18 g
Saturated fat	0.88g
Cholesterol	9.04mg
Fibre	5.69g

1 Preheat the grill. Place the yellow pepper halves under the grill until charred and blistered. Place in a plastic bag to cool. Peel and remove the seeds.

COOK'S TIP
Always cut the stalk ends from peppers and discard the mid-ribs and seeds.

2 Place the pepper flesh in a food processor or blender with the goat's cheese and fromage blanc. Process until smooth. Season with salt and lots of black pepper.

3 Cook the pasta following the manufacturer's instructions until *al dente*. Drain well.

4 Toss with the sauce and serve the dish sprinkled with the toasted flaked almonds.

GREEN LENTIL AND CABBAGE SALAD

This warm crunchy salad makes a satisfying meal if served with crusty French bread or wholemeal rolls.

INGREDIENTS

Serves 4–6
225g/8oz/1¼ cups puy lentils
1.3 litres/2¼ pints/6 cups cold water
1 garlic clove
1 bay leaf
1 onion, peeled and studded with 2 cloves
15ml/1 tbsp olive oil
1 red onion, finely sliced
2 garlic cloves, crushed
15ml/1 tbsp thyme leaves
350g/12oz/3¼ cups cabbage, finely shredded
finely grated rind and juice of 1 lemon
15ml/1 tbsp raspberry vinegar
salt and black pepper

NUTRITION NOTES

Per portion:
Energy	228Kcals/959kJ
Fat	4.38g
Saturated fat	0.44g
Cholesterol	0
Fibre	8.09g

2 Heat the oil in a large pan. Add the red onion, garlic and thyme, and cook for 5 minutes until softened.

4 Stir in the cooked lentils, lemon rind and juice and the raspberry vinegar. Season to taste and serve.

1 Rinse the lentils in cold water and place in a large pan with the water, peeled garlic clove, bay leaf and clove-studded onion. Bring to the boil and cook for about 10 minutes. Reduce the heat, cover the pan, and simmer gently for a further 15–20 minutes. Drain and remove the onion, garlic and bay leaf.

3 Add the cabbage and cook for a further 3–5 minutes until just cooked but still crunchy (al dente).

COOK'S TIP
There are several varieties of cabbage available such as spring, summer, winter, white and red cabbage. White cabbage is excellent in salads, choose one with a firm, compact head and avoid those with loose curling leaves.

Tagliatelle with Milanese Sauce

Ingredients

Serves 4

1 onion, finely chopped
1 celery stick, finely chopped
1 red pepper, seeded and diced
1–2 garlic cloves, crushed
150ml/¼ pint/⅔ cup vegetable or
  chicken stock
400g/14oz can tomatoes
15ml/1 tbsp tomato purée
10ml/2 tsp caster sugar
5ml/1 tsp mixed dried herbs
350g/12oz tagliatelle
115g/4oz button mushrooms, sliced
60ml/4 tbsp dry white wine
115g/4oz lean cooked ham, diced
salt and black pepper
15ml/1 tbsp chopped fresh parsley,
  to garnish

1 Put the chopped onion, celery, pepper and garlic into a saucepan. Add the stock, bring to the boil and cook for 5 minutes or until tender.

Cook's Tip

To reduce the calorie and fat content even more, omit the ham and use sweetcorn kernels or cooked broccoli florets instead.

2 Add the tomatoes, tomato purée, sugar and herbs. Season with salt and pepper. Bring to the boil and simmer for 30 minutes stirring occasionally, until the sauce is thick.

3 Cook the pasta in a large pan of boiling, salted water according to the packet instructions, until al dente. Drain thoroughly.

4 Put the mushrooms into a pan with the white wine, cover and cook for 3–4 minutes until the mushrooms are tender and all the wine has been absorbed.

5 Stir the mushrooms and ham into the tomato sauce and reheat gently over a low heat.

6 Transfer the pasta to a warmed serving dish and spoon on the sauce. Garnish with parsley.

Nutrition Notes

Per portion:

Energy	405Kcals/1700kJ
Fat	3.5g
Saturated Fat	0.8g
Cholesterol	17mg
Fibre	4.5g

LEMON AND GINGER SPICY BEANS

Serves 4

30ml/2 tbsp roughly chopped fresh
  root ginger
3 garlic cloves, roughly chopped
250ml/8fl oz/1 cup cold water
15ml/1 tbsp sunflower oil
1 large onion, thinly sliced
1 red chilli, seeded and finely
  chopped
1.5ml/¼ tsp cayenne pepper
10ml/2 tsp ground cumin
5ml/1 tsp ground coriander
2.5ml/½ tsp ground turmeric
30ml/2 tbsp lemon juice
75g/3oz/3 cups chopped fresh
  coriander
400g/14oz can black-eyed beans,
  drained and rinsed
400g/14oz can aduki beans,
  drained and rinsed
400g/14oz can haricot beans,
  drained and rinsed
salt and black pepper
crusty bread, to serve

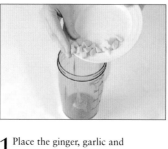

1 Place the ginger, garlic and 60ml/4 tbsp of the cold water in a food processor or blender and process until smooth.

2 Heat the oil in a saucepan. Add the onion and chilli, and cook gently for about 5 minutes until softened.

3 Add the cayenne pepper, cumin, ground coriander and turmeric, and stir-fry for a further 1 minute.

4 Stir in the ginger and garlic paste from the food processor or blender and cook for a further minute.

5 Add the remaining water, lemon juice and fresh coriander, stir well and bring to the boil. Cover the pan tightly and cook for about 5 minutes.

6 Add all the beans and cook for a further 5–10 minutes. Season with salt and pepper, to taste, and serve with crusty bread.

NUTRITION NOTES	
Per portion:	
Energy	281Kcals/1180kJ
Fat	4.3g
Saturated fat	0.42g
Cholesterol	0
Fibre	10.76g

SESAME NOODLE SALAD WITH PEANUTS

An Orient-inspired salad with crunchy vegetables and a light soy dressing. The hot peanuts make a surprisingly successful union with the cold noodles.

——— INGREDIENTS ———

Serves 4

350g/12oz egg noodles
2 carrots, peeled and cut into fine
  julienne strips
½ cucumber, peeled and cut into
  1cm/½ in cubes
115g/4oz celeriac, peeled and cut into
  fine julienne strips
6 spring onions, finely sliced
8 canned water chestnuts, drained and
  finely sliced
175g/6oz/2 cups beansprouts
1 small green chilli, chopped, plus
  1 green chilli, to garnish
30ml/2 tbsp sesame seeds and
  115g/4oz/1 cup peanuts, to serve

For the dressing
15ml/1 tbsp dark soy sauce
15ml/1 tbsp light soy sauce
15ml/1 tbsp clear honey
15ml/1 tbsp rice wine or dry sherry
15ml/1 tbsp sesame oil

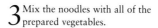

1 Preheat the oven to 200°C/400°F/ Gas 6. Bring a large saucepan of water to the boil, toss in the egg noodles and cook according to the manufacturer's instructions.

2 Drain the noodles, refresh in cold water, then drain again.

3 Mix the noodles with all of the prepared vegetables.

4 For the dressing, combine the ingredients in a bowl, then toss into the vegetable mixture. Divide the salad among four plates.

5 Place the sesame seeds and peanuts on separate baking trays and bake for 5 minutes. Remove the sesame seeds and continue to cook the peanuts for 5 minutes more, or until browned.

6 Sprinkle the sesame seeds and peanuts over each portion and serve at once, garnished with chillies.

NUTRITION NOTES	
Per portion:	
Energy	634Kcals/2664kJ
Fat	28.1g
Saturated fat	4.03g
Cholesterol	0
Fibre	5.33g

SPAGHETTI BOLOGNESE

Serves 8

1 onion, chopped
2–3 garlic cloves, crushed
300ml/½ pint/1¼ cups beef or
  chicken stock
450g/1lb extra-lean minced turkey
  or beef
2 x 400g/14oz cans chopped tomatoes
5ml/1 tsp dried basil
5ml/1 tsp dried oregano
60ml/4 tbsp tomato purée
450g/1lb button mushrooms, quartered
  and sliced
150ml/¼ pint/⅔ cup red wine
450g/1lb spaghetti
salt and black pepper

NUTRITION NOTES

Per portion:
Energy	321Kcals/1350kJ
Fat	4.1g
Saturated Fat	1.3g
Cholesterol	33mg
Fibre	2.7g

1 Put the chopped onion and garlic into a non-stick saucepan with half of the stock. Bring to the boil and cook for 5 minutes until the onion is tender and the stock has reduced completely.

2 Add the turkey or beef and cook for 5 minutes, breaking up the meat with a fork. Add the tomatoes, herbs and tomato purée, bring to the boil, then cover and simmer for 1 hour.

COOK'S TIP
Sautéing vegetables in fat-free stock rather than oil is an easy way of saving calories and fat. Choose fat-free stock to reduce even more.

3 Meanwhile, cook the mushrooms in a non-stick saucepan with the wine for 5 minutes or until the wine has evaporated. Add the mushrooms to the meat with salt and pepper to taste.

4 Cook the pasta in a large pan of boiling salted water for 8–12 minutes until tender. Drain thoroughly. Serve topped with the meat sauce.

RATATOUILLE PENNE BAKE

Serves 6

1 small aubergine
2 courgettes, thickly sliced
200g/7oz firm tofu, cubed
45ml/3 tbsp dark soy sauce
1 garlic clove, crushed
10ml/2 tsp sesame seeds
1 small red pepper, seeded and sliced
1 onion, finely chopped
1–2 garlic cloves, crushed
150ml/¼ pint/⅔ cup vegetable stock
3 firm ripe tomatoes, skinned, seeded
   and quartered
15ml/1 tbsp chopped mixed herbs
225g/8oz penne or other pasta shapes
salt and black pepper
crusty bread, to serve

1 Wash the aubergine and cut into 2.5cm/1in cubes. Put into a colander with the courgettes, sprinkle with salt and leave to drain for 30 minutes.

2 Mix the tofu with the soy sauce, garlic and sesame seeds. Cover and marinate for 30 minutes.

3 Put the pepper, onion and garlic into a saucepan with the stock. Bring to the boil, cover and cook for 5 minutes until tender. Remove the lid and boil until all the stock has evaporated. Add the tomatoes and herbs to the pan and cook for a further 3 minutes, then add the rinsed aubergine and courgettes and cook until tender. Season to taste.

COOK'S TIP
Tofu is a low fat protein, but it is very bland. Marinating adds plenty of flavour – make sure you leave it for the full 30 minutes.

4 Meanwhile, cook the pasta in a large pan of boiling, salted water according to the packet instructions, until al dente, then drain thoroughly. Preheat the grill. Toss the pasta with the vegetables and tofu. Transfer to a shallow ovenproof dish and grill until lightly toasted. Serve with bread.

NUTRITION NOTES	
Per portion:	
Energy	208Kcals/873kJ
Fat	3.7g
Saturated Fat	0.5g
Cholesterol	0
Fibre	3.9g

SWEET AND SOUR PEPPERS WITH PASTA

A tasty and colourful low fat dish – perfect for lunch or supper.

INGREDIENTS

Serves 4

1 red, 1 yellow and 1 orange pepper
1 garlic clove, crushed
30ml/2 tbsp capers
30ml/2 tbsp raisins
5ml/1 tsp wholegrain mustard
rind and juice of 1 lime
5ml/1 tsp clear honey
30ml/2 tbsp chopped fresh coriander
225g/8oz pasta bows
salt and black pepper
shavings of Parmesan cheese, to serve
  (optional)

1 Quarter the peppers and remove the stalks and seeds. Put the quarters into boiling water and cook for 10–15 minutes, until tender. Drain and rinse under cold water, then peel off the skin and cut the flesh into strips lengthways.

2 Put the garlic, capers, raisins, mustard, lime rind and juice, honey, coriander and seasoning into a bowl and whisk together.

3 Cook the pasta in a large pan of boiling, salted water for 10–12 minutes, until *al dente*. Drain thoroughly.

4 Return the pasta to the pan and add the pepper strips and dressing. Heat gently, tossing to mix. Transfer to a warm serving bowl and serve with a few shavings of Parmesan cheese, if using.

NUTRITION NOTES

Per portion:

Energy	268Kcals/1125kJ
Fat	2.0g
Saturated Fat	0.5g
Cholesterol	1.3mg
Fibre	4.3g

PASTA WITH CHICK-PEA SAUCE

This is a delicious, and very speedy, low fat dish. The quality of canned pulses and tomatoes is so good that it is possible to transform them into a very fresh tasting pasta sauce in minutes. Choose whatever pasta shapes you like, although hollow shapes, such as penne (quills) or shells are particularly good with this sauce.

INGREDIENTS

Serves 6

450g/1lb penne or other pasta shapes
30ml/2 tsp olive oil
1 onion, thinly sliced
1 red pepper, seeded and sliced
400g/14oz can chopped tomatoes
425g/15oz can chick-peas
30ml/2 tbsp dry vermouth (optional)
5ml/1 tsp dried oregano
1 large bay leaf
30ml/2 tbsp capers
salt and black pepper
fresh oregano, to garnish

COOK'S TIP
Choose fresh or dried unfilled pasta for this dish. Whichever you choose, cook it in a large saucepan of water, so that the pasta keeps separate and doesn't stick together. Fresh pasta takes about 2–4 minutes to cook and dried pasta about 8–10 minutes. Cook pasta until it is *al dente* – firm and neither too hard nor too soft.

NUTRITION NOTES

Per portion:

Energy	268Kcals/1125kJ
Fat	2.0g
Saturated Fat	0.5g
Cholesterol	1.3mg
Fibre	4.3g

1 Boil the pasta as instructed on the packet, then drain. Meanwhile, heat the oil in a large saucepan and gently fry the onion and pepper for about 5 minutes, stirring occasionally, until softened.

2 Add the tomatoes, chick-peas with their liquid, vermouth (if liked), herbs and capers and stir well.

3 Season to taste and bring to the boil, then simmer for about 10 minutes. Remove the bay leaf and mix in the pasta. Reheat and serve hot, garnished with sprigs of oregano.

Penne with Broccoli and Chilli

───── Ingredients ─────

Serves 4
450g/1 lb small broccoli florets
30ml/2 tbsp stock
1 garlic clove, crushed
1 small red chilli pepper, sliced, or
2.5ml/½ tsp chilli sauce
60ml/4 tbsp natural low fat yogurt
30ml/2 tbsp toasted pine nuts or
cashews
350g/12oz/3¼ cups penne pasta
salt and black pepper

2 Heat the stock and add the crushed garlic and chilli or chilli sauce. Stir over a low heat for 2–3 minutes.

1 Add the pasta to a large pan of lightly salted boiling water and return to the boil. Place the broccoli in a steamer basket over the top. Cover and cook for 8–10 minutes until both are just tender. Drain.

3 Stir in the broccoli, pasta and yogurt. Adjust the seasoning, sprinkle with nuts and serve hot.

───── Nutrition Notes ─────

Per portion:
Energy	403Kcals/1695kJ
Fat	7.87g
Saturated fat	0.89g
Cholesterol	0.6mg
Fibre	5.83g

Creole Jambalaya

───── Ingredients ─────

Serves 6
4 boneless chicken thighs, skinned and
diced
1 large green pepper, seeded and sliced
3 celery sticks, sliced
4 spring onions, sliced
about 300ml/½ pint/1¼ cups chicken
stock
400g/14oz can tomatoes
5ml/1 tsp ground cumin
5ml/1 tsp ground allspice
2.5ml/½ tsp cayenne pepper
5ml/1 tsp dried thyme
300g/10oz/1½ cups long grain rice
200g/7oz cooked, peeled prawns
salt and black pepper

2 Add the pepper, celery and onions with 15ml/1 tbsp stock. Cook for a few minutes to soften, then add the tomatoes, spices and thyme.

1 Fry the chicken in a non-stick pan without fat, turning occasionally, until golden brown.

3 Stir in the rice and stock. Cover closely and cook for about 20 minutes, stirring occasionally, until the rice is tender. Add more stock if necessary.

4 Add the prawns and heat well. Season and serve with a crisp salad.

───── Nutrition Notes ─────

Per portion:
Energy	282Kcals/1185kJ
Fat	3.37g
Saturated fat	0.85g
Cholesterol	51.33mg
Fibre	1.55g

Pappardelle and Provençal Sauce

Ingredients

Serves 4

2 small red onions
150ml/¼ pint/⅔ cup vegetable stock
1–2 garlic cloves, crushed
60ml/4 tbsp red wine
2 courgettes, cut in fingers
1 yellow pepper, seeded and sliced
400g/14oz can tomatoes
10ml/2 tsp fresh thyme
5ml/1 tsp caster sugar
350g/12oz pappardelle or other
    ribbon pasta
salt and black pepper
fresh thyme and 6 black olives, stoned
    and roughly chopped, to garnish

Nutrition Notes

Per portion:

Energy	369Kcals/1550kJ
Fat	2.5g
Saturated Fat	0.4g
Cholesterol	0
Fibre	4.3g

1 Cut each onion into eight wedges through the root end, to hold them together during cooking. Put into a saucepan with the stock and garlic. Bring to the boil, cover and simmer for 5 minutes until tender.

2 Add the red wine, courgettes, yellow pepper, tomatoes, thyme, sugar and seasoning. Bring to the boil and cook gently for 5–7 minutes, shaking the pan occasionally to coat the vegetables with the sauce. (Do not overcook the vegetables as they are much nicer if they remain slightly crunchy.)

3 Cook the pasta in a large pan of boiling, salted water according to the packet instructions, until al dente. Drain thoroughly.

4 Transfer the pasta to warmed serving plates and top with the vegetables. Garnish with fresh thyme and chopped black olives.

Basic Pasta Dough

To make fresh pasta, sift 200g/7oz/1¾ cups plain flour and a pinch of salt on to a work surface and make a well in the centre. Break two eggs into the well, together with 10ml/2 tsp of cold water. Using a fork, beat the eggs gently, then gradually draw in the flour from the sides to make a thick paste. When the mixture becomes too stiff to use a fork, use your hands to mix to a firm dough. Knead for 5 minutes until smooth. Wrap in clear film and leave to rest for 20–30 minutes before rolling out and cutting.

SPAGHETTI ALLA CARBONARA

This is a variation on the classic charcoal burner's spaghetti, using turkey rashers and low fat cream cheese instead of the traditional bacon and egg.

INGREDIENTS

Serves 4

150g/5oz smoked turkey rashers
oil, for frying
1 medium onion, chopped
1–2 garlic cloves, crushed
150ml/¼ pint/⅔ cup chicken stock
150ml/¼ pint/⅔ cup dry white wine
200g/7oz low fat cream cheese
450g/1lb chilli and garlic-flavoured
  spaghetti
30ml/2 tbsp chopped fresh parsley
salt and black pepper
shavings of Parmesan cheese,
  to serve

1 Cut the turkey rashers into 1cm/½in strips. Fry quickly in a non-stick pan for 2–3 minutes. Add the onion, garlic and stock to the pan. Bring to the boil, cover and simmer for about 5 minutes until tender.

2 Add the wine and boil rapidly until reduced by half. Whisk in the cream cheese and season to taste.

4 Return the spaghetti to the pan with the sauce and parsley, toss well and serve immediately with a few thin shavings of Parmesan cheese.

COOK'S TIP
If you can't find chilli and garlic-flavoured spaghetti, use plain spaghetti and add a small amount of raw chilli and garlic in step 4 or use the pasta of your choice.

3 Meanwhile, cook the spaghetti in a large pan of boiling, salted water for 10–12 minutes until *al dente*. Drain thoroughly.

NUTRITION NOTES

Per portion:

Energy	500Kcals/2102kJ
Fat	3.3g
Saturated Fat	0.5g
Cholesterol	21mg
Fibre	4g

THAI FRAGRANT RICE

A lovely, soft, fluffy rice dish, perfumed with delicious and fresh lemon grass.

INGREDIENTS

Serves 4

1 piece lemon grass
2 limes
225g/8oz/1⅓ cups brown basmati rice
15ml/1 tbsp olive oil
1 onion, chopped
2.5cm/1 in piece fresh root ginger,
  peeled and finely chopped
7.5ml/1½ tsp coriander seeds
7.5ml/1½ tsp cumin seeds
750ml/1¼ pints/3⅓ cups vegetable
  stock
60ml/4 tbsp chopped fresh coriander
lime wedges, to serve

COOK'S TIP
Other varieties of rice, such as
white basmati or long grain, can
be used for this dish but you will
need to adjust the cooking times
as necessary.

1 Finely chop the lemon grass and remove the zest from the limes.

2 Rinse the rice in cold water. Drain through a sieve.

3 Heat the oil in a large saucepan and add the onion and spices and cook gently for about 2–3 minutes.

4 Add the rice and cook for a further minute, then add the stock or water and bring to the boil. Reduce the heat to very low and cover the pan. Cook gently for about 30 minutes then check the rice. If it is still crunchy, cover the pan again with the lid and leave for a further 3–5 minutes. Remove from the heat.

5 Stir in the fresh coriander, fluff up the grains, cover and leave for 10 minutes. Serve with lime wedges.

NUTRITION NOTES

Per portion:
Energy	259Kcals/1087kJ
Fat	5.27g
Saturated fat	0.81g
Cholesterol	0
Fibre	1.49g

PUMPKIN AND PISTACHIO RISOTTO

This elegant combination of creamy golden rice and orange pumpkin can be made as pale or bright as you like – simply add different quantities of saffron.

INGREDIENTS

Serves 4
1.2 litres/2 pints/5 cups vegetable stock
    or water
generous pinch of saffron threads
30ml/2 tbsp olive oil
1 onion, chopped
2 garlic cloves, crushed
900g/2 lb pumpkin, peeled, seeded and
    cut into 2cm/¾ in cubes
450g/1 lb/2 cups arborio rice
200ml/7fl oz/⅞ cup dry white wine
15ml/1 tbsp Parmesan cheese, finely
    grated
50g/2oz/½cup pistachios
45ml/3 tbsp chopped fresh marjoram
    or oregano, plus extra leaves, to
    garnish
salt, freshly grated nutmeg and black
    pepper

NUTRITION NOTES

Per portion:

Energy	630Kcals/2646kJ
Fat	15.24g
Saturated fat	2.66g
Cholesterol	3.75mg
Fibre	2.59g

1 Bring the stock or water to the boil and reduce to a low simmer. Ladle a little liquid into a small bowl. Add the saffron threads and leave to infuse.

2 Heat the oil in a saucepan or flame-proof casserole. Add the onion and garlic, and cook gently for 5 minutes until softened. Add the pumpkin and rice and cook for a few more minutes until the rice looks transparent.

3 Pour in the wine and allow it to boil hard. When it is absorbed add a quarter of the stock or water and the infused saffron and liquid. Stir constantly until all the liquid is absorbed.

4 Gradually add a ladleful of stock or water at a time, allowing the rice to absorb the liquid before adding more and stir constantly.

5 Cook the rice for about 25–30 minutes or until al dente. Stir in the Parmesan cheese, cover the pan and leave to stand for 5 minutes.

6 To finish, stir in the pistachios and marjoram or oregano. Season to taste with a little salt, nutmeg and pepper, and sprinkle over a few extra marjoram or oregano leaves.

COOK'S TIP
Italian arborio rice is a special short grain rice that gives an authentic creamy consistency.

FRUITY HAM AND FRENCH BREAD PIZZA

French bread makes a great pizza base. For a really speedy recipe, use ready-prepared pizza topping instead of the tomato sauce and cook the pizzas under a hot grill for a few minutes to melt the cheese, instead of baking them in the oven.

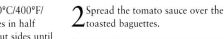

INGREDIENTS

Serves 4

2 small baguettes
300ml/½ pint/1¼ cups tomato sauce
75g/3oz lean sliced cooked ham
4 canned pineapple rings, drained and chopped
½ small green pepper, seeded and cut into thin strips
50g/2oz reduced fat mature Cheddar cheese
salt and black pepper

1 Preheat the oven to 200°C/400°F/ Gas 6. Cut the baguettes in half lengthways and toast the cut sides until crisp and golden.

> **COOK'S TIP**
> If you prefer, omit the ham and substitute cooked chicken, peeled prawns or tuna fish.

2 Spread the tomato sauce over the toasted baguettes.

3 Cut the ham into strips and lay on the baguettes with the pineapple and green pepper. Season to taste with salt and pepper.

4 Grate the cheese and sprinkle on top. Bake for 15–20 minutes until crisp and golden.

NUTRITION NOTES

Per portion:

Energy	111Kcals/468.7kJ
Fat	3.31g
Saturated Fat	1.63g
Cholesterol	18.25mg
Fibre	0.79g

CRACKED WHEAT AND MINT SALAD

INGREDIENTS

Serves 4

250g/9oz/1⅔ cups cracked wheat
4 tomatoes
4 small courgettes, thinly sliced
    lengthways
4 spring onions, sliced on the diagonal
8 ready-to-eat dried apricots, chopped
40g/1½oz/¼ cup raisins
juice of 1 lemon
30ml/2 tbsp tomato juice
45ml/3 tbsp chopped fresh mint
1 garlic clove, crushed
salt and black pepper
sprig of fresh mint, to garnish

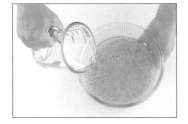

1 Put the cracked wheat into a large bowl. Add enough boiling water to come 2.5cm/1in above the level of the wheat. Leave to soak for 30 minutes, then drain well and squeeze out any excess water in a clean dish towel.

2 Meanwhile, plunge the tomatoes into boiling water for 1 minute and then into cold water. Slip off the skins. Halve, remove the seeds and cores and roughly chop the flesh.

3 Stir the chopped tomatoes, courgettes, spring onions, apricots and raisins into the cracked wheat.

NUTRITION NOTES

Per portion:	
Energy	293Kcals/1231.7kJ
Fat	1.69g
Saturated Fat	0.28g
Fibre	2.25g

4 Put the lemon and tomato juice, mint, garlic clove and seasoning into a small bowl and whisk together with a fork. Pour over the salad and mix well. Chill for at least 1 hour. Serve garnished with a sprig of mint.

CHILLI BEAN BAKE

The contrasting textures of sauce, beans, vegetables and a crunchy cornbread topping make this a memorable meal.

INGREDIENTS

Serves 4
225g/8oz/1¼ cups red kidney beans
1 bay leaf
1 large onion, finely chopped
1 garlic clove, crushed
2 celery sticks, sliced
5ml/1 tsp ground cumin
5ml/1 tsp chilli powder
400g/14oz can chopped tomatoes
15ml/1 tbsp tomato purée
5ml/1 tsp dried mixed herbs
15ml/1 tbsp lemon juice
1 yellow pepper, seeded and diced
salt and black pepper
mixed salad, to serve

For the cornbread topping
175g/6oz/1½ cups corn meal
15ml/1 tbsp wholemeal flour
5ml/1 tsp baking powder
1 egg, beaten
175ml/6fl oz/¾ cup skimmed milk

1 Soak the beans overnight in cold water. Drain and rinse well. Pour 1 litre/1¾ pints/4 cups water into a large, heavy-based saucepan, add the beans and bay leaf and boil rapidly for 10 minutes. Lower the heat, cover and simmer for 35–40 minutes or until the beans are tender.

NUTRITION NOTES

Per portion:

Energy	399Kcals/1675kJ
Protein	22.86g
Fat	4.65g
Saturated Fat	0.86g
Fibre	11.59g

2 Add the onion, garlic, celery, cumin, chilli powder, chopped tomatoes, tomato purée and dried mixed herbs. Half cover the pan with a lid and simmer for a further 10 minutes.

3 Stir in the lemon juice, yellow pepper and seasoning. Simmer for a further 8–10 minutes, stirring occasionally, until the vegetables are just tender. Discard the bay leaf and spoon the mixture into a large casserole.

4 Preheat the oven to 220°C/425°F/ Gas 7. To make the topping, put the corn meal, flour, baking powder and a pinch of salt into a bowl and mix together. Make a well in the centre and add the egg and milk. Mix and pour over the bean mixture. Bake in the oven for 20 minutes or until brown. Serve hot with mixed salad.

SPICY BEAN HOT POT

INGREDIENTS

Serves 4

225g/8oz/3 cups button mushrooms
15ml/1 tbsp sunflower oil
2 onions, sliced
1 garlic clove, crushed
15ml/1 tbsp red wine vinegar
400g/14oz can chopped tomatoes
15ml/1 tbsp tomato purée
15ml/1 tbsp Worcestershire sauce
15ml/1 tbsp wholegrain mustard
15ml/1 tbsp soft dark brown sugar
250ml/8fl oz/1 cup vegetable stock
400g/14oz can red kidney
    beans, drained
400g/14oz can haricot or cannellini
    beans, drained
1 bay leaf
75g/3oz/1/2 cup raisins
salt and black pepper
chopped fresh parsley, to garnish

1 Wipe the mushrooms, then cut them into small pieces. Set aside.

2 Heat the oil in a large saucepan or flameproof casserole, add the onions and garlic and cook over a gentle heat for 10 minutes until soft.

3 Add all the remaining ingredients except the mushrooms and seasoning. Bring to the boil, lower the heat and simmer for 10 minutes.

4 Add the mushrooms and simmer for 5 minutes more. Stir in salt and pepper to taste. Transfer to warm plates and sprinkle with parsley.

NUTRITION NOTES

Per portion:	
Energy	280Kcals/1175kJ
Fat	4.5g
Saturated Fat	0.5g
Cholesterol	0

TOMATO RICE

This dish is delicious and is substantial enough to be eaten as a complete meal on its own.

INGREDIENTS

Serves 4

30ml/2 tbsp corn oil
2.5ml/½ tsp onion seeds
1 onion, sliced
2 tomatoes, sliced
1 orange or yellow pepper, chopped
5ml/1 tsp grated fresh root ginger
1 garlic clove, crushed
5ml/1 tsp chilli powder
30ml/2 tbsp chopped fresh coriander
1 potato, diced
7.5ml/1½ tsp salt
50g/2oz/⅓ cup frozen peas
400g/14oz/2 cups basmati rice, washed
700ml/24fl oz/3 cups water

NUTRITION NOTES

Per portion:

Energy	351Kcals/1475kJ
Fat	6.48g
Saturated fat	0.86g
Cholesterol	0

1 Heat the oil and fry the onion seeds for about 30 seconds. Add the sliced onion and fry for about 5 minutes.

2 Add the next nine ingredients and stir-fry over a medium heat for a further 5 minutes.

3 Add the rice and stir-fry for about 1 minute.

4 Pour in the water and bring to the boil, then lower the heat to medium. Cover and cook for a further 12–15 minutes. Leave the rice to stand for 5 minutes and serve.

PEA AND MUSHROOM PULLAO

It is best to use button mushrooms and petit pois for this delectable rice dish, as they make the pullao look very attractive and appetizing.

INGREDIENTS

Serves 6

450g/1 lb/2¼ cups basmati rice
30ml/2 tbsp vegetable oil
2.5ml/½ tsp black cumin seeds
2 black cardamom pods
2 cinnamon sticks
3 garlic cloves, sliced
5ml/1 tsp salt
1 tomato, sliced
50g/2oz/⅔ cup button mushrooms
75g/3oz/⅓ heaped cup petit pois
750ml/1¼ pints/3⅔ cups water

NUTRITION NOTES

Per portion:

Energy	297Kcals/1246kJ
Fat	4.34g
Saturated fat	0.49g
Cholesterol	0

1 Wash the rice at least twice and set aside in a sieve.

2 Heat the oil in a medium saucepan and add the spices, garlic and salt.

3 Add the sliced tomato and button mushrooms, and stir-fry for about 2–3 minutes.

4 Add the rice and peas, and gently stir around making sure you do not break the rice.

5 Add the water and bring the mixture to the boil. Lower the heat, cover, and continue to cook for a further 15–20 minutes.

Spinach and Hazelnut Lasagne

A vegetarian dish which is hearty enough to satisfy meat-eaters too. Use frozen spinach if you're short of time.

Ingredients

Serves 4
900g/2 lb fresh spinach
300ml/½ pint/1¼ cups vegetable or
   chicken stock
1 medium onion, finely chopped
1 garlic clove, crushed
75g/3oz/¼ cup hazelnuts
30ml/2 tbsp chopped fresh basil
6 sheets lasagne
400g/14oz can chopped tomatoes
200g/7oz/1 cup low fat fromage frais
flaked hazelnuts and chopped parsley,
   to garnish

1 Preheat the oven to 200°C/400°F/ Gas 6. Wash the spinach and place in a pan with just the water that clings to the leaves. Cook the spinach on a fairly high heat for 2 minutes until wilted. Drain well.

2 Heat 30ml/2 tbsp of the stock in a large pan and simmer the onion and garlic until soft. Stir in the spinach, hazelnuts and basil.

3 In a large ovenproof dish, layer the spinach, lasagne and tomatoes. Season well between the layers. Pour over the remaining stock. Spread the fromage frais over the top.

4 Bake the lasagne for about 45 minutes, or until golden brown. Serve hot, sprinkled with lines of flaked hazelnuts and chopped parsley.

Cook's Tip
The flavour of hazelnuts is improved by roasting. Place them on a baking sheet and bake in a moderate oven, or under a hot grill, until light golden.

Nutrition Notes	
Per portion:	
Energy	365Kcals/1532kJ
Fat	17g
Saturated fat	1.46g
Cholesterol	0.5mg
Fibre	8.16g

CALZONE

Makes 4
450g/1 lb/4 cups plain flour
pinch of salt
1 sachet easy-blend yeast
about 350ml/12 fl oz/1½ cups warm
*   water*

For the filling
5ml/1 tsp olive oil
1 medium red onion, thinly sliced
3 medium courgettes, about 350g/12oz
*   total weight, sliced*
2 large tomatoes, diced
150g/5oz mozzarella cheese, diced
15ml/1 tbsp chopped fresh oregano
skimmed milk, to glaze
salt and black pepper

1 To make the dough, sift the flour and salt into a bowl and stir in the yeast. Stir in just enough warm water to mix to a soft dough.

2 Knead for 5 minutes until smooth. Cover and leave in a warm place for about 1 hour, or until doubled in size.

3 Meanwhile, to make the filling, heat the oil and sauté the onion and courgettes for 3–4 minutes. Remove from the heat and add the tomatoes, cheese, oregano and seasoning.

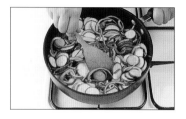

4 Preheat the oven to 220°C/425°F/ Gas 7. Knead the dough lightly and divide into four. Roll out each piece on a lightly floured surface to a 20cm/8in round and place a quarter of the filling on one half.

5 Brush the edges with milk and fold over to enclose the filling. Press firmly to enclose. Brush with milk.

6 Bake on an oiled baking sheet for 15–20 minutes. Serve hot or cold.

— NUTRITION NOTES —

Per portion:
Energy	544Kcals/2285kJ
Fat	10.93g
Saturated fat	5.49g
Cholesterol	24.42mg
Fibre	5.09g

BEAN PURÉE WITH GRILLED CHICORY

The slightly bitter flavours of the radicchio and chicory make a wonderful marriage with the creamy bean purée. Walnut oil adds a nutty taste, but olive oil could also be used.

COOK'S TIP
Other suitable pulses to use are haricot, mung or broad beans.

INGREDIENTS

Serves 4
400g/14oz can cannellini beans
45ml/3 tbsp low fat fromage frais
finely grated rind and juice of
  1 large orange
15ml/1 tbsp finely chopped
  fresh rosemary
4 heads of chicory
2 medium heads of radicchio
10ml/2 tbsp walnut oil
shreds of orange rind, to garnish
  (optional)

1 Drain the beans, rinse, and drain again. Purée the beans in a blender or food processor with the fromage frais, orange rind, orange juice and rosemary. Set aside.

2 Cut the heads of chicory in half lengthwise.

3 Cut each radicchio head into eight wedges. Preheat the grill.

4 Lay out the chicory and radicchio on a baking tray and brush with the walnut oil. Grill for 2–3 minutes. Serve with the purée and scatter over the orange shreds, if using.

NUTRITION NOTES

Per portion:
Energy	103Kcals/432kJ
Protein	6.22g
Fat	1.54g
Saturated Fat	0.4g
Fibre	6.73g

LENTIL BOLOGNESE

A really useful sauce to serve with pasta, as a pancake stuffing or even as a protein-packed sauce for vegetables.

INGREDIENTS

Serves 6
45ml/3 tbsp olive oil
1 onion, chopped
2 garlic cloves, crushed
2 carrots, coarsely grated
2 celery sticks, chopped
115g/4oz/²⁄₃ cup red lentils
400g/14oz can chopped tomatoes
30ml/2 tbsp tomato purée
450ml/³⁄₄ pint/2 cups stock
15ml/1 tbsp fresh marjoram, chopped,
    or 5ml/1 tsp dried marjoram
salt and black pepper

1 Heat the oil in a large saucepan and gently fry the onion, garlic, carrots and celery for about 5 minutes, until they are soft.

NUTRITION NOTES

Per portion:
Energy	103Kcals/432kJ
Fat	2.19g
Saturated Fat	0.85g
Fibre	2.15g

2 Add the lentils, tomatoes, tomato purée, stock, marjoram and seasoning to the pan.

3 Bring the mixture to the boil, then partially cover with a lid and simmer for 20 minutes until thick and soft. Use the sauce as required.

COOK'S TIP
You can easily reduce the fat in this recipe by using less olive oil, or substituting a little of the stock and cooking the vegetables over a low heat in a non-stick frying pan until they are soft.

Vegetable Biryani

This exotic dish made from everyday ingredients will be appreciated by vegetarians and meat-eaters alike. It is extremely low in fat, but packed full of exciting flavours.

Nutrition Notes

Per portion:

Energy	175Kcals/737kJ
Protein	3.66g
Fat	0.78g
Saturated Fat	0.12g
Fibre	0.58g

Ingredients

Serves 4–6

175g/6oz/1 cup long grain rice
2 whole cloves
seeds of 2 cardamom pods
450ml/³⁄4 pint/scant 2 cups vegetable
    stock
2 garlic cloves
1 small onion, roughly chopped
5ml/1 tsp cumin seeds
5ml/1 tsp ground coriander
2.5ml/¹⁄2 tsp ground turmeric
2.5ml/¹⁄2 tsp chilli powder
1 large potato, peeled and cut into
    2.5cm/1in cubes
2 carrots, sliced
¹⁄2 cauliflower, broken into florets
50g/2oz French beans, cut into
    2.5cm/1in lengths
30ml/2 tbsp chopped fresh coriander
30ml/2 tbsp lime juice
salt and black pepper
sprig of fresh coriander, to garnish

Cook's Tip
Substitute other vegetables, if you like. Courgettes, broccoli, parsnip and sweet potatoes would all be excellent choices.

2 Reduce the heat, cover and simmer for 20 minutes, or until all the stock has been absorbed.

3 Meanwhile put the garlic cloves, onion, cumin seeds, coriander, turmeric, chilli powder and seasoning into a blender or coffee grinder together with 30ml/2 tbsp water. Blend to a smooth paste.

1 Put the rice, cloves and cardamom seeds into a large, heavy-based saucepan. Pour over the stock and bring to the boil.

4 Preheat the oven to 180°C/350°F/ Gas 4. Spoon the spicy paste into a flameproof casserole and cook over a low heat for 2 minutes, stirring occasionally.

5 Add the potato, carrots, cauliflower florets, beans and 90ml/6 tbsp water. Cover and cook over a low heat for a further 12 minutes, stirring occasionally. Add the chopped coriander.

6 Remove the cloves and spoon the rice over the vegetables. Sprinkle over the lime juice. Cover and cook in the oven for 25 minutes, or until the vegetables are tender. Fluff up the rice with a fork before serving and garnish with a sprig of fresh coriander.

COCONUT RICE

A delicious alternative to plain boiled rice, brown or white rice will both work well.

INGREDIENTS

Serves 6

450g/1lb/2 cups long grain rice
250ml/8fl oz/1 cup water
475ml/16fl oz/2 cups coconut milk
2.5ml/¹/₂ tsp salt
30ml/2 tbsp granulated sugar
fresh shredded coconut, to garnish

1 Wash the rice in cold water until it runs clear. Place the water, coconut milk, salt and sugar in a heavy-based saucepan or flameproof casserole.

COOK'S TIP
Coconut milk is available in cans, but if you cannot find it, use creamed coconut mixed with water according to the packet instructions.

2 Add the rice, cover and bring to the boil. Reduce the heat to low and simmer for about 15–20 minutes or until the rice is tender to the bite and cooked through.

3 Turn off the heat and allow the rice to rest in the saucepan for a further 5–10 minutes.

4 Fluff up the rice with chopsticks or a fork before serving garnished with shredded coconut.

NUTRITION NOTES

Per portion:

Energy	322.5Kcals/1371kJ
Fat	2.49g
Saturated Fat	1.45g
Cholesterol	0
Fibre	0.68g

JASMINE RICE

Perfectly cooked rice makes an ideal, low fat accompaniment to many low fat dishes such as vegetable chilli and vegetable bolognese.

INGREDIENTS

Serves 6

450g/1lb/2 cups long grain rice
750ml/1¼ pints/3 cups cold water
2.5ml/½ tsp salt

NUTRITION NOTES

Per portion:

Energy	270.8Kcals/1152kJ
Fat	0.75g
Saturated Fat	0
Cholesterol	0
Fibre	0.37g

COOK'S TIP

An electric rice cooker both cooks the rice and keeps it warm. Different sizes and models are available. The top of the range is a non-stick version, which is expensive, but well worth the money if you eat rice a lot.

1 Rinse the rice in several changes of cold water until the water stays clear.

2 Put the rice in a heavy-based saucepan or flameproof casserole and add the water and salt. Bring the rice to a vigorous boil, uncovered, over a high heat.

3 Stir and reduce the heat to low. Cover and simmer for up to 20 minutes, or until all the water has been absorbed. Remove from the heat and leave to stand for 10 minutes.

4 Remove the lid and stir the rice gently with chopsticks or a fork to fluff up and separate the grains.

TAGLIATELLE WITH HAZELNUT PESTO

Hazelnuts are lower in fat than other nuts, which makes them useful for this reduced-fat alternative to pesto sauce.

INGREDIENTS

Serves 4

2 garlic cloves, crushed
25g/1oz/1 cup fresh basil leaves
25g/1oz/¼ cup hazelnuts
200g/7oz/⅞ cup skimmed milk soft cheese
225g/8oz dried tagliatelle, or 450g/1 lb fresh
salt and black pepper

1 Place the garlic, basil, hazelnuts and cheese in a food processor or blender and process to a thick paste.

2 Cook the tagliatelle in lightly salted boiling water until just tender, then drain well.

3 Spoon the sauce into the hot pasta, tossing until melted. Sprinkle with pepper and serve hot.

NUTRITION NOTES

Per portion:
Energy	274Kcals/1155kJ
Fat	5.05g
Saturated fat	0.43g
Cholesterol	0.5mg
Fibre	2.14g

SPAGHETTI WITH TUNA SAUCE

A speedy midweek meal, which can also be made with other pasta shapes.

INGREDIENTS

Serves 4

225g/8oz dried spaghetti, or 450g/1 lb fresh
1 garlic clove, crushed
400g/14oz can chopped tomatoes
425g/15oz can tuna fish in brine, flaked
2.5ml/½ tsp chilli sauce (optional)
4 pitted black olives, chopped
salt and black pepper

> **COOK'S TIP**
> If fresh tuna is available, use 450g/1lb, cut into small chunks, and add after step 2. Simmer for 6–8 minutes, then add the chilli, olives and pasta.

1 Cook the spaghetti in lightly salted boiling water for 12 minutes or until just tender. Drain well and keep hot.

2 Add the garlic and tomatoes to the saucepan and bring to the boil. Simmer, uncovered, for 2–3 minutes.

3 Add the tuna, chilli sauce, if using, the olives and spaghetti. Heat well, add the seasoning and serve hot.

NUTRITION NOTES

Per portion:
Energy	306Kcals/1288kJ
Fat	2.02g
Saturated fat	0.37g
Cholesterol	48.45mg
Fibre	2.46g

BULGUR AND LENTIL PILAF

Bulgur wheat is very easy to cook and can be used in almost any way you would normally use rice, hot or cold. Some of the finer grades need hardly any cooking, so check the pack for cooking times.

INGREDIENTS

Serves 4

5ml/1 tsp olive oil
1 large onion, thinly sliced
2 garlic cloves, crushed
5ml/1 tsp ground coriander
5ml/1 tsp ground cumin
5ml/1 tsp ground turmeric
2.5ml/½ tsp ground allspice
225g/8oz/1¼ cups bulgur wheat
about 750ml/1¼ pints/3⅔ cups stock or
   water
115g/4oz button mushrooms, sliced
115g/4oz/⅔ cup green lentils
salt, black pepper and cayenne

1 Heat the oil in a non-stick saucepan and fry the onion, garlic and spices for 1 minute, stirring.

2 Stir in the bulgur wheat and cook, stirring, for about 2 minutes, until lightly browned. Add the stock or water, mushrooms and lentils.

3 Simmer over a very low heat for about 25–30 minutes, until the bulgur wheat and lentils are tender and all the liquid is absorbed. Add more stock or water, if necessary.

4 Season well with salt, pepper and cayenne and serve hot.

COOK'S TIP
Green lentils can be cooked without presoaking, as they cook quite quickly and keep their shape. However, if you have the time, soaking them first will shorten the cooking time slightly.

NUTRITION NOTES

Per portion:

Energy	325Kcals/1367kJ
Fat	2.8g
Saturated fat	0.33g
Cholesterol	0
Fibre	3.61g

MINTED COUSCOUS CASTLES

Couscous is a fine semolina made from wheat grain, which is usually steamed and served plain with a rich meat or vegetable stew. Here it is flavoured with mint and moulded to make an unusual accompaniment to serve with any savoury dish.

INGREDIENTS

Serves 6

225g/8oz/1¼ cups couscous
475ml/16 fl oz/2 cups boiling stock
15ml/1 tbsp lemon juice
2 tomatoes, diced
30ml/2 tbsp chopped fresh mint
oil, for brushing
salt and black pepper
mint sprigs, to garnish

1 Place the couscous in a bowl and pour over the boiling stock. Cover the bowl and leave to stand for 30 minutes, until all the stock is absorbed and the grains are tender.

2 Stir in the lemon juice with the tomatoes and chopped mint. Adjust the seasoning with salt and pepper.

3 Brush the insides of four cups or individual moulds with oil. Spoon in the couscous mixture and pack down firmly. Chill for several hours.

4 Turn out and serve cold, or alternatively, cover and heat gently in a low oven or microwave, then turn out and serve hot, garnished with mint.

COOK'S TIP

Most packet couscous is now the ready cooked variety, which can be cooked as above, but some types need steaming first, so check the pack instructions.

NUTRITION NOTES

Per portion:

Energy	95Kcals/397kJ
Fat	0.53g
Saturated fat	0.07g
Cholesterol	0
Fibre	0.29g

CORN GRIDDLE PANCAKES

These crisp pancakes are delicious to serve as a snack lunch, or as a light supper with a crisp mixed salad.

INGREDIENTS

Serves 4, makes about 12
115g/4oz/1 cup self-raising flour
1 egg white
150ml/¼ pint/⅔ cup skimmed milk
200g/7oz can sweetcorn, drained
oil, for brushing
salt and black pepper
tomato chutney, to serve

1 Place the flour, egg white and skimmed milk in a food processor or blender with half the sweetcorn and process until smooth.

2 Season the batter well and add the remaining sweetcorn.

3 Heat a frying pan and brush with oil. Drop in tablespoons of batter and cook until set. Turn over the pancakes and cook the other side until golden. Serve hot with tomato chutney.

NUTRITION NOTES

Per portion:

Energy	162Kcals/680kJ
Fat	0.89g
Saturated fat	0.14g
Cholesterol	0.75mg
Fibre	1.49g

BAKED POLENTA WITH TOMATOES

INGREDIENTS

Serves 4
750ml/1¼ pints/3¾ cups stock
175g/6oz/1⅛ cup polenta (coarse corn-meal)
60ml/4 tbsp chopped fresh sage
5ml/1 tsp olive oil
2 beefsteak tomatoes, sliced
15ml/1 tbsp grated Parmesan cheese
salt and black pepper

1 Bring the stock to the boil in a large saucepan, then gradually stir in the polenta.

2 Continue stirring the polenta over a moderate heat for about 5 minutes, until the mixture begins to come away from the sides of the pan. Stir in the chopped sage and season well, then spoon into a lightly oiled, shallow 23 x 33cm/9x13 in tin and spread evenly. Leave to cool.

3 Preheat the oven to 200°C/400°F/ Gas 6. Cut the cooled polenta into 24 squares using a sharp knife.

4 Arrange the polenta overlapping with tomato slices in a lightly oiled, shallow ovenproof dish. Sprinkle with Parmesan and bake for 20 minutes or until golden brown. Serve hot.

NUTRITION NOTES

Per portion:

Energy	200Kcals/842kJ
Fat	3.8g
Saturated fat	0.77g
Cholesterol	1.88mg
Fibre	1.71g

LEMON AND HERB RISOTTO CAKE

This unusual rice dish can be served as a main course with salad, or as a satisfying side dish. It's also good served cold, and packs well for picnics.

INGREDIENTS

Serves 4

1 small leek, thinly sliced
600ml/1 pint/2½ cups chicken stock
225g/8oz/1 cup short grain rice
finely grated rind of 1 lemon
30ml/2 tbsp chopped fresh chives
30ml/2 tbsp chopped fresh parsley
75g/3oz/¼ cup grated mozzarella cheese
salt and black pepper
parsley and lemon wedges, to garnish

1 Preheat the oven to 200°C/400°F/ Gas 6. Lightly oil a 22cm/8½ in round, loose-bottomed cake tin.

2 Cook the leek in a large pan with 45ml/3 tbsp stock, stirring over a moderate heat, to soften. Add the rice and the remaining stock.

3 Bring to the boil. Cover the pan and simmer gently, stirring occasionally, for about 20 minutes, or until all the liquid is absorbed.

4 Stir in the lemon rind, herbs, cheese and seasoning. Spoon into the tin, cover with foil and bake for 30–35 minutes or until lightly browned. Turn out and serve in slices, garnished with parsley and lemon wedges.

COOK'S TIP
The best type of rice to choose for this recipe is the Italian round grain Arborio rice, but if it is not available, use pudding rice instead.

NUTRITION NOTES	
Per portion:	
Energy	280Kcals/1176kJ
Fat	6.19g
Saturated fat	2.54g
Cholesterol	12.19mg
Fibre	0.9g

RICE WITH SEEDS AND SPICES

A change from plain boiled rice, and a colourful accompaniment to serve with spicy curries or grilled meats. Basmati rice gives the best texture and flavour, but you can use ordinary long grain rice instead, if you prefer.

INGREDIENTS

Serves 4

5ml/1 tsp sunflower oil
2.5ml/½ tsp ground turmeric
6 cardamom pods, lightly crushed
5ml/1 tsp coriander seeds, lightly
  crushed
1 garlic clove, crushed
200g/7oz/1 cup basmati rice
400ml/14 fl oz/1⅔ cups stock
115g/4oz/½ cup natural yogurt
15ml/1 tbsp toasted sunflower seeds
15ml/1 tbsp toasted sesame seeds
salt and black pepper
coriander leaves, to garnish

1 Heat the oil in a non-stick pan and fry the spices and garlic for about 1 minute, stirring all the time.

2 Add the rice and stock, bring to the boil then cover and simmer for 15 minutes or until just tender.

3 Stir in the yogurt and the toasted sunflower and sesame seeds. Adjust the seasoning and serve hot, garnished with coriander leaves.

NUTRITION NOTES

Per portion:
Energy	243Kcals/1022kJ
Fat	5.5g
Saturated fat	0.73g
Cholesterol	1.15mg
Fibre	0.57g

COOK'S TIP
Seeds are particularly rich in minerals, so they are a good addition to all kinds of dishes. Light roasting will improve their flavour.

MEAT

Make the most of the wide range of leaner cuts of meat available to make delicious, low fat dishes. Included here are tempting, light and nutritious main courses that are packed with flavour. Try spicy Thai Beef Salad or Skewers of Lamb with Mint for an *al fresco* summer lunch. Ragoût of Veal, Indonesian Pork and Peanut Saté and Venison with Cranberry Sauce make perfect special occasion meals. If you are feeding a family, there are plenty of recipes here that will please, from Roast Pork in a Blanket to Bacon Koftas or Beef and Mushroom Burgers

THAI BEEF SALAD

A hearty salad of beef, laced with a chilli and lime dressing.

INGREDIENTS

Serves 6

75g/3oz lean sirloin steaks
1 red onion, finely sliced
1/2 cucumber, finely sliced
   into matchsticks
1 lemon grass stalk, finely chopped
30ml/2 tbsp chopped spring onions
juice of 2 limes
15–30ml/1–2 tbsp fish sauce
2–4 red chillies, finely sliced, to garnish
fresh coriander, Chinese mustard cress
   and mint leaves, to garnish

NUTRITION NOTES

Per portion:

Energy	101Kcals/424kJ
Fat	3.8g
Saturated Fat	1.7g
Cholesterol	33.4mg
Fibre	0.28g

COOK'S TIP
Rump or fillet steaks would work just as well in this recipe. Choose good-quality lean steaks and remove and discard any visible fat.

1 Grill the sirloin steaks until they are medium-rare, then allow to rest for 10–15 minutes.

2 When cool, thinly slice the beef and put the slices in a large bowl.

3 Add the sliced onion, cucumber matchsticks and lemon grass.

4 Add the spring onions. Toss and season with lime juice and fish sauce. Serve at room temperature or chilled, garnished with the chillies, coriander, mustard cress and mint.

RAGOÛT OF VEAL

If you are looking for a low-calorie dish to treat yourself – or some guests – then this is perfect, and quick, too.

INGREDIENTS

Serves 4

375g/12oz veal fillet or loin
10ml/2 tsp olive oil
10–12 tiny onions, kept whole
1 yellow pepper, seeded and cut
  into eighths
1 orange or red pepper, seeded and
  cut into eighths
3 tomatoes, peeled
  and quartered
4 fresh basil sprigs
30ml/2 tbsp dry martini or sherry
salt and black pepper

NUTRITION NOTES

Per portion:

Energy	158Kcals/665.5kJ
Fat	4.97g
Saturated Fat	1.14g
Cholesterol	63mg
Fibre	2.5g

1 Trim off any fat and cut the veal into cubes. Heat the oil in a frying pan and gently stir-fry the veal and onions until browned.

2 After a couple of minutes, add the peppers and tomatoes. Continue stir-frying for another 4–5 minutes.

COOK'S TIP
Lean beef or pork fillet may be used instead of veal, if you prefer. Shallots can replace the onions.

3 Add half the basil leaves, roughly chopped (keep some for garnish), the martini or sherry, and seasoning. Cook, stirring frequently, for another 10 minutes, or until the meat is tender.

4 Sprinkle with the remaining basil leaves and serve hot.

VENISON WITH CRANBERRY SAUCE

Venison steaks are now readily available. Lean and low in fat, they make a healthy choice for a special occasion. Served with a sauce of fresh seasonal cranberries, port and ginger, they make a dish with a wonderful combination of flavours.

— INGREDIENTS —

Serves 4
1 orange
1 lemon
75g/3oz/1 cup fresh or frozen
    cranberries
5ml/1 tsp grated fresh root ginger
1 thyme sprig, plus extra to garnish
5ml/1 tsp Dijon mustard
60ml/4 tbsp redcurrant jelly
150ml/¼ pint/⅔ cup ruby port
10ml/2 tsp sunflower oil
4 x 90g/3½oz venison steaks
2 shallots, finely chopped
salt and black pepper
mashed potato and broccoli, to serve

— NUTRITION NOTES —

Per portion:

Energy	250Kcals/1055.5kJ
Fat	4.39g
Saturated Fat	1.13g
Cholesterol	50mg
Fibre	1.59g

COOK'S TIP
When frying venison, always remember: the briefer the better. Venison will turn to leather if subjected to fierce heat after it has reached the medium-rare stage. If you dislike any hint of pink, cook it to this stage, then let it rest in a low oven for a few minutes.

1 Pare the rind from half the orange and half the lemon using a vegetable peeler, then cut into very fine strips.

2 Blanch the strips in a small pan of boiling water for about 5 minutes until tender. Drain the strips and refresh under cold water.

3 Squeeze the juice from the orange and lemon, then pour into a small pan. Add the cranberries, ginger, thyme sprig, mustard, redcurrant jelly and port. Cook over a low heat until the jelly melts.

4 Bring the sauce to the boil, stirring occasionally, then cover the pan and reduce the heat. Cook gently for about 15 minutes, until the cranberries are just tender.

VARIATION
When fresh cranberries are unavailable, use redcurrants instead. Stir them into the sauce towards the end of cooking with the orange and lemon rinds.

5 Heat the oil in a heavy-based frying pan, add the venison steaks and cook over a high heat for 2–3 minutes.

6 Turn over the steaks and add the shallots to the pan. Cook the steaks on the other side for 2–3 minutes, depending on whether you like rare or medium-cooked meat.

7 Just before the end of cooking, pour in the sauce and add the strips of orange and lemon rind.

8 Leave the sauce to bubble for a few seconds to thicken slightly, then remove the thyme sprig and adjust the seasoning to taste.

9 Transfer the venison steaks to warmed plates and spoon over the sauce. Garnish with thyme sprigs and serve accompanied by mashed potato and broccoli.

PORK AND CELERY POPOVERS

Lower in fat than they look, and a good way to make the meat go further, these little popovers will be popular with children.

INGREDIENTS

Serves 4
sunflower oil, for brushing
150g/5oz plain flour
1 egg white
250ml/8 fl oz/1 cup skimmed milk
120ml/4 fl oz/½ cup water
350g/12 oz lean minced pork
2 celery sticks, finely chopped
45ml/3 tbsp rolled oats
30ml/2 tbsp snipped chives
15ml/1 tbsp Worcestershire or brown
   sauce
salt and black pepper

1 Preheat the oven to 220°C/425°F/ Gas 7. Brush 12 deep patty tins with a very little oil.

2 Place the flour in a bowl and make a well in the centre. Add the egg white and milk and gradually beat in the flour. Gradually add the water, beating until smooth and bubbly.

3 Place the minced pork, celery, oats, chives, Worcestershire sauce and seasoning in a bowl and mix thoroughly. Mould the mixture into 12 small balls and place in the patty tins.

4 Cook for 10 minutes, remove from the oven and quickly pour the batter into the tins. Cook for a further 20–25 minutes, or until well risen and golden brown. Serve hot with thin gravy and fresh vegetables.

NUTRITION NOTES

Per portion:

Energy	344Kcals/1443kJ
Fat	9.09g
Saturated fat	2.7g
Cholesterol	61.62mg
Fibre	2.37g

BEEF AND MUSHROOM BURGERS

It's worth making your own burgers to cut down on fat – in these the meat is extended with mushrooms for extra fibre.

INGREDIENTS

Serves 4

1 small onion, chopped
150g/5oz/2 cups small cup mushrooms
450g/1 lb lean minced beef
50g/2oz/1 cup fresh wholemeal breadcrumbs
5ml/1 tsp dried mixed herbs
15ml/1 tbsp tomato purée
flour, for shaping
salt and black pepper

1 Place the onion and mushrooms in a food processor and process until finely chopped. Add the beef, bread-crumbs, herbs, tomato purée and seasonings. Process for a few seconds, until the mixture binds together but still has some texture.

2 Divide the mixture into 8–10 pieces, then press into burger shapes using lightly floured hands.

3 Cook the burgers in a non-stick frying pan, or under a hot grill for 12-15 minutes, turning once, until evenly cooked. Serve with relish and salad, in burger buns or pitta bread.

COOK'S TIP
The mixture is quite soft, so handle carefully and use a fish slice for turning to prevent the burgers from breaking up during cooking.

NUTRITION NOTES

Per portion	
Energy	196Kcals/822kJ
Fat	5.9g
Saturated fat	2.21g
Cholesterol	66.37mg
Fibre	1.60g

CURRIED LAMB AND LENTILS

This colourful curry is packed
with protein and low in fat.

INGREDIENTS

Serves 4

8 lean, boneless lamb leg steaks, about
  500g/1¼ lb total weight
1 medium onion, chopped
2 medium carrots, diced
1 celery stick, chopped
15ml/1 tbsp hot curry paste
30ml/2 tbsp tomato purée
475ml/16 fl oz/2 cups stock
175g/6oz/1 cup green lentils
salt and black pepper
fresh coriander leaves, to garnish
boiled rice, to serve

1 In a large, non-stick pan, fry the
lamb steaks without fat until
browned, turning once.

2 Add the vegetables and cook for 2
minutes, then stir in the curry paste,
tomato purée, stock and lentils.

3 Bring to the boil, cover and simmer
gently for 30 minutes until tender.
Add more stock, if necessary. Season
and serve with coriander and rice.

NUTRITION NOTES

Per portion:

Energy	375Kcals/1575kJ
Fat	13.03g
Saturated fat	5.34g
Cholesterol	98.75mg
Fibre	6.11g

GOLDEN PORK AND APRICOT CASSEROLE

The rich golden colour and
warm spicy flavour of this simple
casserole make it ideal for chilly
winter days.

INGREDIENTS

Serves 4

4 lean pork loin chops
1 medium onion, thinly sliced
2 yellow peppers, seeded and sliced
10ml/2 tsp medium curry powder
15ml/1 tbsp plain flour
250ml/8 fl oz/1 cup chicken stock
115g/4oz/⅔ cup dried apricots
30ml/2 tbsp wholegrain mustard
salt and black pepper

1 Trim the excess fat from the pork
and fry without fat in a large, heavy
or non-stick pan until lightly browned.

2 Add the onion and peppers to the
pan and stir over a moderate heat
for 5 minutes. Stir in the curry powder
and the flour.

3 Add the stock, stirring, then add the
apricots and mustard. Cover and
simmer for 25–30 minutes, until tender.
Adjust the seasoning and serve hot,
with rice or new potatoes.

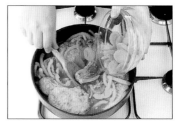

NUTRITION NOTES

Per portion:

Energy	289Kcals/1213kJ
Fat	10.03g
Saturated fat	3.23g
Cholesterol	82.8mg
Fibre	4.86g

COUNTRY PORK WITH PARSLEY COBBLER

This hearty casserole is a complete main course in one pot.

Serves 4
450g/1 lb boneless pork shoulder,
  diced
1 small swede, diced
2 carrots, sliced
2 parsnips, sliced
2 leeks, sliced
2 celery sticks, sliced
750ml/1¼ pint/3⅓ cups boiling beef
  stock
30ml/2 tbsp tomato purée
30ml/2 tbsp chopped fresh parsley
50g/2oz/¼ cup pearl barley
celery salt and black pepper

For the topping
150g/5oz/1 cup plain flour
5ml/1 tsp baking powder
90ml/6 tbsp low fat fromage frais
45ml/3 tbsp chopped fresh parsley

1 Preheat the oven to 180°C/350°F/
Gas 4. Fry the pork without fat, in a
non-stick pan until lightly browned.

2 Add the vegetables to the pan and
stir over a medium heat until lightly
coloured. Tip into a large casserole
dish, then stir in the stock, tomato
purée, parsley and pearl barley.

3 Season with celery salt and pepper,
then cover and place in the oven for
about 1–1¼ hours, until the pork and
vegetables are tender.

4 For the topping, sift the flour and
baking powder with seasoning, then
stir in the fromage frais and parsley
with enough cold water to mix to a soft
dough. Roll out to about 1cm/½ in
thickness and cut into 12–16 triangles.

5 Remove the casserole from the oven
and raise the temperature to 220°C/
425°F/Gas 7.

6 Arrange the triangles over the casserole, overlapping. Bake for 15–20
minutes, until well risen and golden.

────── NUTRITION NOTES ──────

Per portion:
Energy   461Kcals/1936kJ
Fat   10.55g
Saturated fat   3.02g
Cholesterol   77.85mg
Fibre   9.44g

BEEF STRIPS WITH ORANGE AND GINGER

Stir-frying is one of the best ways to cook with the minimum of fat. It's also one of the quickest ways to cook, but you do need to choose tender meat.

INGREDIENTS

Serves 4

450g/1 lb lean beef rump, fillet or sirloin, cut into thin strips
finely grated rind and juice of 1 orange
15ml/1 tbsp light soy sauce
5ml/1 tsp cornflour
2.5cm/1in piece root ginger, finely chopped
10ml/2 tsp sesame oil
1 large carrot, cut into thin strips
2 spring onions, thinly sliced

1 Place the beef strips in a bowl and sprinkle over the orange rind and juice. If possible, leave to marinate for at least 30 minutes.

2 Drain the liquid from the meat and set aside, then mix the meat with the soy sauce, cornflour and ginger.

NUTRITION NOTES

Per portion:	
Energy	175Kcals/730kJ
Fat	6.81g
Saturated fat	2.31g
Cholesterol	66.37mg
Fibre	0.67g

3 Heat the oil in a wok or large frying pan and add the beef. Stir-fry for 1 minute until lightly coloured, then add the carrot and stir-fry for a further 2–3 minutes.

4 Stir in the spring onions and reserved liquid, then cook, stirring, until boiling and thickened. Serve hot with rice noodles or plain boiled rice.

GREEK LAMB PIE

INGREDIENTS

Serves 4

sunflower oil, for brushing
450g/1 lb lean minced lamb
1 medium onion, sliced
1 garlic clove, crushed
400g/14oz can plum tomatoes
30ml/2 tbsp chopped fresh mint
5ml/1 tsp grated nutmeg
350g/12oz young spinach leaves
270g/10 oz packet filo pastry
5ml/1 tsp sesame seeds
salt and black pepper

1 Preheat the oven to 200°C/400°F/ Gas 6. Lightly oil a 22cm/8½ in round spring form tin.

2 Fry the mince and onion without fat in a non-stick pan until golden. Add the garlic, tomatoes, mint, nutmeg and seasoning. Bring to the boil, stirring. Simmer, stirring occasionally, until most of the liquid has evaporated.

3 Wash the spinach and remove any tough stalks, then cook in only the water clinging to the leaves for about 2 minutes, until wilted.

4 Lightly brush each sheet of filo pastry with oil and lay in overlapping layers in the tin, leaving enough overhanging to wrap over the top.

5 Spoon in the meat and spinach, then wrap the pastry over to enclose, scrunching it slightly. Sprinkle with sesame seeds and bake for about 25–30 minutes, or until golden and crisp. Serve hot, with salad or vegetables.

NUTRITION NOTES

Per portion:

Energy	444Kcals/1865kJ
Fat	15.36g
Saturated fat	5.51g
Cholesterol	88.87mg
Fibre	3g

ROAST PORK IN A BLANKET

INGREDIENTS

Serves 4

1.5kg/3 lb lean pork loin joint
1 eating apple, cored and grated
40g/1½oz/¼ cup fresh breadcrumbs
30ml/2 tbsp chopped hazelnuts
15ml/1 tbsp Dijon mustard
15ml/1 tbsp snipped fresh chives
salt and black pepper

1 Cut the skin from the pork leaving a thin layer of fat.

2 Preheat the oven to 220°C/425°F/ Gas 7. Place the meat on a rack in a roasting tin, cover with foil and roast for 1 hour, then reduce the oven temperature to 180°C/350°F/Gas 4.

3 Mix together the apple, breadcrumbs, nuts, mustard, chives and seasoning. Remove the foil and spread the breadcrumb mixture over the fat surface of the meat.

4 Cook the pork for 45–60 minutes, or until the meat juices run clear. Serve in slices with a rich gravy.

NUTRITION NOTES

Per portion:

Energy	367Kcals/1540kJ
Fat	18.73g
Saturated fat	5.19g
Cholesterol	129.38mg
Fibre	1.5g

STUFFED AUBERGINES WITH LAMB

Serves 4

2 aubergines
30ml/2 tbsp sunflower oil
1 onion, sliced
5ml/1 tsp grated fresh root ginger
5ml/1 tsp chilli powder
1 garlic clove, crushed
1.5ml/¼ tsp turmeric
5ml/1 tsp salt
5ml/1 tsp ground coriander
1 tomato, chopped
350g/12oz lean leg of lamb, minced
1 green pepper, roughly chopped
1 orange pepper, roughly chopped
30ml/2 tbsp chopped fresh coriander

For the garnish
½ onion, sliced
2 cherry tomatoes, quartered
fresh coriander leaves

NUTRITION NOTES

Per portion:
Energy	239Kcals/1003kJ
Fat	13.92g
Saturated fat	4.36g
Cholesterol	67.15mg

1 Cut the aubergines in half lengthways and cut out most of the flesh and discard. Place the aubergine shells in a lightly greased ovenproof dish.

2 In a saucepan, heat 15ml/1 tbsp oil and fry the onion until golden. Gradually stir in the ginger, chilli powder, garlic, turmeric, salt and ground coriander. Add the tomato, lower the heat and stir-fry for 5 minutes.

3 Preheat the oven to 180°C/350°F/ Gas 4. Add the minced lamb and stir-fry over a medium heat for a further 7–10 minutes.

4 Add the chopped peppers and fresh coriander to the lamb mixture, and stir well.

5 Spoon the lamb mixture into the aubergine shells and brush the edges of the shells with the remaining oil. Bake in the preheated oven for about 20–25 minutes until cooked through and browned on top.

6 Serve with the garnish ingredients and either a green salad or plain boiled rice.

COOK'S TIP
For a special occasion, stuffed baby aubergines look particularly attractive. Use four small aubergines, leaving the stalks intact, and prepare and cook as described above. Reduce the baking time slightly, if necessary. Large tomatoes or courgettes also make a good alternative to aubergines.

BEEF WITH GREEN BEANS

This easy-to-cook curried dish is a delicious variation on a traditional Indian recipe.

Serves 4

275g/10oz fine green beans, cut into
   2.5cm/1 in pieces
30ml/2 tbsp sunflower oil
1 medium onion, sliced
5ml/1 tsp grated fresh root ginger
1 garlic clove, crushed
5ml/1 tsp chilli powder
6.5ml/1¼ tsp salt
1.5ml/¼ tsp turmeric
2 tomatoes, chopped
450g/1 lb lean beef, cubed
1.2 litres/2 pints/5 cups water
15ml/1 tbsp chopped fresh coriander
1 red pepper, sliced
2 green chillies, chopped

1 Cook the green beans in a saucepan of boiling salted water for about 5 minutes, then drain and set aside.

2 Heat the oil in a large saucepan and fry the sliced onion until golden.

3 Mix together the ginger, garlic, chilli powder, salt, turmeric and chopped tomatoes. Spoon into the onions and stir-fry for about 5–7 minutes.

4 Add the beef and stir-fry for a further 3 minutes. Pour in the water, bring to the boil and lower the heat. Cover and cook for about 45–60 minutes until most of the water has evaporated and the meat is tender.

5 Add the green beans and mix everything together well.

6 Finally, add the red pepper, fresh coriander and chopped green chillies and cook for a further 7–10 minutes stirring occasionally. Serve hot with wholemeal chapatis.

NUTRITION NOTES	
Per portion:	
Energy	241Kcals/1012kJ
Fat	11.6g
Saturated fat	2.89g
Cholesterol	66.96mg

MEXICAN BEEF BURGERS

Nothing beats the flavour and quality of a home-made burger. This version is from Mexico and is delicately seasoned with cumin and fresh coriander.

INGREDIENTS

Makes 4

4 corn on the cob
50g/2oz/1 cup stale white breadcrumbs
90ml/6 tbsp skimmed milk
1 small onion, finely chopped
5ml/1 tsp ground cumin
2.5ml/½ tsp cayenne pepper
2.5ml/½ tsp celery salt
45ml/3 tbsp chopped fresh coriander
900g/2 lb lean minced beef
4 sesame buns
60ml/4 tbsp reduced calorie
   mayonnaise
4 tomato slices
½ iceberg lettuce or other leaves such as
   frisée or Webb's
salt and black pepper
1 large packet corn chips, to serve

1 Cook the corn cobs in a large saucepan of boiling water for about 15 minutes.

2 Combine the breadcrumbs, skimmed milk, onion, cumin, cayenne, celery salt and fresh coriander together in a large bowl.

3 Add the beef and mix by hand until the mixture is evenly blended.

4 Divide the beef mixture into four portions and flatten between sheets of clear film.

5 Preheat a moderate grill and cook for about 10 minutes for medium or 15 minutes for well-done burgers.

6 Split and toast the buns, spread with mayonnaise and sandwich the burgers with the tomato slices, lettuce leaves and seasoning. Serve with corn chips and the corn on the cob.

NUTRITION NOTES

Per portion:

Energy	563Kcals/2363kJ
Fat	18.82g
Saturated fat	5.55g
Cholesterol	133.2mg

PORK STEAKS WITH GREMOLATA

Gremolata is a popular Italian dressing of garlic, lemon and parsley – it adds a hint of sharpness to the pork.

— INGREDIENTS —

Serves 4
30ml/2 tbsp olive oil
4 lean pork shoulder steaks, about
    175g/6oz each
1 onion, chopped
2 garlic cloves, crushed
30ml/2 tbsp tomato purée
400g/14oz can chopped tomatoes
150ml/¼ pint/⅔ cup dry white wine
bouquet garni
3 anchovy fillets, drained and chopped
salt and black pepper
salad leaves, to serve

For the gremolata
45ml/3 tbsp chopped fresh parsley
grated rind of ½ lemon
grated rind of 1 lime
1 garlic clove, chopped

1 Heat the oil in a large flameproof casserole, add the pork steaks and brown on both sides. Remove the steaks from the casserole.

2 Add the onion to the casserole and cook until soft and beginning to brown. Add the garlic and cook for about 1–2 minutes, then stir in the tomato purée, chopped tomatoes and wine. Add the bouquet garni. Bring to the boil, then boil rapidly for a further 3–4 minutes to reduce the sauce and thicken slightly.

3 Return the pork to the casserole, then cover and cook for about 30 minutes. Stir in the anchovies.

4 Cover the casserole and cook for a further 15 minutes, or until the pork is tender. For the gremolata, mix together the parsley, lemon and lime rinds and garlic.

5 Remove the pork steaks and discard the bouquet garni. Reduce the sauce over a high heat, if it is not already thick. Taste and adjust the seasoning if required.

6 Return the pork to the casserole, then sprinkle with the gremolata. Cover and cook for a further 5 minutes, then serve hot with salad leaves.

NUTRITION NOTES	
Per portion:	
Energy	267Kcals/1121kJ
Fat	13.39g
Saturated fat	3.43g
Cholesterol	69mg
Fibre	2.06g

PAN-FRIED MEDITERRANEAN LAMB

The warm summery flavours of the Mediterranean are combined for a simple weekday meal.

--- INGREDIENTS ---

Serves 4

8 lean lamb cutlets
1 medium onion, thinly sliced
2 red peppers, seeded and sliced
400g/14oz can plum tomatoes
1 garlic clove, crushed
45ml/3 tbsp chopped fresh basil leaves
30ml/2 tbsp chopped black olives
salt and black pepper

1 Trim any excess fat from the lamb, then fry without fat in a non-stick pan until golden brown.

2 Add the onion and peppers to the pan. Cook, stirring, for a few minutes to soften, then add the plum tomatoes, garlic and basil.

3 Cover and simmer for 20 minutes or until the lamb is tender. Stir in the olives, season and serve hot with pasta.

--- NUTRITION NOTES ---

Per portion:

Energy	224Kcals/939kJ
Fat	10.17g
Saturated fat	4.32g
Cholesterol	79mg
Fibre	2.48g

BACON KOFTAS

These easy koftas are good for barbecues and summer grills, served with lots of salad.

--- INGREDIENTS ---

Serves 4

225g/8oz lean smoked back bacon,
*   roughly chopped*
75g/3oz/1½ cups fresh wholemeal
*   breadcrumbs*
2 spring onions, chopped
15ml/1 tbsp chopped fresh parsley
finely grated rind of 1 lemon
1 egg white
black pepper
paprika
lemon rind and fresh parsley leaves, to
*   garnish*

1 Place the bacon in a food processor with the breadcrumbs, spring onions, parsley, lemon rind, egg white and pepper. Process the mixture until it is finely chopped and begins to bind together. Alternatively, use a mincer.

2 Divide the bacon mixture into eight even-sized pieces and shape into long ovals around eight wooden or bamboo skewers.

3 Sprinkle the koftas with paprika and cook under a hot grill or on a barbecue for about 8–10 minutes, turning occasionally, until browned and cooked through. Garnish with lemon rind and parsley leaves, then serve hot with lemon rice and salad.

--- NUTRITION NOTES ---

Per portion:

Energy	128Kcals/538kJ
Fat	4.7g
Saturated fat	1.61g
Cholesterol	10.13mg
Fibre	1.33g

SAUSAGE BEANPOT WITH DUMPLINGS

Sausages needn't be totally banned on a low fat diet, but choose them carefully. If you are unable to find a reduced-fat variety, choose turkey sausages instead, and always drain off any fat during cooking.

INGREDIENTS

Serves 4

450g/1 lb half-fat sausages
1 medium onion, thinly sliced
1 green pepper, seeded and diced
1 small red chilli, sliced, or 2.5ml/½ tsp chilli sauce
400g/14oz can chopped tomatoes
250ml/8 fl oz/1 cup beef stock
425g/15oz can red kidney beans, drained
salt and black pepper

For the dumplings

275g/10oz/2½ cups plain flour
10ml/2 tsp baking powder
225g/8oz/1 cup cottage cheese

1 Fry the sausages without fat in a non-stick pan until brown. Add the onion and pepper. Stir in the chilli, tomatoes and stock; bring to the boil.

NUTRITION NOTES

Per portion:

Energy	574Kcals/2409kJ
Fat	13.09g
Saturated fat	0.15g
Cholesterol	52.31mg
Fibre	9.59g

2 Cover and simmer gently for 15–20 minutes, then add the beans and bring to the boil.

3 To make the dumplings, sift the flour and baking powder together and add enough water to mix to a firm dough. Roll out thinly and stamp out 16–18 rounds using a 7.5cm/3in cutter.

4 Place a small spoonful of cottage cheese on each round and bring the edges of the dough together, pinching to enclose. Arrange the dumplings over the sausages in the pan, cover the pan and simmer for 10–12 minutes, until the dumplings are well risen. Serve hot.

SPICY SPRING LAMB ROAST

INGREDIENTS

Serves 6

1.5kg/3–3½lb lean leg spring lamb
5ml/1 tsp chilli powder
1 garlic clove, crushed
5ml/1 tsp ground coriander
5ml/1 tsp ground cumin
5ml/1 tsp salt
10ml/2 tsp desiccated coconut
10ml/2 tsp ground almonds
45ml/3 tbsp low fat natural yogurt
30ml/2 tbsp lemon juice
30ml/2 tbsp sultanas
30ml/2 tbsp corn oil

For the garnish
mixed salad leaves
fresh coriander leaves
2 tomatoes, sliced
1 large carrot, cut into julienne strips
lemon wedges

NUTRITION NOTES

Per portion:

Energy	197Kcals/825kJ
Fat	11.96g
Saturated fat	4.7g
Cholesterol	67.38mg

2 In a medium bowl, mix together the chilli powder, garlic, ground coriander, ground cumin and salt.

3 In a food processor or blender process together the desiccated coconut, ground almonds, yogurt, lemon juice and sultanas until you have a smooth texture.

4 Add the contents of the food processor to the spice mixture together with the corn oil and mix together. Pour this on to the leg of lamb and rub over the meat.

5 Enclose the meat in the foil and place in an ovenproof dish. Cook in the preheated oven for 1½ hours.

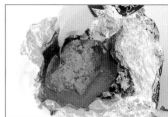

6 Remove the lamb from the oven, open the foil and, using the back of a spoon, spread the mixture evenly over the meat again. Return the lamb, uncovered, to the oven for a further 45 minutes or until it is cooked right through and tender. Slice the meat and serve with the garnish ingredients.

1 Preheat the oven to 180°C/350°F/ Gas 4. Trim off the fat, rinse and pat dry the leg of lamb and set aside on a sheet of foil large enough to enclose the whole joint.

LAMB PIE WITH MUSTARD THATCH

A pleasant change from a classic shepherd's pie – healthier, too.

INGREDIENTS

Serves 4

750g/1½ lb old potatoes, diced
30ml/2 tbsp skimmed milk
15ml/1 tbsp wholegrain or French
    mustard
450g/1 lb lean minced lamb
1 onion, chopped
2 celery sticks, sliced
2 carrots, diced
150ml/¼ pint/⅔ cup beef stock
60ml/4 tbsp rolled oats
15ml/1 tbsp Worcestershire sauce
30ml/2 tbsp fresh chopped rosemary,
    or 10ml/2 tsp dried
salt and black pepper

1 Cook the potatoes in boiling, lightly salted water until tender. Drain and mash until smooth, then stir in the milk and mustard. Meanwhile, preheat the oven to 200°C/400°F/Gas 6.

2 Break up the lamb with a fork and fry without fat in a non-stick pan until lightly browned. Add the onion, celery and carrots to the pan and cook for 2–3 minutes, stirring.

3 Stir in the stock and rolled oats. Bring to the boil, then add the Worcestershire sauce and rosemary and season to taste with salt and pepper.

4 Turn the meat mixture into a 1.8 litre/3 pint/7 cup ovenproof dish and spread over the potato topping evenly, swirling with the edge of a knife. Bake for 30–35 minutes, or until golden. Serve hot with fresh vegetables.

NUTRITION NOTES

Per portion:
Energy	422Kcals/1770kJ
Fat	12.41g
Saturated fat	5.04g
Cholesterol	89.03mg
Fibre	5.07g

INDONESIAN PORK AND PEANUT SATÉ

These delicious skewers of pork are popular street food in Indonesia. They are quick to make and eat.

INGREDIENTS

Serves 4

400g/14oz/2 cups long grain rice
450g/1 lb lean pork
pinch of salt
2 limes, quartered, and a chilli,
   to garnish
115g/4oz green salad, to serve

For the sauce

15ml/1 tbsp sunflower oil
1 small onion, chopped
1 garlic clove, crushed
2.5ml/½ tsp hot chilli sauce
15ml/1 tbsp sugar
30ml/2 tbsp soy sauce
30ml/2 tbsp lemon or lime juice
2.5ml/½ tsp anchovy essence (optional)
60ml/4 tbsp smooth peanut butter

1 Place the rice in a large saucepan, and cover with 900ml/1½ pints/ 3¼ cups of boiling salted water, stir and simmer uncovered for about 15 minutes until the liquid has been absorbed. Switch off the heat, cover and stand for 5 minutes.

2 Slice the pork into thin strips, then thread zig-zag fashion on to sixteen bamboo skewers.

3 To make the sauce, very gently heat the sunflower oil in a pan. Add the onion and cook over a low heat to soften without colouring for about 3–4 minutes. Add the next five ingredients and the anchovy essence, if using. Simmer briefly, then gently stir in the peanut butter.

VARIATION
Indonesian saté can also be prepared with lean beef, chicken or prawns for a delicious alternative.

4 Arrange the skewers on a baking tray and spoon over a third of the sauce. Grill for 6–8 minutes, turning once. Serve on a bed of rice, accompanied by the remaining sauce. Garnish with the limes and chilli and serve with a salad.

NUTRITION NOTES

Per portion:	
Energy	689Kcals/2895kJ
Fat	21.07g
Saturated fat	4.95g
Cholesterol	77.62mg
Fibre	1.39g

RUBY BACON CHOPS

This sweet, tangy sauce works well with lean bacon chops.

INGREDIENTS

Serves 4
1 ruby grapefruit
4 lean bacon loin chops
45ml/3 tbsp redcurrant jelly
black pepper

NUTRITION NOTES

Per portion:	
Energy	215Kcals/904kJ
Fat	8.40g
Saturated fat	3.02g
Cholesterol	20.25mg
Fibre	0.81g

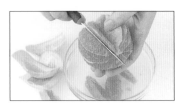

1 Cut away all the peel and pith from the grapefruit, using a sharp knife, and carefully remove the segments, catching the juice in a bowl.

2 Fry the bacon chops in a non-stick frying pan without fat, turning them once, until golden and cooked.

3 Add the reserved grapefruit juice and redcurrant jelly to the pan and stir until melted. Add the grapefruit segments, then season with pepper and serve hot with fresh vegetables.

JAMAICAN BEANPOT

If pumpkin is not available, use any other type of squash, or try swede instead. This recipe is a good one to double – or even treble – for a crowd.

INGREDIENTS

Serves 4
450g/1 lb braising steak, diced
1 small pumpkin, about 450g/1 lb diced flesh
1 medium onion, chopped
1 green pepper, seeded and sliced
15ml/1 tbsp paprika
2 garlic cloves, crushed
2.5ml/1 in piece fresh ginger root, chopped
400g/14oz can chopped tomatoes
115g/4oz baby corn cobs
250ml/8 fl oz/1 cup beef stock
425g/15oz can chick-peas, drained
425g/15oz can red kidney beans, drained
salt and black pepper

1 Fry the diced beef without fat in a large flameproof casserole, stirring to seal it on all sides.

2 Stir in the pumpkin, onion and pepper, cook for a further 2 minutes, then add the paprika, garlic and ginger.

3 Stir in the tomatoes, corn and stock, then bring to the boil. Cover and simmer for 40–45 minutes or until tender. Add the chick-peas and beans and heat thoroughly. Adjust the seasoning with salt and pepper to taste and serve hot with couscous or rice.

NUTRITION NOTES

Per portion:	
Energy	357Kcals/1500kJ
Fat	8.77g
Saturated fat	2.11g
Cholesterol	66.37mg
Fibre	10.63g

BUTTERFLIED CUMIN AND GARLIC LAMB

Ground cumin and garlic give the lamb a wonderful Middle Eastern flavour, although you may prefer a simple oil, lemon and herb marinade instead.

INGREDIENTS

Serves 6
1.75kg/4–4½ lb lean leg of lamb
60ml/4 tbsp olive oil
30ml/2 tbsp ground cumin
4–6 garlic cloves, crushed
salt and black pepper
coriander leaves and lemon wedges,
  to garnish
toasted almond and raisin-studded rice,
  to serve

1 To butterfly the lamb, cut away the meat from the bone using a small sharp knife. Remove any excess fat and the thin, parchment-like membrane. Bat out the meat to an even thickness, then prick the fleshy side of the lamb well with the tip of a knife.

2 In a bowl, mix together the oil, cumin and garlic, and season with pepper. Spoon the mixture all over the lamb, then rub it well into the crevices. Cover and leave to marinate overnight.

3 Preheat the oven to 200°C/400°F/Gas 6. Spread the lamb, skin-side down, on a rack in a roasting tin. Season with salt, and roast for about 45–60 minutes, until crusty brown outside, pink in the centre.

4 Remove the lamb from the oven and leave it to rest for about 10 minutes. Cut into diagonal slices and serve with the toasted almond and raisin-studded rice. Garnish with coriander leaves and lemon wedges.

NUTRITION NOTES	
Per portion:	
Energy	387Kcals/1624kJ
Fat	24.42g
Saturated fat	8.72g
Cholesterol	144.83mg
Fibre	0.14g

COOK'S TIP
The lamb may be barbecued – thread it on to two long skewers and cook on a hot barbecue for 20–25 minutes on each side.

SKEWERS OF LAMB WITH MINT

A delicious way to serve lamb with a Mediterranean twist. This dish could also be cooked on a barbecue and eaten al fresco-style in the garden.

— INGREDIENTS —

Serves 4

300ml/½ pint/1¼ cups low fat natural yogurt
½ garlic clove, crushed
good pinch of saffron powder
30ml/2 tbsp chopped fresh mint
30ml/2 tbsp clear honey
45ml/3 tbsp olive oil
3 lean lamb neck fillets, about 675g/1½ lb
1 aubergine
2 small red onions, quartered
salt and black pepper
small mint leaves, to garnish
lettuce and hot pitta bread, to serve

COOK'S TIP
If using bamboo skewers, soak them in cold water before use to prevent them burning. All lean, not-too-thick cuts of meat such as lamb or chicken grill very well on a barbecue. Meat should be marinated beforehand and left overnight if at all possible.

1 In a shallow dish, mix together the yogurt, garlic, saffron, mint, honey, oil and ground black pepper.

2 Trim the lamb and cut into 2.5cm/1 in cubes. Add to the marinade and stir until well coated. Leave to marinate for at least 4 hours.

3 Cut the aubergine into 2.5cm/1 in cubes and blanch in boiling salted water for 1–2 minutes. Drain well.

4 Preheat the grill. Remove the lamb cubes from the marinade. Thread the lamb, aubergine and onion pieces alternately on to skewers. Grill for about 10–12 minutes, turning and basting occasionally with the marinade, until the lamb is tender. Serve the skewers on a bed of lettuce, garnished with mint leaves and accompanied by hot pitta bread.

— NUTRITION NOTES —

Per portion:

Energy	484Kcals/2032kJ
Fat	30.35g
Saturated fat	12.54g
Cholesterol	143.06mg
Fibre	2.05g

PAN-FRIED PORK WITH PEACHES

INGREDIENTS

Serves 4

400g/14oz/2 cups long grain rice
1 litre/1¾ pints/4 cups chicken stock
4 lean pork chops or loin pieces, about
   200g/7oz each
30ml/2 tbsp vegetable oil
30ml/2 tbsp dark rum or sherry
1 small onion, chopped
3 large ripe peaches
15ml/1 tbsp green peppercorns
15ml/1 tbsp white wine vinegar
salt and black pepper
flat leaf parsley, to garnish

NUTRITION NOTES

Per portion:

Energy	679Kcals/2852kJ
Fat	16.09g
Saturated fat	3.98g
Cholesterol	89.7mg
Fibre	1.84g

1 Place the rice in a large saucepan and cover with 900ml/1½ pints/3¼ cups chicken stock. Stir, bring to a simmer and cook uncovered for about 15 minutes. Switch off the heat, cover, and leave for 5 minutes. Season the pork. Heat a large metal frying pan and moisten the pork with 15ml/1 tbsp of the oil. Cook for about 12 minutes, turning once.

2 Transfer the meat to a warm plate. Pour off the excess fat from the pan and return to the heat. Allow the sediment to sizzle and brown, add the rum or sherry and loosen the sediment with a flat wooden spoon. Pour the pan contents over the meat, cover and keep warm. Wipe the pan clean.

3 Heat the remaining vegetable oil in the pan and soften the onion over a gentle heat.

4 Cover the peaches with boiling water to loosen the skins, then peel, slice and discard the stones.

5 Add the peaches and peppercorns to the onion and cook for about 3–4 minutes, until they begin to soften.

6 Add the remaining chicken stock and simmer briefly. Return the pork and meat juices to the pan, sharpen with vinegar, and season to taste. Serve the pork and peaches with the rice and garnish with flat leaf parsley.

COOK'S TIP
Unripe peaches are unsuitable. A can of sliced peaches may be used instead.

TURKISH LAMB AND APRICOT STEW

The chick-peas and almonds give a delightful crunchiness to this wholesome stew.

INGREDIENTS

Serves 4

1 large aubergine, cubed
30ml/2 tbsp sunflower oil
1 onion, chopped
1 garlic clove, crushed
5ml/1 tsp ground cinnamon
3 whole cloves
450g/1 lb boned leg of lean lamb, cubed
400g/14oz can chopped tomatoes
115g/4oz/⅔ cup ready-to-eat dried apricots
115g/4oz/⅔ cup canned chick-peas, drained
5ml/1 tsp clear honey
salt and black pepper
chopped fresh parsley, and 30ml/2 tbsp chopped almonds, fried in a little oil, to garnish
couscous, to serve

1 Place the aubergine in a colander, sprinkle with salt and leave for 30 minutes. Heat the oil in a flame-proof casserole, add the onion and garlic and fry for about 5 minutes.

NUTRITION NOTES

Per portion:

Energy	360 kcals/1512 kJ
Fat	17.05 g
Saturated fat	5.46g
Cholesterol	88.87mg
Fibre	6.16g

2 Stir in the ground cinnamon and cloves and fry for about 1 minute. Add the lamb and cook for a further 5–6 minutes, stirring occasionally until well browned.

3 Rinse, drain and pat dry the aubergine, add to the pan and cook for about 3 minutes, stirring well. Add the tomatoes, 300ml/½ pint/1¼ cups water, the apricots and seasoning. Bring to the boil, then cover the pan and sim-mer gently for about 45 minutes.

4 Stir in the chick-peas and honey, and cook for a further 15–20 min-utes, or until the lamb is tender. Serve the stew accompanied by couscous mixed with a little chopped parsley and garnished with the almonds.

VARIATION
Grains are very healthy and full of proteins and vitamins. Chick-peas are no exception. This recipe could be adapted by substituting split-peas or lentils for chick-peas.

POULTRY AND GAME

Poultry and game are obvious choices for a health conscious diet, as they are mostly very low in fat and much of the fat they do contain is unsaturated. Chicken, always a favourite choice for family meals, is versatile and economical. Turkey is now available in so many different cuts that it is interchangeable with chicken, and turkey mince can take the place of beef or lamb in bakes and pasta dishes. Game and duck are perfect for special occasions – try Mandarin Sesame Duck or Cider Baked Rabbit. Other tempting dishes include Sticky Ginger Chicken, Turkey Pastitsio, and Chicken, Carrot and Leek Parcels.

BARBECUED CHICKEN

INGREDIENTS

Serves 4 or 8

8 small chicken pieces
2 limes, cut into wedges, 2 red chillies,
  finely sliced, and 2 lemon grass
  stalks, to garnish
rice, to serve

For the marinade
2 lemon grass stalks, chopped
2.5cm/1in piece fresh root ginger
6 garlic cloves
4 shallots
¹/₂ bunch coriander roots
15ml/1 tbsp palm sugar
120ml/4fl oz/¹/₂ cup coconut milk
30ml/2 tbsp fish sauce
30ml/2 tbsp soy sauce

COOK'S TIP

Don't eat the skin of the chicken –
it's only left on to keep the flesh
moist during cooking. Coconut
milk makes a good base for a
marinade or sauce, as it is low in
calories and fat.

NUTRITION NOTES

Per portion (for 8):

Energy	106Kcals/449kJ
Fat	2.05g
Saturated Fat	1.10g
Cholesterol	1.10mg
Fibre	109g

1 To make the marinade, put all the
ingredients into a food processor
and process until smooth.

2 Put the chicken pieces in a dish and
pour over the marinade. Leave in a
cool place to marinate for at least
4 hours or overnight.

3 Preheat the oven to 200°C/400°F/
Gas 6. Put the chicken pieces on a
rack on a baking tray. Brush with
marinade and bake in the oven for
about 20–30 minutes or until the
chicken is cooked and golden brown.
Turn the pieces over halfway through
and brush with more marinade.

4 Garnish with lime wedges, finely
sliced red chillies and lemon grass
stalks. Serve with rice.

TANDOORI CHICKEN KEBABS

This dish originates from the plains of the Punjab at the foot of the Himalayas, where food is traditionally cooked in clay ovens known as tandoors – hence the name.

INGREDIENTS

Serves 4

4 boneless, skinless chicken breasts (about 130g/3¹/₂oz each)
15ml/1 tbsp lemon juice
45ml/3 tbsp tandoori paste
45ml/3 tbsp low fat natural yogurt
1 garlic clove, crushed
30ml/2 tbsp chopped fresh coriander
1 small onion, cut into wedges and separated into layers
10ml/1 tsp oil, for brushing
salt and black pepper
fresh coriander sprigs, to garnish
pilau rice and naan bread, to serve

1 Chop the chicken breasts into 2.5cm/1in cubes, put in a bowl and add the lemon juice, tandoori paste, yogurt, garlic, coriander and seasoning. Cover and leave to marinate in the fridge for 2–3 hours.

2 Preheat the grill to high. Thread alternate pieces of chicken and onion on to four skewers.

COOK'S TIP
Use chopped, boned and skinned chicken thighs, or strips of turkey breasts, for a cheaper and equally low fat alternative.

3 Brush the onions with a little oil, lay the skewers on a grill rack and cook for 10–12 minutes, turning once.

4 Garnish the kebabs with coriander and serve at once with pilau rice and naan bread.

NUTRITION NOTES

Per portion:

Energy	215.7Kcals/911.2kJ
Fat	4.2g
Saturated Fat	0.27g
Cholesterol	122mg
Fibre	0.22g

CHICKEN, CARROT AND LEEK PARCELS

These intriguing parcels may sound a bit fiddly for everyday eating, but actually they take very little time, and you can freeze them ready to cook from frozen when needed.

Serves 4

4 chicken fillets or skinless, boneless
   breast portions
2 small leeks, sliced
2 carrots, grated
2 stoned black olives, chopped
1 garlic clove, crushed
4 anchovy fillets, halved lengthways
salt and black pepper
black olives and herb sprigs, to garnish

1 Preheat the oven to 200°C/400°F/ Gas 6. Season the chicken well.

2 Cut out four sheets of lightly greased greaseproof paper about 23cm/9in square. Divide the leeks equally among them. Put a piece of chicken on top of each.

3 Mix the carrots, olives and garlic together. Season lightly and place on top of the chicken portions. Top each with two of the anchovy fillets.

4 Carefully wrap up each parcel, making sure the paper folds are sealed. Bake the parcels for 20 minutes and serve hot, in the paper, garnished with black olives and herb sprigs.

NUTRITION NOTES	
Per portion:	
Energy	154Kcals/651kJ
Fat	2.37g
Saturated Fat	0.45g
Cholesterol	78.75mg
Fibre	2.1g

COOK'S TIP
Skinless, boneless chicken is low in fat and is an excellent source of protein. Small, skinless turkey breast fillets also work well in this recipe and make a tasty change.

THAI CHICKEN AND VEGETABLE STIR-FRY

INGREDIENTS

Serves 4

1 piece lemon grass (or the rind of
  ½ lemon)
1cm/½in piece fresh root ginger
1 large garlic clove
30ml/2 tbsp sunflower oil
275g/10oz lean chicken,
  thinly sliced
½ red pepper, seeded and
  sliced
½ green pepper, seeded and sliced
4 spring onions, chopped
2 medium carrots, cut into matchsticks
115g/4oz fine green beans
25g/1oz peanuts, lightly crushed
30 ml/2 tbsp oyster sauce
pinch of sugar
salt and black pepper
coriander leaves, to garnish

NUTRITION NOTES

Per portion:

Energy	106Kcals/449kJ
Fat	2.05g
Saturated Fat	1.10g
Cholesterol	1.10mg
Fibre	109g

1 Thinly slice the lemon grass or lemon rind. Peel and chop the ginger and garlic. Heat the oil in a frying pan over a high heat. Add the lemon grass or lemon rind, ginger and garlic, and stir-fry for 30 seconds until brown.

2 Add the chicken and stir-fry for 2 minutes. Then add all the vegetables and stir-fry for 4–5 minutes, until the chicken is cooked and the vegetables are almost cooked.

3 Finally, stir in the peanuts, oyster sauce, sugar and seasoning to taste. Stir-fry for another minute to blend the flavours. Serve at once, sprinkled with the coriander leaves and accompanied by rice.

COOK'S TIP
Make this quick supper dish a little hotter by adding more fresh root ginger, if liked.

DUCK BREAST SALAD

Tender slices of succulent cooked duck breasts served with a salad of mixed pasta, fruit and vegetables, tossed together in a light dressing, ensure that this gourmet dish will impress friends and family alike.

INGREDIENTS

Serves 6

2 small duck breasts, boned
5ml/1 tsp coriander seeds, crushed
350g/12oz rigatoni or penne pasta
150ml/¼ pint/⅔ cup fresh orange juice
15ml/1 tbsp lemon juice
10ml/2 tsp clear honey
1 shallot, finely chopped
1 garlic clove, crushed
1 celery stick, chopped
75g/3oz dried cherries
45ml/3 tbsp port
15ml/1 tbsp chopped fresh mint, plus
    extra to garnish
30ml/2 tbsp chopped fresh coriander,
    plus extra to garnish
1 eating apple, diced
2 oranges, segmented
salt and black pepper

COOK'S TIP
Choose skinless duck breasts to reduce fat and calories. Crush your own spices, such as coriander seeds, to create fresh, aromatic, spicy flavours. Ready-ground spices lose their flavour more quickly than whole spices, which are best freshly ground just before use.

2 Cook the pasta in a large pan of boiling, salted water according to the packet instructions, until *al dente*. Drain thoroughly and rinse under cold running water. Leave to cool.

3 To make the dressing, put the orange juice, lemon juice, honey, shallot, garlic, celery, cherries, port, mint and fresh coriander into a bowl, whisk together and leave to marinate for 30 minutes.

1 Remove the skin and fat from the duck breasts and season with salt and pepper. Rub with coriander seeds. Preheat the grill, then grill the duck for 10 minutes on each side. Wrap in foil and leave for 20 minutes.

4 Slice the duck breasts very thinly. (They should be pink in the centre.)

5 Put the pasta into a large bowl, then add the dressing, diced apple and segments of orange. Toss well to coat the pasta. Transfer the salad to a serving plate with the duck slices and garnish with the extra mint and coriander.

NUTRITION NOTES

Per portion:

Energy	348Kcals/1460kJ
Fat	3.8g
Saturated Fat	0.9g
Cholesterol	55mg
Fibre	3g

FRAGRANT CHICKEN CURRY

In this dish, the mildly spiced sauce is thickened using lentils rather than the traditional onions fried in ghee.

—————— INGREDIENTS ——————

Serves 4–6
75g/3oz/¹/₂ cup red lentils
30ml/2 tbsp mild curry powder
10ml/2 tsp ground coriander
5ml/1 tsp cumin seeds
475ml/16fl oz/2 cups vegetable stock
8 chicken thighs, skinned
225g/8oz fresh shredded spinach, or
    frozen, thawed and well drained
15ml/1 tbsp chopped fresh coriander
salt and black pepper
sprigs of fresh coriander, to garnish
white or brown basmati rice and grilled
    poppadums, to serve

1 Rinse the lentils under cold running water. Put in a large, heavy-based saucepan with the curry powder, ground coriander, cumin seeds and stock.

2 Bring to the boil, then lower the heat. Cover and simmer gently for 10 minutes.

COOK'S TIP
Lentils are an excellent source of fibre, and add colour and texture.

3 Add the chicken and spinach. Replace the cover and simmer gently for a further 40 minutes, or until the chicken has cooked.

4 Stir in the chopped coriander and season to taste. Serve garnished with fresh coriander and accompanied by the rice and grilled poppadums.

TURKEY AND PASTA BAKE

INGREDIENTS

Serves 4

275g/10oz minced turkey
150g/5oz smoked turkey rashers,
 chopped
1–2 garlic cloves, crushed
1 onion, finely chopped
2 carrots, diced
30ml/2 tbsp tomato purée
300ml/1/2 pint/1 1/4 cups chicken stock
225g/8oz rigatoni or penne pasta
30ml/2 tbsp grated Parmesan cheese
salt and black pepper

1 Brown the minced turkey in a non-
stick saucepan, breaking up any
large pieces with a wooden spoon, until
well browned all over.

2 Add the chopped turkey rashers,
garlic, onion, carrots, purée, stock
and seasoning. Bring to the boil, cover
and simmer for 1 hour until tender.

3 Preheat the oven to 180°C/350°F/
Gas 4. Cook the pasta in a large
pan of boiling, salted water according
to the packet instructions, until
al dente. Drain thoroughly and mix
with the turkey sauce.

COOK'S TIP
Minced chicken or extra lean
minced beef work just as well in
this tasty recipe.

4 Transfer to a shallow ovenproof
dish and sprinkle with grated
Parmesan cheese. Bake for 20–30
minutes until lightly browned on top.

NUTRITION NOTES

Per portion:
Energy	391Kcals/1641kJ
Fat	4.9g
Saturated Fat	2.2g
Cholesterol	60mg
Fibre	3.5g

JAMBALAYA

The perfect way to use up left-over cold meat – Jambalaya is a fast, easy-to-make fortifying meal for a hungry family.

INGREDIENTS

Serves 4
45ml/3 tbsp vegetable oil
1 onion, chopped
1 celery stick, chopped
½ red pepper, chopped
400g/14oz/2 cups long grain rice
1 litre/1¾ pints/4 cups chicken stock
15ml/1 tbsp tomato purée
3–4 shakes of Tabasco sauce
225g/8oz cold roast chicken without skin and bone or lean pork, thickly sliced
115g/4oz cooked sausage, such as Chorizo or Kabanos, sliced
75g/3oz/⅜ cup frozen peas

1 Heat the oil in a heavy saucepan and add the onion, celery and pepper. Cook over a gentle heat until soft.

> VARIATION
> Fish and shellfish are also good in a Jambalaya.

2 Add the rice, chicken stock, tomato purée and Tabasco sauce. Simmer uncovered for about 10 minutes.

3 Stir in the cold meat, sausage and peas and simmer for 5 minutes. Switch off the heat, cover and leave to stand for 5 minutes before serving.

NUTRITION NOTES

Per portion:
Energy	699Kcals/2936kJ
Fat	25.71g
Saturated fat	7.2g
Cholesterol	65.46mg
Fibre	1.95g

GRILLED CHICKEN WITH HOT SALSA

This dish originates from
Mexico. Its hot and delicious
fruity flavours form the essence
of Tex-Mex cooking.

―――――― INGREDIENTS ――――――

Serves 4

4 chicken breasts without skin and
  bone, about 175g/6oz each
pinch of celery salt and cayenne pepper
30ml/2 tbsp vegetable oil
fresh coriander, to garnish
corn chips, to serve

For the salsa
275g/10oz watermelon
175g/6oz canteloupe melon
1 small red onion
1–2 green chillies
30ml/2 tbsp lime juice
60ml/4 tbsp chopped fresh coriander
pinch of salt

―――― NUTRITION NOTES ――――

Per portion:

Energy	263Kcals/1106kJ
Fat	10.72g
Saturated fat	2.82g
Cholesterol	64.5mg
Fibre	0.72g

1 Preheat a moderate grill. Slash the chicken breasts deeply to speed up the cooking time.

2 Season the chicken with celery salt and cayenne, brush with oil and grill for about 15 minutes.

3 For the salsa, remove the rind and seeds from the melons. Finely dice the flesh and put it into a bowl.

4 Finely chop the onion, split the chillies (discarding the seeds which contain most of the heat) and chop. Mix with the melon.

5 Add the lime juice and chopped coriander, and season with a pinch of salt. Turn the salsa out into a small mixing bowl.

6 Arrange the grilled chicken on a plate and serve with the salsa and a handful of corn chips. Garnish with sprigs of coriander.

> **COOK'S TIP**
> To capture the spirit of Tex-Mex
> food, cook the chicken over a bar-
> becue and eat shaded from the hot
> summer sun.

MOROCCAN SPICED ROAST POUSSIN

INGREDIENTS

Serves 4

75g/3oz/1 cup cooked long grain rice
1 small onion, chopped finely
finely grated rind and juice of 1 lemon
30ml/2 tbsp chopped mint
45ml/3 tbsp chopped dried apricots
30ml/2 tbsp natural yogurt
10ml/2 tsp ground turmeric
10ml/2 tsp ground cumin
2 x 450g/1lb poussin
salt and black pepper
lemon slices and mint sprigs, to garnish

1 Preheat the oven to 200°C/400°F/ Gas 6. Mix together the rice, onion, lemon rind, mint and apricots. Stir in half each of the lemon juice, yogurt, turmeric, cumin, and salt and pepper.

2 Stuff the poussin with the rice mixture at the neck end only. Any spare stuffing can be served separately. Place the poussin on a rack in a roasting tin.

3 Mix together the remaining lemon juice, yogurt, turmeric and cumin, then brush this over the poussin. Cover loosely with foil and cook in the oven for 30 minutes.

4 Remove the foil and roast for a further 15 minutes, or until golden brown and the juices run clear, not pink, when pierced.

5 Cut the poussin in half with a sharp knife or poultry shears, and serve with the reserved rice. Garnish with lemon slices and fresh mint.

NUTRITION NOTES	
Per portion:	
Energy	219Kcals/919kJ
Fat	6.02g
Saturated fat	1.87g
Cholesterol	71.55mg
Fibre	1.12g

STICKY GINGER CHICKEN

INGREDIENTS

Serves 4

30ml/2 tbsp lemon juice
30ml/2 tbsp light muscovado sugar
5ml/1 tsp grated fresh ginger root
10ml/2 tsp soy sauce
8 chicken drumsticks, skinned
black pepper

NUTRITION NOTES	
Per portion:	
Energy	162Kcals/679kJ
Fat	5.58g
Saturated fat	1.84g
Cholesterol	73mg
Fibre	0.08g

1 Mix together the lemon juice, sugar, ginger, soy sauce and pepper.

2 With a sharp knife, slash the chicken drumsticks about three times through the thickest part, then toss the chicken in the glaze.

3 Cook the chicken on a hot grill or barbecue, turning occasionally and brushing with the glaze, until the chicken is golden and the juices run clear, not pink, when pierced. Serve on a bed of lettuce, with crusty bread.

STIR-FRIED SWEET AND SOUR CHICKEN

INGREDIENTS

Serves 4

275g/10oz Chinese egg noodles
30ml/2 tbsp sunflower oil
3 spring onions, chopped
1 garlic clove, crushed
2.5cm/1 in piece fresh root ginger,
  peeled and grated
5ml/1 tsp hot paprika
5ml/1 tsp ground coriander
3 chicken breasts without skin and
  bone, sliced
115g/4oz/1 cup mange-touts, topped
  and tailed
115g/4oz/1¼ cups baby corn, halved
225g/8oz/2¾ cups beansprouts
15ml/1 tbsp cornflour
45ml/3 tbsp soy sauce
45ml/3 tbsp lemon juice
15ml/1 tbsp sugar
45ml/3 tbsp chopped fresh coriander or
  spring onion, to garnish

1 Bring a large saucepan of salted water to the boil. Add the noodles and cook according to the manufacturer's instructions. Drain and cover.

2 Heat the oil. Add the spring onions and cook over a gentle heat. Mix in the next five ingredients, then stir-fry for about 3–4 minutes.

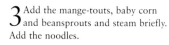

3 Add the mange-touts, baby corn and beansprouts and steam briefly. Add the noodles.

4 Combine the cornflour, soy sauce, lemon juice and sugar in a small bowl. Add to the wok and simmer briefly to thicken. Serve garnished with freshly chopped coriander or spring onion tops.

NUTRITION NOTES

Per portion:

Energy	528Kcals/2218kJ
Fat	15.44g
Saturated fat	2.32g
Cholesterol	48.38mg
Fibre	2.01g

COOK'S TIP
Large wok lids are cumbersome and can be difficult to store in a small kitchen. Consider placing a circle of greaseproof paper against the food surface to keep cooking juices in.
  Be very careful when stir-frying dishes. Timing is very important and overcooking will ruin the flavour. When correctly done the food should be crispy. The high heat used in stir-frying will bring out the natural juices of the vegetables especially if they are fresh.

CHICKEN IN A CASHEW NUT SAUCE

This dish has a deliciously thick and nutty sauce.

INGREDIENTS

Serves 4

2 onions
30ml/2 tbsp tomato purée
50g/2oz/⅓ cup cashew nuts
7.5ml/1½ tsp garam masala
1 garlic clove, crushed
5ml/1 tsp chilli powder
15ml/1 tbsp lemon juice
1.5ml/¼ tsp turmeric
5ml/1 tsp salt
15ml/1 tbsp low fat natural yogurt
30ml/2 tbsp corn oil
15ml/1 tbsp chopped fresh coriander
15ml/1 tbsp sultanas
450g/1 lb chicken without skin and
   bone, cubed
175g/6oz/2½ cups button mushrooms
300ml/½ pint/1¼ cups water
sprig of coriander, to garnish

NUTRITION NOTES

Per portion:

Energy	280Kcals/1176kJ
Fat	14.64g
Saturated fat	2.87g
Cholesterol	64.84mg

1 Cut the onions into quarters and place in a food processor or blender and process for about 1 minute.

2 Add the tomato purée, cashew nuts, garam masala, garlic, chilli powder, lemon juice, turmeric, salt and yogurt to the processed onions.

3 Process all the ingredients in the food processor for a further 1–1½ minutes.

4 In a saucepan, heat the oil, lower the heat to medium and pour in the spice mixture from the food processor.

5 Fry the mixture for about 2 minutes, lowering the heat if necessary.

6 Add the fresh coriander, sultanas and chicken, and continue to stir-fry for a further 1 minute.

7 Add the mushrooms, pour in the water and bring to a simmer. Cover the pan and cook over a low heat for about 10 minutes. Check that the chicken is thoroughly cooked and the sauce is thick. Cook longer if necessary. Serve the chicken garnished with a sprig of coriander.

CHILLI CHICKEN COUSCOUS

Couscous is a very easy alternative to rice and makes a good base for all kinds of ingredients.

———— INGREDIENTS ————

Serves 4
225g/8oz/2 cups couscous
1 litre/1¾ pint/4 cups boiling water
5ml/1 tsp olive oil
400g/14oz chicken without skin and
    bone, diced
1 yellow pepper, seeded and sliced
2 large courgettes, sliced thickly
1 small green chilli, thinly sliced, or
    5ml/1 tsp chilli sauce
1 large tomato, diced
425g/15oz can chick-peas, drained
salt and black pepper
coriander or parsley sprigs to garnish

1 Place couscous in a large bowl and pour over boiling water. Cover and leave to stand for 30 minutes.

2 Heat the oil in a large, non-stick pan and stir fry the chicken quickly to seal, then reduce the heat.

3 Stir in the pepper, courgettes and chilli or sauce and cook for 10 minutes, until the vegetables are softened.

4 Stir in the tomato and chick-peas, then add the couscous. Adjust the seasoning and stir over a moderate heat until hot. Serve garnished with sprigs of fresh coriander or parsley.

NUTRITION NOTES	
Per portion:	
Energy	363Kcals/1525kJ
Fat	8.09g
Saturated fat	1.68g
Cholesterol	57mg
Fibre	4.38g

TURKEY BEAN BAKE

———— INGREDIENTS ————

Serves 4
1 medium aubergine, thinly sliced
15ml/1 tbsp olive oil, for brushing
450g/1 lb turkey breast, diced
1 medium onion, chopped
400g/14oz can chopped tomatoes
425g/15oz can red kidney beans,
    drained
15ml/1 tbsp paprika
15ml/1 tbsp fresh chopped thyme, or
    5ml/1 tsp dried
5ml/1 tsp chilli sauce
350g/12oz/1½ cups Greek-style yogurt
2.5ml/½ tsp grated nutmeg
salt and black pepper

1 Preheat the oven to 190°C/375°F/ Gas 5. Arrange the aubergine in a colander and sprinkle with salt.

2 Leave the aubergine for 30 minutes, then rinse and pat dry. Brush a non-stick pan with oil and fry the aubergine in batches, turning once, until golden.

3 Remove aubergine, add the turkey and onion to the pan, then cook until lightly browned. Stir in the tomatoes, beans, paprika, thyme, chilli sauce, and salt and pepper. In a separate bowl, mix together the yogurt and grated nutmeg.

4 Layer the meat and aubergine in an ovenproof dish, finishing with aubergine. Spread over the yogurt and bake for 50–60 minutes, until golden.

NUTRITION NOTES	
Per portion:	
Energy	370Kcals/1555kJ
Fat	13.72g
Saturated fat	5.81g
Cholesterol	66.5mg
Fibre	7.38g

SPICY MASALA CHICKEN

These chicken pieces are grilled and have a sweet-and-sour taste. They can be served cold with a salad and rice, or hot with mashed potatoes.

INGREDIENTS

Serves 6
12 chicken thighs without skin
90ml/6 tbsp lemon juice
5ml/1 tsp grated fresh root ginger
1 garlic clove, crushed
5ml/1 tsp crushed dried red chillies
5ml/1 tsp salt
5ml/1 tsp soft brown sugar
30ml/2 tbsp clear honey
30ml/2 tbsp chopped fresh coriander
1 green chilli, finely chopped
30ml/2 tbsp sunflower oil
sliced chilli, to garnish

1 Prick the chicken thighs with a fork, rinse, pat dry and set aside in a large bowl.

2 In a large mixing bowl, mix together the lemon juice, ginger, garlic, crushed dried red chillies, salt, sugar and honey.

3 Transfer the chicken thighs to the spice mixture and coat well. Set aside for about 45 minutes.

4 Preheat the grill to medium. Add the fresh coriander and chopped green chilli to the chicken thighs and place them on a flameproof dish.

5 Pour any remaining marinade over the chicken and baste with the oil, using a pastry brush.

6 Grill the chicken thighs under the preheated grill for about 15–20 minutes, turning and basting occasionally, until cooked through and browned.

7 Transfer to a serving dish and garnish with the sliced chilli.

NUTRITION NOTES	
Per portion:	
Energy	189Kcals/795kJ
Fat	9.2g
Saturated fat	2.31g
Cholesterol	73mg

TANDOORI CHICKEN

This popular Indian chicken dish is traditionally cooked in a clay oven called a tandoor. Although the authentic tandoori flavour is very difficult to achieve in conventional ovens, this version still makes a very tasty dish.

── INGREDIENTS ──

Serves 4

4 chicken quarters without skin
175ml/6fl oz/¾ cup low fat natural
    yogurt
5ml/1 tsp garam masala
5ml/1 tsp grated fresh root ginger
1 garlic clove, crushed
7.5ml/1½ tsp chilli powder
1.5ml/¼ tsp turmeric
5ml/1 tsp ground coriander
15ml/1 tbsp lemon juice
5ml/1 tsp salt
a few drops of red food colouring
30ml/2 tbsp corn oil

For the garnish
mixed salad leaves
lime slices
chillies
tomato quarters

1 Rinse and pat dry the chicken quarters. Make two slits into the flesh of each piece, place in a dish and set aside.

2 Mix together the yogurt, garam masala, ginger, garlic, chilli powder, turmeric, ground coriander, lemon juice, salt, red colouring and oil, and beat so that all the ingredients are mixed together well.

3 Cover the chicken quarters with the spice mixture and leave to marinate for about 3 hours.

4 Preheat the oven to 240°C/475°F/ Gas 9. Transfer the chicken pieces to an ovenproof dish.

5 Bake in the preheated oven for about 20–25 minutes or until the chicken is cooked right through and browned on top.

6 Remove from the oven, transfer on to a serving dish, and garnish with the salad leaves, lime and tomato.

NUTRITION NOTES	
Per portion:	
Energy	242Kcals/1018kJ
Fat	10.64g
Saturated fat	2.74g
Cholesterol	81.9mg

TURKEY PASTITSIO

A traditional Greek pastitsio is a rich, high fat dish made with beef mince, but this lighter version is just as tasty.

INGREDIENTS

Serves 4–6

450g/1 lb lean minced turkey
1 large onion, finely chopped
60ml/4 tbsp tomato purée
250ml/8 fl oz/1 cup red wine or stock
5ml/1 tsp ground cinnamon
300g/11oz/2½ cups macaroni
300ml/½ pint/1¼ cups skimmed milk
25g/1oz/2 tbsp sunflower margarine
25g/1oz/3 tbsp plain flour
5ml/1 tsp grated nutmeg
2 tomatoes, sliced
60ml/4 tbsp wholemeal breadcrumbs
salt and black pepper
green salad, to serve

1 Preheat the oven to 220°C/425°F/ Gas 7. Fry the turkey and onion in a non-stick pan without fat, stirring until lightly browned.

2 Stir in the tomato purée, red wine or stock and cinnamon. Season, then cover and simmer for 5 minutes.

3 Cook the macaroni in boiling, salted water until just tender, then drain. Layer with the meat mixture in a wide ovenproof dish.

4 Place the milk, margarine and flour in a saucepan and whisk over a moderate heat until thickened and smooth. Add the nutmeg, and salt and pepper to taste.

5 Pour the sauce evenly over the pasta and meat. Arrange the tomato slices on top and sprinkle lines of breadcrumbs over the surface.

6 Bake for 30–35 minutes, or until golden brown and bubbling. Serve hot with a green salad.

NUTRITION NOTES

Per portion:

Energy	566Kcals/2382kJ
Fat	8.97g
Saturated fat	1.76g
Cholesterol	57.06mg
Fibre	4.86g

TUSCAN CHICKEN

This simple peasant casserole has all the flavours of traditional Tuscan ingredients. The wine can be replaced by chicken stock.

── INGREDIENTS ──

Serves 4

8 chicken thighs, skinned
5ml/1 tsp olive oil
1 medium onion, sliced thinly
2 red peppers, seeded and sliced
1 garlic clove, crushed
300ml/½ pint/1¼ cups passata
150ml/¼ pint/⅔ cup dry white wine
large sprig fresh oregano, or 5ml/1 tsp
*   dried oregano*
400g/14oz can cannelini beans, drained
45ml/3 tbsp fresh breadcrumbs
salt and black pepper

1 Fry the chicken in the oil in a non-stick or heavy pan until golden brown. Remove and keep hot. Add the onion and peppers to the pan and gently sauté until softened, but not brown. Stir in the garlic.

2 Add the chicken, passata, wine and oregano. Season well, bring to the boil then cover the pan tightly.

── NUTRITION NOTES ──

Per portion:

Energy	248Kcals/1045kJ
Fat	7.53g
Saturated fat	2.06g
Cholesterol	73mg
Fibre	4.03g

3 Lower the heat and simmer gently, stirring occasionally for 30–35 minutes or until the chicken is tender and the juices run clear, not pink, when pierced with the point of a knife.

4 Stir in the cannelini beans and simmer for a further 5 minutes until heated through. Sprinkle with the breadcrumbs and cook under a hot grill until golden brown.

MANDARIN SESAME DUCK

Duck is a high fat meat but it is possible to get rid of a good proportion of the fat cooked in this way. (If you remove the skin completely, the meat can be dry.) For a special occasion, duck breasts are a good choice, but they are more expensive.

INGREDIENTS

Serves 4

4 duck leg or boneless breast portions
30ml/2 tbsp light soy sauce
45ml/3 tbsp clear honey
15ml/1 tbsp sesame seeds
4 mandarin oranges
5ml/1 tsp cornflour
salt and black pepper

1 Preheat the oven to 180°C/350°F/ Gas 4. Prick the duck skin all over. Slash the breast skin diagonally at intervals with a sharp knife.

2 Place the duck on a rack in a roasting tin and roast for 1 hour. Mix 15ml/1 tbsp soy sauce with 30ml/2 tbsp honey and brush over the duck. Sprinkle with sesame seeds. Roast for 15–20 minutes, until golden brown.

3 Meanwhile, grate the rind from one mandarin and squeeze the juice from two. Mix in the cornflour, then stir in the remaining soy sauce and honey. Heat, stirring, until thickened and clear. Season. Peel and slice the remaining mandarins. Serve the duck, with the mandarin slices and the sauce.

NUTRITION NOTES

Per portion:

Energy	624Kcals/2621kJ
Fat	48.63g
Saturated fat	12.99g
Cholesterol	256mg
Fibre	0.95g

MINTY YOGURT CHICKEN

INGREDIENTS

Serves 4

8 chicken thigh portions, skinned
15ml/1 tbsp clear honey
30ml/2 tbsp lime or lemon juice
30ml/2 tbsp natural yogurt
60ml/4 tbsp chopped fresh mint
salt and black pepper

1 Slash the chicken flesh at intervals with a sharp knife. Place in a bowl.

2 Mix the lime or honey, lemon juice, yogurt, seasoning and half the mint.

3 Spoon the marinade over the chicken and leave to marinate for 30 minutes. Line the grill pan with foil and cook the chicken under a moderately hot grill until thoroughly cooked and golden brown, turning the chicken occasionally during cooking.

4 Sprinkle with remaining mint, serve with potatoes and tomato salad.

NUTRITION NOTES

Per portion:

Energy	171Kcals/719kJ
Fat	6.74g
Saturated fat	2.23g
Cholesterol	97.90mg
Fibre	0.01g

TURKEY AND TOMATO HOT POT

Here, turkey is turned into tasty meatballs in a rich tomato sauce.

INGREDIENTS

Serves 4

25g/1oz white bread, crusts removed
30ml/2 tbsp skimmed milk
1 garlic clove, crushed
2.5ml/¹/₂ tsp caraway seeds
225g/8oz minced turkey
1 egg white
350ml/12fl oz/1¹/₂ cups chicken stock
400g/14oz can tomatoes
15ml/1 tbsp tomato purée
90g/3¹/₂oz/¹/₂ cup easy-cook rice
salt and black pepper
fresh basil, to garnish
carrot and courgette ribbons, to serve

1 Cut the bread into small cubes and put into a mixing bowl. Sprinkle over the milk and leave to soak for 5 minutes.

2 Add the garlic clove, caraway seeds, turkey and seasoning to the bread. Mix together well.

3 Whisk the egg white until stiff, then fold, half at a time, into the turkey mixture. Chill for 10 minutes.

4 While the turkey mixture is chilling, put the stock, tomatoes and tomato purée into a large saucepan and bring to the boil.

5 Add the rice, stir and cook briskly for about 5 minutes. Turn the heat down to a gentle simmer.

6 Meanwhile, shape the turkey mixture into 16 small balls. Carefully drop them into the tomato stock and simmer for a further 8–10 minutes, or until both the turkey balls and rice are cooked. Garnish with basil, and serve with carrot and courgette ribbons.

COOK'S TIPS
To make carrot and courgette ribbons, cut the vegetables lengthways into thin strips using a vegetable peeler, and blanch or steam until lightly cooked.

Lean minced turkey is low in fat and is a good source of protein. It makes an ideal base for this tasty low fat supper dish. Use minced chicken in place of turkey for an appetizing alternative.

NUTRITION NOTES

Per portion:
Energy	190Kcals/798kJ
Protein	18.04g
Fat	1.88g
Saturated Fat	0.24g
Fibre	10.4g

TURKEY SPIRALS

These little spirals may look difficult, but they're very simple to make, and a very good way to pep up plain turkey.

Serves 4

4 thinly sliced turkey breast steaks, about 90g/3½oz each
20ml/4 tsp tomato purée
15g/½oz/½ cup large basil leaves
1 garlic clove, crushed
15ml/1 tbsp skimmed milk
30ml/2 tbsp wholemeal flour
salt and black pepper
passata or fresh tomato sauce and pasta with fresh basil, to serve

1 Place the turkey steaks on a board. If too thick, flatten them slightly by beating with a rolling pin.

2 Spread each turkey breast steak with tomato purée, then top with a few leaves of basil, a little crushed garlic, and salt and pepper.

3 Roll up firmly around the filling and secure with a cocktail stick. Brush with milk and sprinkle with flour to coat lightly.

4 Place the spirals on a foil-lined grill-pan. Cook under a medium-hot grill for 15–20 minutes, turning them occasionally, until thoroughly cooked. Serve hot, sliced with a spoonful or two of passata or fresh tomato sauce and pasta, sprinkled with fresh basil.

> **COOK'S TIP**
> When flattening the turkey steaks with a rolling pin, place them between two sheets of cling film.

NUTRITION NOTES	
Per portion:	
Energy	123Kcals/518kJ
Fat	1.21g
Saturated fat	0.36g
Cholesterol	44.17mg
Fibre	0.87g

CARIBBEAN CHICKEN KEBABS

These kebabs have a rich, sunshine Caribbean flavour and the marinade keeps them moist without the need for oil. Serve with a colourful salad and rice.

INGREDIENTS

Serves 4

500g/1¼ lb boneless chicken breasts, skinned
finely grated rind of 1 lime
30ml/2 tbsp lime juice
15ml/1 tbsp rum or sherry
15ml/1 tbsp light muscovado sugar
5ml/1 tsp ground cinnamon
2 mangoes, peeled and cubed
rice and salad, to serve

1 Cut the chicken into bite-sized chunks and place in a bowl with the lime rind and juice, rum, sugar and cinnamon. Toss well, cover and leave to stand for 1 hour.

2 Save the juices and thread the chicken on to four wooden skewers, alternating with the mango cubes.

3 Cook the skewers under a hot grill or barbecue for 8–10 minutes, turning occasionally and basting with the juices, until the chicken is tender and golden brown. Serve at once with rice and salad.

COOK'S TIP
The rum or sherry adds a lovely rich flavour, but it is optional so can be omitted if you prefer to make the dish more economical.

NUTRITION NOTES

Per portion:

Energy	218Kcals/918kJ
Fat	4.17g
Saturated fat	1.33g
Cholesterol	53.75mg
Fibre	2.26g

OAT-CRUSTED CHICKEN WITH SAGE

Oats make a good coating for savoury foods, and offer a good way to add extra fibre.

──────── INGREDIENTS ────────

Serves 4
45ml/3 tbsp skimmed milk
10ml/2 tsp English mustard
40g/1½ oz/½ cup rolled oats
45ml/3 tbsp chopped sage leaves
8 chicken thighs or drumsticks, skinned
115g/4oz/½ cup low fat fromage frais
5ml/1 tsp wholegrain mustard
salt and black pepper
fresh sage leaves, to garnish

1 Preheat the oven to 200°C/400°F/ Gas 6. Mix together the milk and English mustard.

2 Mix the oats with 30ml/2 tbsp of the sage and the seasoning on a plate. Brush the chicken with the milk and press into the oats to coat evenly.

3 Place the chicken on a baking sheet and bake for about 40 minutes, or until the juices run clear, not pink, when pierced through the thickest part.

4 Meanwhile, mix together the low fat fromage frais, mustard, remaining sage and seasoning, then serve with the chicken. Garnish the chicken with fresh sage and serve hot or cold.

COOK'S TIP
If fresh sage is not available, choose another fresh herb such as thyme or parsley, instead of using a dried alternative.

──────── NUTRITION NOTES ────────

Per portion:	
Energy	214Kcals/898kJ
Fat	6.57g
Saturated fat	1.81g
Cholesterol	64.64mg
Fibre	0.74g

CHICKEN IN CREAMY ORANGE SAUCE

This sauce is deceptively creamy – in fact it is made with low fat fromage frais, which is virtually fat-free. The brandy adds a richer flavour, but is optional – omit it if you prefer and use orange juice alone.

INGREDIENTS

Serves 4

8 chicken thighs or drumsticks, skinned
45ml/3 tbsp brandy
300ml/½ pint/1¼ cups orange juice
3 spring onions, chopped
10ml/2 tsp cornflour
90ml/6 tbsp low fat fromage frais
salt and black pepper

1 Fry the chicken pieces without fat in a non-stick or heavy pan, turning until evenly browned.

2 Stir in the brandy, orange juice and spring onions. Bring to the boil, then cover and simmer for 15 minutes, or until the chicken is tender and the juices run clear, not pink, when pierced.

3 Blend the cornflour with a little water then mix into the fromage frais. Stir this into the sauce and stir over a moderate heat until boiling.

4 Adjust the seasoning and serve with boiled rice or pasta and green salad.

COOK'S TIP
Cornflour stabilises the fromage frais and helps prevent it curdling.

NUTRITION NOTES

Per portion:
Energy	227Kcals/951kJ
Fat	6.77g
Saturated fat	2.23g
Cholesterol	87.83mg
Fibre	0.17g

AUTUMN PHEASANT

Pheasant is worth buying as it is low in fat, full of flavour and never dry when cooked like this.

INGREDIENTS

Serves 4

1 oven-ready pheasant
2 small onions, quartered
3 celery sticks, thickly sliced
2 red eating apples, thickly sliced
120ml / 4 fl oz / ½ cup stock
15ml / 1 tbsp clear honey
30ml / 2 tbsp Worcestershire sauce
grated nutmeg
30ml / 2 tbsp toasted hazelnuts
salt and black pepper

1 Preheat the oven to 180°C/350°F/ Gas 4. Fry the pheasant without fat in a non-stick pan, turning occasionally until golden. Remove and keep hot.

2 Fry the onions and celery in the pan to brown lightly. Spoon into a casserole and place the pheasant on top. Tuck the apple slices around it.

3 Spoon over the stock, honey and Worcestershire sauce. Sprinkle with nutmeg, salt and pepper, cover and bake for 1¼ –1½ hours or until tender. Sprinkle with nuts and serve hot.

NUTRITION NOTES

Per portion:

Energy	387Kcals/1624kJ
Fat	16.97g
Saturated fat	4.28g
Cholesterol	126mg
Fibre	2.72g

CIDER BAKED RABBIT

Rabbit is a low fat meat and an economical choice for family meals. Chicken joints may be used as an alternative.

INGREDIENTS

Serves 4

450g / 1 lb rabbit joints
15ml / 1 tbsp plain flour
5ml / 1 tsp dry mustard powder
3 medium leeks, thickly sliced
250ml / 8 fl oz / 1 cup dry cider
2 sprigs rosemary
salt and black pepper
fresh rosemary, to garnish

1 Preheat the oven to 180°C/350°F/ Gas 4. Place the rabbit joints in a bowl and sprinkle over the flour and mustard powder. Toss to coat evenly.

2 Arrange the rabbit in one layer in a wide casserole. Blanch the leeks in boiling water, then drain and add to the casserole.

3 Add the cider, rosemary and seasoning, cover, then bake for 1–1¼ hours, or until the rabbit is tender. Garnish with fresh rosemary and serve with jacket potatoes and vegetables.

NUTRITION NOTES

Per portion:

Energy	162Kcals/681kJ
Fat	4.22g
Saturated fat	1.39g
Cholesterol	62.13mg
Fibre	1.27g

CHINESE-STYLE CHICKEN SALAD

INGREDIENTS

Serves 4

4 boneless chicken breasts, about
175g/6oz each
60ml/4 tbsp dark soy sauce
pinch of Chinese five-spice powder
a good squeeze of lemon juice
½ cucumber, peeled and cut into
matchsticks
5ml/1 tsp salt
45ml/3 tbsp sunflower oil
30ml/2 tbsp sesame oil
15ml/1 tbsp sesame seeds
30ml/2 tbsp dry sherry
2 carrots, cut into matchsticks
8 spring onions, shredded
75g/3oz/1 cup beansprouts

For the sauce

60ml/4 tbsp crunchy peanut butter
10ml/2 tsp lemon juice
10ml/2 tsp sesame oil
1.5ml/¼ tsp hot chilli powder
1 spring onion, finely chopped

1 Place the chicken portions in a large saucepan and just cover with water. Add 15ml/1 tbsp of the soy sauce, the Chinese five-spice powder and lemon juice, cover and bring to the boil, then simmer for about 20 minutes.

2 Meanwhile, place the cucumber matchsticks in a colander, sprinkle with the salt and cover with a plate with a weight on top. Leave to drain for about 30 minutes – set the colander in a bowl or on a deep plate to catch any drips that may fall.

3 Lift out the poached chicken with a slotted spoon and leave until cool enough to handle. Remove and discard the skins and bash the chicken lightly with a rolling pin to loosen the fibres. Slice into thin strips and reserve.

4 Heat the oils in a large frying pan or wok. Add the sesame seeds, fry for 30 seconds and then stir in the remaining 45ml/3 tbsp soy sauce and the sherry. Add the carrots and stir-fry for about 2–3 minutes, until just tender. Remove the wok or pan from the heat and reserve until required.

5 Rinse the cucumber well, pat dry with kitchen paper and place in a bowl. Add the spring onions, beansprouts, cooked carrots, pan juices and shredded chicken, and mix together. Transfer to a shallow dish. Cover and chill for about 1 hour, turning the mixture in the juices once or twice.

6 For the sauce, cream the peanut butter with the lemon juice, sesame oil and chilli powder, adding a little hot water to form a paste, then stir in the spring onion. Arrange the chicken mixture on a serving dish and serve with the peanut sauce.

NUTRITION NOTES

Per portion:

Energy	534Kcals/2241kJ
Fat	36.86g
Saturated fat	4.96g
Cholesterol	68.8mg
Fibre	2.91g

CHICKEN BIRYANI

INGREDIENTS

Serves 4

275g/10oz/1½ cups basmati rice, rinsed
2.5ml/½ tsp salt
5 whole cardamom pods
2–3 whole cloves
1 cinnamon stick
45ml/3 tbsp sunflower oil
3 onions, sliced
675g/1½ lb chicken breasts without
   skin and bone, cubed
1.5ml/¼ tsp ground cloves
5 cardamom pods, seeds removed and
   ground
1.5ml/¼ tsp hot chilli powder
5ml/1 tsp ground cumin
5ml/1 tsp ground coriander
2.5ml/½ tsp ground black pepper
3 garlic cloves, finely chopped
5ml/1 tsp finely chopped fresh root
   ginger
juice of 1 lemon
4 tomatoes, sliced
30ml/2 tbsp chopped fresh coriander
150ml/¼ pint/⅔ cup low fat natural
   yogurt
2.5ml/½ tsp saffron strands soaked in
   10ml/2 tsp hot skimmed milk
low fat natural yogurt, 45ml/3 tbsp
   toasted flaked almonds and fresh
   coriander leaves, to garnish

1 Preheat the oven to 190°C/375°F/
Gas 5. Bring a saucepan of water
to the boil and add the rice, salt,
cardamom pods, cloves and cinnamon
stick. Boil for about 2 minutes and
then drain, leaving the whole spices in
the rice.

2 Heat the oil in a frying pan and fry
the onions for about 8 minutes,
until browned. Add the chicken
followed by all the ground spices, the
garlic, ginger and lemon juice. Stir-fry
for a further 5 minutes.

NUTRITION NOTES

Per portion:

Energy	650Kcals/2730kJ
Fat	21.43g
Saturated fat	3.62g
Cholesterol	74.11mg
Fibre	2.95g

3 Transfer the chicken mixture to an
ovenproof casserole and lay the
tomatoes on top. Sprinkle over the
fresh coriander, spoon over the yogurt,
and top with the drained rice.

4 Drizzle the saffron strands and
skimmed milk over the rice and
pour over 150ml/¼ pint/⅔ cup of
water.

5 Cover with a tight-fitting lid and
bake in the oven for about 1 hour.
Transfer to a warmed serving platter
and remove the whole spices from the
rice. Garnish with low fat natural
yogurt, toasted almonds and fresh
coriander leaves.

STIR-FRIED TURKEY WITH MANGE-TOUTS

A quick and easy dish served
with saffron rice.

───── INGREDIENTS ─────

Serves 4

30ml/2 tbsp sesame oil
90ml/6 tbsp lemon juice
1 garlic clove, crushed
1cm/½ in piece fresh root ginger, grated
5ml/1 tsp clear honey
450g/1 lb lean turkey fillets, cut into
    strips
115g/4oz/1 cup mange-touts, trimmed
30ml/2 tbsp groundnut oil
50g/2oz/½ cup cashew nuts
6 spring onions, cut into strips
225g/8oz can water chestnuts, drained
    and thinly sliced
pinch of salt
saffron rice, to serve

1 Mix together the sesame oil, lemon
juice, garlic, ginger and honey in a
shallow non-metallic dish. Add the
turkey and mix well. Cover and leave
to marinate for about 3–4 hours.

2 Blanch the mange-touts in boiling
salted water for 1 minute. Drain
and refresh under cold running water.

3 Drain the marinade from the turkey
strips and reserve the marinade.
Heat the groundnut oil in a wok or
large frying pan, add the cashew nuts,
and stir-fry for about 1–2 minutes.

───── NUTRITION NOTES ─────

Per portion:
Energy	311Kcals/1307kJ
Fat	18.51g
Saturated fat	2.9g
Cholesterol	55.12mg

4 Remove the cashew nuts from the
wok or frying pan using a slotted
spoon and set aside.

5 Add the turkey and stir-fry for
about 3–4 minutes, until golden
brown. Add the mange-touts, spring
onions and water chestnuts with the
reserved marinade. Cook until the
turkey is tender and the sauce is bubbling and hot. Add salt to taste. Stir in
the cashew nuts and serve at once with
saffron rice.

HOT CHICKEN CURRY

This curry has a flavourful thick sauce, and includes red and green peppers for extra colour. Serve with wholemeal chapatis or plain boiled rice.

INGREDIENTS

Serves 4

30ml/2 tbsp corn oil
1.5ml/¼ tsp fenugreek seeds
1.5ml/¼ tsp onion seeds
2 onions, chopped
1 garlic clove, crushed
2.5ml/½ tsp grated fresh root ginger
5ml/1 tsp ground coriander
5ml/1 tsp chilli powder
5ml/1 tsp salt
400g/14oz can tomatoes
30ml/2 tbsp lemon juice
350g/12oz chicken without skin and
   bone, cubed
30ml/2 tbsp chopped fresh coriander
3 green chillies, chopped
½ red pepper, cut into chunks
½ green pepper, cut into chunks
fresh coriander leaves, to garnish

1 Heat the oil in a medium saucepan, and fry the fenugreek and onion seeds until they turn a shade darker. Add the onions, garlic and ginger and fry for about 5 minutes until the onions are golden. Lower the heat to very low.

COOK'S TIP
For a milder version of this delicious curry, simply omit some or all of the fresh green chillies.

2 Meanwhile, in a separate bowl, mix together the ground coriander, chilli powder, salt, tomatoes and lemon juice.

3 Pour this mixture into the pan and turn up the heat to medium. Stir-fry for about 3 minutes.

NUTRITION NOTES

Per portion:
Energy	205Kcals/861kJ
Fat	9.83g
Saturated fat	2.03g
Cholesterol	48.45mg

4 Add the chicken and stir-fry for about 5–7 minutes. Take care not to overcook the chicken.

5 Add the fresh coriander, green chillies and the pepper chunks. Lower the heat, cover, and simmer for about 10 minutes until cooked. Serve hot, garnished with fresh coriander leaves.

FISH AND SEAFOOD

The range of fresh fish available in our supermarkets is impressive, and fish is always a good choice for a healthy low fat diet. Most fish, particularly white fish, is low in fat and is a good source of protein. Oily fish contains more fat than white fish, but contains high levels of essential fatty acids which are vital for good health. Fish is quick and easy to prepare and cook and is ideal for serving with fresh seasonal vegetables as part of a healthy low fat meal. Try Cajun-style Cod, Herby Fishcakes with Lemon Sauce, Mediterranean Fish Cutlets or Curried Prawns in Coconut Milk – just some of the delicious, low fat recipes included in this chapter.

CAJUN-STYLE COD

This recipe works equally well with any firm-fleshed fish – choose low fat fish, such as haddock or monkfish.

INGREDIENTS

Serves 4

4 cod steaks, each weighing about
*   175g/6oz*
30ml/2 tbsp low fat natural yogurt
15ml/1 tbsp lime or lemon juice
1 garlic clove, crushed
5ml/1 tsp ground cumin
5ml/1 tsp paprika
5ml/1 tsp mustard powder
2.5ml/¹/₂ tsp cayenne pepper
2.5ml/¹/₂ tsp dried thyme
2.5ml/¹/₂ tsp dried oregano
non-stick cooking spray
lemon slices, to garnish
new potatoes and a mixed salad,
*   to serve*

NUTRITION NOTES

Per portion:

Energy	137Kcals/577kJ
Protein	28.42g
Fat	1.75g
Saturated Fat	0.26g
Fibre	0.06g

1 Pat the fish dry on kitchen paper. Mix together the yogurt and lime or lemon juice and brush lightly over both sides of the fish.

2 Mix together the crushed garlic, spices and herbs. Coat both sides of the fish with the seasoning mix, rubbing in well.

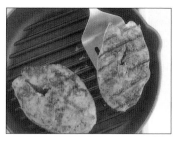

3 Spray a ridged grill pan or heavy-based frying pan with non-stick cooking spray. Heat until very hot. Add the fish and cook over a high heat for 4 minutes, or until the undersides are well browned.

4 Turn the steaks over and cook for a further 4 minutes, or until cooked through. Serve immediately, garnished with lemon and accompanied by new potatoes and a mixed salad.

PLAICE PROVENÇAL

───── INGREDIENTS ─────

Serves 4

4 large plaice fillets
2 small red onions
120ml/4fl oz/½ cup vegetable stock
60ml/4 tbsp dry red wine
1 garlic clove, crushed
2 courgettes, sliced
1 yellow pepper, seeded and sliced
400g/14oz can chopped tomatoes
15ml/1 tbsp chopped fresh thyme
salt and black pepper
potato gratin, to serve

1 Preheat the oven to 180°C/350°F/ Gas 4. Lay the plaice skin-side down and, holding the tail end, push a sharp knife between the skin and flesh in a sawing movement. Hold the knife at a slight angle with the blade towards the skin.

2 Cut each onion into eight wedges. Put into a heavy-based saucepan with the stock. Cover and simmer for 5 minutes. Uncover and continue to cook, stirring occasionally, until the stock has reduced entirely. Add the wine and garlic clove to the pan and continue to cook until the onions are soft.

3 Add the courgettes, yellow pepper, tomatoes and thyme and season to taste. Simmer for 3 minutes. Spoon the sauce into a large casserole.

COOK'S TIP
Skinless white fish fillets such as plaice are low in fat and make an ideal tasty and nutritious basis for many low fat recipes such as this one.

4 Fold each fillet in half and put on top of the sauce. Cover and cook in the oven for 15–20 minutes, until the fish is opaque and flakes easily. Serve with a potato gratin.

NUTRITION NOTES	
Per portion:	
Energy	191Kcals/802kJ
Protein	29.46g
Fat	3.77g
Saturated Fat	0.61g
Fibre	1.97g

Prawns with Vegetables

This is a light and nutritious dish. It is excellent served either on a bed of lettuce leaves, with plain boiled rice or wholemeal chapatis for a healthy meal.

Ingredients

Serves 4

30ml/2 tbsp chopped fresh coriander
5ml/1 tsp salt
2 green chillies, seeded if required
45ml/3 tbsp lemon juice
30ml/2 tbsp vegetable oil
20 cooked king prawns, peeled
1 courgette, thickly sliced
1 onion, cut into 8 chunks
8 cherry tomatoes
8 baby corn
mixed salad leaves, to serve

Nutrition Notes

Per portion:

Energy	109Kcals/458kJ
Fat	6.47g
Saturated fat	0.85g
Cholesterol	29.16mg

1 Place the chopped coriander, salt, green chillies, lemon juice and oil in a food processor or blender and process for a few seconds.

2 Remove the paste from the processor and transfer to a mixing bowl.

3 Add the peeled prawns to the paste and stir to make sure that all the prawns are well coated. Set aside to marinate for about 30 minutes.

4 Preheat the grill to very hot, then turn the heat down to medium.

5 Arrange the vegetables and prawns alternately on four skewers. When all the skewers are ready place them under the preheated grill for about 5–7 minutes until cooked and browned.

6 Serve immediately on a bed of mixed salad leaves.

Cook's Tip
King prawns are a luxury, but worth choosing for a very special dinner party. For a more economical variation, substitute the king prawns with 450g/1 lb/2½ cups peeled prawns.

GRILLED FISH FILLETS

Fish can be grilled beautifully without sacrificing any flavour. This recipe uses a minimum amount of oil to baste the fish.

INGREDIENTS

Serves 4

4 flatfish fillets, such as plaice, sole or flounder, about 115g/4oz each
1 garlic clove, crushed
5ml/1 tsp garam masala
5ml/1 tsp chilli powder
1.5ml/¼ tsp turmeric
2.5ml/½ tsp salt
15ml/1 tbsp finely chopped fresh coriander
15ml/1 tbsp vegetable oil
30ml/2 tbsp lemon juice

1 Line a flameproof dish or grill tray with foil. Rinse and pat dry the fish fillets and put them on the foil-lined dish or tray.

2 In a small bowl, mix together the garlic, garam masala, chilli powder, turmeric, salt, fresh coriander, oil and lemon juice.

3 Using a pastry brush, baste the fish fillets evenly all over with the spice and lemon juice mixture.

COOK'S TIP
Although frozen fish can be used for this dish always try to buy fresh. It is more flavoursome.

4 Preheat the grill to very hot, then lower the heat to medium. Grill the fillets for about 10 minutes, turning as necessary and basting occasionally, until they are cooked right through.

5 Serve immediately with an attractive garnish. This could include grated carrot, tomato quarters and lime slices, if you wish.

NUTRITION NOTES
Per portion:
Energy	143Kcals/599kJ
Fat	5.63g
Saturated fat	0.84g
Cholesterol	47.25mg

MONKFISH AND MUSSEL SKEWERS

Skinless white fish such as monkfish is a good source of protein whilst also being low in calories and fat. These attractive seafood kebabs, flavoured with a light marinade, are excellent grilled or barbecued and served with herby boiled rice and a mixed leaf salad.

INGREDIENTS

Serves 4

450g/1lb monkfish, skinned and boned
5ml/1 tsp olive oil
30ml/2 tbsp lemon juice
5ml/1 tsp paprika
1 garlic clove, crushed
4 turkey rashers
8 cooked mussels
8 raw prawns
15ml/1 tbsp chopped fresh dill
salt and black pepper
lemon wedges, to garnish
salad leaves and long grain and wild
    rice, to serve

1 Cut the monkfish into 2.5cm/1in cubes and place in a shallow glass dish. Mix together the oil, lemon juice, paprika and garlic clove and season.

2 Pour the marinade over the fish and toss to coat evenly. Cover and leave in a cool place for 30 minutes.

3 Cut the turkey rashers in half and wrap each strip around a mussel. Thread on to skewers, alternating with the fish cubes and raw prawns. Preheat the grill to high.

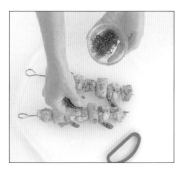

4 Grill the kebabs for 7–8 minutes, turning once and basting with the marinade. Sprinkle with chopped dill and salt. Garnish with lemon wedges and serve with salad and rice.

NUTRITION NOTES	
Per portion:	
Energy	133Kcals/560kJ
Protein	25.46g
Fat	3.23g
Saturated Fat	0.77g
Fibre	0.12g

LEMON SOLE BAKED IN A PAPER CASE

INGREDIENTS

Serves 4

4 lemon sole fillets, each weighing
   about 150g/5oz
½ small cucumber, sliced
4 lemon slices
60ml/4 tbsp dry white wine
sprigs of fresh dill, to garnish
potatoes and braised celery, to serve

For the yogurt hollandaise
150ml/¼ pint low fat natural yogurt
5ml/1 tsp lemon juice
2 egg yolks
5ml/1 tsp Dijon mustard
salt and black pepper

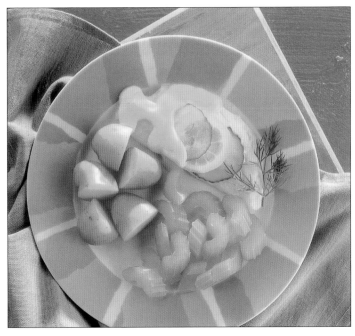

1 Preheat the oven to 180°C/350°F/
Gas 4. Cut out four heart shapes
from non-stick baking paper, each
about 20 x 15cm/8 x 6in.

2 Place a sole fillet on one side of
each paper heart. Arrange the
cucumber and lemon slices on top of
each fillet. Sprinkle with the wine and
close the parcels by turning the edges of
the paper and twisting to secure. Put
on a baking tray and cook in the oven
for 15 minutes.

3 Meanwhile make the hollandaise.
Beat together the yogurt, lemon
juice and egg yolks in a double boiler
or bowl placed over a saucepan. Cook
over simmering water, stirring for
about 15 minutes, or until thickened.
(The sauce will become thinner after
10 minutes, but will thicken again.)

COOK'S TIP
Make sure that the paper parcels
are well sealed, so that none of
the delicious juices can escape.

4 Remove from the heat and stir in
the mustard. Season to taste with
salt and pepper. Open the fish parcels,
garnish with a sprig of dill and serve
accompanied with the sauce, new
potatoes and braised celery.

NUTRITION NOTES

Per portion:	
Energy	185Kcals/779kJ
Protein	29.27g
Fat	4.99g
Saturated Fat	1.58g
Fibre	0.27g

CRUNCHY-TOPPED COD

Colourful and quick to cook, this is ideal for weekday meals.

INGREDIENTS

Serves 4
4 pieces cod fillet, about 115g/4oz
*   each, skinned*
2 medium tomatoes, sliced
50g/2oz/1 cup fresh wholemeal bread-
*   crumbs*
30ml/2 tbsp chopped fresh parsley
finely grated rind and juice of ½ lemon
5 ml/1 tsp sunflower oil
salt and ground black pepper

1 Preheat the oven to 200°C/400°F/ Gas 6. Arrange the cod fillets in a wide, ovenproof dish.

2 Arrange the tomato slices on top. Mix together the breadcrumbs, fresh parsley, lemon rind and juice and the oil with seasoning to taste.

3 Spoon the crumb mixture evenly over the fish, then bake for 15–20 minutes. Serve hot.

NUTRITION NOTES

Per portion:

Energy	130Kcals/546kJ
Fat	2.06g
Saturated fat	0.32g
Cholesterol	52.9mg
Fibre	1.4g

SPECIAL FISH PIE

This fish pie is colourful, healthy and best of all very easy to make. For a more economical version, omit the prawns and replace with more fish fillet.

INGREDIENTS

Serves 4
350g/12oz haddock fillet, skinned
30ml/2 tbsp cornflour
115g/4oz cooked, peeled prawns
198g/7oz can sweetcorn, drained
75g/3oz frozen peas
150ml/¼ pint/⅔ cup skimmed milk
150g/5oz/⅔ cup low fat fromage frais
75g/3oz fresh wholemeal breadcrumbs
40g/1½oz/½ cup grated reduced fat
*   Cheddar cheese*
salt and black pepper

1 Preheat the oven to 190°C/375°F/ Gas 5. Cut the haddock into bite-sized pieces and toss in cornflour to coat evenly.

2 Place the fish, prawns, sweetcorn and peas in an ovenproof dish. Beat together the milk, fromage frais and seasonings, then pour into the dish.

3 Mix together the breadcrumbs and grated cheese then spoon evenly over the top. Bake for 25–30 minutes, or until golden brown. Serve hot with fresh vegetables.

NUTRITION NOTES

Per portion:

Energy	290Kcals/1218kJ
Fat	4.87g
Saturated fat	2.1g
Cholesterol	63.91mg
Fibre	2.61g

HADDOCK AND BROCCOLI CHOWDER

A warming main-meal soup for
hearty appetites.

INGREDIENTS

Serves 4

4 spring onions, sliced
450g/1 lb new potatoes, diced
300ml/½ pint/1¼ cups fish stock or
water
300ml/½ pint/1¼ cups skimmed milk
1 bay leaf
225g/8oz/2 cups broccoli florets, sliced
450g/1 lb smoked haddock fillets,
skinned
198g/7oz can sweetcorn, drained
black pepper
chopped spring onions, to garnish

1 Place the spring onions and potatoes
in a large saucepan and add the
stock, milk and bay leaf. Bring the soup
to the boil, then cover the pan and
simmer for 10 minutes.

2 Add the broccoli to the pan. Cut the
fish into bite-sized chunks and add
to the pan with the sweetcorn.

3 Season the soup well with black
pepper, then cover the pan and
simmer for a further 5 minutes, or until
the fish is cooked through. Remove the
bay leaf and scatter over the spring
onion. Serve hot, with crusty bread.

COOK'S TIP
When new potatoes are not
available, old ones can be used,
but choose a waxy variety which
will not disintegrate.

NUTRITION NOTES

Per portion:

Energy	268Kcals/1124kJ
Fat	2.19g
Saturated fat	0.27g
Cholesterol	57.75mg
Fibre	3.36g

MOROCCAN FISH TAGINE

Tagine is actually the name of the large Moroccan cooking pot used for this type of cooking, but you can use an ordinary casserole instead.

INGREDIENTS

Serves 4
2 garlic cloves, crushed
30ml/2 tbsp ground cumin
30ml/2 tbsp paprika
1 small red chilli (optional)
30ml/2 tbsp tomato purée
60ml/4 tbsp lemon juice
4 cutlets of whiting or cod, about
    175g/6oz each
350g/12oz tomatoes, sliced
2 green peppers, seeded and
    thinly sliced
salt and black pepper
chopped fresh coriander, to garnish

1 Mix together the garlic, cumin, paprika, chilli, tomato purée and lemon juice. Spread this mixture over the fish, then cover and chill for about 30 minutes to let the flavour penetrate.

2 Preheat the oven to 200°C/400°F/ Gas 6. Arrange half of the tomatoes and peppers in a baking dish.

3 Cover with the fish, in one layer, then arrange the remaining tomatoes and pepper on top. Cover the baking dish with foil and bake for about 45 minutes, until the fish is tender. Sprinkle with chopped coriander or parsley to serve.

COOK'S TIP
If you are preparing this dish for a dinner party, it can be assembled completely and stored in the fridge, ready to bake when needed.

NUTRITION NOTES

Per portion:	
Energy	203Kcals/855kJ
Fat	3.34g
Saturated fat	0.29g
Cholesterol	80.5mg
Fibre	2.48g

HERBY FISHCAKES WITH LEMON SAUCE

The wonderful flavour of fresh herbs makes these fishcakes the catch of the day.

INGREDIENTS

Serves 4

350g/12oz potatoes, roughly chopped
75ml/5 tbsp skimmed milk
350g/12oz haddock or hoki
　fillets, skinned
15ml/1 tbsp lemon juice
15ml/1 tbsp creamed horseradish sauce
30ml/2 tbsp chopped fresh parsley
flour, for dusting
115g/4oz/2 cups fresh wholemeal
　breadcrumbs
salt and black pepper
flat leaf parsley sprigs, to garnish
sugar snap peas or mange-tout and a
　sliced tomato and onion salad,
　to serve

For the lemon and chive sauce
thinly pared rind and juice of
　½ small lemon
120ml/4fl oz/½ cup dry white wine
2 thin slices of fresh root ginger
10ml/2 tsp cornflour
30ml/2 tbsp snipped fresh chives

NUTRITION NOTES

Per portion:

Energy	232Kcals/975kJ
Protein	19.99g
Fat	1.99g
Saturated Fat	0.26g
Fibre	3.11g

COOK'S TIP
Dry white wine is a tasty fat-free basis for this herby sauce. Try using cider as an alternative to wine, for a change.

1 Cook the potatoes in a large saucepan of boiling water for 15–20 minutes. Drain and mash with the milk and season to taste.

2 Purée the fish together with the lemon juice and horseradish sauce in a blender or food processor. Mix with the potatoes and parsley.

3 With floured hands, shape the mixture into eight fishcakes and coat with the breadcrumbs. Chill in the fridge for 30 minutes.

4 Preheat the grill to medium and cook the fishcakes for 5 minutes on each side, until browned.

5 To make the sauce, cut the lemon rind into julienne strips and put into a large saucepan together with the lemon juice, wine and ginger. Season to taste with salt and pepper.

6 Simmer, uncovered, for about 6 minutes. Blend the cornflour with 15ml/1 tbsp of cold water, add to the pan and simmer until clear. Stir in the chives immediately before serving.

7 Serve the sauce hot with the fishcakes, garnished with parsley sprigs and accompanied with mange-tout and a tomato and onion salad.

STEAMED FISH WITH CHILLI SAUCE

Steaming is one of the best – and lowest fat – methods of cooking fish. By leaving the fish whole and on the bone, you'll find that all the delicious flavour and moistness is retained.

INGREDIENTS

Serves 6

*1 large or 2 medium, firm fish like bass
   or grouper, scaled and cleaned*
*a fresh banana leaf or large piece
   of foil*
30ml/2 tbsp rice wine
3 red chillies, seeded and finely sliced
2 garlic cloves, finely chopped
*2cm/³⁄₄in piece of fresh root ginger,
   finely shredded*
*2 lemon grass stalks, crushed and
   finely chopped*
2 spring onions, chopped
30ml/2 tbsp fish sauce
juice of 1 lime

For the chilli sauce

10 red chillies, seeded and chopped
4 garlic cloves, chopped
60ml/4 tbsp fish sauce
15ml/1 tbsp sugar
75ml/5 tbsp lime juice

1 Rinse the fish under cold running water. Pat dry with kitchen paper. With a sharp knife, slash the skin of the fish a few times on both sides.

2 Place the fish on the banana leaf or foil. Mix together the remaining ingredients and spread over the fish.

3 Place a small upturned plate in the bottom of a wok or large frying pan, and add about 5cm/2in boiling water. Lay the banana leaf or foil with the fish on top on the plate and cover with a lid. Steam for about 10–15 minutes or until the fish is cooked.

4 Meanwhile, put all the chilli sauce ingredients in a food processor and process until smooth. You may need to add a little cold water.

5 Serve the fish hot, on the banana leaf if liked, with the sweet chilli sauce to spoon over the top.

NUTRITION NOTES	
Per portion:	
Energy	170Kcals/721kJ
Fat	3.46g
Saturated Fat	0.54g
Cholesterol	106mg
Fibre	0.35g

BAKED COD WITH TOMATOES

For the very best flavour, use firm sun-ripened tomatoes for the sauce and make sure it is fairly thick before spooning it over the cod.

─── INGREDIENTS ───

Serves 4

10ml/2 tsp olive oil
1 onion, chopped
2 garlic cloves, finely chopped
450g/1lb tomatoes, peeled, seeded
  and chopped
5ml/1 tsp tomato purée
60ml/4 tbsp dry white wine
60ml/4 tbsp chopped flat leaf parsley
4 cod cutlets
30ml/2 tbsp dried breadcrumbs
salt and black pepper
new potatoes and green salad, to serve

─── NUTRITION NOTES ───

Per portion:

Energy	151Kcals/647kJ
Fat	1.5g
Saturated Fat	0.2g
Cholesterol	55.2mg
Fibre	2.42g

COOK'S TIP
For extra speed, use a 400g/14oz can of chopped tomatoes in place of the fresh tomatoes and 5–10ml/1–2 tsp ready-minced garlic in place of the garlic cloves.

1 Preheat the oven to 190°C/375°F/ Gas 5. Heat the oil in a pan and fry the onion for about 5 minutes. Add the garlic, tomatoes, tomato purée, wine and seasoning.

2 Bring the sauce just to the boil, then reduce the heat slightly and cook, uncovered, for 15–20 minutes until thick. Stir in the parsley.

3 Grease an ovenproof dish, put in the cod cutlets and spoon an equal quantity of the tomato sauce on to each. Sprinkle the dried breadcrumbs over the top.

4 Bake for 20–30 minutes, basting the fish occasionally with the sauce, until the fish is tender and cooked through, and the breadcrumbs are golden and crisp. Serve hot with new potatoes and a green salad.

SEAFOOD PILAF

This all-in-one-pan main course is a satisfying meal for any day of the week. For a special meal, substitute dry white wine for the orange juice.

INGREDIENTS

Serves 4
10ml/2 tsp olive oil
250g/9oz/1¼ cups long grain rice
5ml/1 tsp ground turmeric
1 red pepper, seeded and diced
1 small onion, finely chopped
2 medium courgettes, sliced
150g/5oz/2 cups button mushrooms, halved
350ml/12 fl oz/1½ cups fish or chicken stock
150ml/¼ pint/⅔ cup orange juice
350g/12oz white fish fillets
12 fresh mussels in the shell (or cooked shelled mussels)
salt and ground black pepper
grated rind of 1 orange, to garnish

1 Heat the oil in a large, non-stick pan and fry the rice and turmeric over a low heat for about 1 minute.

2 Add the pepper, onion, courgettes, and mushrooms. Stir in the stock and orange juice. Bring to the boil.

3 Reduce the heat and add the fish. Cover and simmer gently for about 15 minutes, until the rice is tender and the liquid absorbed. Stir in the mussels and heat thoroughly. Adjust the seasoning, sprinkle with orange rind and serve hot.

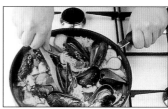

NUTRITION NOTES

Per portion:
Energy	370Kcals/1555kJ
Fat	3.84g
Saturated fat	0.64g
Cholesterol	61.25mg
Fibre	2.08g

SALMON PASTA WITH PARSLEY SAUCE

INGREDIENTS

Serves 4
450g/1 lb salmon fillet, skinned
225g/8oz/3 cups pasta, such as penne or twists
175g/6oz cherry tomatoes, halved
150ml/¼ pint/⅔ cup low fat crème fraîche
45ml/3 tbsp finely chopped parsley
finely grated rind of ½ orange
salt and black pepper

NUTRITION NOTES

Per portion:
Energy	452Kcals/1902kJ
Fat	17.4g
Saturated fat	5.36g
Cholesterol	65.63mg
Fibre	2.56g

1 Cut the salmon into bite-sized pieces, arrange on a heatproof plate and cover with foil.

2 Bring a large pan of salted water to the boil, add the pasta and return to the boil. Place the plate of salmon on top and simmer for 10–12 minutes, until the pasta and salmon are cooked.

3 Drain the pasta and toss with the tomatoes and salmon. Mix together the crème fraîche, parsley, orange rind and pepper to taste, then toss into the salmon and pasta and serve hot or cold.

MEDITERRANEAN FISH CUTLETS

These low fat fish cutlets are well complemented by boiled potatoes, broccoli and carrots.

INGREDIENTS

Serves 4

4 white fish cutlets, about 150g/5oz each
about 150ml/¹⁄4 pint/²⁄3 cup fish stock or dry white wine (or a mixture of the two), for poaching
1 bay leaf, a few black peppercorns and a strip of pared lemon rind, for flavouring

For the tomato sauce
400g/14oz can chopped tomatoes
1 garlic clove, crushed
15ml/1 tbsp pastis or other aniseed-flavoured liqueur
15ml/1 tbsp drained capers
12–16 stoned black olives
salt and black pepper

1 To make the sauce, place the chopped tomatoes, garlic, pastis or liqueur, capers and olives in a saucepan. Season to taste with salt and pepper and cook over a low heat for about 15 minutes, stirring occasionally.

2 Place the fish in a frying pan, pour over the stock and/or wine and add the bay leaf, peppercorns and lemon rind. Cover and simmer for 10 minutes or until it flakes easily.

3 Using a slotted spoon, transfer the fish into a heated dish. Strain the stock into the tomato sauce and boil to reduce slightly. Season the sauce, pour it over the fish and serve immediately, sprinkled with the chopped parsley.

COOK'S TIP
Remove skin from cutlets and reduce the quantity of olives to reduce calories and fat. Use 450g/1lb fresh tomatoes, skinned and chopped, in place of the canned tomatoes.

NUTRITION NOTES	
Per portion:	
Energy	165Kcals/685kJ
Fat	3.55g
Saturated Fat	0.5g
Cholesterol	69mg

BAKED FISH IN BANANA LEAVES

Fish that is prepared in this way is particularly succulent and flavourful. Fillets are used here, rather than whole fish, which is easier for those who don't like to mess about with bones. It is a great dish for a barbecue.

INGREDIENTS

Serves 4

250ml/8fl oz/1 cup coconut milk
30ml/2 tbsp red curry paste
45ml/3 tbsp fish sauce
30ml/2 tbsp caster sugar
5 kaffir lime leaves, torn
4 x 175g/6oz fish fillets, such as snapper
175g/6oz mixed vegetables, such as carrots or leeks, finely shredded
4 banana leaves or pieces of foil
30ml/2 tbsp shredded spring onions, to garnish
2 red chillies, finely sliced, to garnish

NUTRITION NOTES

Per portion:

Energy	258Kcals/1094kJ
Fat	4.31g
Saturated Fat	0.7g
Cholesterol	64.75mg
Fibre	1.23g

COOK'S TIP

Coconut milk is low in calories and fat and so makes an ideal basis for a low fat marinade or sauce. Choose colourful mixed vegetables such as carrots, leeks and red pepper, to make the dish more attractive and appealing.

1 Combine the coconut milk, curry paste, fish sauce, sugar and kaffir lime leaves in a shallow dish.

2 Marinate the fish in this mixture for about 15–30 minutes. Preheat the oven to 200°C/400°F/Gas 6.

3 Mix the vegetables together and lay a portion on top of a banana leaf or piece of foil. Place a piece of fish on top with a little of its marinade.

4 Wrap the fish up by turning in the sides and ends of the leaf and secure with cocktail sticks. (With foil, just crumple the edges together.) Repeat with the rest of the fish.

5 Bake for 20–25 minutes or until the fish is cooked. Alternatively, cook under the grill or on a barbecue. Just before serving, garnish the fish with a sprinkling of spring onions and sliced red chillies.

STUFFED PLAICE ROLLS

Plaice fillets are a good choice for families because they are economical, easy to cook and free of bones. If you prefer, the skin can be removed first.

INGREDIENTS

Serves 4

1 medium courgette, grated
2 medium carrots, grated
60ml/4 tbsp fresh wholemeal
  breadcrumbs
15ml/1 tbsp lime or lemon juice
4 plaice fillets
salt and black pepper

1 Preheat the oven to 200°C/400°F/ Gas 6. Mix together the carrots and courgettes. Stir in the breadcrumbs, lime juice and seasoning.

2 Lay the fish fillets skin side up and divide the stuffing between them, spreading it evenly.

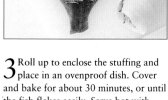

3 Roll up to enclose the stuffing and place in an ovenproof dish. Cover and bake for about 30 minutes, or until the fish flakes easily. Serve hot with new potatoes.

COOK'S TIP
This recipe creates its own delicious juices, but for an extra sauce, stir chopped fresh parsley into a little low fat fromage frais and serve with the fish.

NUTRITION NOTES

Per portion:

Energy	158Kcals/665kJ
Fat	3.22g
Saturated fat	0.56g
Cholesterol	50.4mg
Fibre	1.94g

MACKEREL KEBABS WITH PARSLEY DRESSING

Oily fish such as mackerel are ideal for grilling as they cook quickly and need no extra oil.

INGREDIENTS

Serves 4
450g/1 lb mackerel fillets
finely grated rind and juice of 1 lemon
45ml/3 tbsp chopped fresh parsley
12 cherry tomatoes
8 pitted black olives
salt and black pepper

1 Cut the fish into 4cm/1½in chunks and place in a bowl with half the lemon rind and juice, half of the parsley and some seasoning. Cover the bowl and leave to marinate for 30 minutes.

2 Thread the chunks of fish on to eight long wooden or metal skewers, alternating them with the cherry tomatoes and olives. Cook the kebabs under a hot grill for 3–4 minutes, turning the kebabs occasionally, until the fish is cooked.

3 Mix the remaining lemon rind and juice with the remaining parsley in a small bowl, then season to taste with salt and pepper. Spoon the dressing over the kebabs and serve hot with plain boiled rice or noodles and a leafy green salad.

COOK'S TIP
When using wooden or bamboo kebab skewers, soak them first in a bowl of cold water for a few minutes to help prevent them burning.

NUTRITION NOTES

Per portion:

Energy	268Kcals/1126kJ
Fat	19.27g
Saturated fat	4.5g
Cholesterol	61.88mg
Fibre	1g

PINEAPPLE CURRY WITH SEAFOOD

The delicate sweet and sour flavour of this curry comes from the pineapple, and although it seems an odd combination, it is delicious.

—————— INGREDIENTS ——————

Serves 4

600ml/1 pint/2½ cups coconut milk
30ml/2 tbsp red curry paste
30ml/2 tbsp fish sauce
15ml/1 tbsp sugar
225g/8oz king prawns, shelled and
  deveined
450g/1lb mussels, cleaned and
  beards removed
175g/6oz fresh pineapple, finely
  crushed or chopped
5 kaffir lime leaves, torn
2 red chillies, chopped, and coriander
  leaves, to garnish

1 In a large saucepan, bring half the coconut milk to the boil and heat, stirring, until it separates.

2 Add the red curry paste and cook until fragrant. Add the fish sauce and sugar and continue to cook for a few moments.

3 Stir in the rest of the coconut milk and bring back to the boil. Add the king prawns, mussels, pineapple and kaffir lime leaves.

4 Reheat until boiling and then simmer for 3–5 minutes, until the prawns are cooked and the mussels have opened. Remove any mussels that have not opened and discard. Serve garnished with chillies and coriander.

NUTRITION NOTES	
Per portion:	
Energy	187Kcals/793kJ
Fat	3.5g
Saturated Fat	0.53g
Cholesterol	175.5mg
Fibre	0.59g

CURRIED PRAWNS IN COCONUT MILK

A curry-like dish where the prawns are cooked in a spicy coconut gravy with sweet and sour flavours from the tomatoes.

—————— INGREDIENTS ——————

Serves 4

600ml/1 pint/2½ cups coconut milk
30ml/2 tbsp Thai curry paste
15ml/1 tbsp fish sauce
2.5ml/½ tsp salt
5ml/1 tsp sugar
450g/1lb shelled king prawns, tails left
  intact and deveined
225g/8oz cherry tomatoes
1 chilli, seeded and chopped
juice of ½ lime, to serve
chilli and coriander, to garnish

1 Put half the coconut milk into a pan or wok and bring to the boil.

2 Add the curry paste to the coconut milk, stir until it disperses, then simmer for about 10 minutes.

3 Add the fish sauce, salt, sugar and remaining coconut milk. Simmer for another 5 minutes.

NUTRITION NOTES	
Per portion:	
Energy	184Kcals/778kJ
Fat	3.26g
Saturated Fat	0.58g
Cholesterol	315mg
Fibre	0.6g

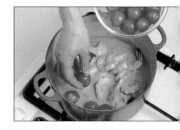

4 Add the prawns, cherry tomatoes and chilli. Simmer gently for about 5 minutes until the prawns are pink and tender.

5 Serve sprinkled with lime juice and garnish with sliced chilli and chopped coriander leaves.

FISH FILLETS WITH A CHILLI SAUCE

Fish fillets, marinated with fresh coriander and lemon juice, then grilled and served with a chilli sauce, are delicious accompanied with saffron rice.

INGREDIENTS

Serves 4

4 flatfish fillets, such as plaice, sole or flounder, about 115g/4oz each
30ml/2 tbsp lemon juice
15ml/1 tbsp finely chopped fresh coriander
15ml/1 tbsp vegetable oil
lime wedges and coriander leaves, to garnish

For the sauce

5ml/1 tsp grated fresh root ginger
30ml/2 tbsp tomato purée
5ml/1 tsp sugar
5ml/1 tsp salt
15ml/1 tbsp chilli sauce
15ml/1 tbsp malt vinegar
300ml/½ pint/1¼ cups water

1 Rinse, pat dry and place the fish fillets in a medium bowl. Add the lemon juice, fresh coriander and oil and rub into the fish. Leave to marinate for at least 1 hour. The flavour will improve if you can leave it for longer.

2 To make the sauce, mix together all the sauce ingredients, pour into a small saucepan and simmer over a low heat for about 6 minutes, stirring occasionally.

3 Preheat the grill to medium. Cook the fillets under the grill for about 5–7 minutes.

4 When the fillets are cooked, remove and arrange them on a warmed serving dish.

5 The chilli sauce should now be fairly thick – about the consistency of a thick chicken soup.

6 Spoon the sauce over the fillets, garnish with the lime wedges and coriander leaves, and serve with rice.

NUTRITION NOTES

Per portion:

Energy	140Kcals/586kJ
Fat	5.28g
Saturated fat	0.78g
Cholesterol	47.25mg

STEAMING MUSSELS WITH A SPICY SAUCE

Serves 4
75ml/5 tbsp red lentils
2 loaves French bread
1.75kg/4–4½ lb/4 pints live mussels
75ml/5 tbsp dry white wine

For the dipping sauce
30ml/2 tbsp sunflower oil
1 small onion, finely chopped
½ celery stick, finely chopped
1 large garlic clove, crushed
5ml/1 tsp medium-hot curry paste

1 Soak the lentils in a bowl filled with plenty of cold water until they are required. Preheat the oven to 150°C/300°F/Gas 2 and put the bread in to warm. Clean the mussels in plenty of cold water and pull off any stray beards. Discard any of the mussels that are damaged.

2 Place the mussels in a large saucepan or flameproof casserole. Add the white wine, cover and steam the mussels for about 8 minutes.

3 Transfer the mussels to a colander over a bowl to collect the juices. Keep warm until required.

4 For the dipping sauce, heat the sunflower oil in a second saucepan, add the onion and celery, and cook for about 3–4 minutes to soften without colouring. Strain the mussel juices into a measuring jug to remove any sand or grit. There will be approximately 400ml/14fl oz/1⅔ cups of liquid.

> **COOK'S TIP**
> Always buy mussels from a reputable supplier and ensure that the shells are tightly closed. Atlantic blue shell mussels are the most common. Small mussels are preferred for their sweet, tender flavour.

5 Add the mussel juices to the saucepan, then add the garlic, curry paste and lentils. Bring to the boil and simmer for a further 10–12 minutes or until the lentils have fallen apart.

6 Tip the mussels out on to four serving plates and serve with the dipping sauce, the warm French bread and a bowl to put the empty shells in.

TUNA AND MIXED VEGETABLE PASTA

INGREDIENTS

Serves 4

10ml/2 tsp olive oil
115g/4oz/1½ cups button
  mushrooms, sliced
1 garlic clove, crushed
½ red pepper, seeded and chopped
15ml/1 tbsp tomato paste
300ml/½ pint/1¼ cups tomato juice
115g/4oz/1 cup frozen peas
15–30ml/1–2 tbsp drained pickled
  green peppercorns, crushed
350g/12oz whole wheat pasta shapes
200g/7oz can tuna chunks in water,
  drained
6 spring onions, diagonally sliced

1 Heat the oil in a pan and gently sauté the mushrooms, garlic and pepper until softened. Stir in the tomato paste, then add the tomato juice, peas and some or all of the crushed peppercorns, depending on how spicy you like the sauce. Bring to the boil, lower the heat and simmer.

2 Bring a large saucepan of lightly salted water to the boil and cook the pasta for about 12 minutes (or according to the instructions on the package), until just tender. When the pasta is almost ready, add the tuna to the sauce and heat through gently. Stir in the spring onions. Drain the pasta, turn it into a heated bowl and pour over the sauce. Toss to mix. Serve at once.

NUTRITION NOTES	
Per portion:	
Energy	354Kcals/1514kJ
Fat	4.5g
Saturated Fat	0.67g
Cholesterol	22.95mg
Fibre	10.35g

SWEET AND SOUR FISH

White fish is high in protein, vitamins and minerals, but low in fat. Serve this tasty, nutritious dish with brown rice and stir-fried cabbage or spinach for a delicious lunch.

INGREDIENTS

Serves 4

60ml/4 tbsp cider vinegar
45ml/3 tbsp light soy sauce
50g/2oz/¼ cup granulated sugar
15ml/1 tbsp tomato purée
25ml/1½ tbsp cornflour
250ml/8fl oz/1 cup water
1 green pepper, seeded and sliced
225g/8oz can pineapple pieces in
  fruit juice
225g/8oz tomatoes, peeled and
  chopped
225g/8oz/2 cups button mushrooms,
  sliced
675g/1½lb chunky haddock fillets,
  skinned
salt and black pepper

1 Preheat the oven to 180°C/350°F/ Gas 4. Mix together the vinegar, soy sauce, sugar and tomato purée in a saucepan. Put the cornflour in a jug, stir in the water, then add the mixture to the saucepan, stirring well. Bring to the boil, stirring constantly until thickened. Lower the heat and simmer the sauce for 5 minutes.

2 Add the green pepper, canned pineapple pieces (with juice) and tomatoes to the pan and stir well. Mix in the mushrooms and heat through. Season to taste with salt and pepper.

3 Place the fish in a single layer in a shallow ovenproof dish, spoon over the sauce and cover with foil. Bake for 15–20 minutes until the fish is tender. Serve immediately.

NUTRITION NOTES	
Per portion:	
Energy	255Kcals/1070kJ
Fat	2g
Saturated Fat	0.5g
Cholesterol	61mg

OATY HERRINGS WITH RED SALSA

Herrings are one of the most economical and nutritious fish. If you buy them ready filleted, they're much easier to eat than the whole fish.

INGREDIENTS

Serves 4
30ml/2 tbsp skimmed milk
10ml/2 tsp Dijon mustard
2 large herrings, filletted
50g/2oz/⅔ cup rolled oats
salt and black pepper

For the salsa
1 small red pepper, seeded
4 medium tomatoes
1 spring onion, chopped
15ml/1 tbsp lime juice
5ml/1 tsp caster sugar

1 Preheat the oven to 200°C/400°F/ Gas 6. To make the salsa, place the pepper, tomatoes, spring onion, lime juice, sugar and seasoning in a food processor. Process until finely chopped.

2 Mix the milk and mustard, and the oats and pepper. Dip fillets into the mustard mixture, then oats to coat.

3 Place on a baking sheet, then bake for 20 minutes. Serve with the salsa.

NUTRITION NOTES	
Per portion:	
Energy	261Kcals/1097kJ
Fat	15.56g
Saturated fat	3.17g
Cholesterol	52.65mg
Fibre	2.21g

SPICED RAINBOW TROUT

Farmed rainbow trout are very good value and cook very quickly on a grill or barbecue. Herring and mackerel can be cooked in this way too.

INGREDIENTS

Serves 4
4 large rainbow trout fillets (about 150g/5oz each)
15ml/1 tbsp ground coriander
1 garlic clove, crushed
30ml/2 tbsp finely chopped fresh mint
5ml/1 tsp paprika
175g/6oz/¾ cup natural yogurt
salad and pitta bread, to serve

1 With a sharp knife, slash the flesh of the fish fillets through the skin fairly deeply at intervals.

2 Mix together the coriander, garlic, mint, paprika and yogurt. Spread this mixture evenly over the fish and leave to marinate for about an hour.

3 Cook the fish under a moderately hot grill or on a barbecue, turning occasionally, until crisp and golden. Serve hot with a crisp salad and some warmed pitta bread.

> **COOK'S TIP**
> If you are using the grill, it is best to line the grill pan with foil before cooking the trout.

NUTRITION NOTES	
Per portion:	
Energy	188Kcals/792kJ
Fat	5.66g
Saturated fat	1.45g
Cholesterol	110.87mg
Fibre	0.05g

HOKI BALLS IN TOMATO SAUCE

This quick meal is a good choice for young children, as you can guarantee no bones. If you like, add a dash of chilli sauce.

INGREDIENTS

Serves 4

*450g/1 lb hoki or other white fish
    fillets, skinned*
*60ml/4 tbsp fresh wholemeal bread-
    crumbs*
*30ml/2 tbsp snipped chives or spring
    onion*
400g/14oz can chopped tomatoes
*50g/2oz/¼ cup button mushrooms,
    sliced*
salt and black pepper

1 Cut the fish fillets into large chunks and place in a food processor. Add the wholemeal breadcrumbs, chives or spring onion. Season to taste with salt and pepper and process until the fish is finely chopped, but still has some texture left.

2 Divide the fish mixture into about 16 even-sized pieces, then mould them into balls with your hands.

3 Place the tomatoes and mushrooms in a wide saucepan and cook over a medium heat until boiling. Add the fish balls, cover and simmer for about 10 minutes, until cooked. Serve hot.

COOK'S TIP
Hoki is a good choice for this dish but if it's not available, use cod, haddock or whiting instead.

NUTRITION NOTES

Per portion:

Energy	138Kcals/580kJ
Fat	1.38g
Saturated fat	0.24g
Cholesterol	51.75mg
Fibre	1.89g

TUNA AND CORN FISH CAKES

These economical little tuna fish cakes are quick to make. Either use fresh mashed potatoes, or make a storecupboard version with instant mash.

―――― INGREDIENTS ――――

Serves 4

*300g/11oz/1¼ cups cooked mashed
   potatoes*
*200g/7oz can tuna fish in soya oil,
   drained*
*115g/4oz/¼ cup canned or frozen
   sweetcorn*
30ml/2 tbsp chopped fresh parsley
*50g/2oz/1 cup fresh white or brown
   breadcrumbs*
salt and black pepper
lemon wedges, to serve

1 Place the mashed potato in a bowl and stir in the tuna fish, sweetcorn and chopped parsley.

2 Season to taste with salt and pepper, then shape into eight patty shapes with your hands.

3 Spread out the breadcrumbs on a plate and press the fish cakes into the breadcrumbs to coat lightly, then place on a baking sheet.

4 Cook the fish cakes under a moderately hot grill until crisp and golden brown, turning once. Serve hot with lemon wedges and fresh vegetables.

COOK'S TIP
For simple storecupboard variations which are just as nutritious, try using canned sardines, red or pink salmon, or smoked mackerel in place of the tuna.

―――― NUTRITION NOTES ――――

Per portion:

Energy	203Kcals/852kJ
Fat	4.62g
Saturated fat	0.81g
Cholesterol	21.25mg
Fibre	1.82g

FISH AND VEGETABLE KEBABS

INGREDIENTS

Serves 4

275g/10oz cod fillets, or any other
firm, white fish fillets
45ml/3 tbsp lemon juice
5ml/1 tsp grated fresh root ginger
2 green chillies, very finely chopped
15ml/1 tbsp very finely chopped fresh
coriander
15ml/1 tbsp very finely chopped fresh
mint
5ml/1 tsp ground coriander
5ml/1 tsp salt
1 red pepper
1 green pepper
½ cauliflower
8 button mushrooms
8 cherry tomatoes
15ml/1 tbsp soya oil
1 lime, quartered, to garnish

COOK'S TIP
Use different vegetables to the ones
suggested, if wished. Try baby corn
instead of mushrooms and broccoli
in place of the cauliflower.

1 Cut the fish fillets into large chunks using a sharp knife.

2 In a large mixing bowl, blend together the lemon juice, ginger, chopped green chillies, fresh coriander, mint, ground coriander and salt. Add the fish chunks and leave to marinate for about 30 minutes.

3 Cut the red and green peppers into large squares and divide the cauliflower into individual florets.

4 Preheat the grill to hot. Arrange the prepared vegetables alternately with the fish pieces on four skewers.

5 Baste the kebabs with the oil and any remaining marinade. Transfer to a flameproof dish and grill for about 7–10 minutes or until the fish is cooked right through. Garnish with the lime quarters, and serve the kebabs either on their own or with saffron rice.

NUTRITION NOTES

Per portion:	
Energy	130Kcals/546kJ
Fat	4.34g
Saturated fat	0.51g
Cholesterol	32.54mg

GLAZED GARLIC PRAWNS

A fairly simple and quick dish to prepare, it is best to peel the prawns as this helps them to absorb maximum flavour. Serve as a main course with a variety of accompaniments, or with a salad as a starter.

INGREDIENTS

Serves 4

15ml/1 tbsp sunflower oil
3 garlic cloves, roughly chopped
3 tomatoes, chopped
2.5ml/½ tsp salt
5ml/1 tsp crushed dried red chillies
5ml/1 tsp lemon juice
15ml/1 tbsp mango chutney
1 green chilli, chopped
15–20 cooked king prawns, peeled
fresh coriander leaves and 2 chopped
    spring onions, to garnish

NUTRITION NOTES

Per portion:

Energy	90Kcals/380kJ
Fat	3.83g
Saturated fat	0.54g
Cholesterol	30.37mg

1 Heat the oil in a medium saucepan, and add the chopped garlic.

2 Lower the heat. Add the chopped tomatoes along with the salt, crushed chillies, lemon juice, mango chutney and chopped fresh chilli.

3 Finally add the prawns, turn up the heat and stir-fry quickly until they are heated through.

4 Transfer to a serving dish. Serve immediately garnished with fresh coriander leaves and chopped spring onions.

COD CREOLE

INGREDIENTS

Serves 4

450g/1 lb cod fillets, skinned
15ml/1 tbsp lime or lemon juice
10ml/2 tsp olive oil
1 medium onion, finely chopped
1 green pepper, seeded and sliced
2.5ml/½ tsp cayenne pepper
2.5ml/½ tsp garlic salt
400g/14oz can chopped tomatoes

NUTRITION NOTES

Per portion:

Energy	130Kcals/546kJ
Fat	2.61g
Saturated fat	0.38g
Cholesterol	51.75mg
Fibre	1.61g

1 Cut the cod fillets into bite-sized chunks and sprinkle with the lime or lemon juice.

2 In a large, non-stick pan, heat the olive oil and fry the onion and pepper gently until softened. Add the cayenne pepper and garlic salt.

3 Stir in the cod with the chopped tomatoes. Bring to the boil, then cover and simmer for about 5 minutes, or until the fish flakes easily. Serve with boiled rice or potatoes.

FIVE-SPICE FISH

Chinese mixtures of spicy, sweet and sour flavours are particularly successful with fish, and dinner is ready in minutes.

INGREDIENTS

Serves 4

4 white fish fillets, such as cod, haddock
  or hoki (about 175g/6oz each)
5ml/1 tsp Chinese five-spice powder
20ml/4 tsp cornflour
15ml/1 tbsp sesame or sunflower oil
3 spring onions, shredded
5ml/1 tsp finely chopped root ginger
150g/5oz button mushrooms, sliced
115g/4oz baby corn cobs, sliced
30ml/2 tbsp soy sauce
45ml/3 tbsp dry sherry or apple juice
5ml/1 tsp sugar
salt and black pepper

1 Toss the fish in the five-spice powder and cornflour to coat.

2 Heat the oil in a frying pan or wok and stir-fry the onions, ginger mushrooms and corn cobs for about 1 minute. Add the fish and cook for 2–3 minutes, turning once.

3 Mix together the soy sauce, sherry and sugar then pour over the fish. Simmer for 2 minutes, adjust the seasoning, then serve with noodles and stir-fried vegetables.

NUTRITION NOTES

Per portion:

Energy	213Kcals/893kJ
Fat	4.41g
Saturated fat	0.67g
Cholesterol	80.5mg
Fibre	1.08g

GRILLED SNAPPER WITH MANGO SALSA

Serves 4

350g/12oz new potatoes
3 eggs
115g/4 oz green beans, topped, tailed
  and halved
4 red snapper, about 350g/12oz each,
  scaled and gutted
30ml/2 tbsp olive oil
175g/6oz mixed lettuce leaves
10 cherry tomatoes, to serve
salt and black pepper

For the salsa

45ml/3 tbsp chopped fresh coriander
1 ripe mango, peeled, stoned and diced
½ red chilli, seeded and chopped
2.5cm/1 in fresh root ginger, grated
juice of 2 limes
generous pinch of celery salt

—— NUTRITION NOTES ——

Per portion:	
Energy	405Kcals/1702kJ
Fat	15.59g
Saturated fat	2.06g
Cholesterol	163.62mg
Fibre	2.03g

1 Place the potatoes in a large saucepan and cover with cold salted water. Bring to the boil and simmer for about 15–20 minutes. Drain and set aside.

2 Bring a second large pan of salted water to the boil. Put in the eggs and boil for 4 minutes.

3 Add the beans and cook for a further 6 minutes, so that the eggs have had a total of 10 minutes. Remove the eggs from the pan, cool, peel and cut into quarters. Drain the beans and set aside.

4 Preheat a moderate grill. Slash each snapper three times on either side, moisten with oil and cook for about 12 minutes, turning once.

5 For the dressing, place the coriander in a food processor or blender. Add the mango, chilli, ginger, lime juice and celery salt, and process until smooth.

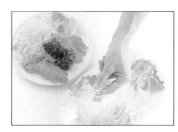

6 Moisten the lettuce leaves with olive oil, and divide them among four large plates.

7 Arrange the snapper over the lettuce and season to taste. Halve the new potatoes and tomatoes, and distribute them with the beans and quartered hard-boiled eggs over the salad. Serve with the salsa dressing.

SALMON RISOTTO WITH CUCUMBER

Any rice can be used for risotto, although the creamiest ones are made with short grain arborio and carnaroli rice. Fresh tarragon and cucumber combine well to bring out the flavour of the salmon.

INGREDIENTS

Serves 4

25g/1oz/2 tbsp sunflower margarine
1 small bunch spring onions, white part
  only, chopped
½ cucumber, peeled, seeded and
  chopped
400g/14oz/1¼ cups short grain
  risotto rice
900ml/1½ pints/3¾ cups chicken or
  fish stock
150ml/¼ pint/⅔ cup dry white wine
450g/1 lb salmon fillet, skinned and
  diced

COOK'S TIP
Long grain rice can also be used for this recipe. Reduce the stock to 750ml/1¼ pints/3⅔ cups.

1 Heat the margarine in a large saucepan, and add the spring onions and cucumber. Cook for about 2–3 minutes without colouring.

2 Add the rice, stock and wine and return to the boil.

NUTRITION NOTES

Per portion:

Energy	653Kcals/2742kJ
Fat	19.88g
Saturated fat	6.99g
Cholesterol	70.63mg
Fibre	0.91g

3 Simmer the wine and stock mixture for about 10 minutes, stirring occasionally. Stir in the diced salmon and tarragon. Continue cooking for a further 5 minutes, then switch off the heat. Cover and leave to stand for 5 minutes before serving.

JAMAICAN COD STEAKS WITH RAGOUT

Spicy hot from Kingston town,
this is a fast fish dish.

——————— **INGREDIENTS** ———————

Serves 4
finely grated zest of ½ orange
30ml/2 tbsp black peppercorns
15ml/1 tbsp allspice berries or
 Jamaican pepper
2.5ml/½ tsp salt
4 cod fillet steaks, about 175g/6oz each
groundnut oil, for frying
new potatoes, to serve (optional)
45ml/3 tbsp chopped fresh parsley,
 to garnish

For the ragout
30ml/2 tbsp groundnut oil
1 medium onion, chopped
2.5cm/1 in piece fresh root ginger,
 peeled and grated
450g/1 lb fresh pumpkin, peeled,
 deseeded and chopped
3–4 shakes of Tabasco sauce
30ml/2 tbsp soft brown sugar
15ml/1 tbsp vinegar

1 For the ragout, heat the oil in a heavy saucepan and add the onion and ginger. Cover and cook, stirring, for 3–4 minutes until soft.

2 Add the chopped pumpkin, Tabasco sauce, brown sugar and vinegar, cover and cook over a low heat for about 10–12 minutes until softened.

3 Combine the orange zest, peppercorns, allspice or Jamaican pepper and salt, then crush coarsely using a pestle and mortar. (Alternatively, coarsely grind the peppercorns in a pepper mill and combine with the zest and seasoning.)

4 Sprinkle the spice mixture over both sides of the fish and moisten with a little oil.

5 Heat a large frying pan and dry-fry the cod steaks for about 12 minutes, turning once.

6 Serve the cod steaks with a spoonful of pumpkin ragout and new potatoes, if required, and garnish the ragout with chopped fresh parsley.

——————— **NUTRITION NOTES** ———————

Per portion:

Energy	324Kcals/1360kJ
Fat	14.9g
Saturated fat	2.75g
Cholesterol	80.5mg
Fibre	1.92g

COOK'S TIP
This recipe can be adapted using any types of firm pink or white fish that is available, such as haddock, whiting, monkfish, halibut or tuna.

TUNA FISH AND FLAGEOLET BEAN SALAD

Two cans of tuna fish form the basis of this delicious and easy-to-make storecupboard salad.

INGREDIENTS

Serves 4

90ml/6 tbsp reduced calorie
   mayonnaise
5ml/1 tsp mustard
30ml/2 tbsp capers
45ml/3 tbsp chopped fresh parsley
pinch of celery salt
2 x 200g/7oz cans tuna fish in brine,
   drained
3 little gem lettuces
400g/14oz can flageolet beans, drained
12 cherry tomatoes, halved
400g/14oz can baby artichoke hearts,
   halved
toasted sesame bread or sticks, to serve

NUTRITION NOTES

Per portion:

Energy	299Kcals/1255kJ
Fat	13.91g
Saturated fat	2.12g
Cholesterol	33mg
Fibre	6.36g

1 Combine the mayonnaise, mustard, capers and parsley in a mixing bowl. Season to taste with celery salt.

2 Flake the tuna into the dressing and toss gently.

3 Arrange the lettuce leaves on four plates, then spoon the tuna mixture on to the leaves.

COOK'S TIP
If flageolet beans are not available, use cannellini beans.

4 Spoon the flageolet beans to one side, followed by the tomatoes and artichoke hearts.

5 Serve with slices of toasted sesame bread or sticks.

VEGETABLES AND VEGETARIAN DISHES

Vegetarian food provides a tasty and nutritious choice at mealtimes for everyone and is especially tempting when it is low in fat too. Choose from delicious vegetable dishes such as Mixed Mushroom Ragoût, Devilled Onions en Croûte and Courgettes in Citrus Sauce or tempting low fat vegetarian meals such as Autumn Glory, Ratatouille Pancakes, and Tofu and Green Bean Curry.

HERBY BAKED TOMATOES

INGREDIENTS

Serves 4–6

675g/1½ lb large red and yellow
  tomatoes
10ml/2 tsp red wine vinegar
2.5ml/½ tsp wholegrain mustard
1 garlic clove, crushed
10ml/2 tsp chopped fresh parsley
10ml/2 tsp snipped fresh chives
25g/1oz/½ cup fresh fine white
  breadcrumbs, for topping
salt and black pepper

NUTRITION NOTES

Per portion:	
Energy	37Kcals/156kJ
Fat	0.49g
Saturated Fat	0.16g
Cholesterol	0
Fibre	1.36g

1 Preheat the oven to 200°C/400°F/
Gas 6. Thickly slice the tomatoes
and arrange half of them in a 900ml/
1½ pint/3¾ cup ovenproof dish.

COOK'S TIP
Use wholemeal breadcrumbs in
place of white, for added colour,
flavour and fibre. Use 5–10ml/
1–2 tsp mixed dried herbs, if fresh
herbs are not available.

2 Mix the vinegar, mustard, garlic
and seasoning together. Stir in
10ml/2 tsp cold water. Sprinkle the
tomatoes with half the parsley and
chives, then drizzle over half the
dressing.

3 Lay the remaining tomato slices on
top, overlapping them slightly.
Drizzle with the remaining dressing.

4 Sprinkle over the breadcrumbs.
Bake for 25 minutes or until the
topping is golden. Sprinkle with the
remaining parsley and chives. Serve
immediately, garnished with sprigs
of parsley.

POTATO GRATIN

The flavour of Parmesan is wonderfully strong, so a little goes a long way. Leave the cheese out altogether for an almost fat-free dish.

INGREDIENTS

Serves 4
1 garlic clove
5 large baking potatoes, peeled
45ml/3tbsp freshly grated Parmesan
  cheese
600ml/1 pint/2½ cups vegetable or
  chicken stock
pinch of grated nutmeg
salt and black pepper

1 Preheat the oven to 200°C/400°F/ Gas 6. Halve the garlic clove and rub over the base and sides of a large shallow gratin dish.

2 Slice the potatoes very thinly and arrange a third of them in the dish. Sprinkle with a little grated Parmesan cheese, and season with salt and pepper. Pour over some of the stock to prevent the potatoes from discolouring.

3 Continue layering the potatoes and cheese as before, then pour over the rest of the stock. Sprinkle with the grated nutmeg.

4 Bake in the preheated oven for about 1¼–1½ hours or until the potatoes are tender and the tops well browned.

NUTRITION NOTES

Per portion:
Energy	178Kcals/749kJ
Protein	9.42g
Fat	1.57g
Saturated Fat	0.30g
Fibre	1.82g

COOK'S TIP
For a potato and onion gratin, thinly slice one medium onion and layer with the potato.

MIXED MUSHROOM RAGOÛT

These mushrooms are delicious served hot or cold and can be prepared up to two days in advance.

INGREDIENTS

Serves 4

1 small onion, finely chopped
1 garlic clove, crushed
5ml/1 tsp coriander seeds, crushed
30ml/2 tbsp red wine vinegar
15ml/1 tbsp soy sauce
15ml/1 tbsp dry sherry
10ml/2 tsp tomato purée
10ml/2 tsp soft light brown sugar
150ml/¼ pint/⅔ cup vegetable stock
115g/4oz baby button mushrooms
115g/4oz chestnut mushrooms, quartered
115g/4oz oyster mushrooms, sliced
salt and black pepper
coriander sprig, to garnish

NUTRITION NOTES

Per portion:

Energy	41Kcals/172kJ
Protein	2.51g
Fat	0.66g
Saturated Fat	0.08g
Fibre	1.02g

COOK'S TIP
There are many types of fresh mushrooms available and all are low in calories and fat. They add flavour and colour to many low fat dishes such as this tasty ragoût.

1 Put the first nine ingredients into a large saucepan. Bring to the boil and reduce the heat. Cover and simmer for 5 minutes.

2 Uncover the saucepan and simmer for 5 more minutes, or until the liquid has reduced by half.

3 Add the baby button and chestnut mushrooms and simmer for 3 minutes. Stir in the oyster mushrooms and cook for a further 2 minutes.

4 Remove the mushrooms from the pan with a slotted spoon and transfer them to a serving dish. Keep warm, if serving hot.

5 Boil the juices for about 5 minutes, or until reduced to about 75ml/ 5 tbsp. Season to taste.

6 Allow to cool for 2–3 minutes, then pour over the mushrooms. Serve hot or well chilled, garnished with a sprig of coriander.

Devilled Onions en Croûte

Fill crisp bread cups with tender button onions tossed in a mustardy glaze. Try other low fat mixtures of vegetables, such as ratatouille, for a delicious change.

Ingredients

Serves 4

12 thin slices of white or
  wholemeal bread
225g/8oz button onions or shallots
150ml/¼ pint/⅔ cup vegetable stock
15ml/1 tbsp dry white wine or
  dry sherry
2 turkey rashers, cut into thin strips
10ml/2 tsp Worcestershire sauce
5ml/1 tsp tomato purée
1.5ml/¼ tsp prepared English mustard
salt and black pepper
sprigs of flat leaf parsley, to garnish

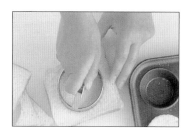

1 Preheat the oven to 200°C/400°F/ Gas 6. Stamp out the bread into rounds with a 7.5cm/3in fluted biscuit cutter and use to line a 12–cup patty tin.

2 Cover each bread case with non-stick baking paper and fill with baking beans. Bake blind for 5 minutes. Remove the paper and beans and bake for a further 5 minutes, until lightly browned and crisp.

3 Meanwhile, put the button onions or shallots in a bowl and cover with boiling water. Leave for 3 minutes, then drain and rinse under cold water. Trim off their top and root ends and slip them out of their skins.

4 Simmer the onions and stock in a covered saucepan for 5 minutes. Uncover and cook, stirring occasionally until the stock has reduced entirely. Add all the remaining ingredients, except the flat leaf parsley, and cook for 2–3 minutes.

5 Fill the toast cups with the devilled onions. Serve hot, garnished with sprigs of flat leaf parsley.

Nutrition Notes

Per portion:

Energy	178Kcals/749kJ
Protein	9.42g
Fat	1.57g
Saturated Fat	0.30g
Fibre	1.82g

KOHLRABI STUFFED WITH PEPPERS

If you haven't sampled kohlrabi, or have only eaten it in stews where its flavour is lost, this dish is recommended. The slightly sharp flavour of the peppers are an excellent foil to the more earthy flavour of the kohlrabi.

— INGREDIENTS —

Serves 4

4 small kohlrabies, about 175g–225g/
  6–8oz each
about 400ml/14fl oz/²⁄₃ cup hot
  vegetable stock
15ml/1 tbsp sunflower oil
1 onion, chopped
1 small red pepper, seeded and sliced
1 small green pepper, seeded and sliced
salt and black pepper
flat leaf parsley, to garnish (optional)

— NUTRITION NOTES —

Per portion:
Energy	112Kcals/470kJ
Fat	4.63g
Saturated Fat	0.55g
Cholesterol	0
Fibre	5.8g

1 Preheat the oven to 180°C/350°F/ Gas 4. Trim and top and tail the kohlrabies and arrange in the base of a medium-sized ovenproof dish.

2 Pour over the stock to come about halfway up the vegetables. Cover and braise in the oven for about 30 minutes, until tender. Transfer to a plate and allow to cool, reserving the stock.

3 Heat the oil in a frying pan and fry the onion for 3–4 minutes over a gentle heat, stirring occasionally. Add the peppers and cook for a further 2–3 minutes, until the onion is lightly browned.

4 Add the reserved vegetable stock and a little seasoning and simmer, uncovered, over a moderate heat until the stock has almost evaporated.

5 Scoop out the insides of the kohlrabies and chop roughly. Stir into the onion and pepper mixture, taste and adjust the seasoning. Arrange the shells in a shallow ovenproof dish.

6 Spoon the filling into the kohlrabi shells. Put in the oven for 5–10 minutes to heat through and then serve, garnished with a sprig of flat leaf parsley, if liked.

COURGETTES IN CITRUS SAUCE

If baby courgettes are unavailable, you can use larger ones, but they should be cooked whole so that they don't absorb too much water. After cooking, halve them lengthways and cut into 10cm/4in lengths. These tender, baby courgettes served in a very low fat sauce make this a tasty and low fat accompaniment to grilled fish fillets.

NUTRITION NOTES

Per portion:

Energy	33Kcals/138kJ
Protein	2.18g
Fat	0.42g
Saturated Fat	0.09g
Fibre	0.92g

INGREDIENTS

Serves 4

350g/12oz baby courgettes
4 spring onions, finely sliced
2.5cm/1in fresh root ginger, grated
30ml/2 tbsp cider vinegar
15ml/1 tbsp light soy sauce
5ml/1 tsp soft light brown sugar
45ml/3 tbsp vegetable stock
finely grated rind and juice of ½ lemon
   and ½ orange
5ml/1 tsp cornflour

1 Cook the courgettes in lightly salted boiling water for 3–4 minutes, or until just tender. Drain well.

2 Meanwhile, put all the remaining ingredients, except the cornflour, into a small saucepan and bring to the boil. Simmer for 3 minutes.

3 Blend the cornflour with 10ml/2 tsp cold water and add to the sauce. Bring to the boil, stirring continuously, until the sauce has thickened.

4 Pour the sauce over the courgettes and heat gently, shaking the pan to coat them evenly. Transfer to a warmed serving dish and serve.

COOK'S TIP
Use baby sweetcorn or aubergines in place of the courgettes for an appetizing change.

COURGETTE AND ASPARAGUS PARCELS

To appreciate the aroma, these paper parcels should be broken open at the table.

INGREDIENTS

Serves 4

2 medium courgettes
1 medium leek
225g/8oz young asparagus, trimmed
4 tarragon sprigs
4 whole garlic cloves, unpeeled
1 egg, beaten, to glaze
salt and black pepper

NUTRITION NOTES

Per portion:

Energy	110 Kcals/460kJ
Protein	6.22g
Fat	2.29g
Saturated Fat	0.49g
Fibre	6.73g

1 Preheat the oven to 200°C/400°F/ Gas 6. Using a potato peeler, carefully slice the courgettes lengthways into thin strips.

2 Cut the leek into very fine julienne strips and cut the asparagus evenly into 5cm/2in lengths.

3 Cut out four sheets of greaseproof paper measuring 30 x 38cm/ 12 x 15in and fold in half. Draw a large curve to make a heart shape when unfolded. Cut along the inside of the line and open out.

4 Divide the courgettes, asparagus and leek evenly between each paper heart, positioning the filling on one side of the fold line, and topping each with a sprig of tarragon and an unpeeled garlic clove. Season to taste.

5 Brush the edges lightly with the beaten egg and fold over.

6 Twist the edges together so that each parcel is completely sealed. Lay the parcels on a baking sheet and cook for 10 minutes. Serve immediately.

COOK'S TIP
Experiment with other vegetable combinations, if you like.

AUTUMN GLORY

Glorious pumpkin shells summon up the delights of autumn and look too good to throw away, so use one as a serving pot. Pumpkin and pasta make marvellous partners, especially as a main course served from the baked shell.

INGREDIENTS

Serves 4–6
1 pumpkin, about 2kg/4–4½lb
1 onion, sliced
2.5cm/1in fresh root ginger
15ml/1 tbsp extra virgin olive oil
1 courgette, sliced
115g/4oz sliced mushrooms
400g/14oz can chopped tomatoes
75g/3oz/1 cup pasta shells
450ml/¾ pint/2 cups stock
60ml/4 tbsp fromage frais
30ml/2 tbsp chopped fresh basil
salt and black pepper

NUTRITION NOTES

Per portion (6 servings):
Energy	140Kcals/588kJ
Fat	4.29g
Saturated Fat	1.17g
Cholesterol	2.5mg
Fibre	4.45g

COOK'S TIP
Use reduced fat or very low fat fromage frais to cut the calories and fat. Cook the onion, ginger and pumpkin flesh in 30–45ml/ 2–3 tbsp vegetable stock in place of the oil, to cut the calories and fat more.

1 Preheat the oven to 180°C/350°F/ Gas 4. Cut the top off the pumpkin with a large sharp knife, then scoop out and discard the seeds.

2 Using a small sharp knife and a sturdy tablespoon, extract as much of the pumpkin flesh as possible, then chop it into chunks.

3 Bake the pumpkin shell with its lid on for 45 minutes to 1 hour until the inside begins to soften.

4 Meanwhile make the filling. Gently fry the onion, ginger and pumpkin chunks in the olive oil for about 10 minutes, stirring occasionally.

5 Add the courgette and mushrooms and cook for a further 3 minutes, then stir in the tomatoes, pasta shells and stock. Season well, bring to the boil, then cover and simmer gently for another 10 minutes.

6 Stir the fromage frais and basil into the pasta and spoon the mixture into the pumpkin. (It may not be possible to fit all the filling into the pumpkin shell; serve the rest separately if this is the case.)

VEGETABLES À LA GRECQUE

This simple side salad is made with winter vegetables, but you can vary it according to the season. This combination of vegetables makes an ideal, low fat side salad to serve with grilled lean meat or poultry, or with thick slices of fresh, crusty bread.

INGREDIENTS

Serves 4
175ml/6fl oz/³⁄₄ cup white wine
5ml/1 tsp olive oil
30ml/2 tbsp lemon juice
2 bay leaves
sprig of fresh thyme
4 juniper berries
450g/1lb leeks, trimmed and cut into
   2.5cm/1in lengths
1 small cauliflower, broken into florets
4 celery sticks, sliced on the diagonal
30ml/2 tbsp chopped fresh parsley
salt and black pepper

1 Put the wine, oil, lemon juice, bay leaves, thyme and juniper berries into a large, heavy-based saucepan and bring to the boil. Cover and let simmer for 20 minutes.

2 Add the leeks, cauliflower and celery. Simmer very gently for 5–6 minutes or until just tender.

NUTRITION NOTES

Per portion:

Energy	88Kcals/368kJ
Protein	4.53g
Fat	2.05g
Saturated Fat	0.11g
Fibre	4.42g

3 Remove the vegetables with a slotted spoon and transfer them to a serving dish. Briskly boil the cooking liquid for 15–20 minutes, or until reduced by half. Strain.

4 Stir the parsley into the liquid and season with salt and pepper to taste. Pour over the vegetables and leave to cool. Chill in the fridge for at least 1 hour before serving.

COOK'S TIP
Choose a dry or medium-dry white wine for best results.

ROASTED MEDITERRANEAN VEGETABLES

For a really colourful dish, try these vegetables roasted in olive oil with garlic and rosemary. The flavour is wonderfully intense.

INGREDIENTS

Serves 6
1 each red and yellow pepper
2 Spanish onions
2 large courgettes
1 large aubergine or 4 baby aubergines,
  trimmed
1 fennel bulb, thickly sliced
2 beef tomatoes
8 fat garlic cloves
30ml/2 tbsp olive oil
fresh rosemary sprigs
black pepper
lemon wedges and black olives
  (optional), to garnish

1 Halve and seed the peppers, then cut them into large chunks. Peel the onions and cut into thick wedges.

NUTRITION NOTES

Per portion:	
Energy	120Kcals/504kJ
Fat	5.2g
Saturated Fat	0.68g
Cholesterol	0

2 Cut the courgettes and aubergines into large chunks.

3 Preheat the oven to 220°C/425°F/ Gas 7. Spread the peppers, onions, courgettes, aubergines and fennel in a lightly oiled, shallow ovenproof dish or roasting pan, or, if liked, arrange in rows to make a colourful design.

4 Cut each tomato in half and place, cut-side up, with the vegetables.

5 Tuck the garlic cloves among the vegetables, then brush them with the olive oil. Place some sprigs of rosemary among the vegetables and grind over some black pepper, particularly on the tomatoes.

6 Roast for 20–25 minutes, turning the vegetables halfway through the cooking time. Serve from the dish or on a flat platter, garnished with lemon wedges. Scatter some black olives over the top, if you like.

RATATOUILLE PANCAKES

These pancakes are made slightly thicker than usual to hold the juicy vegetable filling. By using cooking spray, you can control the amount of fat you are using and keep it to a minimum.

INGREDIENTS

Serves 4

75g/3oz/²⁄₃ cup plain flour
pinch of salt
25g/1oz/¹⁄₄ cup medium oatmeal
1 egg
300ml/¹⁄₂ pint/1¹⁄₄ cups skimmed milk
non-stick cooking spray
mixed salad, to serve

For the filling
1 large aubergine, cut into 2.5cm/
*   1in cubes*
1 garlic clove, crushed
2 medium courgettes, sliced
1 green pepper, seeded and sliced
1 red pepper, seeded and sliced
75ml/5 tbsp vegetable stock
200g/7oz can chopped tomatoes
5ml/1 tsp cornflour
salt and black pepper

NUTRITION NOTES

Per portion:	
Energy	182Kcals/767kJ
Protein	9.36g
Fat	3.07g
Saturated Fat	0.62g
Fibre	4.73g

COOK'S TIP
Adding oatmeal to the batter mixture adds flavour, colour and texture to the cooked pancakes. If you like, wholemeal flour may be used in place of white flour to add extra fibre and flavour too.

1 Sift the flour and a pinch of salt into a bowl. Stir in the oatmeal. Make a well in the centre, add the egg and half the milk and mix to a smooth batter. Gradually beat in the remaining milk. Cover the bowl and leave to stand for 30 minutes.

2 Spray an 18cm/7in heavy-based frying pan with cooking spray. Heat the pan, then pour in just enough batter to cover the base of the pan thinly. Cook for 2–3 minutes, until the underside is golden brown. Flip over and cook for a further 1–2 minutes.

3 Slide the pancake out on to a plate lined with non-stick baking paper. Stack the other pancakes on top as they are made, interleaving each with non-stick baking paper. Keep warm.

4 For the filling, put the aubergine in a colander and sprinkle well with salt. Leave to stand on a plate for 30 minutes. Rinse thoroughly and drain well.

5 Put the garlic clove, courgettes, peppers, stock and tomatoes into a large saucepan. Simmer uncovered, stirring occasionally, for 10 minutes. Add the aubergine and cook for a further 15 minutes. Blend the cornflour with 10ml/2 tsp water and stir into the saucepan. Simmer for 2 minutes. Season to taste.

6 Spoon some of the ratatouille mixture into the middle of each pancake. Fold each one in half, then in half again to make a cone shape. Serve hot with a mixed salad.

CONCERTINA GARLIC POTATOES

With a low fat topping these would make a superb meal in themselves or could be enjoyed as a nutritious accompaniment to grilled fish or meat.

─── INGREDIENTS ───

Serves 4
4 baking potatoes
2 garlic cloves, cut into slivers
60ml/4 tbsp low fat fromage frais
60ml/4 tbsp low fat natural yogurt
30ml/2 tbsp snipped chives
6–8 watercress sprigs, finely chopped
  (optional)

─── NUTRITION NOTES ───

Per portion:
Energy   195Kcals/815kJ
Fat   3.5g
Saturated Fat   2g
Cholesterol   10mg

1 Preheat the oven to 200°C/400°F/ Gas 6. Slice each potato at about 5mm/¹⁄₄in intervals, cutting not quite to the base, so that they retain their shape. Slip the slivers of the garlic between the cuts in the potatoes.

2 Place the garlic-filled potatoes in a roasting tin and bake for 1–1¹⁄₄ hours or until soft when tested with a knife. Meanwhile, mix the low fat fromage frais and yogurt in a bowl, then stir in the snipped chives, along with the watercress, if using.

3 Serve the baked potatoes on individual plates, with a dollop of the yogurt and fromage frais mixture on top of each.

COOK'S TIP
The most suitable potatoes for baking are of the floury variety. Some of the best include Estima, Cara and Kerr's Pink.

POTATO, LEEK AND TOMATO BAKE

─── INGREDIENTS ───

Serves 4
675g/1¹⁄₂lb potatoes
2 leeks, sliced
3 large tomatoes, sliced
a few fresh rosemary sprigs, crushed
1 garlic clove, crushed
300ml/¹⁄₂ pint/1¹⁄₄ cups vegetable stock
15ml/1 tbsp olive oil
salt and black pepper

─── NUTRITION NOTES ───

Per portion:
Energy   180Kcals/740kJ
Fat   3.5g
Saturated Fat   0.5g
Cholesterol   0

1 Preheat the oven to 180°C/350°F/ Gas 4 and grease a 1.2 litre/ 2 pint/5 cup shallow ovenproof dish. Scrub and thinly slice the potatoes. Layer them with the leeks and tomatoes in the dish, scattering some rosemary between the layers and ending with a layer of potatoes.

2 Add the garlic to the stock, stir in salt if needed and pepper to taste, then pour over the vegetables. Brush the top layer of potatoes with olive oil.

3 Bake for 1¹⁄₄–1¹⁄₂ hours until the potatoes are tender and the topping is golden and slightly crisp.

MUSHROOM AND OKRA CURRY

This simple but delicious curry with its fresh gingery mango relish is best served with plain basmati rice.

INGREDIENTS

Serves 4

4 garlic cloves, roughly chopped
2.5cm/1in piece fresh root ginger, peeled and roughly chopped
1–2 red chillies, seeded and chopped
175ml/6fl oz/³⁄₄ cup water
15ml/1 tbsp sunflower oil
5ml/1 tsp coriander seeds
5ml/1 tsp cumin seeds
5ml/1 tsp ground cumin
2 cardamom pods, seeds removed and crushed
pinch of ground turmeric
400g/14oz can chopped tomatoes
450g/1lb mushrooms, quartered if large
225g/8oz okra, trimmed and cut into 1cm/¹⁄₂in slices
30ml/2 tbsp chopped fresh coriander
basmati rice, to serve

For the mango relish
1 large ripe mango, about 500g/1¹⁄₄lb
1 small garlic clove, crushed
1 onion, finely chopped
10ml/2 tsp grated fresh root ginger
1 fresh red chilli, seeded and finely chopped
pinch of salt and sugar

1 For the mango relish, peel the mango and then cut off the fruit from the stone. Put the mango into a bowl and mash with a fork, or use a food processor.

2 Add the rest of the relish ingredients to the mango, mix well and set aside.

3 Place the garlic, ginger, chillies and 45ml/3 tbsp of the water into a blender and blend until smooth. Heat the oil in a large pan. Add the coriander and cumin seeds and allow them to sizzle for a few seconds, then add the ground cumin, cardamom seeds and turmeric and cook for 1 minute more.

4 Add the paste from the blender, the tomatoes, remaining water, mushrooms and okra. Stir and bring to the boil. Reduce the heat, cover and simmer for 5 minutes. Uncover, turn up the heat slightly and cook for another 5–10 minutes until the okra is tender. Stir in the fresh coriander and serve with rice and the mango relish.

NUTRITION NOTES	
Per portion:	
Energy	139Kcals/586kJ
Fat	4.6g
Saturated Fat	0.63g
Cholesterol	0
Fibre	6.96g

TOFU AND GREEN BEAN CURRY

This exotic curry is simple and quick to make. This recipe uses beans and mushrooms, but you can use almost any kind of vegetable such as aubergines, bamboo shoots or broccoli.

INGREDIENTS

Serves 4

350ml/12fl oz/1½ cups coconut milk
15ml/1 tbsp red curry paste
45ml/3 tbsp fish sauce
10ml/2 tsp sugar
225g/8oz button mushrooms
115g/4oz French beans, trimmed
175g/6oz bean curd, rinsed and cut
    into 2cm/¾in cubes
4 kaffir lime leaves, torn
2 red chillies, seeded and sliced
coriander leaves, to garnish

NUTRITION NOTES

Per portion:

Energy	100Kcals/420kJ
Fat	3.36g
Saturated Fat	0.48g
Cholesterol	0
Fibre	1.35g

1 Put about one third of the coconut milk in a wok or saucepan. Cook until it starts to separate and an oily sheen appears.

2 Add the red curry paste, fish sauce and sugar to the coconut milk. Mix together thoroughly.

3 Add the mushrooms. Stir and cook for 1 minute.

4 Stir in the rest of the coconut milk and bring back to the boil.

COOK'S TIP
Use 5–10ml/1–2 tsp hot chilli powder, if fresh red chillies aren't available. When preparing fresh chillies, wear rubber gloves and wash hands, work surfaces and utensils thoroughly afterwards. Chillies contain volatile oils which can irritate and burn sensitive areas, especially eyes.

5 Add the French beans and cubes of bean curd and simmer gently for another 4–5 minutes.

6 Stir in the kaffir lime leaves and chillies. Serve garnished with the coriander leaves.

VEGETARIAN CASSOULET

Every town in south-west France has its own version of this popular classic. Warm French bread is all that you need to accompany this hearty low fat vegetable version.

INGREDIENTS

Serves 4–6

400g/14oz/2 cups dried haricot beans
1 bay leaf
2 onions
3 whole cloves
2 garlic cloves, crushed
5ml/1 tsp olive oil
2 leeks, thickly sliced
12 baby carrots
115g/4oz button mushrooms
400g/14oz can chopped tomatoes
15ml/1 tbsp tomato purée
5ml/1 tsp paprika
15ml/1 tbsp chopped fresh thyme
30ml/2 tbsp chopped fresh parsley
115g/4oz/2 cups fresh white
  breadcrumbs
salt and black pepper

NUTRITION NOTES

Per portion:	
Energy	325Kcals/1378kJ
Fat	3.08g
Saturated Fat	0.46g
Cholesterol	0
Fibre	15.68g

COOK'S TIP
If you're short of time, use canned haricot beans – you'll need two 400g/14oz cans. Drain, reserving the bean juices and make up to 400ml/14fl oz/1²/₃ cups with vegetable stock.

1 Soak the beans overnight in plenty of cold water. Drain and rinse under cold running water. Put them in a saucepan with 1.75 litres/3 pints/7½ cups of cold water and the bay leaf. Bring to the boil and cook rapidly for 10 minutes.

2 Peel one of the onions and spike with the cloves. Add to the beans, then reduce the heat. Cover and simmer gently for 1 hour, until the beans are almost tender. Drain, reserving the stock but discarding the bay leaf and onion.

3 Chop the remaining onion and put it into a large flameproof casserole together with the crushed garlic and olive oil. Cook gently for 5 minutes, or until softened.

4 Preheat the oven to 160°C/325°F/Gas 3. Add the leeks, carrots, mushrooms, chopped tomatoes, tomato purée, paprika and thyme to the casserole, then pour in about 400ml/14fl oz/1²/₃ cups of the reserved stock.

5 Bring to the boil, cover and simmer gently for 10 minutes. Stir in the cooked beans and parsley. Season to taste with salt and pepper.

6 Sprinkle the breadcrumbs over the top and bake uncovered for 35 minutes or until the topping is golden brown and crisp.

Vegetable Ribbons

This may just tempt a few fussy eaters to eat up their vegetables!

Ingredients

Serves 4

3 medium carrots
3 medium courgettes
120ml/4 fl oz/½ cup chicken stock
30ml/2 tbsp chopped fresh parsley
salt and black pepper

1 Using a vegetable peeler or sharp knife, cut the carrots and courgettes into thin ribbons.

2 Bring the stock to the boil in a large saucepan and add the carrots. Return the stock to the boil, then add the courgettes. Boil rapidly for 2–3 minutes, or until the vegetable ribbons are just tender.

3 Stir in the parsley, season lightly and serve hot.

Nutrition Notes

Per portion:

Energy	35Kcals/144kJ
Fat	0.53g
Saturated fat	0.09g
Cholesterol	0
Fibre	2.19g

Veggie Burgers

Ingredients

Serves 4

115g/4oz cup mushrooms, finely chopped
1 small onion, chopped
1 small courgette, chopped
1 carrot, chopped
25g/1oz unsalted peanuts or cashews
115g/4oz/2 cups fresh breadcrumbs
30ml/2 tbsp chopped fresh parsley
5ml/1 tsp yeast extract
salt and black pepper
fine oatmeal or flour, for shaping

1 Cook the mushrooms in a non-stick pan without oil, stirring, for 8–10 minutes to drive off all the moisture.

2 Process the onion, courgette, carrot and nuts in a food processor until beginning to bind together.

3 Stir in the mushrooms, breadcrumbs, parsley, yeast extract and seasoning to taste. With the oatmeal or flour, shape into four burgers. Chill.

4 Cook the burgers in a non-stick frying pan with very little oil or under a hot grill for 8–10 minutes, turning once, until the burgers are cooked and golden brown. Serve hot with a crisp salad.

Nutrition Notes

Per portion:

Energy	126Kcals/530kJ
Fat	3.8g
Saturated fat	0.73g
Cholesterol	0
Fibre	2.21g

CRACKED WHEAT AND FENNEL

This salad incorporates both sweet and savoury flavours. It can be served either as a side-dish or as a starter with warm pitta bread.

INGREDIENTS

Serves 4

115g/4oz/¼ cup cracked wheat
1 large fennel bulb, finely chopped
115g/4oz green beans, chopped and blanched
1 small orange
1 garlic clove, crushed
30ml/2 tbsp sunflower oil
15ml/1 tbsp white wine vinegar
salt and black pepper
½ red or orange pepper, seeded and finely chopped, to garnish

NUTRITION NOTES

Per portion:
Energy   180Kcals/755kJ
Fat   6.32 g
Saturated fat   0.8g
Cholesterol   0
Fibre   2.31g

1 Place the wheat in a bowl and cover with boiling water. Leave for about 10–15 minutes. Drain well and squeeze out any excess water.

2 While still slightly warm, stir in the chopped fennel and green beans. Finely grate the orange rind into a bowl. Peel and segment the orange and stir into the salad.

3 Add the crushed garlic to the orange rind, then add the sunflower oil, white wine vinegar, and seasoning to taste, and mix thoroughly. Pour the dressing over the salad, mix well. Chill the salad for 1–2 hours.

4 Serve the salad sprinkled with the chopped red or orange pepper.

COOK'S TIP
When buying green beans, choose young, crisp ones.

PROVENÇAL PAN BAGNA

A wholemeal French baguette, filled with salad and sardines, provides protein, fibre, vitamins and minerals and gives a completely new meaning to the term "packed lunch".

INGREDIENTS

Serves 4

1 wholemeal baguette or 3 large
    wholemeal rolls
2 garlic cloves, crushed
45ml/3 tbsp olive oil
1 small onion, thinly sliced
2 tomatoes, sliced
7.5cm/3in length of cucumber, sliced
115g/4oz canned sardines in
    tomato sauce
30ml/2 tbsp chopped fresh parsley
ground black pepper

1 Cut the baguette into three equal pieces, then slice each piece in half lengthways. If using rolls, split them in half. Squash down the crumb on the inside of the bread to make a shallow hollow for the filling. Mix the garlic with the oil, then brush over the inside of the bread.

2 Lay slices of onion, tomato and cucumber on one half of the bread. Top with the sardines in tomato sauce. If you are concerned about the bones in the fish, you could slice open the sardines and remove the larger pieces, but it makes sound nutritional sense to leave them, as they are edible and are an excellent source of calcium.

3 Sprinkle the parsley over the fish and season with pepper. Sandwich the bread halves back together and wrap tightly in foil or clear film. Chill for at least 30 minutes before eating.

NUTRITION NOTES	
Per portion:	
Energy	320Kcals/1340KJ
Fat	17.5g
Saturated Fat	3.5g
Cholesterol	30.5mg

MASALA MASHED POTATOES

These potatoes are very versatile and will perk up any meal.

INGREDIENTS

Serves 4

3 potatoes
15ml/1 tbsp chopped fresh mint and
    coriander, mixed
5ml/1 tsp mango powder
5ml/1 tsp salt
5ml/1 tsp crushed black peppercorns
1 red chilli, chopped
1 green chilli, chopped
50g/2oz/4 tbsp low fat margarine

NUTRITION NOTES

Per portion:
Energy	94Kcals/394kJ
Fat	5.8g
Saturated fat	1.25g
Cholesterol	0.84mg

1 Place the potatoes in a large saucepan and cover with water. Bring to the boil and cook until soft enough to be mashed. Drain, then mash well.

2 Blend together the mint, coriander, mango powder, salt, peppercorns, chillies and margarine in a small bowl.

3 Stir the mixture into the mashed potatoes and stir together thoroughly with a fork.

4 Serve warm as an accompaniment to meat or vegetarian dishes.

COOK'S TIP
Mango powder is available in specialist Indian shops.

SPICY CABBAGE

An excellent vegetable accompaniment, this dish can also be served as a warm side salad.

INGREDIENTS

Serves 4

50g/2oz/4 tbsp low fat margarine
2.5ml/½ tsp white cumin seeds
3–8 dried red chillies, to taste
1 small onion, sliced
225g/8oz/2½ cups shredded cabbage
2 carrots, grated
2.5ml/½ tsp salt
30ml/2 tbsp lemon juice

NUTRITION NOTES

Per portion:
Energy	92Kcals/384kJ
Fat	6.06g
Saturated fat	1.28g
Cholesterol	0.84mg

1 Melt the low fat margarine in a medium saucepan and fry the white cumin seeds and dried red chillies for about 30 seconds.

2 Add the sliced onion and fry for about 2 minutes. Add the cabbage and carrots, and stir-fry for a further 5 minutes or until the cabbage is soft.

3 Finally, stir in the salt and lemon juice, and serve either hot or warm.

RED CABBAGE IN PORT AND RED WINE

A sweet and sour, spicy red cabbage dish, with the added crunch of walnuts.

INGREDIENTS

Serves 6

15ml/1 tbsp walnut oil
1 onion, sliced
2 whole star anise
5ml/1 tsp ground cinnamon
pinch of ground cloves
450g/1 lb/5 cups, finely shredded red
  cabbage
30ml/2 tbsp dark brown sugar
45ml/3 tbsp red wine vinegar
300ml/½ pint/1¼ cups red wine
150ml/¼ pint/⅔ cup port
2 pears, cut into 1cm/½ in cubes
115g/4oz/⅔ cup raisins
115g/4oz/½ cup walnut halves
salt and black pepper

NUTRITION NOTES

Per portion:

Energy	336Kcals/1409kJ
Fat	15.41g
Saturated fat	1.58g
Cholesterol	0
Fibre	4.31g

1 Heat the oil in a large flameproof casserole. Add the onion and cook gently for about 5 minutes until softened.

2 Add the star anise, cinnamon, cloves and cabbage, and cook for a further 3 minutes.

3 Stir in the sugar, vinegar, red wine and port. Cover the pan and simmer gently for a further 10 minutes, stirring occasionally.

4 Stir in the cubed pears and raisins, and cook for a further 10 minutes or until the cabbage is tender. Season to taste. Mix in the walnut halves and serve immediately.

> **COOK'S TIP**
> If you are unable to buy prepackaged walnut halves, buy whole ones and cut them in half.

CRUSTY LEEK AND CARROT GRATIN

Tender leeks are mixed with a creamy caraway sauce and given a crunchy carrot topping.

---------- INGREDIENTS ----------

Serves 4–6

675g/1½ lb leeks, cut into 5cm/2 in
  pieces
150ml/¼ pint/⅔ cup vegetable stock or
  water
45ml/3 tbsp dry white wine
5ml/1 tsp caraway seeds
pinch of salt
275ml/10fl oz/1¼ cups skimmed milk,
  or as required
25g/1oz/2 tbsp sunflower margarine
25g/1oz/¼ cup plain flour

For the topping

115g/4oz/2 cups fresh wholemeal
  breadcrumbs
15g/4oz/2 cups grated carrot
30ml/2 tbsp chopped fresh parsley
75g/3oz/¾ cup coarsely grated Edam
30ml/2 tbsp flaked almonds

------ NUTRITION NOTES ------	
Per portion:	
Energy	314Kcals/1320kJ
Fat	15.42g
Saturated fat	6.75g
Cholesterol	30.75mg
Fibre	6.98g

1 Place the leeks in a large saucepan and add the stock or water, wine, caraway seeds and salt. Bring to a simmer, cover and cook for about 5–7 minutes until the leeks are just tender.

2 With a slotted spoon, transfer the leeks to an ovenproof dish. Boil the remaining liquid to half the original volume, then make up to 350ml/ 12fl oz/1½ cups with skimmed milk.

3 Preheat the oven to 180°C/350°F/ Gas 4. Melt the sunflower margarine in a flameproof casserole, stir in the flour and cook without allowing it to colour for about 1–2 minutes. Gradually add the stock and milk, stirring well after each addition, until you have a smooth sauce.

4 Simmer the sauce for about 5–6 minutes, stirring constantly until thickened and smooth, then pour the sauce over the leeks in the dish.

5 For the topping, mix all the ingredients together in a bowl and sprinkle over the leeks. Bake for about 20–25 minutes until golden.

SPICY JACKET POTATOES

INGREDIENTS

Serves 2–4
2 large baking potatoes
5ml/1 tsp sunflower oil
1 small onion, finely chopped
2.5cm/1in piece fresh ginger root, grated
5ml/1 tsp ground cumin
5ml/1 tsp ground coriander
2.5ml/½ tsp ground turmeric
garlic salt
natural yogurt and fresh coriander
    sprigs, to serve

1 Preheat the oven to 190°C/375°F/ Gas 5. Prick the potatoes with a fork. Bake for 40 minutes, or until soft.

2 Cut the potatoes in half and scoop out the flesh. Heat the oil in a non-stick pan and fry the onion for a few minutes to soften. Stir in the ginger, cumin, coriander and turmeric.

3 Stir over a low heat for about 2 minutes, then add the potato flesh, and garlic salt, to taste.

4 Cook the potato mixture for a further 2 minutes, stirring occasionally. Spoon the mixture back into the potato shells and top each with a spoonful of natural yogurt and a sprig or two of fresh coriander. Serve hot.

NUTRITION NOTES

Per portion:
Energy	212Kcals/890kJ
Fat	2.54g
Saturated fat	0.31g
Cholesterol	0.4mg
Fibre	3.35g

TWO BEANS PROVENÇAL

INGREDIENTS

Serves 4
5ml/1 tsp olive oil
1 small onion, finely chopped
1 garlic clove, crushed
225g/8oz French beans
225g/8oz runner beans
2 tomatoes, skinned and chopped
salt and black pepper

NUTRITION NOTES

Per portion:
Energy	68Kcals/286kJ
Fat	1.76g
Saturated fat	0.13g
Cholesterol	0
Fibre	5.39g

1 Heat the oil in a heavy-based, or non-stick, pan and sauté the chopped onion over a medium heat until softened but not browned.

2 Add the garlic, the French and runner beans and the tomatoes, then season well and cover tightly.

3 Cook over a fairly low heat, shaking the pan occasionally, for about 30 minutes, or until the beans are tender. Serve hot.

SPRING VEGETABLE STIR-FRY

A colourful, dazzling medley of
fresh, delicious and sweet young
vegetables.

INGREDIENTS

Serves 4
15ml/1 tbsp groundnut oil
1 garlic clove, sliced
2.5cm/1 in piece fresh root ginger,
 finely chopped
115g/4oz/2 cups baby carrots
115g/4oz patty-pan squash
115g/4oz/1¼ cups baby corn
115g/4oz green beans, topped and
 tailed
115g/4oz/1¼ cups sugar-snap peas,
 topped and tailed
115g/4oz young asparagus, cut into
 7.5cm/3 in pieces
8 spring onions, trimmed and cut into
 5cm/2 in pieces
115g/4oz cherry tomatoes

For the dressing
juice of 2 limes
15ml/1 tbsp clear honey
15ml/1 tbsp soy sauce
5ml/1 tsp sesame oil

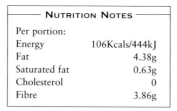

NUTRITION NOTES	
Per portion:	
Energy	106Kcals/444kJ
Fat	4.38g
Saturated fat	0.63g
Cholesterol	0
Fibre	3.86g

1 Heat the groundnut oil in a wok or
large frying pan. Add the garlic and
ginger and stir-fry for about 1 minute.

2 Add the carrots, patty-pan squash,
baby corn and beans, and stir-fry
for a further 3–4 minutes.

3 Add the sugar-snap peas, asparagus,
spring onions and cherry tomatoes,
and stir-fry for a further 1–2 minutes.

4 For the dressing, mix all the ingredients together and add to the pan.

5 Stir well then cover the pan. Cook
for 2–3 minutes more until the
vegetables are just tender but still crisp.

BEETROOT AND CELERIAC GRATIN

INGREDIENTS

Serves 6
350g/12oz raw beetroot
350g/12oz celeriac
4 thyme sprigs
6 juniper berries, crushed
120ml/4fl oz/½ cup fresh orange juice
120ml/4fl oz/½ cup vegetable stock
salt and black pepper

NUTRITION NOTES

Per portion:	
Energy	37Kcals/157kJ
Fat	0.31g
Saturated fat	0
Cholesterol	0
Fibre	3.28g

1 Preheat the oven to 190°C/375°F/ Gas 5. Peel and slice the beetroot very finely. Quarter and peel the celeriac and slice very finely.

2 Fill a 25cm/10 in diameter cast iron or ovenproof frying pan with layers of beetroot and celeriac slices, sprinkling with the thyme, juniper and seasoning between each layer.

3 Mix the orange juice and stock together and pour over the gratin. Place over a medium heat and bring to the boil. Boil for about 2 minutes.

4 Cover with foil and place in the oven for about 15–20 minutes. Remove the foil and raise the oven temperature to 200°C/400°F/Gas 6. Cook for a further 10 minutes until tender. Serve garnished with a few extra crushed juniper berries and a sprig of thyme, if you like.

BOMBAY SPICED POTATOES

This Indian potato dish uses a wonderfully aromatic mixture of whole and ground spices. Look out for mustard and black onion seeds in specialist food shops.

INGREDIENTS

Serves 4

4 large potatoes, cut into chunks
60ml/4 tbsp sunflower oil
1 garlic clove, finely chopped
10ml/2 tsp brown mustard seeds
5ml/1 tsp black onion seeds (optional)
5ml/1 tsp turmeric
5ml/1 tsp ground cumin
5ml/1 tsp ground coriander
5ml/1 tsp fennel seeds
good squeeze of lemon juice
salt and black pepper
chopped fresh coriander and lemon
   wedges, to garnish

1 Bring a saucepan of salted water to the boil, add the potatoes and simmer for about 4 minutes, until just tender. Drain well.

2 Heat the oil in a large frying pan and add the garlic along with all the whole and ground spices. Fry gently for about 1–2 minutes, stirring until the mustard seeds start to pop.

3 Add the potatoes and stir-fry over a moderate heat for about 5 minutes, until heated through and well coated with the spicy oil.

4 Season well and sprinkle over the lemon juice. Garnish with chopped coriander and lemon wedges. Serve as an accompaniment to curries or other strong-flavoured dishes.

NUTRITION NOTES

Per portion:

Energy	373kcals/1149kJ
Fat	12.49g
Saturated fat	1.49g
Cholesterol	0
Fibre	2.65g

SPANISH CHILLI POTATOES

INGREDIENTS

Serves 4

1kg/2¼lb new or salad potatoes
60ml/2 tbsp olive oil
1 onion, finely chopped
2 garlic cloves, crushed
15ml/1 tbsp tomato purée
200g/7oz can chopped tomatoes
15ml/1 tbsp red wine vinegar
2–3 small dried red chillies, seeded and
   finely chopped, or 5–10ml/1–2 tsp
   hot chilli powder
5ml/1 tsp paprika
salt and black pepper
flat leaf parsley sprig, to garnish

NUTRITION NOTES

Per portion:

Energy	301Kcals/1266kJ
Fat	12.02g
Saturated fat	1.6g
Cholesterol	0
Fibre	3.54g

1 Halve the potatoes if large, then place in a large saucepan and cover with water. Bring to the boil, then simmer for about 10–12 minutes or until just tender. Drain well and leave to cool, then cut in half and reserve.

2 Heat the oil in a large pan and add the onions and garlic. Fry gently for about 5–6 minutes, until just softened. Stir in the next five ingredients, and simmer for about 5 minutes.

3 Add the potatoes and mix into the sauce mixture until well coated. Cover and simmer gently for about 8–10 minutes, or until the potatoes are tender. Season well and transfer to a warmed serving dish. Serve garnished with a sprig of flat leaf parsley.

BROCCOLI CAULIFLOWER GRATIN

Broccoli and cauliflower make an attractive combination, and this dish is much lighter than a classic cauliflower cheese.

INGREDIENTS

Serves 4
1 small cauliflower (about 250g/9oz)
1 small head broccoli (about 250g/9oz)
150g/5oz/½ cup natural low fat yogurt
75g/3oz/1 cup grated reduced fat
 Cheddar cheese
5ml/1 tsp wholegrain mustard
30ml/2 tbsp wholemeal breadcrumbs
salt and black pepper

1 Break the cauliflower and broccoli into florets and cook in lightly salted, boiling water for 8–10 minutes, until just tender. Drain well and transfer to a flameproof dish.

2 Mix together the yogurt, grated cheese and mustard, then season the mixture with pepper and spoon over the cauliflower and broccoli.

3 Sprinkle the breadcrumbs over the top and place under a moderately hot grill until golden brown. Serve hot.

COOK'S TIP
When preparing the cauliflower and broccoli, discard the tougher part of the stalk, then break the florets into even-sized pieces, so they cook evenly.

NUTRITION NOTES

Per portion:
Energy	144Kcals/601kJ
Fat	6.5g
Saturated fat	3.25g
Cholesterol	16.5mg
Fibre	3.25g

MUSHROOM AND FENNEL HOTPOT

Marvellous flavours permeate this unusual vegetarian main course or accompaniment. Mushrooms provide useful amounts of vitamins, minerals and fibre.

INGREDIENTS

Serves 4

25g/1oz dried shiitake mushrooms
1 small head of fennel or 4 celery sticks
30ml/2 tbsp olive oil
12 shallots, peeled
225g/8oz/2 cups button mushrooms, trimmed and halved
300ml/½ pint/1¼ cups dry cider
25g/1oz sun-dried tomatoes
30ml/2 tbsp sun-dried tomato paste
1 bay leaf
chopped fresh parsley, to garnish

1 Place the dried mushrooms in a bowl. Pour over boiling water to cover and set aside for 10 minutes.

2 Roughly chop the fennel or celery sticks and heat the oil in a flame-proof casserole. Add the shallots and fennel or celery and sauté for about 10 minutes over a moderate heat until the mixture is softened and lightly browned. Add the button mushrooms and fry for 2–3 minutes.

3 Drain the dried mushrooms, reserving the liquid. Cut up any large pieces and add to the pan.

NUTRITION NOTES

Per portion:

Energy	170Kcals/715KJ
Fat	11.5g
Saturated Fat	1.5g
Cholesterol	0

4 Pour in the cider and stir in the sun-dried tomatoes and the paste. Add the bay leaf. Bring to the boil, then lower the heat, cover the casserole and simmer gently for about 30 minutes.

5 If the mixture seems dry, stir in the reserved liquid from the soaked mushrooms. Reheat briefly, then remove the bay leaf and serve, sprinkled with plenty of chopped parsley.

Middle-Eastern Vegetable Stew

A spiced dish of mixed vegetables which can be served as a side dish or as a vegetarian main course. Children may prefer less chilli.

— Ingredients —

Serves 4–6
45ml/3 tbsp vegetable or chicken stock
1 green pepper, seeded and sliced
2 medium courgettes, sliced
2 medium carrots, sliced
2 celery sticks, sliced
2 medium potatoes, diced
400g/14oz can chopped tomatoes
5ml/1 tsp chilli powder
30ml/2 tbsp chopped fresh mint
15ml/1 tbsp ground cumin
400g/14oz can chick-peas, drained
salt and black pepper
mint sprigs, to garnish

1 Heat the vegetable or chicken stock in a large flameproof casserole until boiling, then add the sliced pepper, courgettes, carrot and celery. Stir over a high heat for 2–3 minutes, until the vegetables are just beginning to soften.

2 Add the potatoes, tomatoes, chilli powder, mint and cumin. Add the chick-peas and bring to the boil.

3 Reduce the heat, cover the casserole and simmer for 30 minutes, or until all the vegetables are tender. Season to taste with salt and pepper and serve hot garnished with mint leaves.

Cook's Tip
Chick-peas are traditional in this type of Middle-Eastern dish, but if you prefer, red kidney beans or haricot beans can be used instead.

— Nutrition Notes —

Per portion:
Energy	168Kcals/703kJ
Fat	3.16g
Saturated fat	0.12g
Cholesterol	0
Fibre	6.13g

SUMMER VEGETABLE BRAISE

Tender, young vegetables are ideal for quick cooking in a minimum of liquid. Use any mixture of the family's favourite vegetables, as long as they are of similar size.

INGREDIENTS

Serves 4

175g/6oz/2½ cups baby carrots
175g/6oz/2 cups sugar-snap peas or
*   mangetout*
115g/4oz/1¼ cups baby corn cobs
90ml/6 tbsp vegetable stock
10ml/2 tsp lime juice
salt and black pepper
chopped fresh parsley parsley and
*   snipped fresh chives, to garnish*

1 Place the carrots, peas and baby corn cobs in a large heavy-based saucepan with the vegetable stock and lime juice. Bring to the boil.

2 Cover the pan and reduce the heat, then simmer for 6–8 minutes, shaking the pan occasionally, until the vegetables are just tender.

3 Season the vegetables to taste with salt and pepper, then stir in the chopped fresh parsley and snipped fresh chives. Cook the vegetables for a few seconds more, stirring them once or twice until the herbs are well mixed, then serve at once with grilled lamb chops or roast chicken.

COOK'S TIP
You can make this dish in the winter too, but cut larger, tougher vegetables into chunks and cook for slightly longer.

NUTRITION NOTES

Per portion:
Energy	36Kcals/152kJ
Fat	0.45g
Saturated fat	0
Cholesterol	0
Fibre	2.35g

NEW POTATO PARCELS

These delicious potatoes may be cooked in individual portions.

INGREDIENTS

Serves 4
16–20 very small potatoes in their skins
45ml/3 tbsp olive oil
1–2 sprigs each of thyme, tarragon and oregano, or 15ml/1 tbsp mixed dried herbs
salt and black pepper

NUTRITION NOTES

Per portion:

Energy	206Kcals/866kJ
Fat	11.49g
Saturated fat	1.54g
Cholesterol	0
Fibre	1.5g

1 Preheat the oven to 200°C/400°F/ Gas 6. Grease one large sheet or four small sheets of foil.

2 Put the potatoes in a large bowl and add in the rest of the ingredients and seasoning. Mix well so the potatoes are thoroughly coated.

3 Put the potatoes on the foil and seal up the parcel(s). Place on a baking sheet and bake for about 40–50 minutes. The potatoes will stay warm for quite some time if left wrapped up.

COOK'S TIP
This dish can also be cooked on a barbecue, if you like.

STIR-FRIED FLORETS WITH HAZELNUTS

INGREDIENTS

Serves 4
175g/6oz/1½ cups cauliflower florets
175g/6oz/1½ cups broccoli florets
15ml/1 tbsp sunflower oil
25g/1oz/¼ cup hazelnuts, finely chopped
¼ red chilli, finely chopped, or 5ml/ 1 tsp chilli powder (optional)
60ml/4 tbsp very low fat crème fraîche or fromage frais
salt and black pepper
a little paprika, to garnish

NUTRITION NOTES

Per portion:

Energy	146Kcals/614kJ
Fat	11.53g
Saturated fat	0.94g
Cholesterol	0.15mg
Fibre	2.84g

1 Make sure the cauliflower and broccoli florets are all of an even size. Heat the oil in a saucepan or wok and toss the florets over a high heat for 1 minute.

2 Reduce the heat and continue stir-frying for another 5 minutes, then add the hazelnuts, chilli, if using, and seasoning to taste.

3 Fry the cauliflower and broccoli florets until crisp and nearly tender, then stir in the crème fraîche or fromage frais and just heat through. Serve at once, sprinkled with the paprika.

COOK'S TIP
The crisper these florets are the better, so cook them just long enough to make them piping hot, and give them time to absorb all the flavours.

ROSEMARY ROASTIES

These unusual roast potatoes use far less fat than traditional roast potatoes, and because they still have their skins they not only absorb less oil but have more flavour too.

INGREDIENTS

Serves 4

1kg/2 lb small red potatoes
10ml/2 tsp walnut or sunflower oil
30ml/2 tbsp fresh rosemary leaves
salt and paprika

1 Preheat the oven to 240°C/475°F/ Gas 9. Leave the potatoes whole with the peel on, or if large, cut in half. Place the potatoes in a large pan of cold water and bring to the boil. Drain well.

2 Drizzle the walnut or sunflower oil over the potatoes and shake the pan to coat them evenly.

3 Tip the potatoes into a shallow roasting tin. Sprinkle with rosemary, salt and paprika. Roast for 30 minutes or until crisp. Serve hot.

NUTRITION NOTES

Per portion:

Energy	205Kcals/865kJ
Fat	2.22g
Saturated fat	0.19g
Cholesterol	0
Fibre	3.25g

BAKED COURGETTES IN PASSATA

INGREDIENTS

Serves 4

5ml/1 tsp olive oil
3 large courgettes, thinly sliced
½ small red onion, finely chopped
300ml/½ pint/1¼ cups passata
30ml/2 tbsp chopped fresh thyme
garlic salt and black pepper
fresh thyme sprigs, to garnish

1 Preheat the oven to 190°C/375°F/ Gas 5. Brush an ovenproof dish with olive oil. Arrange half the courgettes and onion in the dish.

2 Spoon half the passata over the vegetables and sprinkle with some of the fresh thyme, then season to taste with garlic salt and pepper.

3 Arrange the remaining courgettes and onion in the dish on top of the passata, then season to taste with more garlic salt and pepper. Spoon over the remaining passata and spread evenly.

4 Cover the dish with foil, then bake for 40–45 minutes, or until the courgettes are tender. Garnish with sprigs of thyme and serve hot.

NUTRITION NOTES

Per portion:

Energy	49Kcals/205kJ
Fat	1.43g
Saturated fat	0.22g
Cholesterol	0
Fibre	1.73g

CHINESE SPROUTS

If you are bored with plain boiled Brussels sprouts, try pepping them up with this unusual stir-fried method, which uses the minimum of oil.

─────── INGREDIENTS ───────

Serves 4

1 lb Brussels sprouts, shredded
1 tsp sesame or sunflower oil
2 scallions, sliced
½ tsp Chinese five-spice powder
1 tbsp light soy sauce

1 Trim the Brussels sprouts, then shred them finely using a large sharp knife or shred in a food processor.

2 Heat the oil and add the sprouts and onions, then stir-fry for about 2 minutes, without browning.

3 Stir in the five-spice powder and soy sauce, then cook, stirring, for 2–3 minutes more, until just tender.

4 Serve hot, with broiled meats or fish, or Chinese dishes.

COOK'S TIP
Brussels sprouts are rich in Vitamin C, and this is a good way to cook them to preserve the vitamins. Larger sprouts cook particularly well by this method, and cabbage can also be cooked this way.

─────── NUTRITION NOTES ───────

Per portion:

Energy	58Kcals/243kJ
Fat	2.38g
Saturated fat	0.26g
Cholesterol	0
Fiber	4.67g

LEMONY VEGETABLE PARCELS

ves 4
edium carrots
nall rutabaga
rge parsnip
ek, sliced
ly grated rind of ½ lemon
sp lemon juice
sp whole-grain mustard
sp walnut or sunflower oil
and black pepper

Preheat the oven to 375°F. Peel the root vegetables and cut into ½ in bes. Place in a large bowl, then add sliced leek.

Stir the lemon rind and juice and the mustard into the vegetables and ix well, then season to taste.

3 Cut four 12 in squares of nonstick baking paper and brush them lightly with the oil.

4 Divide the vegetables among them. Roll up the paper from one side, then twist the ends firmly to seal.

5 Place the parcels on a baking sheet and bake for 50–55 minutes, or until the vegetables are just tender. Serve hot, with roast or broiled meats.

NUTRITION NOTES	
Per portion	
Energy	78Kcals/326kJ
Fat	2.06g
Saturated fat	0.08g
Cholesterol	0
Fiber	5.15g

ROOT VEGETABLE CASSEROLE

Potatoes, carrots and parsnips are all complex carbohydrates and make a hearty, sustaining vegetable dish, high in fibre and vitamin C. The carrots are also an excellent source of beta-carotene, which is converted to vitamin A in the body.

INGREDIENTS

Serves 4

225g/8oz carrots
225g/8oz parsnips
15ml/1 tbsp sunflower oil
knob of butter
15ml/1 tbsp demerara sugar
450g/1lb baby new potatoes, scrubbed
225g/8oz small onions, peeled
400ml/14fl oz/1⅔ cup vegetable stock
15ml/1 tbsp Worcestershire sauce
15ml/1 tbsp tomato purée
5ml/1 tsp wholegrain mustard
2 bay leaves
salt and ground black pepper
chopped parsley, to garnish

COOK'S TIP
Other vegetables could be added, such as leeks, mushrooms, sweet potato or celery. When they are in season, shelled chestnuts make a delicious addition.

1 Peel the carrots and parsnips and cut into large chunks.

2 Heat the oil, butter and sugar in a pan. Stir until the sugar dissolves.

3 Add the potatoes, onions, carrots and parsnips. Sauté for 10 minutes until the vegetables look glazed.

NUTRITION NOTES	
Per portion:	
Energy	215Kcals/895KJ
Fat	5.5g
Saturated Fat	1g
Cholesterol	3mg

4 Mix the vegetable stock, Worcestershire sauce, tomato purée and mustard in a jug. Stir well, then pour over the vegetables. Add the bay leaves. Bring to the boil, then lower the heat, cover and cook gently for about 30 minutes until the vegetables are tender.

5 Remove the bay leaves, add salt and pepper to taste and serve, sprinkled with the parsley.

WINTER VEGETABLE STIR-FRY

russels sprouts are not always
opular, but taste absolutely
elicious when steamed and
wiftly stir-fried. As a bonus,
ore of their vitamin B and C
ontent is preserved.

INGREDIENTS

erves 4
50g/12oz Brussels sprouts
 courgettes
5ml/1 tbsp sunflower or nut oil
2 shallots, peeled
 garlic clove, crushed
nall piece of fresh root ginger, peeled
 and finely chopped
5g/1oz/¼ cup walnut pieces

1 If necessary, trim the sprouts and
remove any dirty outside leaves.

2 Cut the courgettes into even-size
diagonal slices.

3 Steam the Brussels sprouts for
about 7–10 minutes, or until they
re just tender. Drain, if necessary, and
set aside.

4 Heat the oil in a frying pan or
wok. Add the shallots and courgettes and stir-fry for 2–3 minutes.

5 Add the sprouts, garlic and ginger
and stir-fry for 2 minutes more.
Scatter over the walnut pieces, toss
them with the vegetable mixture and
serve immediately.

NUTRITION NOTES

Per portion:
Energy	125Kcals/530KJ
Fat	8.5g
Saturated Fat	1g
Cholesterol	0

COOK'S TIP
Choose small, tight Brussels
sprouts which don't need to be
trimmed or have their outside
leaves removed. The darker outside leaves are rich in vitamins
and minerals. Shredded cabbage
could be used instead of Brussels
sprouts, and chestnuts in place of
walnuts. Vacuum-packed chestnuts are cooked and ready to use.

VEGETABLES WITH AROMATIC SEEDS

A healthy diet should include plenty of vegetables to provide fibre as well as vitamins and minerals. Here, spices transform everyday vegetables.

INGREDIENTS

Serves 4

1½ lb small new potatoes
1 small cauliflower
6oz green beans
4oz frozen peas
small piece of fresh ginger root
2 tbsp sunflower oil
2 tsp cumin seeds
2 tsp black mustard seeds
2 tbsp sesame seeds
juice of 1 lemon
ground black pepper
fresh cilantro, to garnish (optional)

1 Scrub the potatoes, cut the cauliflower into small florets, and trim and halve the green beans.

2 Cook the vegetables in separate pans of lightly salted boiling water until tender, allowing, 15–20 minutes for the potatoes, 8–10 minutes for the cauliflower and 4–5 minutes for the beans and peas. Drain thoroughly.

3 Using a small, sharp knife, peel and finely chop the fresh ginger.

4 Heat the oil. Add the ginger and seeds. Fry until they start to pop.

5 Add the vegetables and stir-fry for 2–3 minutes. Sprinkle over the lemon juice and season with pepper. Garnish with cilantro, if using.

> COOK'S TIP
> Other vegetables could be used, such as zucchini, leeks or broccoli. Buy whatever looks freshest and do not store vegetables for long periods as their vitamin content will deteriorate.

NUTRITION NOTES	
Per portion:	
Energy	285Kcals/1200KJ
Fat	12.5g
Saturated Fat	1.5g
Cholesterol	0

Baked Mushrooms with Oat Stuffing

t mushrooms, rich in B-group
amins, have a wonderful
vor and are perfect for this
ty stuffing.

Ingredients

ves 4

sp sunflower oil
arge flat mushrooms, wiped
nion, chopped
arlic clove, crushed
cup rolled oats
z can chopped tomatoes
vith herbs
sp hot pepper sauce
cup pine nuts
cup freshly grated Parmesan
heese
t and ground black pepper

1 Preheat the oven to 375°F. Use a little of the oil to grease a shallow ovenproof dish lightly. The dish should be large enough to hold all the mushroom caps in a single layer. Remove the mushroom stalks, chop them roughly and set them aside. Reserve the whole mushroom caps.

2 Heat the oil in a small saucepan and sauté the onion, garlic and mushroom stalks until softened and lightly browned. Stir in the oats and cook for 1 minute more.

3 Stir in the tomatoes and hot pepper sauce and add salt and pepper to taste. Arrange the mushroom caps, gills uppermost, in the prepared dish. Divide the stuffing mixture among them.

4 Sprinkle the pine nuts and Parmesan cheese over the stuffed mushrooms. Bake for 25 minutes until the mushrooms are tender and the topping is golden brown.

Nutrition Notes	
Per portion:	
Energy	190Kcals/785KJ
Fat	13.5g
Saturated Fat	3g
Cholesterol	6.5mg

MUSHROOM, LEEK AND CASHEW RISOTTO

INGREDIENTS

Serves 4

225g/8oz/1⅓ cups brown rice
900ml/1½ pints/3¾ cups vegetable
  stock or a mixture of stock and dry
  white wine in the ratio 5:1
15ml/1 tbsp walnut or hazelnut oil
2 leeks, sliced
225g/8oz/2 cups mixed wild or
  cultivated mushrooms, trimmed
  and sliced
50g/2oz/½ cup cashew nuts
grated rind of 1 lemon
30ml/2 tbsp chopped fresh thyme
25g/1oz/scant ¼ cup pumpkin seeds
salt and ground black pepper
fresh thyme leaves and lemon wedges,
  to garnish

1 Place the brown rice in a large saucepan, pour in the vegetable stock (or stock and wine), and bring to the boil. Lower the heat and cook gently for about 30 minutes, until all the stock has been absorbed and the rice grains are tender.

2 About 6 minutes before the rice is cooked, heat the oil in a large frying pan, add the leeks and mushrooms and fry over a gentle heat for 3–4 minutes.

3 Add the cashew nuts, lemon rind and chopped thyme to the vegetables and cook for 1–2 minutes more. Season with salt and pepper.

4 Drain off any excess stock from the cooked rice and stir in the vegetable mixture. Turn into a serving dish. Scatter the pumpkin seeds over the top and garnish with the fresh thyme sprigs and lemon wedges. Serve at once.

NUTRITION NOTES

Per portion:

Energy	395Kcals/1645KJ
Fat	14g
Saturated Fat	2.5g
Cholesterol	0

MUSHROOM AND MIXED NUT ROAST

INGREDIENTS

rves 4

ml/3 tbsp sunflower seeds
ml/3 tbsp sesame seeds
ml/2 tbsp sunflower oil, plus extra
for greasing
onion, roughly chopped
celery sticks, roughly chopped
green pepper, seeded and chopped
5g/8oz/2 cups mixed mushrooms,
chopped
garlic clove, crushed
5g/4oz/2 cups fresh wholemeal
breadcrumbs
5g/4oz/1 cup chopped mixed nuts
0g/2oz/¹/₃ cup sultanas
mall piece of fresh root ginger, peeled
and finely chopped
ml/2 tsp coriander seeds, crushed
ml/2 tbsp light soy sauce
egg, beaten
lt and ground black pepper
lery and coriander leaves, to garnish

or the tomato sauce
00g/14oz can chopped tomatoes
spring onions, chopped
ml/2 tbsp chopped fresh coriander

NUTRITION NOTES

Per portion:

Energy	460Kcals/1925KJ
Fat	37.5g
Saturated Fat	4.5g
Cholesterol	53mg

2 Preheat the oven to 190°C/375°F/
Gas 5. Heat the oil in a frying
pan, add the onion, celery, pepper,
mushrooms and garlic and cook over
a gentle heat for about 5 minutes until
the onion has softened.

4 Press the mixture evenly into the
tin and bake for 45 minutes. Make
the sauce. Heat the tomatoes in a small
saucepan, add the spring onions and
fresh coriander and season to taste.

1 Grease and line a 675g/1½lb loaf
tin. Sprinkle the sunflower and
sesame seeds on the base.

3 Mix the breadcrumbs and nuts in a
large bowl. Tip in the contents of
the frying pan, then stir in the sultanas,
ginger, coriander seeds and soy sauce.
Bind with the egg, then season.

5 When the loaf is cooked, loosen it
with a knife, then allow to cool for
a few minutes. Turn out on to a serving
dish and garnish with the celery and
coriander leaves. Serve with the warm
tomato sauce.

SALADS

Salads are healthy and refreshing and can be served either as accompaniments to other dishes or as perfect low fat meals in themselves. Presented here is a wonderful selection of recipes: vegetarian delights include Marinated Cucumber Salad and a fresh, fast and filling Fruit and Fiber Salad; there are fish and seafood dishes, such as Shrimp Noodle Salad and a tasty Thai-style Seafood Salad with Fragrant Herbs; and healthy salads made with grains and rice, such as Bulgur Salad with Oranges and Brown Rice Salad with Fruit, which are hearty enough to serve as a meal on their own.

MARINATED CUCUMBER SALAD

Sprinkling cucumbers with salt draws out some of the water and makes them softer and sweeter.

INGREDIENTS

Serves 6

2 medium cucumbers
15ml/1 tbsp salt
90g/3¹/₂oz/¹/₂ cup granulated sugar
175ml/6fl oz/³/₄ cup dry cider
15ml/1 tbsp cider vinegar
45ml/3 tbsp chopped fresh dill
pinch of pepper

NUTRITION NOTES

Per portion:	
Energy	111Kcals/465kJ
Fat	0.14g
Saturated Fat	0.01g
Fibre	0.62g

1 Slice the cucumbers thinly and place them in a colander, sprinkling salt between each layer. Put the colander over a bowl and leave to drain for 1 hour.

2 Thoroughly rinse the cucumber under cold running water to remove excess salt, then pat dry on absorbent kitchen paper.

COOK'S TIP
As a shortcut, leave out the method for salting cucumber described in step 1.

3 Gently heat the sugar, cider and vinegar in a saucepan, until the sugar has dissolved. Remove from the heat and leave to cool. Put the cucumber slices in a bowl, pour over the cider mixture and leave to marinate for about 2 hours.

4 Drain the cucumber and sprinkle with the dill and pepper to taste. Mix well and transfer to a serving dish. Chill in the fridge until ready to serve.

TURNIP SALAD WITH HORSERADISH

The robust-flavoured turnip partners well with the taste of horseradish and caraway seeds. This salad is delicious with cold roast beef or smoked trout.

INGREDIENTS

Serves 4

350g/12oz medium turnips
2 spring onions, white part only, chopped
15ml/1 tbsp caster sugar
salt
30ml/2 tbsp horseradish cream
10ml/2 tsp caraway seeds

NUTRITION NOTES

Per portion:

Energy	48.25Kcals/204kJ
Fat	1.26g
Saturated Fat	0.09g
Cholesterol	1mg
Fibre	2.37g

1 Peel, slice and shred the turnips – or grate them if you wish.

COOK'S TIP

If turnips are not available, giant white radish (mooli) can be used as a substitute. For extra sweetness, try red onion instead of spring onions.

2 Add the spring onions, sugar and salt, then rub together with your hands to soften the turnip.

3 Fold in the horseradish cream and caraway seeds and serve.

FRUIT AND FIBER SALAD

Fresh, fast and filling, this salad makes a great supper or snack.

————— INGREDIENTS —————

Serves 6
8oz red or white cabbage, or a mixture
   of both
3 medium carrots
1 pear
1 red-skinned eating apple
1 7oz can cannellini beans, drained
¼ cup chopped dates

For the dressing
½ tsp dry English mustard
2 tsp honey
2 tbsp orange juice
1 tsp white wine vinegar
½ tsp paprika
salt and black pepper

1 Shred the cabbage very finely, discarding the core and tough ribs.

2 Cut the carrots into very thin strips, about 2in long.

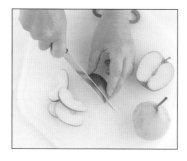

3 Quarter, core and slice the pear and the apple, leaving the peel on.

4 Put the fruit and vegetables in a bowl with the beans and dates. Mix well.

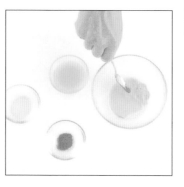

5 To make the dressing, blend the mustard with the honey until smooth. Add the orange juice, vinegar, paprika and seasoning and mix well.

6 Pour the dressing over the salad and toss to coat. Chill in the fridge for 30 minutes before serving.

————— NUTRITION NOTES —————

Per portion:	
Energy	137Kcals/574kJ
Fat	0.87g
Saturated fat	0.03g
Fiber	6.28g

COOK'S TIP

Use other canned beans, such as red kidney beans or chickpeas, in place of the cannellini beans. Add ½ tsp ground spice, such as chili powder, cumin or coriander, for extra flavor. Add 1 tsp finely grated orange or lemon rind to the dressing, for extra flavor.

AUBERGINE SALAD

An appetizing and unusual salad that you will find yourself making over and over again.

INGREDIENTS

Serves 6

2 aubergines
15ml/1 tbsp oil
30ml/2 tbsp dried shrimps, soaked
  and drained
15ml/1 tbsp coarsely chopped garlic
30ml/2 tbsp freshly squeezed lime juice
5ml/1 tsp palm sugar
30ml/2 tbsp fish sauce
1 hard-boiled egg, chopped
4 shallots, thinly sliced into rings
coriander leaves, to garnish
2 red chillies, seeded and sliced,
  to garnish

COOK'S TIP
For an interesting variation, try using salted duck's or quail's eggs, cut in half, instead of chopped hen's eggs.

1 Grill or roast the aubergines until charred and tender.

2 When cool enough to handle, peel away the skin and slice the aubergine into thick pieces.

3 Heat the oil in a small frying pan, add the drained shrimps and the garlic and fry until golden. Remove from the pan and set aside.

4 To make the dressing, put the lime juice, palm sugar and fish sauce in a small bowl and whisk together.

5 To serve, arrange the aubergine on a serving dish. Top with the chopped egg, shallot rings and dried shrimp mixture. Drizzle over the dressing and garnish with coriander and red chillies.

NUTRITION NOTES

Per portion:

Energy	70.5Kcals/295kJ
Fat	3.76g
Saturated Fat	0.68g
Cholesterol	57mg
Fibre	1.20g

BAMBOO SHOOT SALAD

This salad, which has a hot and sharp flavour, originated in north-east Thailand. Use fresh young bamboo shoots if you can find them, otherwise substitute canned bamboo shoots.

—— INGREDIENTS ——

Serves 4

400g/14oz can whole bamboo shoots
25g/1oz glutinous rice
30ml/2 tbsp chopped shallots
15ml/1 tbsp chopped garlic
45ml/3 tbsp chopped spring onions
30ml/2 tbsp fish sauce
30ml/2 tbsp lime juice
5ml/1 tsp granulated sugar
2.5ml/½ tsp dried flaked chillies
20–25 small mint leaves
15ml/1 tbsp toasted sesame seeds

1 Rinse and drain the bamboo shoots, then slice and set aside.

2 Dry roast the rice in a frying pan until it is golden brown. Remove and grind to fine crumbs with a pestle and mortar.

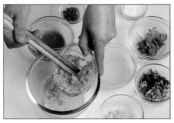

3 Tip the rice into a bowl, add the shallots, garlic, spring onions, fish sauce, lime juice, granulated sugar, chillies and half the mint leaves.

COOK'S TIP
Omit the sesame seeds to reduce calories and fat. Use ready-minced or "lazy" garlic instead of crushing your own.

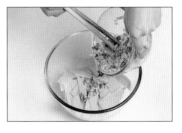

4 Mix thoroughly, then pour over the bamboo shoots and toss together. Serve sprinkled with sesame seeds and the remaining mint leaves.

—— NUTRITION NOTES ——

Per portion:

Energy	73.5Kcals/308kJ
Fat	2.8g
Saturated Fat	0.41g
Cholesterol	0
Fibre	2.45g

BULGUR WHEAT SALAD WITH ORANGES

Bulgur wheat makes an excellent
alternative to rice or pasta.

———————— INGREDIENTS ————————

Serves 6
1 small green pepper
150g/5oz/1 cup bulgur wheat
600ml/1 pint/2½ cups water
½ cucumber, diced
15g/½oz/½ cup chopped fresh mint
40g/1½oz/⅓ cup flaked almonds, toasted
grated rind and juice of 1 lemon
2 seedless oranges
salt and black pepper
mint sprigs, to garnish

1 Using a sharp vegetable knife,
carefully halve and seed the green
pepper. Cut it on a board into small
cubes and put to one side.

2 Place the bulgur wheat in a
saucepan and add the water. Bring
to the boil, lower the heat, cover and
simmer for 10–15 minutes until tender.
Alternatively, place the bulgur wheat in
a heatproof bowl, pour over boiling
water and leave to soak for 30 minutes.
Most, if not all, of the water should be
absorbed; drain off any excess.

3 Toss the bulgur wheat with the
cucumber, green pepper, mint and
toasted almonds in a serving bowl. Add
the grated lemon rind and juice.

4 Cut the rind from the oranges, then
working over the bowl to catch
the juice, cut the oranges into neat
segments. Add to the bulgur mixture,
then season and toss lightly. Garnish
with the mint sprigs.

———— NUTRITION NOTES ————

Per portion:

Energy	160Kcals/672kJ
Fat	4.3g
Saturated Fat	0.33g
Cholesterol	0

BROWN RICE SALAD WITH FRUIT

An Oriental-style dressing gives this colourful rice salad extra piquancy. Whole grains like brown rice are unrefined, so they retain their natural fibre, vitamins and minerals.

INGREDIENTS

Serves 4–6

115g/4oz/²⁄₃ cup brown rice
1 small red pepper, seeded and diced
200g/7oz can sweetcorn niblets, drained
45ml/3 tbsp sultanas
225g/8oz can pineapple pieces in fruit juice
15ml/1 tbsp light soy sauce
5ml/1 tsp sunflower oil
10ml/2 tsp hazelnut oil
1 garlic clove, crushed
5ml/1 tsp finely chopped fresh root ginger
ground black pepper
4 spring onions, sliced, to garnish

COOK'S TIP
Hazelnut oil, which contains mainly monounsaturated fats, adds a wonderful flavour.

1 Cook the brown rice in a large saucepan of lightly salted boiling water for about 30 minutes, or until it is tender. Drain thoroughly and cool. Meanwhile, prepare the garnish by slicing the spring onions at an angle and setting aside.

2 Tip the rice into a bowl and add the red pepper, sweetcorn and sultanas. Drain the pineapple pieces, reserving the juice, add them to the rice mixture and toss lightly.

3 Pour the reserved pineapple juice into a clean screw-top jar. Add the soy sauce, sunflower and hazelnut oils, garlic and root ginger. Add some salt and pepper, then close the jar tightly and shake well to combine.

4 Pour the dressing over the salad and toss well. Scatter the spring onions over the top.

NUTRITION NOTES

Per portion:

Energy	245Kcals/1029kJ
Fat	4.25g
Saturated Fat	0.6g
Cholesterol	0

SEAFOOD SALAD WITH FRAGRANT HERBS

INGREDIENTS

Serves 6

250ml/8fl oz/1 cup fish stock or water
250g/12oz squid, cleaned and cut
  into rings
12 uncooked king prawns, shelled
12 scallops
50g/2oz bean thread noodles, soaked in
  warm water for 30 minutes
½ cucumber, cut into thin sticks
1 lemon grass stalk, finely chopped
2 kaffir lime leaves, finely shredded
2 shallots, finely sliced
juice of 1–2 limes
30ml/2 tbsp fish sauce
30ml/2 tbsp chopped spring onions
30ml/2 tbsp chopped coriander leaves
12–15 mint leaves, roughly torn
4 red chillies, seeded and sliced
coriander sprigs, to garnish

1 Pour the stock or water into a medium saucepan, set over a high heat and bring to the boil.

2 Cook each type of seafood separately in the stock. Don't overcook – it takes only a few minutes for each seafood. Remove and set aside.

3 Drain the bean thread noodles and cut them into short lengths, about 5cm/2in long. Combine the noodles with the cooked seafood.

4 Add all the remaining ingredients, mix together well and serve garnished with coriander sprigs.

NUTRITION NOTES

Per portion:

Energy	78Kcals/332kJ
Fat	1.12g
Saturated Fat	0.26g
Cholesterol	123mg
Fibre	0.37g

COOK'S TIP
Use other prepared seafood, such as mussels and cockles, in place of the prawns or scallops. If fresh chillies are not available, use 10–15ml/2–3 tsp of hot chilli powder or, alternatively, use ready-chopped chillies.

GREEN PAPAYA SALAD

There are many variations of this salad in south-east Asia. As green papaya is not easy to get hold of, shredded carrots, cucumber or green apple may be substituted. Serve this salad with raw white cabbage and rice.

INGREDIENTS

Serves 4

1 medium green papaya
4 garlic cloves
15ml/1 tbsp chopped shallots
3–4 red chillies, seeded and sliced
2.5ml/½ tsp salt
2–3 French or runner beans, cut into
   2cm/¾in lengths
2 tomatoes, cut into wedges
45ml/3 tbsp fish sauce
15ml/1 tbsp caster sugar
juice of 1 lime
30ml/2 tbsp crushed roasted peanuts
sliced red chillies, to garnish

1 Peel the papaya and cut in half lengthways, scrape out the seeds with a spoon and finely shred the flesh.

2 Grind the garlic, shallots, chillies and salt together in a large mortar with a pestle.

NUTRITION NOTES

Per portion:
Energy	96Kcals/402kJ
Fat	4.2g
Saturated Fat	0.77g
Cholesterol	0

3 Add the shredded papaya a little at a time and pound until it becomes slightly limp and soft.

4 Add the sliced beans and tomatoes and lightly crush. Season with fish sauce, sugar and lime juice.

5 Transfer the salad to a serving dish, sprinkle with crushed peanuts and garnish with chillies.

COOK'S TIP
If you do not have a large pestle and mortar, use a bowl and crush the shredded papaya with a wooden meat tenderizer or the end of a rolling pin.

THAI-STYLE CHICKEN SALAD

This salad comes from Chiang Mai, a city in the north-east of Thailand. It's hot and spicy, and wonderfully aromatic. Choose strong-flavoured leaves, such as curly endive or rocket, for the salad.

INGREDIENTS

Serves 6
450g/1lb minced chicken breast
1 lemon grass stalk, finely chopped
3 kaffir lime leaves, finely chopped
4 red chillies, seeded and chopped
60ml/4 tbsp lime juice
30ml/2 tbsp fish sauce
15ml/1 tbsp roasted ground rice
2 spring onions, chopped
30ml/2 tbsp coriander leaves
mixed salad leaves, cucumber and
   tomato slices, to serve
mint sprigs, to garnish

1 Heat a large non-stick frying pan. Add the minced chicken and cook in a little water.

2 Stir constantly until cooked, which will take about 7–10 minutes.

-COOK'S TIP
Use sticky (glutinous) rice to make roasted ground rice. Put the rice in a frying pan and dry roast until golden brown. Remove and grind to a powder with a pestle and mortar or in a food processor. Keep in a glass jar in a cool dry place and use as required.

3 Transfer the cooked chicken to a large bowl and add the rest of the ingredients. Mix thoroughly.

4 Serve on a bed of mixed salad leaves, cucumber and tomato slices, garnished with mint sprigs.

NUTRITION NOTES

Per portion:

Energy	106Kcals/446kJ
Fat	1.13g
Saturated Fat	0.28g
Cholesterol	52.5mg
Fibre	0.7g

FRUITY PASTA AND PRAWN SALAD

Orange cantaloupe or Charentais melon look spectacular in this salad. Or try a mixture of ogen, cantaloupe and water melon.

INGREDIENTS

Serves 6

175g/6oz pasta shapes
225g/8oz/2 cups frozen prawns, thawed and drained
1 large or 2 small melons
30ml/2 tbsp olive oil
15ml/1 tbsp tarragon vinegar
30ml/2 tbsp snipped fresh chives or chopped parsley
herb sprigs, to garnish
shredded Chinese leaves, to serve

NUTRITION NOTES

Per portion:

Energy	167Kcals/705kJ
Fat	4.72g
Saturated Fat	0.68g
Cholesterol	105mg
Fibre	2.08g

1 Cook the pasta in boiling salted water according to the instructions on the packet. Drain well and allow to cool.

COOK'S TIP
Use wholewheat pasta in place of white pasta, and mussels or scallops in place of prawns.

2 Peel the prawns and discard the shells.

3 Halve the melon(s) and remove the seeds with a teaspoon. Scoop the flesh into balls with a melon baller and mix with the prawns and pasta.

4 Whisk the oil, vinegar and chopped herbs together. Pour on to the prawn mixture and turn to coat. Cover and chill for at lesat 30 minutes.

5 Meanwhile, shred the Chinese leaves and use to line a shallow bowl or the empty melon shells. Pile the prawn mixture on to the Chinese leaves and garnish with herb sprigs.

PRAWN NOODLE SALAD

A light, refreshing salad with all the tangy flavour of the sea. Instead of prawns, try squid, scallops, mussels or crab.

INGREDIENTS

Serves 4
115g/4oz cellophane noodles, soaked in hot water until soft
16 cooked prawns, peeled
1 small red pepper, seeded and cut into strips
½ cucumber, cut into strips
1 tomato, cut into strips
2 shallots, finely sliced
salt and black pepper
coriander leaves, to garnish

For the dressing
15ml/1 tbsp rice vinegar
30ml/2 tbsp fish sauce
30ml/2 tbsp fresh lime juice
pinch of salt
2.5ml/½ tsp grated fresh root ginger
1 lemon grass stalk, finely chopped
1 red chilli, seeded and finely sliced
30ml/2 tbsp roughly chopped mint
a few sprigs of tarragon, roughly chopped
15ml/1 tbsp snipped chives

1 Make the dressing by combining all the ingredients in a small bowl or jug; whisk well.

2 Drain the noodles, then plunge them in a saucepan of boiling water for 1 minute. Drain, rinse under cold running water and drain again well.

3 In a large bowl, combine the noodles with the prawns, red pepper, cucumber, tomato and shallots. Lightly season with salt and pepper, then toss with the dressing.

4 Spoon the noodles on to individual plates. Garnish with a few coriander leaves and serve at once.

NUTRITION NOTES

Per portion:
Energy	164.5Kcals/697kJ
Fat	2.9g
Saturated Fat	0.79g
Cholesterol	121mg
Fibre	1.86g

COOK'S TIP
Prawns are available ready-cooked and often shelled. To cook prawns, boil them for 5 minutes. Leave them to cool in the cooking liquid, then gently pull off the tail shell and twist off the head.

CACHUMBAR

Cachumbar is a salad relish most commonly served with Indian curries. There are many versions; this one will leave your mouth feeling cool and fresh after a spicy meal.

INGREDIENTS

Serves 4

3 ripe tomatoes
2 chopped spring onions
1.5ml/¹/₄ tsp caster sugar
salt
45ml/3 tbsp chopped fresh coriander

NUTRITION NOTES

Per portion:

Energy	9.5Kcals/73.5kJ
Fat	0.23g
Saturated Fat	0.07g
Cholesterol	0
Fibre	0.87g

1 Remove the tough cores from the bottom of the tomatoes with a small sharp-pointed knife.

COOK'S TIP
Cachumbar also makes a fine accompaniment to fresh crab, lobster and shellfish.

2 Halve the tomatoes, remove the seeds and dice the flesh.

3 Combine the tomatoes with the spring onions, sugar, salt and chopped coriander. Serve at room temperature.

WARM CHICKEN LIVER SALAD

Although warm salads may seem over-fussy or trendy, there are times when they are just right. Serve this delicious combination as either a starter or a light meal, with hunks of bread to dip into the dressing.

INGREDIENTS

Serves 4

115g/4oz each fresh young spinach
   leaves, rocket and lollo rosso lettuce
2 pink grapefruit
90ml/6 tbsp sunflower oil
10ml/2 tsp sesame oil
10ml/2 tsp soy sauce
225g/8oz chicken livers, chopped
salt and black pepper

1 Wash, dry and tear up all the leaves. Mix them together well in a large salad bowl.

2 Carefully cut away all the peel and white pith from the grapefruit, then neatly segment them catching all the juices in a bowl. Add the grapefruit segments to the leaves in the bowl.

3 To make the dressing, mix together 60ml/4 tbsp of the sunflower oil with the sesame oil, soy sauce, seasoning and grapefruit juice to taste.

4 Heat the rest of the sunflower oil in a small pan and cook the liver, stirring gently, until firm and lightly browned.

5 Tip the chicken livers and dressing over the salad and serve at once.

NUTRITION NOTES

Per portion:

Energy	266Kcals/1107kJ
Fat	20.10g
Saturated Fat	2.74g
Cholesterol	213.75mg

WATERCRESS POTATO SALAD BOWL

New potatoes are equally good hot or cold, and this colourful, nutritious salad is an ideal way of making the most of them.

INGREDIENTS

Serves 4

450g/1 lb small new potatoes, unpeeled
1 bunch watercress
200g/7oz/1½ cups cherry tomatoes, halved
30ml/2 tbsp pumpkin seeds
45ml/3 tbsp low fat fromage frais
15ml/1 tbsp cider vinegar
5ml/1 tsp soft light brown sugar
salt and paprika

1 Cook the potatoes in lightly salted, boiling water until just tender, then drain and leave to cool.

2 Toss together the potatoes, watercress, tomatoes and pumpkin seeds.

3 Place the fromage frais, vinegar, sugar, salt and paprika in a screw-topped jar and shake well to mix. Pour over the salad just before serving.

NUTRITION NOTES

Per portion:

Energy	150Kcals/630kJ
Fat	4.15g
Saturated fat	0.81g
Cholesterol	0.11mg
Fibre	2.55g

COOK'S TIP
If you are packing this salad for a picnic, take the dressing in the jar and toss in just before serving.

FENNEL AND HERB COLESLAW

Serve this delicious vegetarian salad as an accompaniment, or turn it into a main meal with the addition of some low fat cottage cheese and thick slices of crisp red-skinned apples.

INGREDIENTS

Serves 4

175g/6oz fennel
2 spring onions
175g/6oz white cabbage
115g/4oz celery
175g/6oz carrots
50g/2oz sultanas
2.5ml/½ tsp caraway seeds (optional)
15ml/1 tbsp chopped fresh parsley
45ml/3 tbsp fat-free French dressing
5ml/1 tsp lemon juice
salt and ground black pepper
shreds of spring onion, to garnish

VARIATION
Use reduced fat mayonnaise in place of the French dressing.

1 Using a sharp knife, cut the fennel and spring onions into thin slices.

NUTRITION NOTES

Per portion:	
Energy	74Kcals/315KJ
Fat	0.5g
Saturated Fat	0.05g
Cholesterol	0

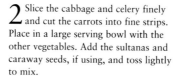

2 Slice the cabbage and celery finely and cut the carrots into fine strips. Place in a large serving bowl with the other vegetables. Add the sultanas and caraway seeds, if using, and toss lightly to mix.

3 Stir in the chopped parsley, French dressing and lemon juice and mix well, then season with salt and pepper. Cover and chill for 3 hours to allow the flavours to mingle, then serve, garnished with spring onion shreds.

SWEET POTATO AND CARROT SALAD

INGREDIENTS

Serves 4

1 sweet potato, peeled and roughly
   diced
2 carrots, cut into thick diagonal slices
3 tomatoes
8–10 iceberg lettuce leaves
75g/3oz/³⁄₄ cup canned chick-peas,
   drained

For the dressing

15ml/1 tbsp clear honey
90ml/6 tbsp low fat natural yogurt
2.5ml/½ tsp salt
5ml/1 tsp coarsely ground black pepper

For the garnish

15ml/1 tbsp walnuts
15ml/1 tbsp sultanas
1 small onion, cut into rings

NUTRITION NOTES

Per portion:

Energy	176Kcals/741kJ
Fat	4.85g
Saturated fat	0.58g
Cholesterol	0.85mg

1 Place the potatoes in a large saucepan and cover with water. Bring to the boil and cook until soft but not mushy, cover the pan and set aside. Boil the carrots for a few minutes making sure they remain crunchy. Add to the sweet potatoes.

3 Slice the tops off the tomatoes, then scoop out and discard the seeds. Roughly chop the flesh.

5 For the dressing, blend together all the ingredients and beat together with a fork.

2 Drain the water from the sweet potatoes and carrots, and place together in a bowl.

4 Line a glass bowl with the lettuce leaves. Mix together the sweet potatoes, carrots, chick-peas and tomatoes, and place in the bowl.

6 Spoon the dressing over the salad or serve it in a separate bowl, if desired. Garnish the salad with the walnuts, sultanas and onion rings.

BEETROOT, CHICORY AND ORANGE SALAD

A refreshing salad which goes well with grilled meats or fish. Alternatively, arrange it prettily on individual plates and serve as a summer starter.

──── INGREDIENTS ────

Serves 4
2 medium cooked beetroot, diced
2 heads chicory, sliced
1 large orange
60ml/4 tbsp natural low fat yogurt
10ml/2 tsp wholegrain mustard
salt and black pepper

1 Mix together the diced cooked beetroot and sliced chicory in a large serving bowl.

2 Finely grate the rind from the orange. With a sharp knife, remove all the peel and white pith. Cut out the segments, catching the juice in a bowl. Add the segments to the salad.

3 Add the orange rind, yogurt, mustard and seasonings to the orange juice, mix thoroughly, then spoon over the salad.

> **COOK'S TIP**
> Fresh baby spinach leaves or rocket could be used in place of the chicory, if you prefer.

──── NUTRITION NOTES ────

Per portion:
Energy	41Kcals/172kJ
Fat	0.60g
Saturated fat	0.08g
Cholesterol	0.60mg
Fibre	1.42g

ROASTED PEPPER SALAD

This colourful salad is very easy and can be made up to a day in advance, as the sharp-sweet dressing mingles with the mild pepper flavours.

──── INGREDIENTS ────

Serves 4
3 large red, green and yellow peppers,
* halved and seeded*
115g/4oz feta cheese, diced or
* crumbled*
15ml/1 tbsp sherry vinegar or red wine
* vinegar*
15ml/1 tbsp clear honey
salt and black pepper

2 Lift the peppers into a plastic bag and close the end. Leave until cool, then peel off and discard the skin.

1 Arrange the pepper halves in a single layer, skin side upwards, on a baking sheet. Place the peppers under a hot grill until the skin is blackened and beginning to blister.

3 Arrange the peppers on a platter and scatter the cheese over them. Mix together the vinegar, honey and seasonings, then sprinkle over the salad. Chill until ready to serve.

──── NUTRITION NOTES ────

Per portion:
Energy	110Kcals/462kJ
Fat	6.15g
Saturated fat	3.65g
Cholesterol	20.13mg
Fibre	1.84g

CABBAGE SLAW WITH DATE AND APPLE

Three types of cabbage are shredded together for serving raw, so that the maximum amount of vitamin C is retained in this cheerful salad.

INGREDIENTS

Serves 6–8
¼ small white cabbage, shredded
¼ small red cabbage, shredded
¼ small Savoy cabbage, shredded
175g/6oz/1 cup dried stoned dates
3 eating apples
juice of 1 lemon
10ml/2 tsp caraway seeds

For the dressing
60ml/4 tbsp olive oil
15ml/1 tbsp cider vinegar
5ml/1 tsp clear honey
salt and ground black pepper

1 Finely shred all the cabbages and place them in a large salad bowl.

2 Chop the dates and add them to the cabbage.

3 Core the eating apples and slice them thinly into a mixing bowl. Add the lemon juice and toss together to prevent discoloration before adding to the salad bowl.

4 Make the dressing. Combine the oil, vinegar and honey in a screw-top jar. Add salt and pepper, then close the jar tightly and shake well. Pour the dressing over the salad, toss lightly, then sprinkle with the caraway seeds and toss again.

COOK'S TIP
Support local orchards by looking out for different home-grown apples.

NUTRITION NOTES
Per portion:

Energy	200Kcals/835KJ
Fat	8g
Saturated Fat	1g
Cholesterol	0

SPROUTED SEED SALAD

If you sprout beans, lentils and whole grains it increases their nutritional value, and they make a deliciously crunchy salad.

INGREDIENTS

Serves 4
2 eating apples
115g/4oz alfalfa sprouts
115g/4oz beansprouts
115g/4oz aduki beansprouts
¼ cucumber, sliced
1 bunch watercress, trimmed
1 carton mustard and cress, trimmed

For the dressing
150ml/¼ pint/⅔ cup low fat
  natural yogurt
juice of ½ lemon
bunch of chives, snipped
30ml/2 tbsp chopped fresh herbs
ground black pepper

1 Core and slice the apples and mix with the other salad ingredients.

2 Mix the dressing ingredients in a jug. Drizzle over the salad and toss together just before serving.

NUTRITION NOTES
Per portion:

Energy	85Kcals/355KJ
Fat	1.5g
Saturated Fat	0.5g
Cholesterol	1.5mg

FATTOUSH

This Middle-Eastern mixed salad is traditionally topped with pieces of unleavened bread to soak up the dressing. It provides the perfect solution of what to do with slightly stale pitta breads.

─── INGREDIENTS ───

Serves 4
2 wholemeal pitta breads
1 iceberg or cos lettuce, torn
    into pieces
1 green pepper, seeded
10cm/4in length of cucumber
4 tomatoes
4 spring onions
a few black olives, to garnish

For the dressing
60ml/4 tbsp olive oil
45ml/3 tbsp freshly squeezed
    lemon juice
2 garlic cloves, crushed
45ml/3 tbsp finely chopped
    fresh parsley
30ml/2 tbsp finely chopped fresh mint
few drops of harissa or chilli sauce
    (optional)
salt and ground black pepper

COOK'S TIP
Any salad leaves can be used instead of lettuce. Try young spinach or Swiss chard.

2 Place the lettuce in a large bowl. Chop the green pepper, cucumber, tomatoes and spring onions roughly, making sure they are all about the same size. Add them to the lettuce and toss together well.

4 Just before serving the dish, pour the dressing from the jar over the salad and toss well to combine together. Scatter pieces of pitta bread over the salad and garnish with the black olives.

─── NUTRITION NOTES ───

Per portion:
Energy	225Kcals/935KJ
Fat	13g
Saturated Fat	2g
Cholesterol	0

1 Grill or toast the pitta breads on both sides until crisp and golden. Cut into rough squares and set aside.

3 Make the dressing by shaking all the ingredients together in a screw-top jar.

GREEN GREEN SALAD

You could make this lovely dish at any time of the year using imported or frozen vegetables and still get a pretty, healthy – and unusual – salad.

INGREDIENTS

Serves 4

175g/6oz shelled broad beans
115g/4oz French or flat beans,
    quartered
115g/4oz mange-tout
8–10 small fresh mint leaves
3 spring onions, chopped
60ml/4 tbsp green olive oil
15ml/1 tbsp cider vinegar
15ml/1 tbsp chopped fresh mint, or
    5 ml/1 tsp dried
1 garlic clove, crushed
salt and black pepper

1 Plunge the broad beans into a saucepan of boiling water and bring back to the boil. Remove from the heat immediately and plunge into cold water. Drain. Repeat with the French or flat beans.

NUTRITION NOTES

Per portion:
Energy	153Kcals/635kJ
Fat	11.5g
Saturated Fat	1.65g
Cholesterol	0mg

2 Mix together the blanched beans, the raw mange-tout, mint leaves and spring onions.

3 Mix together the olive oil, vinegar, chopped mint, garlic and seasoning thoroughly, then pour over the salad and toss well. Chill until ready to serve.

MANGO, PRAWN AND TOMATO SALAD

INGREDIENTS

Serves 4

1 large mango
225g/8oz extra large cooked tiger
  prawns, peeled and deveined
16 cherry tomatoes, halved
fresh mint, to garnish

For the dressing
15ml/1 tbsp white wine vinegar
2.5ml/½ tsp clear honey
15ml/1 tbsp mango or apricot chutney
15ml/1 tbsp chopped fresh mint
15ml/1 tbsp chopped fresh lemon balm
45ml/3 tbsp olive oil
salt and ground black pepper

NUTRITION NOTES

Per portion:

Energy	230Kcals/960KJ
Fat	10g
Saturated Fat	1.5g
Cholesterol	45.5mg

1 Using a sharp knife, peel, stone and dice the mango carefully. Mix with the tiger prawns and cherry tomatoes in a bowl. Toss lightly to mix, then cover and chill.

2 Make the salad dressing by mixing the vinegar, clear honey, chutney and fresh herbs in a bowl. Gradually whisk in the oil, then add salt and pepper to taste.

3 Spoon the prawn mixture into the dressing and toss lightly, then divide among serving dishes. Garnish with the fresh mint sprigs and serve.

COOK'S TIP
If you use frozen prawns, thaw them in a colander, then drain thoroughly on kitchen paper before use or the water will dilute the salad dressing and spoil the flavour.

CHICKEN AND CRANBERRY SALAD

INGREDIENTS

Serves 4

4 boned chicken breasts, total weight
  about 675g/1½lb
300ml/½ pint/1¼ cups stock or a
  mixture of stock and white wine
fresh herb sprigs
200g/7oz mixed salad leaves
50g/2oz/½ cup chopped walnuts
  or hazelnuts

For the dressing
30ml/2 tbsp olive oil
15ml/1 tbsp walnut or hazelnut oil
15ml/1 tbsp raspberry or red
  wine vinegar
30ml/2 tbsp cranberry relish
salt and ground black pepper

1 Skin the chicken breasts. Pour the stock (or stock and wine mixture) into a large shallow saucepan. Add the herbs and bring the liquid to simmering point. Poach the chicken breasts for about 15 minutes until cooked through. Alternatively, leave the skin on the breasts and grill or roast them until tender, then remove the skin.

2 Arrange the salad leaves on four plates. Slice each chicken breast neatly, keeping the slices together, then place each breast on top of a portion of salad, fanning the slices out slightly.

3 Make the dressing by shaking all the ingredients together in a screw-top jar. Spoon a little dressing over each salad and sprinkle with the walnuts or hazelnuts.

NUTRITION NOTES

Per portion:

Energy	365Kcals/1530KJ
Fat	22g
Saturated Fat	3.5g
Cholesterol	64.5mg

TWO PEAR SALAD

Serves 4

2 courgettes, grated
2 avocados
2 ripe eating pears
1 large carrot

For the dressing

250ml/8fl oz/1 cup low fat
   natural yogurt
60ml/4 tbsp reduced-calorie
   mayonnaise
grated rind of 1 lemon
8–10 chives, snipped
30ml/2 tbsp chopped fresh mint
ground black pepper
4 mint sprigs, to garnish

1 Pile the grated courgettes on to four individual serving plates.

2 Cut the avocados in half, then remove the stones and peel. Slice each half lengthways. Core and slice the pears. Arrange avocado and pear slices on top of each courgette salad.

3 Peel the carrot, then use the peeler to peel off fine ribbons.

4 Make the dressing. Mix the yogurt and mayonnaise together in a bowl, then stir in the lemon rind, chives and chopped mint. Season with pepper. Drizzle some of the dressing over each salad and garnish with a mint sprig. Serve immediately.

COOK'S TIP
If the salad is not to be served straight away, sprinkle the avocado with lemon juice or the flesh will discolour.

NUTRITION NOTES

Per portion:
Energy	260Kcals/1090KJ
Fat	19.5g
Saturated Fat	3g
Cholesterol	2.5g

FOUR SEASONS SALAD PLATTER

Fresh vegetable salads are packed with vitamin C. Include some protein foods and serve with a hunk of fresh wholemeal bread for a well-balanced snack or simple lunch.

INGREDIENTS

Serves 4

4 chicory leaves
115g/4oz French beans, lightly cooked
7.5cm/3in length of cucumber, cut into sticks
6 cherry tomatoes
1 hard-boiled egg, halved

Carrot and Radish Salad
2 carrots
2 radishes
15ml/1 tbsp chopped mixed nuts

Beetroot and Onion Salad
2–3 cooked beetroot, sliced
15ml/1 tbsp balsamic or wine vinegar
2–3 spring onions, finely chopped
30ml/2 tbsp chopped fresh parsley

Mushroom and Thyme Salad
75g/3oz/³⁄₄ cup button mushrooms, sliced
30ml/2 tbsp lemon juice
15ml/1 tbsp chopped fresh thyme

Tuna and Haricot Bean Salad
90g/3½oz can tuna in oil
200g/7oz can haricot beans
½ red onion, thinly sliced
30ml/2 tbsp chopped fresh parsley

NUTRITION NOTES

Per portion:	
Energy	405Kcals/1690KJ
Fat	13.5g
Saturated Fat	2.5g
Cholesterol	122.5mg

1 Grate the carrots and radishes. Mix together with the nuts in a bowl.

2 Sprinkle the beetroot with vinegar, add the spring onions and parsley and toss lightly.

3 Mix the mushrooms with the lemon juice and thyme.

4 Drain the tuna and beans, tip them both into a bowl and toss with the onion and parsley.

5 Divide the chicory leaves between two large salad plates. Add a portion of each salad, arranging them attractively with the French beans, cucumber sticks, tomatoes and egg halves. Serve with wholemeal bread.

CITRUS GREEN SALAD WITH CROÛTONS

Wholemeal croûtons add a delicious crunch to leaf salads. The kumquats or orange segments provide a colour contrast as well as a good helping of vitamin C.

INGREDIENTS

Serves 4–6
4 kumquats or 2 seedless oranges
200g/7oz mixed green salad leaves
4 slices of wholemeal bread,
 crusts removed
30–45ml/2–3 tbsp pine nuts,
 lightly toasted

For the dressing
grated rind of 1 lemon and
 15ml/1tbsp juice
45ml/3 tbsp olive oil
5ml/1 tsp wholegrain mustard
1 garlic clove, crushed

1 Thinly slice the kumquat, or peel and segment the oranges.

NUTRITION NOTES

Per portion:	
Energy	250Kcals/1000KJ
Fat	15g
Saturated Fat	2g
Cholesterol	0

2 Tear all the salad leaves into bite-size pieces and place together in a large salad bowl.

3 Toast the bread on both sides and cut into cubes. Add to the salad leaves with the sliced kumquats or orange segments.

4 Shake all the dressing ingredients together in a jar. Pour over the salad just before serving and scatter the toasted pine nuts over the top.

BEAN SALAD WITH TOMATO DRESSING

All pulses are a good source of vegetable protein, and minerals.

INGREDIENTS

Serves 4
115g/4oz French beans
425g/15oz can mixed pulses, drained
 and rinsed
2 celery sticks, finely chopped
1 small onion, finely chopped
3 tomatoes, chopped
45ml/3 tbsp chopped fresh parsley,
 to garnish

For the dressing
45ml/3 tbsp olive oil
10ml/2 tsp red wine vinegar
1 garlic clove, crushed
15ml/1 tbsp tomato chutney
salt and ground black pepper

1 Remove the ends from the French beans, then cook the beans in boiling water for 5–6 minutes (or steam for 10 minutes) until tender. Drain, then refresh under cold running water and cut into thirds.

2 Place the French beans and pulses in a large bowl. Add the celery, onion and tomatoes and toss lightly.

3 Shake the dressing ingredients together in a jar. Pour over the salad and sprinkle with the parsley.

> **COOK'S TIP**
> Cans of mixed pulses include several different types such as chick-peas, pinto, black-eye, red kidney, soya and aduki beans, and save the hassle of long soaking and cooking which dried beans require.

NUTRITION NOTES

Per portion:	
Energy	175Kcals/740KJ
Fat	9.5g
Saturated Fat	1.5g
Cholesterol	0

HOT DESSERTS

When we talk of desserts and puddings we tend to imagine deliciously rich, creamy, calorie-laden treats which are well out of reach if you are following a low fat diet. However, it is very easy to create delicious, low fat desserts, full of flavour, colour and appeal that will satisfy a sweet tooth any day. We include a tasty selection of hot desserts, including temptations such as Sultana and Couscous Pudding, Baked Apples in Honey and Lemon, Cinnamon and Apricot Soufflés, Blueberry and Orange Crêpe Baskets, and Blushing Pears.

STRAWBERRY AND APPLE CRUMBLE

A high-fibre, healthier version of the classic apple crumble. Raspberries can be used instead of strawberries, either fresh or frozen.

INGREDIENTS

Serves 4
450g/1lb cooking apples
150g/5oz/1¼ cups strawberries
30ml/2 tbsp granulated sugar
2.5ml/½ tsp ground cinnamon
30ml/2 tbsp orange juice
custard or yogurt, to serve

For the crumble
45ml/3 tbsp plain wholemeal flour
50g/2oz/⅔ cup porridge oats
25g/1oz/⅛ cup low fat spread

1 Preheat the oven to 180°C/350°F/ Gas 4. Peel, core and slice the apples. Halve the strawberries.

2 Toss together the apples, strawberries, sugar, cinnamon and orange juice. Tip into a 1.2 litre/ 2 pint/5 cup ovenproof dish, or four individual dishes.

NUTRITION NOTES

Per portion:	
Energy	182.3Kcals/785kJ
Fat	4g
Saturated Fat	0.73g
Cholesterol	0.5mg
Fibre	3.87g

3 Combine the flour and oats in a bowl and mix in the low fat spread with a fork.

4 Sprinkle the crumble evenly over the fruit. Bake for 40–45 minutes (20–25 minutes for individual dishes), until golden brown and bubbling. Serve warm with custard or yogurt.

SULTANA AND COUSCOUS PUDDING

Most couscous on the market now is the pre-cooked variety, which needs only the minimum of cooking, but check the packet instructions first to make sure. Serve hot, with yogurt or skimmed-milk custard.

INGREDIENTS

Serves 4

50g/2oz/⅓ cup sultanas
475ml/16fl oz/2 cups apple juice
90g/3½oz/1 cup couscous
2.5ml/½ tsp mixed spice

1 Lightly grease four 250ml/8fl oz/ 1 cup pudding basins or one 1 litre/1¾ pint/4 cup pudding basin. Put the sultanas and apple juice in a pan.

2 Bring the apple juice to the boil, then cover the pan and leave to simmer gently for 2–3 minutes to plump up the fruit. Using a slotted spoon, lift out about half the fruit and put it in the bottom of the basin(s).

3 Add the couscous and mixed spice to the pan and bring back to the boil, stirring. Cover and leave over a low heat for 8–10 minutes, or until the liquid has been absorbed.

NUTRITION NOTES

Per portion:

Energy	130.5Kcals/555kJ
Fat	0.40g
Saturated Fat	0
Cholesterol	0
Fibre	0.25g

4 Spoon the couscous into the basin(s), spread it level, then cover the basin(s) tightly with foil. Put the basin(s) in a steamer over boiling water, cover and steam for about 30 minutes. Run a knife around the edges, turn the puddings out carefully and serve.

COOK'S TIP

As an alternative, use chopped ready-to-eat dried apricots or pears, in place of the sultanas. Use unsweetened pineapple or orange juice in place of the apple juice.

CHUNKY APPLE BAKE

This filling, economical family pudding is a good way to use up slightly stale bread – any type of bread will do, but wholemeal is richer in fibre.

INGREDIENTS

Serves 4
450g/1lb cooking apples
75g/3oz wholemeal bread
115g/4oz/¹/₂ cup cottage cheese
45ml/3 tbsp light muscovado sugar
200ml/7fl oz/scant 1 cup semi-
  skimmed milk
5ml/1 tsp demerara sugar

NUTRITION NOTES

Per portion:

Energy	172.5Kcals/734.7kJ
Fat	2.5g
Saturated Fat	1.19g
Cholesterol	7.25mg
Fibre	2.69g

1 Preheat the oven to 220°C/425°F/ Gas 7. Peel the apples, cut them into quarters and remove the cores.

2 Roughly chop the apples into even-sized pieces, about 1cm/¹/₂in across.

3 Trim the crusts from the bread, then cut into 1cm/¹/₂in dice.

4 Toss together the apples, bread, cottage cheese and muscovado sugar.

5 Stir in the milk, then tip the mixture into a wide ovenproof dish. Sprinkle with the demerara sugar.

6 Bake the pudding for about 30–35 minutes, or until golden brown and bubbling. Serve hot.

COOK'S TIP
You may need to adjust the amount of milk used, depending on the dryness of the bread; the more stale the bread, the more milk it will absorb.

Baked Apples in Honey and Lemon

A classic mix of flavours in a healthy, traditional family pudding. Serve warm, with skimmed-milk custard or low fat frozen yogurt.

Ingredients

Serves 4

4 medium cooking apples
15ml/1 tbsp clear honey
grated rind and juice of 1 lemon
15ml/1 tbsp low fat spread
skimmed-milk custard, to serve

1 Preheat the oven to 180°C/350°F/ Gas 4. Remove the cores from the apples, leaving them whole.

2 With a cannelle or sharp knife, cut lines through the apple skin at intervals. Put the apples in an oven-proof dish.

3 Mix together the honey, lemon rind, juice and low fat spread.

4 Spoon the mixture into the apples and cover the dish with foil or a lid. Bake for 40–45 minutes, or until the apples are tender. Serve with skimmed-milk custard.

APPLE AND BLACKCURRANT PANCAKES

These pancakes are made with a wholewheat batter and are filled with a delicious fruit mixture.

INGREDIENTS

Makes 10

115g/4oz/1 cup plain wholemeal flour
300ml/½ pint/1¼ cups skimmed milk
1 egg, beaten
15ml/1 tbsp sunflower oil, plus extra
  for greasing
half fat crème fraîche, to serve
  (optional)
toasted nuts or sesame seeds, for
  sprinkling (optional)

For the filling

450g/1lb cooking apples
225g/8oz blackcurrants
30–45ml/2–3 tbsp water
30ml/2 tbsp demerara sugar

1 To make the pancake batter, put the flour in a mixing bowl and make a well in the centre.

2 Add a little of the milk with the egg and the oil. Beat the flour into the liquid, then gradually beat in the rest of the milk, keeping the batter smooth and free from lumps. Cover the batter and chill while you prepare the filling.

> **COOK'S TIP**
> If you wish, substitute other combinations of fruit for apples and blackcurrants.

3 Quarter, peel and core the apples. Slice them into a pan and add the blackcurrants and water. Cook over a gentle heat for 10–15 minutes until the fruit is soft. Stir in enough demerara sugar to sweeten.

NUTRITION NOTES	
Per portion:	
Energy	120Kcals/505kJ
Fat	3g
Saturated Fat	0.5g
Cholesterol	25mg

4 Lightly grease a non-stick pan with just a smear of oil. Heat the pan, pour in about 30ml/2 tbsp of the batter, swirl it around and cook for about 1 minute. Flip the pancake over with a palette knife and cook the other side. Put on a sheet of kitchen paper and keep hot while cooking the remaining pancakes.

5 Fill the pancakes with the apple and blackcurrant mixture and roll them up. Serve with a dollop of crème fraîche, if using, and sprinkle with nuts or sesame seeds, if liked.

CINNAMON AND APRICOT SOUFFLÉS

Don't expect these to be difficult simply because they're soufflés – they really couldn't be easier, and, best of all, they're very low in calories.

INGREDIENTS

Serves 4

3 eggs
115g/4oz/1/2 cup apricot fruit spread
finely grated rind of 1/2 lemon
5ml/1 tsp ground cinnamon
extra cinnamon, to decorate

NUTRITION NOTES

Per portion:

Energy	102Kcals/429kJ
Fat	4.97g
Saturated Fat	1.42g
Cholesterol	176.25mg
Fibre	0

1 Preheat the oven to 190°C/375°F/ Gas 5. Lightly grease four individual soufflé dishes and dust them lightly with flour.

2 Separate the eggs and put the yolks in a bowl with the fruit spread, lemon rind and cinnamon.

3 Whisk hard until the mixture is thick and pale in colour.

4 Place the egg whites in a clean bowl and whisk them until they are stiff enough to hold soft peaks.

5 Using a large metal spoon or spatula, fold the egg whites evenly into the yolk mixture.

6 Divide the soufflé mixture between the prepared dishes and bake for 10–15 minutes, until well risen and golden brown. Serve immediately, dusted with a little extra cinnamon.

COOK'S TIP
Puréed fresh or well-drained canned fruit can be used instead of the apricot spread, but make sure the mixture is not too wet, or the soufflés will not rise properly.

FLOATING ISLANDS IN HOT PLUM SAUCE

An unusual pudding that is simpler to make than it looks. The plum sauce can be made in advance, and reheated just before you cook the meringues.

INGREDIENTS

Serves 4
450g/1 lb red plums
300ml/½ pint/1¼ cups apple juice
2 egg whites
30ml/2 tbsp concentrated apple juice
freshly grated nutmeg, to sprinkle

NUTRITION NOTES	
Per portion:	
Energy	90Kcals/380kJ
Fat	0.3g
Saturated fat	0
Cholesterol	0
Fibre	1.69g

1 Halve the plums and remove the stones. Place them in a wide saucepan, with the apple juice.

2 Bring to the boil, then cover and simmer gently until the plums have become tender.

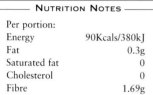

3 Meanwhile, place the egg whites in a clean, dry bowl and whisk them until they hold soft peaks.

4 Gradually whisk in the concentrated apple juice, whisking until the meringue holds fairly firm peaks.

5 Using a tablespoon, scoop the meringue mixture into the gently simmering plum sauce. You may need to cook the "islands" in two batches.

6 Cover and simmer gently for about 2–3 minutes, until the meringues are set. Serve immediately, sprinkled with a little freshly grated nutmeg.

> COOK'S TIP
> A bottle of concentrated apple juice is a useful storecupboard sweetener, but if you don't have any, use a little clear honey instead.

LATTICED PEACHES

INGREDIENTS

Serves 6
For the pastry
115g/4oz/1 cup all-purpose flour
45ml/3 tbsp butter or margarine
45ml/3 tbsp low fat plain yogurt
30ml/2 tbsp orange juice
skimmed milk, for brushing

For the filling
3 ripe peaches or nectarines
45ml/3 tbsp ground almonds
30ml/2 tbsp low fat plain yogurt
finely grated rind of 1 small orange
1.25ml/¼ tsp almond extract

For the sauce
1 ripe peach or nectarine
45ml/3 tbsp orange juice

NUTRITION NOTES

Per portion:
Energy	192Kcals/806kJ
Fat	9.6g
Saturated Fat	4.07g
Cholesterol	15.92mg

1 Sift the flour into a bowl and use your fingers to rub in the butter or margarine. Stir in the yogurt and orange juice to make a firm dough.

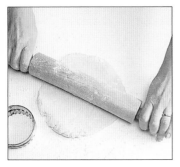

2 Roll out half of the pastry and cut out rounds about 7.5cm /3in across. Place on a lightly greased baking sheet.

3 Skin and halve the peaches or nectarines. Mix together the almonds, yogurt, orange rind and almond extract. Spoon the mixture into the hollows of each fruit half.

4 Place each peach or nectarine half cut-side down on a pastry round. Cut thin pastry strips and arrange on top to form a lattice. Brush with milk to secure firmly. Chill for 30 minutes.

5 Heat the oven to 200°C/400°F/Gas 6. Brush the fruit with milk. Bake for 15 minutes, until golden brown.

6 For the sauce, skin a ripe peach or nectarine and halve it to remove the pit. Place the flesh in a food processor with the orange juice and purée it until smooth. Serve the peaches or nectarines hot with the sauce spooned around.

BLUEBERRY AND ORANGE CRÊPE BASKETS

Impress your guests with these pretty, fruit-filled crêpes. When blueberries are out of season, replace them with other soft fruit, such as raspberries.

INGREDIENTS

Serves 6
150g/5oz/1¼ cups plain flour
pinch of salt
2 egg whites
200ml/7fl oz/⁷⁄₈ cup skimmed milk
150ml/¼ pint/²⁄₃ cup orange juice
oil, for frying
yogurt or light crème fraîche, to serve

For the filling
4 medium oranges
225g/8oz/2 cups blueberries

1 Preheat the oven to 200°C/400°F/ Gas 6. To make the pancakes, sift the flour and salt into a bowl. Make a well in the centre and add the egg whites, milk and orange juice. Whisk hard, until all the liquid has been incorporated and the batter is smooth and bubbly.

2 Lightly grease a heavy or non-stick pancake pan and heat it until it is very hot. Pour in just enough batter to cover the base of the pan, swirling it to cover the pan evenly.

3 Cook until the pancake has set and is golden, then turn it to cook the other side. Remove the pancake to a sheet of kitchen paper. Cook the remaining batter to make 6–8 pancakes.

4 Place six small ovenproof bowls or moulds on a baking sheet and lay the pancakes over these. Bake them in the oven for about 10 minutes, until they are crisp and set into shape. Lift the 'baskets' off the moulds.

5 Pare a thin piece of orange rind from one orange and cut it into fine strips. Blanch the strips in boiling water for 30 seconds, rinse them in cold water and set them aside. Cut all the peel and white pith from the oranges.

6 Divide the oranges into segments, catching the juice, combine with the blueberries and warm them gently. Spoon the fruit into the baskets and scatter the rind over the top. Serve with yogurt or light crème fraîche.

COOK'S TIP
Don't fill the pancake baskets until you're ready to serve them, because they will absorb the fruit juice and begin to soften.

NUTRITION NOTES

Per portion:
Energy	157.3Kcals/668.3kJ
Fat	2.20g
Saturated Fat	0.23g
Cholesterol	0.66mg
Fibre	2.87g

FILO CHIFFON PIE

Filo pastry is low in fat and is
very easy to use. Keep a pack in
the freezer, ready to make
impressive desserts like this one.

─────── INGREDIENTS ───────

Serves 6
500g/1¼lb rhubarb
5ml/1 tsp mixed spice
finely grated rind and juice of 1 orange
15ml/1 tbsp granulated sugar
15g/½oz/1 tbsp butter
3 filo pastry sheets

1 Preheat the oven to 200°C/400°F/
Gas 6. Chop the rhubarb into
2.5cm/1in pieces and put them in
a bowl.

2 Add the mixed spice, orange rind
and juice and sugar. Tip the rhubarb
into a 1 litre/1¾ pint/4 cup pie dish.

─────── NUTRITION NOTES ───────

Per portion:	
Energy	71Kcals/299kJ
Fat	2.5g
Saturated Fat	1.41g
Cholesterol	5.74mg
Fibre	1.48g

3 Melt the butter and brush it over
the pastry. Lift the pastry on to the
pie dish, butter-side up, and crumple it
up decoratively to cover the pie.

┌─────────────────────────────┐
VARIATION
Other fruit can be used in this pie –
just prepare depending on type.
└─────────────────────────────┘

4 Put the dish on a baking sheet and
bake for 20 minutes, until golden
brown. Reduce the heat to 180°C/350°F/
Gas 4 and bake for a further 10–15
minutes, until the rhubarb is tender.

BLUSHING PEARS

Pears poached in rosé wine and sweet spices absorb all the subtle flavours and turn a delightful soft pink colour.

INGREDIENTS

Serves 6

6 firm eating pears
300ml/½ pint/1¼ cups rosé wine
150ml/¼ pint/⅔ cup cranberry or
    clear apple juice
strip of thinly pared orange rind
1 cinnamon stick
4 whole cloves
1 bay leaf
75ml/5 tbsp caster sugar
small bay leaves, to decorate

1 Thinly peel the pears with a sharp knife or vegetable peeler, leaving the stalks attached.

2 Pour the wine and cranberry or apple juice into a large heavy-based saucepan. Add the orange rind, cinnamon stick, cloves, bay leaf and sugar.

3 Heat gently, stirring all the time, until the sugar has dissolved. Add the pears and stand them upright in the pan. Pour in enough cold water to barely cover them. Cover and cook gently for 20–30 minutes, or until just tender, turning and basting occasionally.

4 Using a slotted spoon, gently lift the pears out of the syrup and transfer to a serving dish.

5 Bring the syrup to the boil and boil rapidly for 10–15 minutes, or until it has reduced by half.

6 Strain the syrup and pour over the pears. Serve hot or well-chilled, decorated with small bay leaves.

NUTRITION NOTES

Per portion:
Energy	148Kcals/620kJ
Fat	0.16g
Saturated Fat	0
Fibre	2.93g

COOK'S TIP
Check the pears by piercing with a skewer or sharp knife towards the end of the poaching time, because some may cook more quickly than others. Serve straight away, or leave to cool in the syrup and then chill.

SNOW-CAPPED APPLES

Serves 4
4 small Bramley cooking apples
90ml /6 tbsp orange marmalade or jam
2 egg whites
50g/2oz/4 tbsp caster sugar

1 Preheat the oven to 180°C/350°F/
Gas 4. Core the apples and score
through the skins around the middle
with a sharp knife.

2 Place in a wide ovenproof dish and
spoon 15ml/1 tbsp marmalade into
the centre of each. Cover and bake for
35–40 minutes, or until tender.

3 Whisk the egg whites in a large
bowl until stiff enough to hold soft
peaks. Whisk in the sugar, then fold in
the remaining marmalade.

4 Spoon the meringue over the apples,
then return to the oven for 10–15
minutes, or until golden. Serve hot.

NUTRITION NOTES	
Per portion:	
Energy	165Kcals/394kJ
Fat	0.16g
Saturated fat	0
Cholesterol	0
Fibre	1.9g

STRAWBERRY APPLE TART

Serves 4–6
150g/5oz/1¼ cups self-raising flour
50g/2oz/⅔ cup rolled oats
50g/2oz/4 tbsp sunflower margarine
2 medium Bramley cooking apples,
  about 450g/1 lb total weight
200g/7oz/2 cups strawberries, halved
50g/2oz/4 tbsp caster sugar
15ml/1 tbsp cornflour

1 Preheat the oven to 200°C/400°F/
Gas 6. Mix together the flour and
oats in a large bowl and rub in the margarine evenly. Stir in just enough cold
water to bind the mixture to a firm
dough. Knead lightly until smooth.

2 Roll out the pastry and line a
23cm/9in loose-based flan tin. Trim
the edges, prick the base and line with
greaseproof paper and baking beans.
Roll out the pastry trimmings and
stamp out heart shapes using a cutter.

3 Bake the pastry case for 10 minutes,
remove paper and beans and bake
for 10–15 minutes or until golden
brown. Bake the hearts until golden.

4 Peel, core and slice the apples. Place
in a pan with the strawberries,
sugar and cornflour. Cover and cook
gently, stirring, until the fruit is just
tender. Spoon into the pastry case and
decorate with pastry hearts.

NUTRITION NOTES	
Per portion:	
Energy	382Kcals/1602kJ
Fat	11.93g
Saturated fat	2.18g
Cholesterol	0.88mg
Fibre	4.37g

GOLDEN GINGER COMPÔTE

Warm, spicy and full of sun-ripened ingredients – this is the perfect winter dessert.

INGREDIENTS

Serves 4

200g/7oz/2 cups kumquats
200g/7oz/1¼ cups dried apricots
30ml/2 tbsp sultanas
400ml/14fl oz/1⅔ cups water
1 orange
2.5cm/1 in piece fresh root ginger
4 cardamom pods
4 cloves
30ml/2 tbsp clear honey
15ml/1 tbsp flaked almonds, toasted

NUTRITION NOTES

Per portion:

Energy	196Kcals/825kJ
Fat	2.84g
Saturated fat	0.41g
Cholesterol	0
Fibre	6.82g

1 Wash the kumquats and, if they are large, cut them in half. Place them in a saucepan with the apricots, sultanas and water. Bring to the boil.

2 Pare the rind thinly from the orange, peel and grate the ginger, crush the cardamom pods and add to the pan, with the cloves.

3 Reduce the heat, cover the pan and simmer gently for about 30 minutes, or until the fruit is tender.

4 Squeeze the juice from the orange and add to the pan with honey to sweeten to taste, sprinkle with flaked almonds, and serve warm.

VARIATION
Use ready-to-eat dried apricots, but reduce the liquid to 300ml/½ pint/1¼ cups, and add 5 minutes before the end.

NECTARINES WITH SPICED RICOTTA

This easy dessert is good at any time of year – use canned peach halves if fresh nectarines are out of season.

INGREDIENTS

Serves 4

4 ripe nectarines or peaches
115g/4oz/½ cup ricotta cheese
15ml/1 tbsp light brown sugar
2.5ml/½ tsp ground star anise,
  to decorate

NUTRITION NOTES

Per portion:	
Energy	92Kcals/388kJ
Fat	3.27g
Saturated fat	0
Cholesterol	14.38mg
Fibre	1.65g

1 Cut the nectarines or peaches, if using, in half and remove the stones. Do this carefully with a sharp knife and a steady hand.

2 Arrange the nectarines or peaches, cut-side upwards, in a shallow flameproof dish or on a baking sheet.

3 Place the ricotta cheese in a small mixing bowl. Stir the light brown sugar into the ricotta cheese. Using a teaspoon, spoon equal amounts of the mixture into the hollow of each nectarine or peach half.

4 Sprinkle with the star anise. Cook under a moderately hot grill for 6–8 minutes, or until the nectarines or peaches are hot. Serve warm.

COOK'S TIP
Star anise has a warm, rich flavour – if you can't get it, use ground cloves or ground allspice as an alternative.

SPICED RED FRUIT COMPÔTE

INGREDIENTS

Serves 4

4 ripe red plums, halved
225g/8oz/2 cups strawberries, halved
225g/8oz/1¼ cups raspberries
30ml/2 tbsp light muscovado sugar
30 ml/2 tbsp cold water
1 cinnamon stick
3 pieces star anise
6 cloves

NUTRITION NOTES

Per portion:

Energy	90Kcals/375kJ
Fat	0.32g
Saturated fat	0
Cholesterol	0
Fibre	3.38g

1 Place the plums, strawberries and raspberries in a heavy-based pan with the sugar and water.

2 Add the cinnamon stick, star anise and cloves to the pan and heat gently, without boiling, until the sugar dissolves and the fruit juices run.

3 Cover the pan and leave the fruit to infuse over a very low heat for about 5 minutes. Remove the spices from the compote before serving warm with natural yogurt or fromage frais.

RHUBARB SPIRAL COBBLER

INGREDIENTS

Serves 4

675g/1½ lb rhubarb, sliced
50g/2oz/4 tbsp caster sugar
45ml/3 tbsp orange juice
200g/7oz/1¾ cups self-raising flour
30ml/2 tbsp caster sugar
about 200g/7oz/1 cup natural yogurt
grated rind of 1 medium orange
30ml/2 tbsp demerara sugar
5ml/1 tsp ground ginger

1 Preheat the oven to 200°C/400°F/ Gas 6. Cook the rhubarb, sugar and orange juice in a covered pan until tender. Tip into an ovenproof dish.

2 To make the topping, mix the flour and caster sugar, then stir enough of the yogurt to bind to a soft dough.

3 Roll out on a floured surface to a 25cm/10in square. Mix the orange rind, demerara sugar and ginger, then sprinkle this over the dough.

4 Roll up quite tightly, then cut into about 10 slices using a sharp knife. Arrange the slices over the rhubarb.

5 Bake in the oven for 15–20 minutes, or until the spirals are well risen and golden brown. Serve warm, with yogurt or custard.

NUTRITION NOTES

Per portion:

Energy	320Kcals/1343kJ
Fat	1.2g
Saturated fat	0.34g
Cholesterol	2mg
Fibre	3.92g

COCONUT AND LEMON DUMPLINGS

INGREDIENTS

Serves 4

For the dumplings
75g/3oz/⅓ cup cottage cheese
1 egg white
25g/1oz/2 tbsp low fat margarine
15ml/1 tbsp light brown sugar
30ml/2 tbsp self-raising wholemeal
   flour
finely grated rind of ½ lemon
30ml/2 tbsp desiccated coconut,
   toasted, plus extra, to decorate

For the sauce
225g/8oz can apricot halves in natural
   juice
15ml/1 tbsp lemon juice

NUTRITION NOTES

Per portion:	
Energy	162Kcals/681kJ
Fat	9.5g
Saturated fat	5.47g
Cholesterol	33.69mg
Fibre	2.21g

1 Half-fill a steamer with boiling water and put it on to boil, or place a heatproof dish over a saucepan of boiling water.

2 Beat together the cottage cheese, egg white and margarine.

3 Stir in the sugar, flour, lemon rind and coconut, mixing evenly to form a fairly firm dough.

4 Place eight to twelve spoonfuls of the mixture in the steamer or on the dish, leaving space between them.

5 Cover the steamer or pan tightly with a lid or a plate and steam for about 10 minutes, until the dumplings have risen and are firm to the touch.

6 Meanwhile make the sauce: put the apricots in a food processor or blender, and process until smooth. Stir in the lemon juice. Pour into a small pan and heat until boiling, then serve with the dumplings. Sprinkle with extra coconut to decorate.

WARM BAGELS WITH POACHED APRICOTS

INGREDIENTS

Serves 4

a few strips of orange peel
225g/8oz/1⅓ cups ready-to-eat dried
  apricots
250ml/8fl oz/1 cup fresh orange juice
2.5ml/½ tsp orange flower water
2 cinnamon and raisin bagels
20ml/4 tsp reduced-sugar orange
  marmalade
60ml/4 tbsp half-fat crème fraîche or
  soured cream
15g/½oz/2 tbsp chopped pistachio nuts,
  to decorate

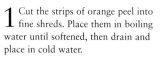

1 Cut the strips of orange peel into fine shreds. Place them in boiling water until softened, then drain and place in cold water.

3 Split the bagels in half horizontally. Lay one half, crumb uppermost, on each serving plate. Spread 5ml/1 tsp orange marmalade on each bagel.

2 Preheat the oven to 160°C/325°F/ Gas 3. Combine the apricots and orange juice in a small saucepan. Heat gently for about 10 minutes until the juice has reduced and looks syrupy. Allow to cool, then stir in the orange flower water. Meanwhile, place the bagels on a baking sheet and warm in the oven for 5–10 minutes.

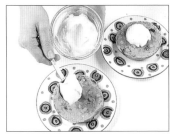

4 Spoon 15ml/1 tbsp crème fraîche or soured cream into the centre of each bagel and place a quarter of the apricot compôte at the side. Scatter orange peel and pistachio nuts over the top to decorate. Serve immediately.

NUTRITION NOTES

Per portion:
Energy	260Kcals/1090KJ
Fat	9g
Saturated Fat	4g
Cholesterol	51.5mg

CRISPY PEACH BAKE

A golden, crisp-crusted, family pudding that's made in minutes, from storecupboard ingredients.

NUTRITION NOTES

Per portion:

Energy	184Kcals/772kJ
Fat	8.42g
Saturated fat	4.26g
Cholesterol	17.25mg

INGREDIENTS

Serves 4

415g/14½oz can peach slices in juice
30ml/2 tbsp sultanas
1 cinnamon stick
strip of fresh orange rind
25g/1oz/2 tbsp low fat margarine
50g/2oz/1½ cups cornflakes
15ml/1 tbsp sesame seeds

COOK'S TIP

If you don't have a cinnamon stick, sprinkle in about 2.5ml/ ½ tsp ground cinnamon instead.

1 Drain the peaches, reserving the juice, and arrange the peach slices in a shallow ovenproof dish.

2 Preheat the oven to 200°C/400°F/ Gas 6. Place the peach juice, sultanas, cinnamon stick and orange rind in a saucepan and bring to the boil. Simmer, uncovered, for about 3–4 minutes, to reduce the liquid by about half. Remove the cinnamon stick and orange rind, and spoon the syrup over the peaches.

3 Melt the low fat margarine in a small pan and stir in the cornflakes and sesame seeds.

4 Spread the cornflake mixture over the fruit. Bake for about 15–20 minutes, or until the topping is crisp and golden. Serve hot.

Baked Blackberry Cheesecake

This light cheesecake is best made with wild blackberries, but cultivated ones will do. You can also substitute them for other soft fruit such as raspberries or loganberries.

INGREDIENTS

Serves 5

175g/6oz/³⁄₄ cup cottage cheese
150g/5oz/²⁄₃ cup low fat natural yogurt
15ml/1 tbsp wholemeal flour
30ml/2 tbsp golden caster sugar
1 egg
1 egg white
finely grated rind and juice of ½ lemon
200g/7oz/2 cups blackberries

NUTRITION NOTES

Per portion:

Energy	94Kcals/394kJ
Fat	1.67g
Saturated fat	1.03g
Cholesterol	5.75mg
Fibre	1.71g

1 Preheat the oven to 180°C/350°F/ Gas 4. Lightly grease and line the base of an 18cm/7 in cake tin.

2 Whizz the cottage cheese in a food processor or blender until smooth, or rub it through a sieve.

3 Add the yogurt, flour, sugar, egg and egg white, and mix. Add the lemon rind and juice, and blackberries, reserving a few for decoration.

4 Tip the mixture into the prepared tin and bake it for about 30–35 minutes, or until just set. Turn off the oven and leave for 30 minutes.

5 Run a knife around the edge of the cheesecake, and then turn it out.

6 Remove the lining paper and place the cheesecake on a warm serving plate. Decorate with the reserved blackberries and serve it warm.

> **COOK'S TIP**
> If you prefer to use canned blackberries, choose those preserved in natural juice and drain the fruit well before adding it to the cheesecake mixture. The juice may be served with the cheesecake, but this will increase the total calories.

Hot Plum Batter

Other fruits can be used in place of plums, depending on the season. Canned black cherries are also a convenient storecupboard substitute.

Ingredients

Serves 4

450g/1 lb ripe red plums, quartered
  and stoned
200ml/7 fl oz/⅞ cup skimmed milk
60ml/4 tbsp skimmed milk powder
15ml/1 tbsp light muscovado sugar
5ml/1 tsp vanilla essence
75g/3oz self-raising flour
2 egg whites
icing sugar, to sprinkle

1 Preheat the oven to 220°C/425°F/ Gas 7. Lightly oil a wide, shallow ovenproof dish and add the plums.

2 Pour the milk, milk powder, sugar, vanilla, flour and egg whites into a food processor. Process until smooth.

3 Pour the batter over the plums. Bake for 25–30 minutes, or until well risen and golden. Sprinkle with icing sugar and serve immediately.

Nutrition Notes

Per portion:

Energy	195Kcals/816kJ
Fat	0.48g
Saturated fat	0.12g
Cholesterol	2.8mg
Fibre	2.27g

Glazed Apricot Sponge

Proper puddings are usually very high in saturated fat, but this one uses the minimum of oil and no eggs.

Ingredients

Serves 4

10ml/2 tsp golden syrup
411g/14½oz can apricot halves in
  fruit juice
150g/5oz/1¼ cup self-raising flour
75g/3oz/1½ cups fresh breadcrumbs
90g/3½oz/⅔ cup light muscovado
  sugar
5ml/1 tsp ground cinnamon
30ml/2 tbsp sunflower oil
175ml/6 fl oz/¾ cup skimmed milk

1 Preheat the oven to 180°C/350°F/ Gas 4. Lightly oil a 900ml/1½ pint/3¾ cup pudding basin. Spoon in the syrup.

2 Drain the apricots and reserve the juice. Arrange about 8 halves in the basin. Purée the rest of the apricots with the juice and set aside.

3 Mix the flour, breadcrumbs, sugar and cinnamon then beat in the oil and milk. Spoon into the basin and bake for 50–55 minutes, or until firm and golden. Turn out and serve with the puréed fruit as a sauce.

Nutrition Notes

Per portion:

Energy	364Kcals/1530kJ
Fat	6.47g
Saturated fat	0.89g
Cholesterol	0.88mg
Fibre	2.37g

CHERRY PANCAKES

Serves 4

50g/2oz/½ cup plain flour
50g/2oz/⅓ cup wholemeal flour
pinch of salt
1 egg white
150ml/¼ pint/⅔ cup skimmed milk
150ml/¼ pint/⅔ cup water
15ml/1 tbsp sunflower oil for frying
low fat fromage frais, to serve

For the filling

425g/15oz can black cherries in juice
7.5ml/1½ tsp arrowroot

NUTRITION NOTES

Per portion:

Energy	173Kcals/725kJ
Fat	3.33g
Saturated fat	0.44g
Cholesterol	0.75mg
Fibre	2.36g

1 Sift the flours and salt into a bowl, adding any bran left in the sieve to the bowl at the end.

2 Make a well in the centre of the flour and add the egg white. Gradually beat in the milk and water, whisking hard until all the liquid is incorporated and the batter is smooth and frothy.

3 Heat a non-stick frying pan with a small amount of oil until the pan is very hot. Pour in just enough batter to cover the base of the pan, swirling the pan to cover the base evenly.

4 Cook until the pancake is set and golden, and then turn to cook the other side. Remove to a sheet of kitchen paper and then cook the remaining batter, to make about eight pancakes.

5 For the filling, drain the cherries, reserving the juice. Blend about 30ml/2 tbsp of the juice from the can of cherries with the arrowroot in a saucepan. Stir in the rest of the juice. Heat gently, stirring, until boiling. Stir over a moderate heat for about 2 minutes, until thickened and clear.

6 Add the cherries to the sauce and stir until thoroughly heated. Spoon the cherries into the pancakes and fold them into quarters.

COOK'S TIP
If fresh cherries are in season, cook them gently in enough apple juice just to cover them, and then thicken the juice with arrowroot as in Step 5. The basic pancakes will freeze very successfully between layers of kitchen paper or greaseproof paper.

SOUFFLÉED RICE PUDDING

INGREDIENTS

Serves 4

65g/2½oz/¼ cup short grain rice
45ml/3 tbsp clear honey
750ml/1¼ pints/3⅔ cups skimmed milk
1 vanilla pod or 2.5ml/½ tsp vanilla
  essence
2 egg whites
5ml/1 tsp freshly grated nutmeg

NUTRITION NOTES

Per portion:

Energy	163Kcals/683kJ
Fat	0.62g
Saturated fat	0.16g
Cholesterol	3.75mg
Fibre	0.08g

1 Place the rice, honey and milk in a heavy or non-stick saucepan, and bring the milk to the boil. Add the vanilla pod, if using it.

2 Reduce the heat and put the lid on the pan. Leave to simmer gently for about 1–1¼ hours, stirring occasionally to prevent sticking, until most of the liquid has been absorbed.

3 Remove the vanilla pod, or if using vanilla essence, add this to the rice mixture now. Preheat the oven to 220°C/425°F/Gas 7.

4 Place the egg whites in a clean, dry bowl and whisk them until they hold soft peaks.

5 Using either a large metal spoon or spatula, carefully fold the egg whites evenly into the rice and milk mixture and tip into a 1 litre/1¾ pint/ 4 cup ovenproof dish.

6 Sprinkle with grated nutmeg and bake for about 15–20 minutes, until the pudding is well risen and golden brown. Serve hot.

COOK'S TIP
Be very careful when simmering skimmed milk. With so little fat, it tends to boil over very easily. Use semi-skimmed if you wish.

CRUNCHY GOOSEBERRY CRUMBLE

Gooseberries are perfect for traditional family puddings like this one. When they are out of season, other fruits such as apple, plums or rhubarb could be used instead.

INGREDIENTS

Serves 4

500g/1¼ lb/5 cups gooseberries
50g/2oz/4 tbsp caster sugar
75g/3oz/1 cup rolled oats
75g/3oz/¾ cup wholemeal flour
60ml/4 tbsp sunflower oil
50g/2oz/4 tbsp demerara sugar
30ml/2 tbsp chopped walnuts
natural yogurt or custard, to serve

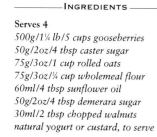

1 Preheat the oven to 200°C/400°F/ Gas 6. Place the gooseberries in a pan with the caster sugar. Cover the pan and cook over a low heat for 10 minutes, until the gooseberries are just tender. Tip into an ovenproof dish.

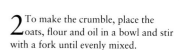

2 To make the crumble, place the oats, flour and oil in a bowl and stir with a fork until evenly mixed.

3 Stir in the demerara sugar and walnuts, then spread evenly over the gooseberries. Bake for 25–30 minutes, or until golden and bubbling. Serve hot with yogurt, or custard made with skimmed milk.

COOK'S TIP
The best cooking gooseberries are the early small, firm green ones.

NUTRITION NOTES

Per portion:

Energy	422Kcals/1770kJ
Fat	18.5g
Saturated fat	2.32g
Cholesterol	0
Fibre	5.12g

GINGERBREAD UPSIDE DOWN PUDDING

A proper pudding goes down well on a cold winter's day. This one is quite quick to make and looks very impressive.

INGREDIENTS

Serves 4–6
sunflower oil, for brushing
15ml/1 tbsp soft brown sugar
4 medium peaches, halved and stoned,
   or canned peach halves
8 walnut halves

For the base
130g/4½oz/½ cup wholemeal flour
2.5ml/½ tsp bicarbonate of soda
7.5ml/1½ tsp ground ginger
5ml/1 tsp ground cinnamon
115g/4oz/½ cup molasses sugar
1 egg
120ml/4 fl oz/½ cup skimmed milk
50ml/2 fl oz/¼ cup sunflower oil

1 Preheat the oven to 175°C/350°F/ Gas 4. For the topping, brush the base and sides of a 23cm/9in round springform cake tin with oil. Sprinkle the sugar over the base.

2 Arrange the peaches cut-side down in the tin with a walnut half in each.

3 For the base, sift together the flour, bicarbonate of soda, ginger and cinnamon, then stir in the sugar. Beat together the egg, milk and oil, then mix into the dry ingredients until smooth.

4 Pour the mixture evenly over the peaches and bake for 35–40 minutes, until firm to the touch. Turn out onto a serving plate. Serve hot with yogurt or custard.

NUTRITION NOTES

Per portion:

Energy	432Kcals/1812kJ
Fat	16.54g
Saturated fat	2.27g
Cholesterol	48.72mg
Fibre	4.79g

PLUM FILO POCKETS

INGREDIENTS

Serves 4

*115g/4oz/½ cup skimmed milk soft
 cheese*
15ml/1 tbsp light muscovado sugar
2.5ml/½ tsp ground cloves
8 large, firm plums, halved and stoned
8 sheets filo pastry
sunflower oil, for brushing
icing sugar, to sprinkle

1 Preheat the oven to 220°C/425°F/
Gas 7. Mix together the cheese,
sugar and cloves.

2 Sandwich the plum halves back
together in twos with a spoonful of
the cheese mixture.

3 Spread out the pastry and cut into
16 pieces, about 23cm/9in square.
Brush one lightly with oil and place a
second at a diagonal on top. Repeat
with the remaining squares.

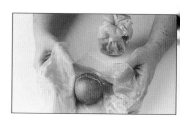

4 Place a plum on each pastry square,
and pinch corners together. Place on
baking sheet. Bake for 15–18 minutes,
until golden, then dust with icing sugar.

NUTRITION NOTES	
Per portion:	
Energy	188Kcals/790kJ
Fat	1.87g
Saturated fat	0.27g
Cholesterol	0.29mg
Fibre	2.55g

APPLE COUSCOUS PUDDING

This unusual mixture makes a
delicious family pudding with a
rich fruity flavour, but virtually
no fat.

INGREDIENTS

Serves 4

600ml/1 pint/2½ cups apple juice
115g/4oz/⅔ cup couscous
40g/1½ oz/¼ cup sultanas
2.5ml/½ tsp mixed spice
*1 large Bramley cooking apple, peeled,
 cored and sliced*
30ml/2 tbsp demerara sugar
natural low fat yogurt, to serve

1 Preheat the oven to 200°C/400°F/
Gas 6. Place the apple juice, couscous, sultanas and spice in a pan and
bring to the boil, stirring. Cover and
simmer for 10–12 minutes, until all the
free liquid is absorbed.

2 Spoon half the couscous mixture
into a 1.2 litre/2 pint/5 cup ovenproof dish and top with half the apple
slices. Top with remaining couscous.

3 Arrange the remaining apple slices
overlapping over the top and sprinkle with demerara sugar. Bake for
25–30 minutes or until golden brown.
Serve hot, with yogurt.

NUTRITION NOTES	
Per portion:	
Energy	194Kcals/815kJ
Fat	0.58g
Saturated fat	0.09g
Cholesterol	0
Fibre	0.75g

FRUITY BREAD PUDDING

A delicious family favourite pud from grandmother's day, with a lighter, healthier touch.

INGREDIENTS

Serves 4

75g/3oz/⅔ cup mixed dried fruit
150ml/¼ pint/⅔ cup apple juice
115g/4oz stale brown or white bread, diced
5ml/1 tsp mixed spice
1 large banana, sliced
150ml/¼ pint/⅔ cup skimmed milk
15ml/1 tbsp demerara sugar
natural low fat yogurt, to serve

1 Preheat the oven to 200°C/400°F/ Gas 6. Place the dried fruit in a small pan with the apple juice and bring to the boil.

2 Remove the pan from the heat and stir in the bread, spice and banana Spoon the mixture into a shallow 1.2 litre/2 pint/5 cup ovenproof dish and pour over the milk.

3 Sprinkle with demerara sugar and bake for 25–30 minutes, until firm and golden brown. Serve hot or cold with natural yogurt.

COOK'S TIP
Different types of bread will absorb varying amounts of liquid, so you may need to adjust the amount of milk to allow for this.

NUTRITION NOTES

Per portion:

Energy	190Kcals/800kJ
Fat	0.89g
Saturated fat	0.21g
Cholesterol	0.75mg
Fibre	1.8g

SPICED PEARS IN CIDER

Any variety of pear can be used for cooking, but it is best to choose firm pears for this recipe, or they will break up easily – Conference are a good choice.

─────── INGREDIENTS ───────

Serves 4

4 medium firm pears
250ml/8 fl oz/1 cup dry cider
thinly pared strip of lemon rind
1 cinnamon stick
30ml/2 tbsp light muscovado sugar
5ml/1 tsp arrowroot
ground cinnamon, to sprinkle

1 Peel the pears thinly, leaving them whole with the stalks on. Place in a pan with the cider, lemon rind and cinnamon. Cover and simmer gently, turning the pears occasionally for 15–20 minutes, or until tender.

2 Lift out the pears. Boil the syrup, uncovered to reduce by about half. Remove the lemon rind and cinnamon stick, then stir in the sugar.

3 Mix the arrowroot with 15ml/1 tbsp cold water in a small bowl until smooth, then stir into the syrup. Bring to the boil and stir over the heat until thickened and clear.

4 Pour the sauce over the pears and sprinkle with ground cinnamon. Leave to cool slightly, then serve warm with low fat fromage frais.

COOK'S TIP
Whole pears look very impressive, but if you prefer, they can be halved and cored before cooking. This will shorten the cooking time slightly.

─── NUTRITION NOTES ───
Per portion:
Energy	102Kcals/428kJ
Fat	0.18g
Saturated fat	0.01g
Cholesterol	0
Fibre	1.65g

BANANA, MAPLE AND LIME PANCAKES

Pancakes are a treat any day of the week, and they can be made in advance and stored in the freezer for convenience.

INGREDIENTS

Serves 4
115g/4oz/1 cup plain flour
1 egg white
250ml/8 fl oz/1 cup skimmed milk
50ml/2 fl oz/¼ cup cold water
sunflower oil, for frying

For the filling
4 bananas, sliced
45ml/3 tbsp maple syrup or golden syrup
30ml/2 tbsp lime juice
strips of lime rind, to decorate

1 Beat together the flour, egg white, milk and water until smooth and bubbly. Chill until needed.

2 Heat a small amount of oil in a non-stick frying pan and pour in enough batter just to coat the base. Swirl it around the pan to coat evenly.

3 Cook until golden, then toss or turn and cook the other side. Place on a plate, cover with foil and keep hot while making the remaining pancakes.

4 To make the filling, place the bananas, syrup and lime juice in a pan and simmer gently for 1 minute. Spoon into the pancakes and fold into quarters. Sprinkle with shreds of lime rind to decorate. Serve hot, with yogurt or low fat fromage frais.

COOK'S TIP
Pancakes freeze well. To store for later use, interleave them with non-stick baking paper, overwrap and freeze for up to 3 months.

NUTRITION NOTES

Per portion:
Energy	282Kcals/1185kJ
Fat	2.79g
Saturated fat	0.47g
Cholesterol	1.25mg
Fibre	2.12g

SOUFFLÉED ORANGE SEMOLINA

Semolina has a poor reputation as a rather dull, sloppy pudding, but cooked like this you would hardly recognise it.

INGREDIENTS

Serves 4

50g/2oz/¼ cup semolina
600ml/1 pint/2½ cups semi-skimmed milk
30ml/2 tbsp light muscovado sugar
1 large orange
1 egg white

1 Preheat the oven to 200°C/400°F/ Gas 6. Place the semolina in a non-stick pan with the milk and sugar. Stir over a moderate heat until thickened and smooth. Remove from the heat.

2 Grate a few long shreds of orange rind from the orange and save for decoration. Finely grate the remaining rind. Cut all the peel and white pith from the orange and remove the segments. Stir into the semolina with the orange rind.

3 Whisk the egg white until stiff but not dry, then fold lightly and evenly into the mixture. Spoon into a 1 litre/ 1¼ pint/4 cup ovenproof dish and bake for 15–20 minutes, until risen and golden brown. Serve immediately.

COOK'S TIP
When using the rind of citrus fruit, scrub the fruit thoroughly before use, or buy unwaxed fruit.

NUTRITION NOTES

Per portion:
Energy	158Kcals/665kJ
Fat	2.67g
Saturated fat	1.54g
Cholesterol	10.5mg
Fibre	0.86g

COLD DESSERTS

There is such a vast range of ready-made desserts available today that it may hardly seem worth making your own, but it is definitely well worth the effort. In no time at all, you can make and enjoy a wide variety of nutritious low fat delicious cold desserts, such as Rhubarb and Orange Water-ice, Apple and Blackberry Terrine, Mandarins in Syrup and Raspberry Vacherin.

APRICOT DELICE

A fluffy mousse base with a layer of fruit jelly on top makes this dessert doubly delicious.

INGREDIENTS

Serves 8

2 x 400g/14oz cans apricots in
   natural juice
60ml/4 tbsp sugar
25ml/5 tbsp lemon juice
25ml/5 tsp powdered gelatine
425g/15oz low fat ready-to-serve
   custard
150ml/¼ pint/²⁄₃ cup Greek-style
   yogurt
1 apricot, sliced, and fresh mint sprig,
   to decorate
whipped cream, to decorate (optional)

NUTRITION NOTES

Per portion:
Energy	155Kcals/649kJ
Fat	0.63g
Saturated Fat	0.33g
Fibre	0.9g

COOK'S TIP
Use reduced fat Greek yogurt
to cut calories and fat. Add the
finely grated rind of 1 lemon
to the mixture, for extra flavour.
Peaches or pears are good
alternatives to apricots.

1 Line the base of a 1.2 litre/2 pint/ 5 cup heart-shaped or round cake tin with non-stick baking paper.

2 Drain the apricots, reserving the juice. Put the apricots in a food processor or blender fitted with a metal blade, together with the sugar and 60ml/4 tbsp of the apricot juice. Blend to a smooth purée.

3 Measure 30ml/2 tbsp of the apricot juice into a small bowl. Add the lemon juice, then sprinkle over 10ml/ 2 tsp of the gelatine. Leave for about 5 minutes, until spongy.

4 Stir the gelatine into half of the purée and pour into the prepared tin. Chill in the fridge for 1½ hours, or until firm.

5 Sprinkle the remaining 15ml/3 tsp of gelatine over 60ml/4 tbsp of the apricot juice. Leave for about 5 minutes until spongy. Mix the remaining apricot purée with the custard, yogurt and gelatine. Pour on to the layer of set fruit purée and chill for 3 hours.

6 Dip the cake tin into hot water for a few seconds and unmould the delice on to a serving plate and peel off the lining paper. Decorate with the sliced apricot and mint sprig; for a special occasion, pipe whipped cream round the edge.

MELON, GINGER AND GRAPEFRUIT

This pretty fruit combination is very light and refreshing for any summer meal.

INGREDIENTS

Serves 4

500g/1¼ lbs diced watermelon flesh
2 ruby or pink grapefruit
2 pieces stem ginger in syrup
30ml/2 tbsp stem ginger syrup

NUTRITION NOTES

Per portion:
Energy	76Kcals/324.5kJ
Fat	0.42g
Saturated Fat	0.125g
Cholesterol	0
Fibre	0.77g

1 Remove any seeds from the watermelon and discard. Cut the fruit into bite-size chunks. Set aside.

2 Using a small sharp knife, cut away all the peel and white pith from the grapefruits and carefully lift out the segments, catching any juice in a bowl.

3 Finely chop the stem ginger and put in a serving bowl with the melon cubes and grapefruit segments, also adding the juice.

4 Spoon over the ginger syrup and toss the fruits lightly to mix evenly. Chill before serving.

COOK'S TIP
Take care to toss the fruits gently – grapefruit segments will break up easily and the appearance of the dish will be spoiled.

MANGO AND GINGER CLOUDS

The sweet, perfumed flavour of ripe mango combines beautifully with ginger, and this low fat dessert makes the very most of them both.

INGREDIENTS

Serves 6
3 ripe mangoes
3 pieces stem ginger
45ml/3 tbsp stem ginger syrup
75g/3oz/½ cup silken tofu
3 egg whites
6 pistachio nuts, chopped

1 Cut the mangoes in half, remove the stones and peel. Roughly chop the mango flesh.

2 Put the chopped mango in a food processor bowl, with the ginger, syrup and tofu. Process the mixture until smooth and spoon into a mixing bowl.

3 Put the egg whites in a bowl and whisk them until they form soft peaks. Fold them lightly into the mango mixture.

4 Spoon the mixture into wide dishes or glasses and chill before serving, sprinkled with the chopped pistachios.

NUTRITION NOTES

Per portion:
Energy	112Kcals/472kJ
Fat	3.5g
Saturated Fat	0.52g
Cholesterol	0
Fibre	2.25g

COOK'S TIP
This dessert can be served lightly frozen. If you prefer not to use ginger, omit the ginger pieces and syrup and use 45ml/3 tbsp clear honey instead.

GOOSEBERRY CHEESE COOLER

INGREDIENTS

Serves 4

500g/1¼lb/4 cups fresh or frozen
  gooseberries
1 small orange
15ml/1 tbsp clear honey
250g/9oz/1 cup half-fat cottage cheese

NUTRITION NOTES

Per portion:

Energy	123Kcals/525kJ
Fat	1.29g
Saturated Fat	0.69g
Cholesterol	3.25mg
Fibre	3.64g

1 Top and tail the gooseberries and place them in a pan. Finely grate the rind from the orange and squeeze out the juice, then add them both to the pan. Cover the pan and cook gently, stirring occasionally, until the fruit is tender.

2 Remove from the heat and stir in the honey. Purée the gooseberries with their juice in a blender or food processor until almost smooth. Cool.

3 Press the cottage cheese through a sieve until smooth. Stir half the cooled gooseberry purée into the cheese.

4 Spoon the cheese mixture into four serving glasses. Top each with gooseberry purée. Serve chilled.

COOK'S TIP
If fresh or frozen gooseberries are not available, canned ones are often packed in heavy syrup, so substitute a different fresh fruit.

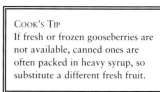

MANGO AND LIME SORBET IN LIME SHELLS

This richly flavoured sorbet looks pretty served in the lime shells, but is also good served in scoops for a more traditional presentation.

Serves 4
4 large limes
1 medium-size ripe mango
7.5ml/½ tsp powdered gelatine
2 egg whites
15ml/1 tbsp granulated sugar
lime rind strips, to decorate

1 Cut a thick slice from the top of each of the limes, and then cut a thin slice from the bottom end so that the limes will stand upright. Squeeze out the juice, then use a small knife to remove all the white membrane from the centre.

2 Halve, stone, peel and chop the mango, then purée the flesh in a blender or food processor with 30ml/2 tbsp of the lime juice. Dissolve the gelatine in 45ml/3 tbsp of lime juice and stir it into the mango mixture.

3 Whisk the egg whites until they hold soft peaks. Whisk in the sugar, then quickly fold the egg-white mixture into the mango mixture. Spoon the sorbet into the lime shells. (Any leftover sorbet that will not fit in can be frozen in small ramekins.)

COOK'S TIP
If you have any lime juice left over, it will freeze well for future use. Pour into a freezer container, seal and freeze for up to six months.

4 Wrap the shells in clear film and put in the freezer until the sorbet is firm. Before serving, allow the shells to stand at room temperature for about 10 minutes; decorate them with strips of lime rind.

NUTRITION NOTES

Per portion:
Energy	50.5Kcals/215kJ
Fat	0.09g
Saturated Fat	0.3g
Cholesterol	0
Fibre	1g

RHUBARB AND ORANGE WATER-ICE

Pretty pink rhubarb, with sweet oranges and honey – the perfect sweet ice.

INGREDIENTS

Serves 4
350g/12oz rhubarb
1 medium orange
15ml/1 tbsp clear honey
5ml/1 tsp/1 sachet powdered gelatine
orange slices, to decorate

COOK'S TIP
Most pink, forced rhubarb is naturally quite sweet, but if yours is not, you can add a little more honey, sugar or artificial sweetener to taste.

1 Trim the rhubarb and slice into 2.5cm/1in lengths. Put the pieces in a pan without adding water.

NUTRITION NOTES

Per portion:
Energy	36Kcals/155kJ
Fat	0.12g
Saturated Fat	0
Cholesterol	0
Fibre	1.9g

2 Finely grate the rind from the orange and squeeze out the juice. Add about half the orange juice and all the grated rind to the rhubarb in the pan and allow to simmer until the rhubarb is just tender. Stir in the honey.

3 Heat the remaining orange juice and sprinkle in the gelatine to dissolve it. Stir into the rhubarb. Turn the whole mixture into a rigid freezer container and freeze it for about 2 hours until slushy.

4 Remove the mixture from the freezer and beat it well to break up the ice crystals. Return to the freezer and freeze again until firm. Allow the water-ice to soften slightly at room temperature before serving.

ICED ORANGES

The ultimate fat-free treat –
these delectable orange sorbets
served in fruit shells were origi-
nally sold in the beach cafés in
the south of France.

INGREDIENTS

Serves 8
150g/5oz/²⁄₃ cup granulated sugar
juice of 1 lemon
14 medium oranges
8 fresh bay leaves, to decorate

NUTRITION NOTES

Per portion:

Energy	139Kcals/593kJ
Fat	0.17g
Saturated Fat	0
Cholesterol	0
Fibre	3g

COOK'S TIP
Use crumpled kitchen paper to
keep the shells upright.

1 Put the sugar in a heavy-based
saucepan. Add half the lemon juice,
then add 120ml/4fl oz/½ cup water.
Cook over a low heat until the sugar
has dissolved. Bring to the boil and boil
for 2–3 minutes until the syrup is clear.

2 Slice the tops off eight of the
oranges to make "hats". Scoop out
the flesh of the oranges and reserve.
Freeze the empty orange shells and
"hats" until needed.

3 Grate the rind of the remaining
oranges and add to the syrup.
Squeeze the juice from the oranges, and
from the reserved flesh. There should
be 750ml/1¼ pints/3 cups. Squeeze
another orange or add bought orange
juice, if necessary.

4 Stir the orange juice and remaining
lemon juice, with 90ml/6 tbsp water
into the syrup. Taste, adding more
lemon juice or sugar as desired. Pour
the mixture into a shallow freezer
container and freeze for 3 hours.

5 Turn the orange sorbet mixture into
a bowl and whisk thoroughly to
break up the ice crystals. Freeze for
4 hours more, until firm, but not solid.

6 Pack the mixture into the hollowed-
out orange shells, mounding it up,
and set the "hats" on top. Freeze the
sorbet shells until ready to serve. Just
before serving, push a skewer into the
tops of the "hats" and push in a bay
leaf, to decorate.

APPLE AND BLACKBERRY TERRINE

Apples and blackberries are a classic autumn combination; they really complement each other. This pretty, three-layered terrine can be frozen, so you can enjoy it at any time of year.

INGREDIENTS

Serves 6

500g/1½lb cooking or eating apples
300ml/½ pint/1¼ cups sweet cider
15ml/1 tbsp clear honey
5ml/1 tsp vanilla essence
200g/7oz fresh or frozen and thawed blackberries
15ml/1 tbsp/1 sachet powdered gelatine
2 egg whites
apple slices and blackberries, to decorate

NUTRITION NOTES

Per portion:	
Energy	72Kcals/306kJ
Fat	0.13g
Saturated Fat	0
Cholesterol	0
Fibre	2.1g

COOK'S TIP

For a quicker version, the mixture can be set without layering. Purée the apples and blackberries together, stir the dissolved gelatine and whisked egg whites into the mixture, turn the whole thing into the tin and leave the mixture to set.

1 Peel, core and chop the apples and place them in a saucepan, with half the cider. Bring the cider to the boil, and then cover the pan and let the apples simmer gently on a medium heat until tender.

2 Tip the apples into a blender or food processor and process them to a smooth purée. Stir in the honey and vanilla. Add half the blackberries to half the apple purée, and then process the mixture again until smooth. Sieve.

3 Heat the remaining cider until it is almost boiling, then sprinkle the powdered gelatine over and stir until the gelatine has completely dissolved. Add half the gelatine and cider liquid to the apple purée and half to the blackberry purée.

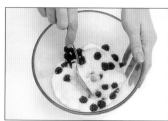

4 Leave the purées to cool until almost set. Whisk the egg whites until they are stiff, then quickly fold them into the apple purée. Remove half the purée to another bowl. Stir the remaining whole blackberries into half the apple purée, and then turn this into a 1.75 litre/3 pint/7½ cup loaf tin.

5 Top with the blackberry purée and spread it evenly. Finally, add a layer of the apple purée and smooth it evenly. To make sure the layers remain clearly separated, you can freeze each one until firm before adding the next.

6 Freeze until firm. To serve, allow to stand at room temperature for about 20 minutes to soften, then serve in thick slices, decorated with apples and blackberries.

QUICK APRICOT WHIP

INGREDIENTS

Serves 4

400g/14oz can apricot halves in juice
15ml/1 tbsp Grand Marnier or brandy
175g/6oz/³⁄4 cup low fat yogurt
30ml/2 tsp flaked almonds

NUTRITION NOTES

Per portion:

Energy	114Kcals/480kJ
Fat	4.6g
Saturated Fat	0.57g
Cholesterol	0
Fibre	1.45g

1 Drain the juice from the apricots and place the fruit and liqueur in a blender or food processor.

2 Process the apricots until they are completely smooth.

3 Put alternate spoonfuls of the fruit purée and yogurt into four tall glasses or glass dishes, swirling them together slightly to give a marbled effect.

4 Lightly toast the almonds until they are golden-brown. Let them cool slightly and then sprinkle them on top of the desserts.

COOK'S TIP
If you prefer to omit the liqueur, add a little of the fruit juice from the can.

MANDARINS IN SYRUP

Mandarins, tangerines, clementines, mineolas; any of these lovely citrus fruits are suitable for this recipe.

INGREDIENTS

Serves 4

10 mandarin oranges
15ml/1 tbsp icing sugar
10ml/2 tsp orange-flower water
15ml/1 tbsp chopped pistachio nuts

1 Thinly pare a little of the rind from one mandarin and cut it into fine shreds for decoration. Squeeze the juice from two mandarins and set aside.

2 Peel the remaining fruit, removing as much of the white pith as possible. Arrange the peeled fruit whole in a wide dish.

3 Mix the mandarin juice, sugar and orange-flower water and pour it over the fruit. Cover the dish and chill for at least an hour.

4 Blanch the shreds of mandarin rind in boiling water for 30 seconds. Drain, leave to cool and then sprinkle them over the mandarins, with the pistachio nuts, to serve.

NUTRITION NOTES

Per portion:

Energy	53.25Kcals/223.5kJ
Fat	2.07g
Saturated Fat	0.28g
Cholesterol	0
Fibre	0.38g

COOK'S TIP
Mandarin oranges look very attractive if you leave them whole, but you may prefer to separate the segments.

CRUNCHY FRUIT LAYER

Serves 2

1 peach or nectarine
75g/3oz/1 cup crunchy toasted
  oat cereal
150ml/¼ pint/⅔ cup low fat
  natural yogurt
15ml/1 tbsp jam
15ml/1 tbsp fruit juice

— NUTRITION NOTES —	
Per portion:	
Energy	240Kcals/1005kJ
Fat	3g
Saturated Fat	1g
Cholesterol	3mg

1 Remove the stone from the peach or nectarine and cut the fruit into bite-size pieces with a sharp knife.

2 Divide the chopped fruit between two tall glasses, reserving a few pieces for decoration.

3 Sprinkle the oat cereal over the fruit in an even layer, then top with the low fat yogurt.

4 Stir the jam and the fruit juice together in a jug, then drizzle the mixture over the yogurt. Decorate with the reserved peach or nectarine pieces and serve at once.

RASPBERRY MUESLI LAYER

As well as being a delicious, low fat, high-fibre dessert, this recipe can also be served for a quick, healthy breakfast.

INGREDIENTS

Serves 4

225g/8oz/2¼ cups fresh or frozen and
    thawed raspberries
225g/8oz/1 cup low fat natural yogurt
75g/3oz/½ cup Swiss-style muesli

1 Reserve four raspberries for decoration, then spoon a few raspberries into each of four stemmed glasses or glass dishes.

2 Top the raspberries with a spoonful of yogurt in each glass.

3 Sprinkle a layer of muesli mixture over the yogurt.

4 Repeat with the remaining raspberries and other ingredients, finishing with muesli. Top each dish with a whole raspberry.

COOK'S TIP
This recipe can be made in advance and stored in the fridge for several hours, or overnight if you're serving it for breakfast.

NUTRITION NOTES

Per portion:

Energy	114Kcals/483kJ
Fat	1.7g
Saturated Fat	0.48g
Cholesterol	2.25mg
Fibre	2.6g

YOGURT SUNDAES WITH PASSION FRUIT

Here is a sundae you can enjoy every day! The frozen yogurt has less fat and fewer calories than traditional ice cream, and the fruits provide vitamins A and C.

—————— INGREDIENTS ——————

Serves 4
350g/12oz strawberries, hulled
  and halved
2 passion fruit, halved
10ml/2 tsp icing sugar (optional)
2 ripe peaches, stoned and chopped
8 scoops (about 350g/12oz) vanilla or
  strawberry frozen yogurt

COOK'S TIP
Choose reduced fat or virtually fat free frozen yogurt or ice cream, to cut the calories and fat.

1 Purée half the strawberries. Scoop out the passion fruit pulp and add it to the coulis. Sweeten, if necessary.

—————— NUTRITION NOTES ——————

Per portion:
Energy   135Kcals/560kJ
Fat   1g
Saturated Fat   0.5g
Cholesterol   3.5mg

2 Spoon half the remaining strawberries and half the chopped peaches into four tall sundae glasses. Top each dessert with a scoop of frozen yogurt. Set aside a few choice pieces of fruit for decoration, and use the rest to make a further layer on the top of each sundae. Top each sundae with a final scoop of frozen yogurt.

3 Pour over the passion fruit coulis and decorate the sundaes with the remaining strawberries and pieces of peach. Serve immediately.

FRUIT FONDUE WITH HAZELNUT DIP

—————— INGREDIENTS ——————

Serves 2
selection of fresh fruit for dipping, such
  as satsumas, kiwi fruit, grapes
  and physalis (cape gooseberries)
50g/2oz/¹/₂ cup reduced fat soft cheese
150ml/5fl oz/1¹/₄ cup low fat
  hazelnut yogurt
5ml/1 tsp vanilla essence
5ml/1 tsp caster sugar

—————— NUTRITION NOTES ——————

Per portion (dip only):
Energy   170Kcals/714kJ
Fat   4g
Saturated Fat   2.5g
Cholesterol   6.5mg

1 First prepare the fruit. Peel and segment the satsumas, removing as much of the white pith as possible. Quarter the kiwi fruits, wash the grapes and peel back the papery casing on the physalis.

2 Beat the soft cheese with the yogurt, vanilla essence and sugar in a bowl. Spoon the mixture into a glass serving dish set on a platter or into small pots on individual plates.

3 Arrange the prepared fruits around the dip and serve immediately.

Pineapple, Allspice and Lime

Fresh pineapple is easy to prepare and always looks very festive, so this dish is perfect for easy entertaining.

--- Nutrition Notes ---

Per portion:

Energy	39Kcals/163kJ
Fat	0.12g
Saturated Fat	0
Cholesterol	0
Fibre	0.68g

--- Ingredients ---

Serves 4
1 ripe medium pineapple
1 lime
15ml/1 tbsp dark muscovado sugar
5ml/1 tsp ground allspice

1 Cut the pineapple lengthways into quarters and remove the core.

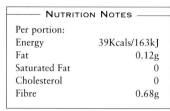

2 Loosen the fruit by sliding a knife between it and the skin. Cut the pineapple flesh into thick slices.

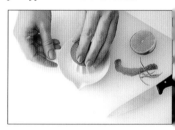

3 Remove a few shreds of rind from the lime and set aside, then squeeze out the juice.

4 Sprinkle the pineapple with the lime juice and rind, muscovado sugar and allspice. Serve immediately, or chill for up to 1 hour.

PAPAYA SKEWERS WITH PASSION FRUIT

Tropical fruits, full of natural sweetness, make a simple dessert.

INGREDIENTS

Serves 6

3 ripe papayas
10 small passion fruit or kiwi fruit
30ml/2 tbsp lime juice
30ml/2 tbsp icing sugar
30ml/2 tbsp white rum
lime slices, to decorate (optional)

NUTRITION NOTES

Per portion:

Energy	83Kcals/351kJ
Fat	0.27g
Saturated Fat	0
Cholesterol	0
Fibre	2.8g

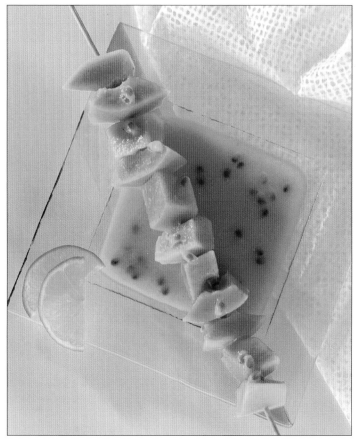

1 Cut the papayas in half and scoop out the seeds. Peel and cut the flesh into even-size chunks. Thread the chunks on to six bamboo skewers.

2 Halve eight of the passion fruit or kiwi fruit and scoop out the insides. Purée for a few seconds in a blender or food processor.

3 Press the passion fruit or kiwi fruit pulp through a sieve and discard the seeds. Add the lime juice, icing sugar and white rum, then stir the coulis well until the sugar has dissolved.

4 Spoon a little of the coulis on to six serving plates. Place the skewers on top. Scoop the flesh from the remaining passion fruit or kiwi fruit and spoon it over. Decorate with lime slices.

RASPBERRY VACHERIN

Meringue rounds filled with orange-flavoured low fat fromage frais and fresh raspberries make this a perfect dinner party dessert.

INGREDIENTS

Serves 6
3 egg whites
175g/6oz/³/₄ cup caster sugar
5ml/1 tsp chopped almonds
icing sugar, for dusting
raspberry leaves, to decorate (optional)

For the filling
175g/6oz/³/₄ cup low fat soft cheese
15–30ml/1–2 tbsp clear honey
15–30ml/1–2 tbsp Cointreau
120ml/4fl oz/¹/₂ cup low fat
   fromage frais
225g/8oz raspberries

NUTRITION NOTES

Per portion:

Energy	197Kcals/837.5kJ
Fat	1.02g
Saturated Fat	0.36g
Cholesterol	1.67mg
Fibre	1g

COOK'S TIP
When making the meringue, whisk the egg whites until they are so stiff that you can turn the bowl upside-down without them falling out.

1 Preheat the oven to 140°C/275°F/ Gas 1. Draw a 20cm/8in circle on two pieces of non-stick baking paper. Turn the paper over so the marking is on the underside and use it to line two heavy baking sheets.

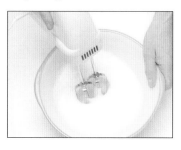

2 Whisk the egg whites in a clean bowl until very stiff, then gradually whisk in the caster sugar to make a stiff meringue mixture.

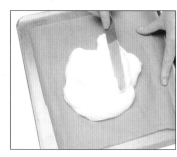

3 Spoon the mixture on to the circles on the prepared baking sheets, spreading the meringue evenly to the edges. Sprinkle one meringue round with the chopped almonds.

4 Bake for 1¹/₂–2 hours until crisp and dry, and then carefully lift the meringue rounds off the baking sheets. Peel away the paper and cool the meringues on a wire rack.

5 To make the filling, cream the soft cheese with the honey and liqueur in a bowl. Gradually fold in the fromage frais and the raspberries, reserving three berries for decoration.

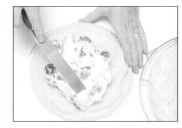

6 Place the plain meringue round on a board, spread with the filling and top with the nut-covered round. Dust with the icing sugar, transfer to a serving plate and decorate with the reserved raspberries and a sprig of raspberry leaves, if you like.

COOL GREEN FRUIT SALAD

A sophisticated, simple fruit salad for any time of year.

INGREDIENTS

Serves 6

3 Ogen or Galia melons
115g/4oz green seedless grapes
2 kiwi fruit
1 star fruit
1 green-skinned eating apple
1 lime
175ml/6fl oz/³⁄4 cup sparkling grape
 juice

NUTRITION NOTES

Per portion:
Energy	67Kcals/285kJ
Fat	0.27g
Saturated Fat	0
Cholesterol	0
Fibre	1.22g

1 Cut the melons in half and scoop out the seeds. Keeping the shells intact, scoop out the fruit with a melon baller, or scoop it out with a spoon and cut into bite-size cubes. Set aside the melon shells.

COOK'S TIP
If you're serving this dessert on a hot summer day, serve the filled melon shells nestling on a platter of crushed ice to keep them beautifully cool.

2 Remove any stems from the grapes, and, if they are large, cut them in half. Peel and chop the kiwi fruit. Thinly slice the star fruit. Core and thinly slice the apple and place the slices in a bowl, with the melon, grapes, kiwi fruit and star fruit.

3 Thinly pare the rind from the lime and cut it into fine strips. Blanch the strips in boiling water for 30 seconds, then drain them and rinse in cold water. Squeeze the juice from the lime and toss it into the fruit. Mix gently.

4 Spoon the prepared fruit into the melon shells and chill in the fridge until required. Just before serving, spoon the sparkling grape juice over the fruit and scatter it with the blanched lime rind.

THREE FRUIT COMPÔTES

INGREDIENTS

Each Compôte Serves 1
ORANGE AND PRUNE COMPÔTE
1 orange
50g/2oz ready-to-eat prunes
75ml/5 tbsp orange juice

PEAR AND KIWI FRUIT COMPÔTE
1 ripe eating pear
1 kiwi fruit
60ml/4 tbsp apple or pineapple juice

GRAPEFRUIT AND STRAWBERRY COMPÔTE
1 ruby grapefruit
115g/4oz strawberries
60ml/4 tbsp orange juice

To serve
low fat natural yogurt and toasted
  hazelnuts

NUTRITION NOTES

Per portion (minus topping):

Orange and Prune

Energy	155Kcals/650kJ
Fat	0.5g
Saturated Fat	0
Cholesterol	0

Pear and Kiwi Fruit

Energy	100Kcals/405kJ
Fat	0.5g
Saturated Fat	0
Cholesterol	0

Grapefruit and Strawberry

Energy	110Kcals/465kJ
Fat	0.5g
Saturated Fat	0
Cholesterol	0

COOK'S TIP
Choose fresh-pressed fruit juices
or squeeze your own fruit juice
using a blender or food processor.

1 For the orange and prune compôte,
segment the orange and place in a
bowl with the prunes.

2 For the pear and kiwi fruit compôte,
peel the pear and cut it into wedges,
and peel and slice the kiwi fruit.

3 For the grapefruit and strawberry
compôte, segment the grapefruit
and halve the strawberries.

4 Put your selected fruits together in a
bowl and pour over the fruit juice.

5 Serve the chosen fruit compôte
topped with a spoonful of low fat
natural yogurt and a sprinking of
chopped toasted hazelnuts, to decorate.

Prune and Orange Pots

This simple, storecupboard dessert can be made in minutes. Serve straight away or, for the best result, chill it for about half an hour before serving.

Ingredients

Serves 4

225g/8oz/1½ cups ready-to-eat dried prunes
150ml/¼ pint/⅔ cup orange juice
225g/8oz/1 cup low fat natural yogurt
shreds of orange rind, to decorate

Nutrition Notes

Per portion:	
Energy	112Kcals/474kJ
Fat	0.62g
Saturated Fat	0.34g
Cholesterol	2.25mg
Fibre	2.8g

1 Remove the stones from the prunes and roughly chop them. Place them in a pan with the orange juice.

2 Bring the juice to the boil, stirring. Reduce the heat, cover and leave to simmer for 5 minutes, until the prunes are tender and the liquid has reduced by half.

3 Remove from the heat, allow to cool slightly and then beat well with a wooden spoon, until the fruit breaks down to a rough purée.

Cook's Tip
This dessert can also be made with other ready-to-eat dried fruit, such as apricots or peaches. For a special occasion, add a dash of brandy or Cointreau with the yogurt.

4 Transfer the purée mixture to a bowl. Stir in the low fat yogurt, swirling the yogurt and fruit purée together lightly to give an attractive marbled effect.

5 Spoon the mixture into individual dishes or stemmed glasses, smoothing the tops.

6 Top each pot with a few shreds of orange rind, to decorate. Chill before serving.

Tropical Foamy Yogurt Ring

An impressive, light and colourful tropical dessert with a truly fruity flavour.

── Ingredients ──

Serves 6
For the yogurt ring
175ml/6fl oz/³/₄ cup tropical fruit juice
15ml/1 tbsp/1 sachet powdered gelatine
3 egg whites
150g/5oz low fat natural yogurt
finely grated rind of 1 lime

For the filling
1 mango
2 kiwi fruit
10–12 physalis cape gooseberries
juice of 1 lime

1 Place the tropical fruit juice in a small pan and sprinkle the powdered gelatine over. Heat gently until the gelatine has dissolved.

2 Whisk the egg whites in a clean, dry bowl until they hold soft peaks. Continue whisking hard, while gradually adding the yogurt and lime rind.

3 Continue whisking hard and pour in the hot gelatine and the egg white and yogurt mixture in a steady stream, until everything is smooth and evenly mixed.

4 Quickly pour the mixture into a 1.5 litre/2½ pint/6¼ cup ring mould. Chill the mould in the fridge until set. The mixture will separate into two layers.

5 Halve, stone, peel and dice the mango. Peel and slice the kiwi fruit. Remove the outer leaves from the physalis and cut in half. Toss all the fruits together and stir in the lime juice.

6 Run a knife around the edge of the ring to loosen the mixture. Dip the tin quickly into cold water and then turn the chilled yogurt mould out on to a serving plate. Spoon all the prepared fruit into the centre of the ring and serve immediately.

── Nutrition Notes ──

Per portion:
Energy	83.5Kcals/355kJ
Fat	0.67g
Saturated Fat	0.27g
Cholesterol	2.16mg
Fibre	1.77g

Cook's Tip
Any mixture of fruit works in this recipe, depending on the season. In summer try using apple juice in the ring mixture and fill it with luscious, red summer fruits.

STRAWBERRY ROSE-PETAL PASHKA

This lighter version of a traditional Russian dessert is ideal for dinner parties – make it a day or two in advance for best results.

INGREDIENTS

Serves 4

350g/12oz/1½ cups cottage cheese
175g/6oz/¾ cup low fat natural yogurt
30ml/2 tbsp clear honey
2.5ml/½ tsp rose-water
275g/10oz strawberries
handful of scented pink rose petals, to decorate

NUTRITION NOTES

Per portion:

Energy	150.5Kcals/634kJ
Fat	3.83g
Saturated Fat	2.32g
Cholesterol	0.13mg
Fibre	0.75g

COOK'S TIP
The flowerpot shape is traditional for pashka, but you could make it in any shape – the small porcelain heart-shaped moulds with draining holes usually reserved for *coeurs à la crème* make a pretty alternative.

1 Drain any free liquid from the cottage cheese and tip the cheese into a sieve. Use a wooden spoon to rub it through the sieve into a bowl.

2 Stir the yogurt, honey and rose-water into the cheese.

3 Roughly chop about half the strawberries and stir them into the cheese mixture.

4 Line a new, clean flowerpot or a sieve with muslin and tip the cheese mixture in. Leave it to drain over a bowl for several hours, or overnight.

5 Invert the flowerpot or sieve on to a serving plate, turn out the pashka and remove the muslin.

6 Decorate the pashka with strawberries and rose petals. Serve chilled.

FLUFFY BANANA AND PINEAPPLE MOUSSE

This light, low fat mousse looks very impressive but is really very easy to make, especially with a food processor. You could try substituting the canned pineapple chunks for other canned fruits such as peaches or apricots.

INGREDIENTS

Serves 6

2 ripe bananas
225g/8oz/1 cup cottage cheese
*425g/15oz can pineapple chunks or
  pieces in juice*
15ml/1 tbsp/1 sachet powdered gelatine
2 egg whites

NUTRITION NOTES

Per portion:

Energy	110Kcals/464kJ
Fat	1.6g
Saturated fat	0.98g
Cholesterol	4.88mg
Fibre	0.51g

1 Tie a double band of non-stick baking paper around a 600ml/1 pint/2½ cup soufflé dish, to come 5cm/2 in above the rim.

2 Peel and chop one banana and place it in a food processor or blender with the cottage cheese. Process until smooth.

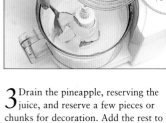

3 Drain the pineapple, reserving the juice, and reserve a few pieces or chunks for decoration. Add the rest to the banana mixture and process for a few seconds until finely chopped. Transfer the mixture to a large bowl.

4 Dissolve the gelatine in 60ml/4 tbsp of the reserved pineapple juice. Stir the gelatine quickly into the fruit mixture with a spoon.

5 In a separate bowl, quickly whisk the egg whites until they hold soft peaks, then fold them lightly and evenly into the fruit mixture. Tip the mousse into the prepared dish, smooth the surface and chill until set.

6 When the mousse is set, carefully remove the paper collar. Decorate the mousse with the reserved banana and pineapple.

> COOK'S TIP
> For a simpler way of serving, use a 1 litre/1¾ pint/4 cup serving dish, but do not tie a collar around the edge.

ROSE-SCENTED FRUIT COMPÔTE

Rose-scented tea gives this dessert a lovely subtle flavour.

INGREDIENTS

Serves 4

5ml/1 tsp rose pouchong tea
5ml/1 tsp rose water (optional)
50g/2oz/¼ cup sugar
5ml/1 tsp lemon juice
5 dessert apples
175g/6oz/1½ cups fresh raspberries

NUTRITION NOTES

Per portion:	
Energy	141Kcals/591kJ
Fat	0.34g
Saturated fat	0
Cholesterol	0
Fibre	3.94g

1 Warm a large tea pot. Add the rose pouchong tea and 900ml/1½ pints/ 3¾ cups of boiling water together with the rose water, if using. Allow to stand and infuse for about 4 minutes.

3 Peel and quarter the apples, then remove the cores.

5 Transfer the apples and syrup to a large metal baking tray and leave to cool to room temperature.

6 Pour the cooled apples and syrup into a bowl, add the raspberries and mix to combine. Spoon into individual glass dishes or bowls and serve.

> **COOK'S TIP**
> If fresh raspberries are out of season, use the same weight of frozen fruit or a 400g/14oz can of well-drained fruit.

2 Measure the sugar and lemon juice into a stainless steel saucepan. Strain in the tea and stir to dissolve the sugar.

4 Add the apples to the syrup and poach for about 5 minutes.

CREAMY MANGO CHEESECAKE

Cheesecakes are always a
favourite but sadly they are often
high in fat. This one is the
exception.

INGREDIENTS

Serves 4
115g/4oz/1¼ cups rolled oats
40g/1½oz/3 tbsp sunflower margarine
30ml/2 tbsp clear honey
1 large ripe mango
300g/10oz/1¼ cups low fat soft cheese
150g/5oz/⅔ cup low fat natural
  yogurt
finely grated rind of 1 small lime
45ml/3 tbsp apple juice
20ml/4 tsp powdered gelatine
fresh mango and lime slices, to decorate

1 Preheat the oven to 200°C/400°F/
Gas 6. Mix together the oats,
margarine and honey. Press the mixture
into the base of a 20cm/8in loose-
bottomed cake tin. Bake for 12–15
minutes, until lightly browned. Cool.

2 Peel, stone and roughly chop the
mango. Place the chopped mango,
cheese, yogurt and lime rind in a food
processor and process until smooth.

3 Heat the apple juice until boiling,
sprinkle the gelatine over it, stir to
dissolve, then stir into cheese mixture.

4 Pour the cheese mixture into the tin
and chill until set, then turn out on
to a serving plate. Decorate the top
with mango and lime slices.

NUTRITION NOTES

Per portion:
Energy	422Kcals/1774kJ
Fat	11.37g
Saturated fat	2.2g
Cholesterol	2.95mg
Fibre	7.15g

FRUDITÉS WITH HONEY DIP

INGREDIENTS

Serves 4
225g/8oz/1 cup Greek-style yogurt
45ml/3 tbsp clear honey
selection of fresh fruit for dipping such
  as apples, pears, tangerines, grapes,
  figs, cherries, strawberries and kiwi
  fruit

NUTRITION NOTES

Per portion:
Energy	161Kcals/678kJ
Fat	5.43g
Saturated fat	3.21g
Cholesterol	7.31mg
Fibre	2.48g

1 Place the yogurt in a dish, beat until
smooth, then stir in the honey,
leaving a little marbled effect.

2 Cut the fruits into wedges or bite-
sized pieces or leave whole.

3 Arrange the fruits on a platter with
the bowl of dip in the centre. Serve
chilled.

FIGS AND PEARS IN HONEY

INGREDIENTS

Serves 4
1 lemon
90ml/6 tbsp clear honey
1 cinnamon stick
1 cardamom pod
2 pears
3 fresh figs, halved

NUTRITION NOTES

Per portion:

Energy	108kcals/465kJ
Fat	0.2g
Saturated fat	0
Protein	0.73g
Fibre	2.2g

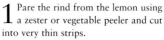

1 Pare the rind from the lemon using a zester or vegetable peeler and cut into very thin strips.

2 Place the lemon rind, honey, cinnamon stick, cardamom pod and 350ml/12fl oz/1½ cups water in a pan and boil, uncovered, for about 10 minutes until reduced by about half.

3 Cut the pears into eighths, discarding the core. Place in the syrup, add the figs and simmer for 5 minutes until the fruit is tender.

4 Transfer the fruit to a serving bowl. Continue cooking the liquid until syrupy, then discard the cinnamon stick and pour over the figs and pears. Chill before serving.

SUMMER FRUIT SALAD ICE CREAM

This beautiful ice cream contains delicious mixed summer fruits.

INGREDIENTS

Serves 6

900g/2 lb/8 cups mixed soft summer
  fruit, such as raspberries, strawberries, blackcurrants and redcurrants
2 eggs, separated
225g/8oz/1 cup low fat Greek-style
  yogurt
175ml/6fl oz/³⁄4 cup red grape juice
15ml/1 tbsp/1 sachet powdered gelatine

NUTRITION NOTES

Per portion:

Energy	133Kcals/558kJ
Fat	5.69g
Saturated fat	2.72g
Cholesterol	78.02mg
Fibre	3.6g

1 Reserve half the fruit and purée the rest in a food processor or blender, or rub it through a sieve to make a smooth purée.

2 Whisk the egg yolks and yogurt into the fruit purée.

3 Heat the grape juice until almost boiling. Remove from the heat, sprinkle the gelatine over the juice and stir to dissolve the gelatine completely.

4 Whisk the dissolved gelatine into the fruit purée. Pour into a freezer container. Freeze until slushy.

5 Whisk the egg whites until they are stiff. Quickly fold them into the half-frozen mixture.

6 Return to the freezer and freeze until almost firm. Scoop into individual dishes or glasses and decorate with the reserved soft fruits.

COOK'S TIP
Red grape juice has a good flavour and improves the colour of the ice, but if it is not available, use cranberry, apple or orange juice instead.

GRAPE CHEESE WHIP

INGREDIENTS

Serves 4

150g/5oz/1 cup black or green seedless grapes, plus 4 sprigs
2 egg whites
15ml/1 tbsp caster sugar
finely grated rind and juice of ½ lemon
225g/8oz/1 cup skimmed milk soft
  cheese
45ml/3 tbsp clear honey
30ml/2 tbsp brandy (optional)

NUTRITION NOTES

Per portion:

Energy	135Kcals/563kJ
Fat	0
Saturated fat	0
Cholesterol	0.56mg
Fibre	0

1 Brush the sprigs of grapes lightly with egg white and sprinkle with sugar to coat. Leave to dry.

2 Mix together the lemon rind and juice, cheese, honey and brandy. Chop the remaining grapes and stir in.

3 Whisk the egg whites until stiff enough to hold soft peaks. Fold the whites into the grape mixture, then spoon into serving glasses.

4 Top with sugar-frosted grapes and serve chilled.

STRAWBERRIES IN SPICED GRAPE JELLY

INGREDIENTS

Serves 4

450ml/¾ pint/1⅞cups red grape juice
1 cinnamon stick
1 small orange
15ml/1 tbsp/1 envelope gelatine
225g/8oz strawberries, chopped
strawberries and orange rind, to
  decorate

1 Place the grape juice in a pan with the cinnamon. Thinly pare the rind from the orange and add to the pan. Infuse over a very low heat for 10 minutes, then remove the flavourings.

2 Squeeze the juice from the orange and sprinkle over the gelatine. Stir into the grape juice to dissolve. Allow to cool until just beginning to set.

3 Stir in the strawberries and quickly tip into a 1 litre/1¾pint/4 cup mould or serving dish. Chill until set.

4 To turn out, dip the mould quickly into hot water and invert on to a serving plate. Decorate with fresh strawberries and shreds of orange rind.

NUTRITION NOTES

Per portion:

Energy	85Kcals/355kJ
Fat	0.2g
Saturated fat	0
Cholesterol	0
Fibre	1.04g

PEARS IN MAPLE AND YOGURT SAUCE

INGREDIENTS

Serves 6

6 firm pears
15ml/1 tbsp lemon juice
250ml/8fl oz/1 cup sweet white wine or cider
thinly pared rind of 1 lemon
1 cinnamon stick
30ml/2 tbsp maple syrup
2.5ml/½ tsp arrowroot
150g/5oz/⅔ cup low fat Greek-style yogurt

NUTRITION NOTES

Per portion:
Energy	132Kcals/556kJ
Fat	2.4g
Saturated fat	1.43g
Cholesterol	3.25mg
Fibre	2.64g

1 Thinly peel the pears, leaving them whole and with stalks intact. Brush them with lemon juice, to prevent them from browning. Use a potato peeler or small knife to scoop out the core from the base of each pear.

2 Place the pears in a wide, heavy saucepan and pour over the wine or cider, with enough cold water almost to cover the pears.

3 Add the lemon rind and cinnamon stick, and then bring to the boil. Reduce the heat, and simmer the pears gently for about 30–40 minutes, or until tender. Turn the pears occasionally. Lift the pears out carefully, draining them well.

4 Bring the liquid to the boil and boil uncovered to reduce to about 120ml/4fl oz/½ cup.

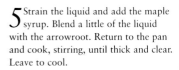

5 Strain the liquid and add the maple syrup. Blend a little of the liquid with the arrowroot. Return to the pan and cook, stirring, until thick and clear. Leave to cool.

6 Slice each pear about three-quarters of the way through, leaving the slices attached at the stem end. Fan each pear out on a serving plate.

7 Stir 30ml/2 tbsp of the cooled syrup into the yogurt and spoon it around the pears. Drizzle with the remaining syrup and serve immediately.

COOK'S TIP
Poach the pears in advance, and have the cooled syrup ready to spoon on to the plates just before serving. The cooking time of this dish will vary, depending upon the type and ripeness of the pears. The pears should be ripe, but still firm – over-ripe ones will not keep their shape well.

FRAGRANT RICE WITH MANGO PURÉE

Nuts, dried fruit, cardamom and rosewater make this Indian-style rice pudding a real treat.

INGREDIENTS

Serves 6
2 ripe mangoes
50g/2oz/¹⁄₃ cup basmati rice
1.5 litres/2½ pints/6 cups semi-skimmed milk
50g/2oz/¹⁄₃ cup demerara sugar
50g/2oz/¹⁄₃ cup sultanas
5ml/1 tsp rosewater
5 cardamom pods
45ml/3 tbsp orange juice
20g/³⁄₄oz/scant ¹⁄₄ cup flaked almonds, toasted
20g/³⁄₄oz/scant ¹⁄₄ cup pistachio nuts, chopped

1 Using a sharp knife, peel, slice and stone the mangoes.

2 Preheat the oven to 150°C/300°F/ Gas 2. Put the basmati rice in an ovenproof dish. Boil the milk then pour it over the rice. Bake uncovered for 2 hours until the rice has become soft and mushy.

3 Remove the dish from the oven and stir in the demerara sugar and sultanas, with half the rosewater. Crush the cardamom pods, extract the seeds and stir them into the rice mixture. Allow to cool.

4 Place the mango flesh in a blender or food processor. Add the orange juice and remaining rosewater. Blend until smooth.

5 Divide the mango purée among six individual glass serving dishes. Spoon the rice pudding mixture evenly over the top. Leave to chill thoroughly in the fridge or a cool place.

6 When ready to serve, scatter the toasted almonds and chopped pistachio nuts over the top of each pudding.

NUTRITION NOTES

Per portion:
Energy	300Kcals/1260KJ
Fat	8g
Saturated Fat	3g
Cholesterol	17.5mg

FRESH CITRUS JELLY

Fresh fruit jellies really are worth the effort – they make a stunning fat-free dessert and are also rich in vitamins.

INGREDIENTS

Serves 4

3 oranges
1 lemon
1 lime
300ml/½ pint/1¼ cups water
75g/3oz/⅓ cup golden caster sugar
15ml/1 tbsp/1 sachet powdered gelatine
extra slices of fruit, to decorate

NUTRITION NOTES

Per portion:	
Energy	136Kcals/573kJ
Fat	0.21g
Saturated fat	0
Cholesterol	0
Fibre	2.13g

1 With a sharp knife, cut all the peel and white pith from one orange and carefully remove the segments. Arrange all of the segments in the base of a 900ml/1½ pint/3¾ cup mould or dish.

2 Remove some shreds of citrus rind with a zester and reserve them for decoration. Grate the remaining rind from the lemon and lime and one orange. Place all the grated rind in a saucepan with the water and sugar.

3 Heat gently until the sugar has dissolved. Remove from the heat. Squeeze the juice from all the rest of the fruit and stir it into the pan.

4 Strain the liquid into a measuring jug to remove the rind (you should have about 600ml/1 pint/2½ cups: if necessary, make up the amount with water). Sprinkle the gelatine over the liquid and stir until dissolved.

5 Pour a little of the jelly over the orange segments and chill until it has set. Leave the remaining jelly at room temperature to cool, but do not allow it to set.

6 Pour the remaining cooled jelly into the dish and chill until set. To serve, turn out the jelly and decorate it with the reserved citrus rind shreds and slices of citrus fruit.

COOK'S TIP
To speed up the setting of the fruit segments in jelly, stand the dish in a bowl of ice.

AUTUMN PUDDING

Summer pudding is far too good to be reserved for the soft fruit season. Here is an autumn version, with apples, plums and blackberries, which makes a high-fibre dessert full of vitamins.

─────── INGREDIENTS ───────

Serves 6

450g/1lb eating apples
450g/1lb plums, halved and stoned
225g/8oz blackberries, hulled
60ml/4 tbsp apple juice
sugar or honey, to sweeten (optional)
8 slices of wholemeal bread,
  crusts removed
mint sprig and blackberry, to decorate
half-fat crème fraîche, to serve

1 Quarter the apples, remove the cores and peel, then slice them into a saucepan. Add the plums, blackberries and apple juice. Cover and cook gently for 10–15 minutes until tender. Sweeten, if necessary, with a little sugar or honey, although the fruit should be sweet enough.

2 Line the bottom and sides of a 1.2 litre/2 pint/5 cup pudding basin with 6–7 slices of bread, cut to fit. Press together tightly.

3 Spoon the fruit into the basin. Pour in just enough juice to moisten. Reserve any remaining juice.

4 Cover the fruit completely with the remaining bread. Fit a plate on top, so that it rests on the bread just below the rim. Stand the basin in a larger bowl to catch any juice. Place a weight on the plate and chill overnight.

5 Turn the pudding out on to a plate and pour the reserved juice over any areas which have not absorbed the juice. Decorate with the mint sprig and blackberry and serve with crème fraîche.

─────── NUTRITION NOTES ───────

Per portion:

Energy	185Kcals/765KJ
Fat	1.5g
Saturated Fat	0.5g
Cholesterol	0

Emerald Fruit Salad

Serves 4

30ml/2 tbsp lime juice
30ml/2 tbsp clear honey
2 green eating apples, cored and sliced
1 small ripe Ogen melon, diced
2 kiwi fruit, sliced
1 star fruit, sliced
mint sprigs, to decorate

1 Mix together the lime juice and honey in a large bowl, then toss the apple slices in this.

2 Stir in the melon, kiwi fruit and star fruit. Place in a glass serving dish and chill before serving.

3 Decorate with mint sprigs and serve with yogurt or fromage frais.

Cook's Tip
Starfruit is best when fully ripe – look for plump, yellow fruit.

Nutrition Notes	
Per portion:	
Energy	93Kcals/390kJ
Fat	0.48g
Saturated fat	0
Cholesterol	0
Fibre	2.86g

Peach and Ginger Pashka

This simpler adaptation of a Russian Easter favourite is made with much lighter ingredients than the traditional version.

Serves 4–6

350g/12oz/1½ cups low fat cottage cheese
2 ripe peaches or nectarines
90g/3½oz/⅓ cup low fat natural yogurt
2 pieces stem ginger in syrup, drained and chopped
30ml/2 tbsp stem ginger syrup
2.5ml/½ tsp vanilla essence
peach slices and toasted flaked almonds, to decorate

Nutrition Notes	
Per portion:	
Energy	142Kcals/600kJ
Fat	1.63g
Saturated fat	0.22g
Cholesterol	1.77mg
Fibre	1.06g

1 Drain the cottage cheese and rub through a sieve into a bowl. Stone and roughly chop the peaches.

2 Mix together the chopped peaches, cottage cheese, yogurt, ginger, syrup and vanilla essence.

3 Line a new, clean flowerpot or a sieve with a piece of clean, fine cloth such as muslin.

4 Tip in the cheese mixture, then wrap over the cloth and place a weight on top. Leave over a bowl in a cool place to drain overnight. To serve, unwrap the cloth and invert the pashka on to a plate. Decorate with peach slices and almonds.

PLUM AND PORT SORBET

Rather a grown-up sorbet, this one, but you could use fresh, still red grape juice in place of the port if you prefer.

INGREDIENTS

Serves 4–6
*1kg/2 lb ripe red plums, halved and
    stoned*
75g/3oz/6 tbsp caster sugar
45ml/3 tbsp water
*45ml/3 tbsp ruby port or red wine
crisp, sweet biscuits, to serve*

1 Place the plums in a pan with the sugar and water. Stir over a gentle heat until the sugar is melted, then cover and simmer gently for about 5 minutes, until the fruit is soft.

2 Turn into a food processor and purée until smooth, then stir in the port. Cool completely, then tip into a freezer container and freeze until firm around the edges.

3 Spoon into the food processor and process until smooth. Return to the freezer and freeze until solid.

4 Allow to soften slightly at room temperature for 15–20 minutes before serving in scoops, with sweet biscuits.

NUTRITION NOTES	
Per portion:	
Energy	166Kcals/699kJ
Fat	0.25g
Saturated fat	0
Cholesterol	0
Fibre	3.75g

TOFU BERRY BRULÉE

This is a lighter variation of a classic dessert, usually forbidden on a low fat diet, using tofu, which is low in fat and free from cholesterol. Use any soft fruits in season.

INGREDIENTS

Serves 4

300g/11oz packet silken tofu
45ml/3 tbsp icing sugar
225g/8oz/1½ cups red berry fruits,
    such as raspberries, strawberries and
    redcurrants
about 75ml/5 tbsp demerara sugar

1 Place the tofu and icing sugar in a food processor or blender and process until smooth.

2 Stir in the fruits and spoon into a 900ml/1½ pint/3¾ cup flameproof dish. Sprinkle the top with enough demerara sugar to cover evenly.

3 Place under a very hot grill until the sugar melts and caramelises. Chill before serving.

COOK'S TIP
Choose silken tofu rather than firm tofu as it gives a smoother texture in this type of dish. Firm tofu is better for cooking in chunks.

NUTRITION NOTES

Per portion:

Energy	180Kcals/760kJ
Fat	3.01g
Saturated fat	0.41g
Cholesterol	0
Fibre	1.31g

APRICOT MOUSSE

This light, fluffy dessert can be made with any dried fruits instead of apricots – try dried peaches, prunes or apples.

INGREDIENTS

Serves 4
300g/10oz/1½ cups ready-to-eat dried apricots
300ml/½ pint/1¼ cups fresh orange juice
200g/7oz/⅞ cup low fat fromage frais
2 egg whites
mint sprigs, to decorate

1 Place the apricots in a saucepan with the orange juice and heat gently until boiling. Cover and simmer gently for 3 minutes.

2 Cool slightly. Place in a food processor or blender and process until smooth. Stir in the fromage frais.

3 Whisk the egg whites until stiff enough to hold soft peaks, then fold into the apricot mixture.

4 Spoon into four stemmed glasses or one large serving dish. Chill before serving.

COOK'S TIP
To make a speedier fool-type dish, omit the egg whites and simply swirl together the apricot mixture and fromage frais.

NUTRITION NOTES

Per portion:

Energy	180Kcals/757kJ
Fat	0.63g
Saturated fat	0.06g
Cholesterol	0.5mg
Fibre	4.8g

APPLE FOAM WITH BLACKBERRIES

Any seasonal soft fruit can be used for this if blackberries are not available.

INGREDIENTS

Serves 4

225g/8oz blackberries
150ml/¼ pint/⅔ cup apple juice
5ml/1 tsp powdered gelatine
15ml/1 tbsp clear honey
2 egg whites

1 Place the blackberries in a pan with 60ml/4 tbsp of the apple juice and heat gently until the fruit is soft. Remove from the heat, cool and chill.

2 Sprinkle the gelatine over the remaining apple juice in a small pan and stir over a low heat until dissolved. Stir in the honey.

3 Whisk the egg whites until they hold stiff peaks. Continue whisking hard and pour in the hot gelatine mixture gradually, until well mixed.

4 Quickly spoon the foam into rough mounds on individual plates. Chill. Serve with the blackberries and juice spooned around.

COOK'S TIP
Make sure that you dissolve the gelatine over a very low heat. It must not boil, or it will lose its setting ability.

NUTRITION NOTES

Per portion:
Energy	49Kcals/206kJ
Fat	0.15g
Saturated fat	0
Cholesterol	0
Fibre	1.74g

BANANA HONEY YOGURT ICE

Serves 4–6
4 ripe bananas, chopped roughly
15ml/1 tbsp lemon juice
30ml/2 tbsp clear honey
250g/9oz/1 cup Greek-style yogurt
2.5ml/½ tsp ground cinnamon
crisp biscuits, flaked hazelnuts and
*   banana slices, to serve*

1 Place the bananas in a food processor or blender with the lemon juice, honey, yogurt and cinnamon. Process until smooth and creamy.

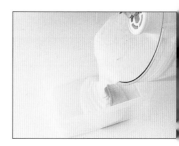

3 Return to the freezer until firm. Allow to soften at room temperature for 15 minutes, then serve in scoops, with crisp biscuits, flaked hazelnuts and banana slices.

NUTRITION NOTES	
Per portion:	
Energy	138Kcals/580kJ
Fat	7.37g
Saturated fat	3.72g
Cholesterol	8.13mg
Fibre	0.47g

2 Pour the mixture into a freezer container and freeze until almost solid. Spoon back into the food processor and process again until smooth.

AUTUMN PUDDING

Serves 6
10 slices white or brown bread, at least
*   1 day old*
1 Bramley cooking apple, peeled, cored
*   and sliced*
225g/8oz ripe red plums, halved and
*   stoned*
225g/8oz blackberries
60ml/4 tbsp water
75g/3oz/6 tbsp caster sugar

2 Place the bread round in the base of a 1.2 litre/2 pint/5 cup pudding basin, then overlap the fingers around the sides, saving some for the top.

5 Cover the mould with a saucer and place weights on top. Chill the pudding overnight. Turn out on to a serving plate and serve with low fat yogurt or fromage frais.

3 Place the apple, plums, blackberries, water and sugar in a pan, heat gently until the sugar dissolves, then simmer gently for 10 minutes, or until soft. Remove from the heat.

1 Remove the crusts from the bread and use a biscuit cutter to stamp out a 7.5cm/3in round from one slice. Cut the remaining slices in half.

4 Reserve the juice and spoon the fruit into the bread-lined basin. Top with the reserved bread, then spoon over the reserved fruit juices.

NUTRITION NOTES	
Per portion:	
Energy	197Kcals/830kJ
Fat	1.1g
Saturated fat	0.2g
Cholesterol	0
Fibre	2.84g

FRUITED RICE RING

This unusual rice pudding looks beautiful turned out of a ring mould but if you prefer, stir the fruit into the rice and serve in individual dishes.

INGREDIENTS

Serves 4

65g/2½oz/5 tbsp short grain rice
900ml/1½ pint/3¾ cups semi-skimmed milk
1 cinnamon stick
175g/6oz/1½ cups dried fruit salad
175ml/6 fl oz/¾ cup orange juice
45ml/3 tbsp caster sugar
finely grated rind of 1 small orange

1 Place the rice, milk and cinnamon stick in a large pan and bring to the boil. Cover and simmer, stirring occasionally, for about 1½ hours, until no free liquid remains.

2 Meanwhile, place the fruit and orange juice in a pan and bring to the boil. Cover and simmer very gently for about 1 hour, until tender and no free liquid remains.

3 Remove the cinnamon stick from the rice and stir in the sugar and orange rind.

4 Tip the fruit into the base of a lightly oiled 1.5 litre/2½ pint/6 cup ring mould. Spoon the rice over, smoothing down firmly. Chill.

5 Run a knife around the edge of the mould and turn out the rice carefully on to a serving plate.

NUTRITION NOTES

Per portion:

Energy	343Kcals/1440kJ
Fat	4.4g
Saturated fat	2.26g
Cholesterol	15.75mg
Fibre	1.07g

RASPBERRY PASSION FRUIT SWIRLS

If passion fruit is not available, this simple dessert can be made with raspberries alone.

INGREDIENTS

Serves 4

300g/11oz/2½ cups raspberries
2 passion fruit
400g/14oz/1⅔ cups low fat fromage frais
30ml/2 tbsp caster sugar
raspberries and sprigs of mint, to decorate

1 Mash the raspberries in a small bowl with a fork until the juice runs. Scoop out the passion fruit pulp into a separate bowl with the fromage frais and sugar and mix well.

2 Spoon alternate spoonfuls of the raspberry pulp and the fromage frais mixture into stemmed glasses or one large serving dish, stirring lightly to create a swirled effect.

3 Decorate each dessert with a whole raspberry and a sprig of fresh mint. Serve chilled.

COOK'S TIP
Over-ripe, slightly soft fruit can also be used in this recipe. Use frozen raspberries when fresh are not available, but thaw first.

NUTRITION NOTES	
Per portion:	
Energy	110Kcals/462kJ
Fat	0.47g
Saturated fat	0.13g
Cholesterol	1mg
Fibre	2.12g

RED BERRY SPONGE TART

When soft berry fruits are in season, try making this delicious
sponge tart. Serve warm from
the oven with scoops of low fat
vanilla ice cream, if you wish.

────── INGREDIENTS ──────

Serves 4

softened butter, for greasing
450g/1 lb/4 cups soft berry fruits such
as raspberries, blackberries, blackcur-
rants, redcurrants, strawberries or
blueberries
2 eggs, at room temperature
50g/2oz/¼ cup caster sugar, plus extra
to taste (optional)
15ml/1 tbsp plain flour
25g/1oz/¼ cup ground almonds
vanilla ice cream, to serve (optional)

┌─────── NUTRITION NOTES ───────┐
Per portion:
Energy   219Kcals/919kJ
Fat   11.31g
Saturated fat   2.05g
Cholesterol   112.6mg
Fibre   4.49g
└──────────────────────────────┘

┌──────────────────────────────┐
VARIATION
When berry fruits are out of season, use bottled fruits, but ensure
that they are very well drained
before use.
└──────────────────────────────┘

1 Preheat the oven to 190°C/375°F/
Gas 5. Brush a 23cm/9 in flan tin
with softened butter and line the bottom
with a circle of non-stick baking paper.
Scatter the fruit in the base of the tin
with a little sugar if the fruits are tart.

2 Whisk the eggs and sugar together
for about 3–4 minutes or until they
leave a thick trail across the surface.
Combine the flour and almonds, then
fold into the egg mixture with a spatula
– retaining as much air as possible.

3 Spread the mixture on top of the
fruit base and bake in the preheated
oven for about 15 minutes. Turn out
on to a serving plate and serve, with
low fat vanilla ice cream if you like.

┌──────────────────────────────┐
COOK'S TIP
Fresh soft berry fruits are best
used on the day of purchase. If
you purchase them in traditional
punnets, avoid any badly stained
containers.
└──────────────────────────────┘

RASPBERRY-PASSION FRUIT CHINCHILLAS

Few desserts are so strikingly easy to make as this one: beaten egg whites and sugar baked in a dish, turned out and served with a handful of soft fruit and ready-made custard from a carton.

INGREDIENTS

Serves 4

25g/1oz/2 tbsp butter, softened
5 egg whites
150g/5oz/⅔ cup caster sugar
2 passion fruit
675g/1½ lb/6 cups fresh raspberries
250ml/8fl oz/1 cup low fat ready-made
   custard from a carton or can
skimmed milk, as required
icing sugar, for dusting

NUTRITION NOTES	
Per portion:	
Energy	309Kcals/1296kJ
Fat	5.74g
Saturated fat	3.3g
Cholesterol	15.81mg
Fibre	4.47g

1 Preheat the oven to 180°C/350°F/ Gas 4. With a brush, paint four 300ml/½ pint/1¼ cup soufflé dishes with a visible layer of soft butter.

2 Whisk the egg whites in a mixing bowl until firm. (You can use an electric mixer.) Add the sugar a little at a time and whisk into a firm meringue.

3 Halve the passion fruit, take out the seeds with a spoon and fold them into the meringue.

4 Turn the meringue out into the four prepared dishes, stand them in a deep roasting tin which has been half-filled with boiling water and bake for about 10 minutes.

5 Turn the chinchillas out upside-down on to individual plates.

6 Top the chinchillas with the fresh raspberries. Thin the custard with a little skimmed milk and pour around the edge. Dredge with icing sugar and serve warm or cold.

COOK'S TIP
If raspberries are out of season, use either fresh, bottled or canned soft berry fruit such as strawberries, blueberries or redcurrants.

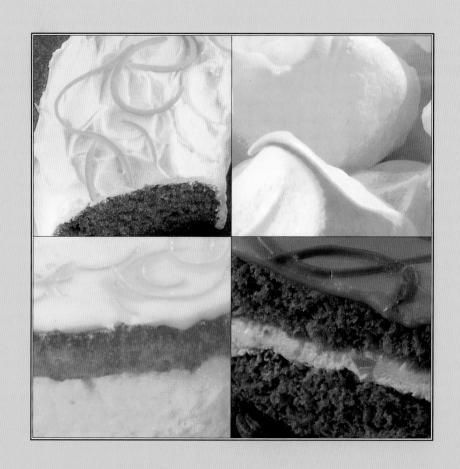

CAKES AND BAKES

We tend to think of cakes and bakes being out of bounds for those following a low fat diet, but you will be pleased to learn that this is not the case at all. There are many ways of creating delicious cakes and bakes without the need for high fat mixtures, and all the cakes and bakes in this chapter, both sweet and savoury, are low in fat. Choose from tempting recipes for such delights as Tia Maria Gâteau, Coffee Sponge Drops, Muscovado Meringues, and Chocolate and Banana Brownies.

IRISH WHISKEY CAKE

This moist rich fruit cake is drizzled with whiskey as soon as it comes out of the oven.

INGREDIENTS

Serves 12

115g/4oz/²⁄₃ cup glacé cherries
175g/6oz/1 cup dark muscovado sugar
115g/4oz/²⁄₃ cup sultanas
115g/4oz/²⁄₃ cup raisins
115g/4oz/¹⁄₂ cup currants
300ml/¹⁄₂ pint/1¹⁄₄ cups cold tea
300g/10oz/2¹⁄₂ cups self-raising
   flour, sifted
1 egg
45ml/3 tbsp Irish whiskey

COOK'S TIP
If time is short, use hot tea and soak the fruit for just 2 hours.

1 Mix the cherries, sugar, dried fruit and tea in a large bowl. Leave to soak overnight until all the tea has been absorbed into the fruit.

NUTRITION NOTES

Per portion:

Energy	265Kcals/1115kJ
Fat	0.88g
Saturated Fat	0.25g
Cholesterol	16mg
Fibre	1.48g

2 Preheat the oven to 180°C/350°F/ Gas 4. Grease and line a 1kg/2¹⁄₄lb loaf tin. Add the flour, then the egg to the fruit mixture and beat thoroughly until well mixed.

3 Pour the mixture into the prepared tin and bake for 1¹⁄₂ hours or until a skewer inserted into the centre of the cake comes out clean.

4 Prick the top of the cake with a skewer and drizzle over the whiskey while the cake is still hot. Allow to stand for about 5 minutes, then remove from the tin and cool on a wire rack.

ANGEL CAKE

A delicious light cake to serve as a dessert for a special occasion.

INGREDIENTS

Serves 10

40g/1½oz/⅓ cup cornflour
40g/1½oz/⅓ cup plain flour
8 egg whites
225g/8oz/1 cup caster sugar, plus extra
    for sprinkling
5ml/1 tsp vanilla essence
90ml/6 tbsp orange-flavoured glacé
    icing, 4–6 physalis and a little icing
    sugar, to decorate

1 Preheat the oven to 180°C/350°F/ Gas 4. Sift both flours on to a sheet of greaseproof paper.

2 Whisk the egg whites in a large, clean, dry bowl until very stiff, then gradually add the sugar and vanilla essence, whisking until the mixture is thick and glossy.

3 Gently fold in the flour mixture with a large metal spoon. Spoon into an ungreased 25cm/10in angel cake tin, smooth the surface and bake for about 45–50 minutes, until the cake springs back when lightly pressed.

COOK'S TIP
If you prefer, omit the glacé icing and physalis and simply dust the cake with a little icing sugar – it is delicious to serve as a coffee-time treat, and also makes the perfect accompaniment to vanilla yogurt ice cream for a dessert.

4 Sprinkle a piece of greaseproof paper with caster sugar and set an egg cup in the centre. Invert the cake tin over the paper, balancing it carefully on the egg cup. When cold, the cake will drop out of the tin. Transfer it to a plate, spoon over the glacé icing, arrange the physalis on top and then dust with icing sugar and serve.

NUTRITION NOTES	
Per portion:	
Energy	139Kcals/582kJ
Fat	0.08g
Saturated Fat	0.01g
Cholesterol	0
Fibre	0.13g

TIA MARIA GÂTEAU

A feather-light coffee sponge with a creamy liqueur-flavoured filling.

INGREDIENTS

Serves 8
75g/3oz/³/₄ cup plain flour
30ml/2 tbsp instant coffee powder
3 eggs
115g/4oz/¹/₂ cup caster sugar
coffee beans, to decorate (optional)

For the filling
175g/6oz/³/₄ cup low fat soft cheese
15ml/1 tbsp clear honey
15ml/1 tbsp Tia Maria liqueur
50g/2oz/¹/₄ cup stem ginger,
   roughly chopped

For the icing
225g/8oz/1³/₄ cups icing sugar, sifted
10ml/2 tsp coffee essence
15ml/1 tbsp water
5ml/1 tsp reduced fat cocoa powder

NUTRITION NOTES

Per portion:	
Energy	226Kcals/951kJ
Fat	3.14g
Saturated Fat	1.17g
Cholesterol	75.03mg
Fibre	0.64g

COOK'S TIP
When folding in the flour mixture in step 3, be careful not to remove the air, as it helps the cake to rise.

1 Preheat the oven to 190°C/375°F/ Gas 5. Grease and line a 20cm/8in deep round cake tin. Sift the flour and coffee powder together on to a sheet of greaseproof paper.

2 Whisk the eggs and sugar in a bowl with a hand-held electric whisk until thick and mousse-like. (When the whisk is lifted, a trail should remain on the surface of the mixture for at least 15 seconds.)

3 Gently fold in the flour mixture with a metal spoon. Turn the mixture into the prepared tin. Bake the sponge for 30–35 minutes or until it springs back when lightly pressed. Turn on to a wire rack to cool completely.

4 To make the filling, mix the soft cheese with the honey in a bowl. Beat until smooth, then stir in the Tia Maria and chopped stem ginger.

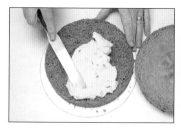

5 Split the cake in half horizontally and sandwich the two halves together with the Tia Maria filling.

6 Make the icing. In a bowl, mix the icing sugar and coffee essence with enough water to make a consistency that will coat the back of a wooden spoon. Pour three-quarters of the icing over the cake, spreading it evenly to the edges. Stir the cocoa into the remaining icing until smooth. Spoon into a piping bag fitted with a writing nozzle and pipe the mocha icing over the coffee icing. Decorate with coffee beans, if liked.

CHOCOLATE AND ORANGE ANGEL CAKE

This light-as-air sponge with its fluffy icing is virtually fat free, yet tastes heavenly.

INGREDIENTS

Serves 10

25g/1oz/¼ cup plain flour
15g/½oz/2 tbsp reduced fat
  cocoa powder
15g/½oz/2 tbsp cornflour
pinch of salt
5 egg whites
2.5ml/½ tsp cream of tartar
115g/4oz/scant ½ cup caster sugar
blanched and shredded rind of
  1 orange, to decorate

For the icing
200g/7oz/1 cup caster sugar
1 egg white

NUTRITION NOTES

Per portion:

Energy	53Kcals/644kJ
Fat	0.27g
Saturated Fat	0.13g
Fibre	0.25g

COOK'S TIP
Make sure you do not over-beat the egg whites. They should not be stiff but should form soft peaks, so that the air bubbles can expand further during cooking and help the cake to rise.

1 Preheat the oven to 180°C/350°F/ Gas 4. Sift the flour, cocoa powder, cornflour and salt together three times. Beat the egg whites in a large clean, dry bowl until foamy. Add the cream of tartar, then whisk until soft peaks form.

2 Add the caster sugar to the egg whites a spoonful at a time, whisking after each addition. Sift a third of the flour and cocoa mixture over the meringue and gently fold in. Repeat, sifting and folding in the flour and cocoa mixture two more times.

3 Spoon the mixture into a non-stick 20cm/8in ring mould and level the top. Bake for 35 minutes or until springy to the touch. Turn upside-down on to a wire rack and leave to cool in the tin. Carefully ease out of the tin.

4 For the icing, put the sugar in a pan with 75ml/5 tbsp cold water. Stir over a low heat until dissolved. Boil until the syrup reaches a temperature of 120°C/240°F on a sugar thermometer, or when a drop of the syrup makes a soft ball when dropped into a cup of cold water. Remove from the heat.

5 Whisk the egg white until stiff. Add the syrup in a thin stream, whisking all the time. Continue to whisk until the mixture is very thick and fluffy.

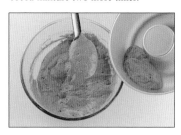

6 Spread the icing over the top and sides of the cooled cake. Sprinkle the orange rind over the top of the cake and serve.

CINNAMON APPLE GÂTEAU

Make this lovely cake for an autumn celebration.

INGREDIENTS

Serves 8
3 eggs
115g/4oz/1/2 cup caster sugar
75g/3oz/3/4 cup plain flour
5ml/1 tsp ground cinnamon

For the filling and topping
4 large eating apples
60ml/4 tbsp clear honey
15ml/1 tbsp water
75g/3oz/1/2 cup sultanas
2.5ml/1/2 tsp ground cinnamon
350g/12oz/1 1/2 cups low fat soft cheese
60ml/4 tbsp reduced fat fromage frais
10ml/2 tsp lemon juice
45ml/3 tbsp apricot glaze
mint sprig, to decorate

1 Preheat the oven to 190°C/375°F/ Gas 5. Grease and line a 23cm/9in sandwich cake tin. Place the eggs and caster sugar in a bowl and beat with a hand-held electric whisk until thick and mousse-like. (When the whisk is lifted, a trail should remain on the surface of the mixture for at least 15 seconds.)

NUTRITION NOTES

Per portion:
Energy	244 Kcals/1023kJ
Fat	4.05g
Saturated Fat	1.71g
Cholesterol	77.95mg
Fibre	1.50g

2 Sift the flour and cinnamon over the egg mixture and fold in with a large spoon. Pour into the prepared tin and bake for 25–30 minutes or until the cake springs back when lightly pressed. Turn the cake on to a wire rack to cool.

3 To make the filling, peel, core and slice three of the apples and put them in a saucepan. Add 30ml/2 tbsp of the honey and the water. Cover and cook over a gentle heat for about 10 minutes. Add the sultanas and cinnamon, stir well, replace the lid and leave to cool.

4 Put the soft cheese in a bowl with the remaining honey, the fromage frais and half the lemon juice. Beat until the mixture is smooth.

5 Halve the cake horizontally, place the bottom half on a board and drizzle over any liquid from the apples. Spread with two-thirds of the cheese mixture, then top with the apple filling. Fit the top of the cake in place.

6 Swirl the remaining cheese mixture over the top of the sponge. Core and slice the remaining apple, sprinkle with lemon juice and use to decorate the edge of the cake. Brush the apple with the apricot glaze and place mint sprigs on top, to decorate.

COOK'S TIP
Apricot glaze is useful for brushing over any kind of fresh fruit topping or filling. Place a few spoonfuls of apricot jam in a small pan along with a squeeze of lemon juice. Heat the jam, stirring until it is melted and runny. Pour the melted jam into a wire sieve set over a bowl. Stir the jam with a wooden spoon to help it go through. Return the strained jam to the pan. Keep the glaze warm until needed.

SNOWBALLS

These light and airy little mouthfuls make an excellent accompaniment to low fat yogurt ice cream.

────────── INGREDIENTS ──────────

Makes about 20
2 egg whites
115g/4oz/¹/₂ cup caster sugar
15ml/1 tbsp cornflour, sifted
5ml/1 tsp white wine vinegar
1.5ml/¹/₄ tsp vanilla essence

1 Preheat the oven to 150C°/300°F/ Gas 2. Line two baking sheets with non-stick baking paper. Whisk the egg whites in a large grease-free bowl until very stiff, using an electric whisk.

2 Add the sugar, whisking until the meringue is very stiff. Whisk in the cornflour, vinegar and vanilla essence.

3 Drop teaspoonfuls of the mixture on to the baking sheets, shaping them into mounds, and bake for 30 minutes until crisp.

4 Remove from the oven and leave to cool on the baking sheet. When the snowballs are cold, remove them from the baking paper with a palette knife.

┌──────── NUTRITION NOTES ────────┐
Per portion:
Energy   29Kcals/24kJ
Fat   0.01g
Saturated Fat   0
Cholesterol   0

MUSCOVADO MERINGUES

These light brown meringues are extremely low in fat and are delicious served on their own or sandwiched together with a fresh fruit and soft cheese filling.

INGREDIENTS

Makes about 20

115g/4oz/²/₃ cup light muscovado sugar
2 egg whites
5ml/1 tsp finely chopped walnuts

NUTRITION NOTES

Per portion:

Energy	30Kcals/124kJ
Fat	0.34g
Saturated Fat	0.04g
Cholesterol	0
Fibre	0.02g

1 Preheat the oven to 160°C/325°F/ Gas 3. Line two baking sheets with non-stick baking paper. Press the sugar through a metal sieve into a bowl.

2 Whisk the egg whites in a clean, dry bowl until very stiff and dry, then whisk in the sugar, about 15ml/1 tbsp at a time, until the meringue is very thick and glossy.

4 Sprinkle the meringues with the chopped walnuts. Bake for 30 minutes. Cool for 5 minutes on the baking sheets, then leave to cool on a wire rack.

COOK'S TIP
For a sophisticated filling, mix 115g/4oz/¹/₂ cup low fat soft cheese with 15ml/1 tbsp icing sugar. Chop 2 slices of fresh pineapple and add to the mixture. Use to sandwich the meringues together in pairs.

3 Spoon small mounds of the mixture on to the prepared baking sheets.

LEMON SPONGE FINGERS

These tangy, light sponge fingers are virtually fat-free and perfect to serve either as an accompaniment to low fat desserts, or to serve with coffee.

NUTRITION NOTES

Per portion:

Energy	33Kcals/137kJ
Fat	0.57g
Saturated Fat	0.16g
Cholesterol	19.30mg
Fibre	0.08g

INGREDIENTS

Makes about 20
2 eggs
75g/3oz/½ cup caster sugar
grated rind of 1 lemon
50g/2oz/½ cup plain flour, sifted
caster sugar, for sprinkling

1 Preheat the oven to 190°C/375°F/ Gas 5. Line two baking sheets with non-stick baking paper.

2 Whisk the eggs, sugar and lemon rind together with an electric whisk until the mixture is thick and mousse-like and leaves a thick trail on the surface for at least 15 seconds.

3 Carefully fold in the flour with a large metal spoon. Place the mixture in a large piping bag fitted with a 1cm/½in plain nozzle and pipe into finger lengths on the baking sheets.

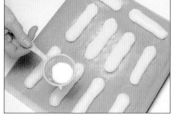

4 Dust the fingers with caster sugar and bake for 6–8 minutes until golden brown.

VARIATION
To make Spice Fingers, omit the lemon rind and fold in 5ml/1 tsp mixed spice with the flour.

APRICOT SPONGE BARS

These fingers are delicious at tea time – the apricots keep them moist for several days.

INGREDIENTS

Makes 18

225g/8oz/2 cups self-raising flour
115g/4oz/½ cup soft light brown sugar
50g/2oz/½ cup semolina
175g/6oz/1 cup ready-to-eat dried
  apricots, chopped
30ml/2 tbsp clear honey
30ml/2 tbsp malt extract
2 eggs
60ml/4 tbsp skimmed milk
60ml/4 tbsp sunflower oil
a few drops of almond essence
30ml/2 tbsp flaked almonds

1 Preheat the oven to 160°C/325°F/ Gas 3. Lightly grease and then line an 18 x 28cm/7 x 11in baking tin.

2 Sift the flour into a bowl and mix in the sugar, semolina and apricots. Make a well in the centre and add the honey, malt extract, eggs, milk, oil and almond essence. Mix the ingredients together thoroughly until smooth.

3 Spoon the mixture into the tin, spreading it to the edges, then sprinkle over the flaked almonds.

4 Bake for 30–35 minutes, or until the centre springs back when lightly pressed. Remove from the tin and turn on to a wire rack to cool. Cut into 18 slices using a sharp knife.

COOK'S TIP
If you can't find pre-soaked apricots, just chop ordinary dried apricots soak them in boiling water for 1 hour, then drain and add to the mixture.

NUTRITION NOTES	
Per portion:	
Energy	153Kcals/641kJ
Fat	4.56g
Saturated Fat	0.61g
Cholesterol	21.5mg
Fibre	1.27g

COFFEE SPONGE DROPS

These are delicious on their own, but taste even better with a filling made by mixing low fat soft cheese with drained and chopped stem ginger.

INGREDIENTS

Makes 12
50g/2oz/¹/2 cup plain flour
15ml/1 tbsp instant coffee powder
2 eggs
75g/3oz/6 tbsp caster sugar

For the filling
115g/4oz/¹/2 cup low fat soft cheese
40g/1¹/2oz/¹/4 cup chopped
   stem ginger

COOK'S TIP
As an alternative to stem ginger in the filling, try walnuts.

1 Preheat the oven to 190°C/375°F/ Gas 5. Line two baking sheets with non-stick baking paper. Make the filling by beating together the soft cheese and stem ginger. Chill until required. Sift the flour and instant coffee powder together.

NUTRITION NOTES
Per portion:	
Energy	69Kcals/290kJ
Fat	1.36g
Saturated Fat	0.50g
Cholesterol	33.33mg
Fibre	0.29g

2 Combine the eggs and caster sugar in a bowl. Beat with a hand-held electric whisk until thick and mousse-like. (When the whisk is lifted, a trail should remain on the surface of the mixture for at least 15 seconds.)

3 Carefully add the sifted flour and coffee mixture and gently fold in with a metal spoon, being careful not to knock out any air.

4 Spoon the mixture into a piping bag fitted with a 1cm/¹/2in plain nozzle. Pipe 4cm/1¹/2in rounds on the baking sheets. Bake for 12 minutes. Cool on a wire rack, then sandwich together with the filling.

CHOCOLATE AND BANANA BROWNIES

Nuts traditionally give brownies their chewy texture. Here oat bran is used instead, creating a low fat, moist, moreish, yet healthy alternative.

INGREDIENTS

Serves 9

75ml/5 tbsp reduced fat cocoa powder
15ml/1 tbsp caster sugar
75ml/5 tbsp skimmed milk
3 large bananas, mashed
215g/7¹/₂oz/1 cup soft light brown sugar
5ml/1 tsp vanilla essence
5 egg whites
75g/3oz/³/₄ cup self-raising flour
75g/3oz/³/₄ cup oat bran
15ml/1 tbsp icing sugar, for dusting

NUTRITION NOTES

Per portion:	
Energy	230Kcals/968kJ
Fat	2.15g
Saturated Fat	0.91g
Fibre	1.89g

COOK'S TIPS
Store these brownies in an airtight tin for a day before eating – they improve with keeping.

You'll find reduced fat cocoa powder in health food stores. If you can't find it, ordinary cocoa powder will work just as well, but, of course, the fat content will be much higher!

1 Preheat the oven to 180°C/350°F/ Gas 4. Line a 20cm/8in square tin with non-stick baking paper.

2 Blend the reduced fat cocoa powder and caster sugar with the skimmed milk. Add the bananas, soft light brown sugar and vanilla essence.

3 Lightly beat the egg whites with a fork. Add the chocolate mixture and continue to beat well. Sift the flour over the mixture and fold in with the oat bran. Pour into the prepared tin.

4 Cook in the preheated oven for 40 minutes or until firm. Cool in the tin for 10 minutes, then turn out on to a wire rack. Cut into squares and lightly dust with icing sugar before serving.

Peach Swiss Roll

A feather-light sponge enclosing peach jam – delicious at tea time.

Ingredients

Serves 6–8

3 eggs
115g/4oz/½ cup caster sugar
75g/3oz/¾ cup plain flour, sifted
15ml/1 tbsp boiling water
90ml/6 tbsp peach jam
icing sugar, for dusting (optional)

Nutrition Notes

Per portion:

Energy	178Kcals/746kJ
Fat	2.45g
Saturated Fat	0.67g
Cholesterol	82.50mg
Fibre	0.33g

Cook's Tip
To decorate the Swiss roll with glacé icing, put 115g/4oz glacé icing in a piping bag fitted with a small writing nozzle and pipe lines over the top.

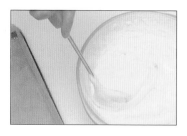

2 Carefully fold in the flour with a large metal spoon, then add the boiling water in the same way.

3 Spoon into the prepared tin, spread evenly to the edges and bake for about 10–12 minutes until the cake springs back when lightly pressed.

5 Neatly trim the edges of the cake. Make a neat cut two-thirds of the way through the cake, about 1cm/½in from the short edge nearest you.

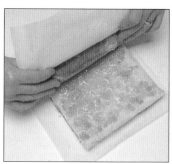

6 Spread the cake with the peach jam and roll up quickly from the partially cut end. Hold in position for a minute, making sure the join is underneath. Cool on a wire rack. Decorate with glacé icing (see Cook's Tip) or dust with icing sugar before serving.

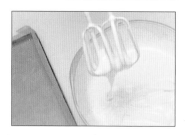

1 Preheat the oven to 200°C/400°F/ Gas 6. Grease a 30 x 20cm/12 x 8in Swiss roll tin and line with non-stick baking paper. Combine the eggs and sugar in a bowl. Beat with a hand-held electric whisk until thick and mousse-like. (When the whisk is lifted, a trail should remain on the surface of the mixture for at least 15 seconds.)

4 Spread a sheet of greaseproof paper on a flat surface, sprinkle it with caster sugar, then invert the cake on top. Peel off the lining paper.

LEMON CHIFFON CAKE

Lemon mousse provides a tangy filling for this light lemon sponge.

INGREDIENTS

Serves 8
2 eggs
75g/3oz/6 tbsp caster sugar
grated rind of 1 lemon
50g/2oz/¹/₂ cup sifted plain flour
lemon shreds, to decorate

For the filling
2 eggs, separated
75g/3oz/6 tbsp caster sugar
grated rind and juice of 1 lemon
30ml/2 tbsp water
15ml/1 tbsp gelatine
125ml/4fl oz/¹/₂ cup low fat
   fromage frais

For the icing
15ml/1 tbsp lemon juice
115g/4oz/scant 1 cup icing sugar, sifted

1 Preheat the oven to 180°C/350°F/ Gas 4. Grease and line a 20cm/8in loose-bottomed cake tin. Whisk the eggs, sugar and lemon rind together with a hand-held electric whisk until thick and mousse-like. Gently fold in the flour, then turn the mixture into the prepared tin.

2 Bake for 20–25 minutes until the cake springs back when lightly pressed in the centre. Turn on to a wire rack to cool. Once cold, split the cake in half horizontally and return the lower half to the clean cake tin.

3 Make the filling. Put the egg yolks, sugar, lemon rind and juice in a bowl. Beat with a hand-held electric whisk until thick, pale and creamy.

4 Pour the water into a heat-proof bowl and sprinkle the gelatine on top. Leave until spongy, then stir over simmering water until dissolved. Cool, then whisk into the yolk mixture. Fold in the fromage frais. When the mixture begins to set, whisk the egg whites to soft peaks. Fold the egg whites into the mousse mixture.

5 Pour the lemon mousse over the sponge in the cake tin, spreading it to the edges. Set the second layer of sponge on top and chill until set.

6 Slide a palette knife dipped in hot water between the tin and the cake to loosen it, then carefully transfer the cake to a serving plate. Make the icing by adding enough lemon juice to the icing sugar to make a mixture thick enough to coat the back of a wooden spoon. Pour over the cake and spread evenly to the edges. Decorate with the lemon shreds.

NUTRITION NOTES

Per portion:

Energy	202Kcals/849kJ
Fat	2.81g
Saturated Fat	0.79g
Cholesterol	96.41mg
Fibre	0.20g

COOK'S TIP
The mousse should be just setting when the egg whites are added. Speed up this process by placing the bowl of mousse in iced water.

BANANA AND GINGERBREAD SLICES

Very quick to make and
deliciously moist due to the
addition of bananas.

INGREDIENTS

Makes 20
275g/10oz/2 cups plain flour
20ml/4 tsp ground ginger
10ml/2 tsp mixed spice
5ml/1 tsp bicarbonate of soda
115g/4oz/¹/₂ cup soft light brown sugar
60ml/4 tbsp sunflower oil
30ml/2 tbsp molasses or black treacle
30ml/2 tbsp malt extract
2 eggs
60ml/4 tbsp orange juice
3 bananas
115g/4oz/²/₃ cup raisins

NUTRITION NOTES

Per portion:
Energy	148Kcals/621kJ
Fat	3.07g
Saturated Fat	0.53g
Cholesterol	19.30mg
Fibre	0.79g

VARIATION
To make Spiced Honey and
Banana Cake: omit the ground
ginger and add another 5ml/1 tsp
mixed spice; omit the malt extract
and the molasses or treacle and
add 60ml/4 tbsp strong-flavoured
clear honey instead; and replace
the raisins with either sultanas, or
coarsely chopped ready-to-eat
dried apricots, or semi-dried
pineapple. If you choose to use
the pineapple, then you could also
replace the orange juice with fresh
pineapple juice.

1 Preheat the oven to 180°C/350°F/
Gas 4. Lightly grease and line an
18 x 28cm/7 x 11in baking tin.

2 Sift the flour into a bowl with the
spices and bicarbonate of soda. Mix
in the sugar with some of the flour and
sift it all into the bowl.

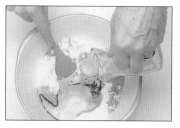

3 Make a well in the centre, add the
oil, molasses or black treacle, malt
extract, eggs and orange juice and mix
together thoroughly.

4 Mash the bananas, add them to
the bowl with the raisins and mix
well together.

5 Pour the mixture into the prepared
tin and bake for about 35–40
minutes, until the centre springs back
when lightly pressed.

6 Leave the cake in the tin to cool for
5 minutes, then turn out on to a
wire rack and leave to cool completely.
Cut into 20 slices.

COOK'S TIP
The flavour of this cake develops
as it keeps, so if you can, store it
for a few days before eating.

GREEK HONEY AND LEMON CAKE

INGREDIENTS

Makes 16 slices
40g/1½oz/3 tbsp sunflower margarine
60ml/4 tbsp clear honey
finely grated rind and juice of 1 lemon
150ml/¼ pint/⅔ cup skimmed milk
150g/5oz/1¼ cups plain flour
7.5ml/1½ tsp baking powder
2.5ml/½ tsp grated nutmeg
50g/2oz/¼ cup semolina
2 egg whites
10ml/2 tsp sesame seeds

1 Preheat the oven to 200°C/400°F/ Gas 6. Lightly oil a 19cm/7½in square deep cake tin (pan) and line the base with non-stick baking paper.

2 Place the margarine and 45ml/3 tbsp of the honey in a saucepan and heat gently until melted. Reserve 15ml/1 tbsp lemon juice, then stir in the rest with the lemon rind and milk.

3 Sift together the flour, baking powder and nutmeg, then beat in with the semolina. Whisk the egg whites until they form soft peaks, then fold evenly into the mixture.

4 Spoon into the tin and sprinkle with sesame seeds. Bake for 25–30 minutes, until golden brown. Mix the reserved honey and lemon juice and drizzle over the cake while warm. Cool in the tin, then cut into fingers to serve.

NUTRITION NOTES

Per portion:
Energy	82Kcals/342kJ
Fat	2.62g
Saturated fat	0.46g
Cholesterol	0.36mg
Fibre	0.41g

STRAWBERRY ROULADE

INGREDIENTS

Serves 6
4 egg whites
115g/4oz/⅔ cup golden caster sugar
75g/3oz/¾ cup plain flour
30ml/2 tbsp orange juice
115g/4oz/1 cup strawberries, chopped
150g/5oz/¼ cup low fat fromage frais
caster sugar, for sprinkling
strawberries, to decorate

1 Preheat the oven to 200°C/400°F/ Gas 6. Oil a 23 x 33cm/9 x 13in Swiss roll tin and line with non-stick baking paper.

2 Place the egg whites in a large bowl and whisk until they form soft peaks. Gradually whisk in the sugar. Fold in half of the sifted flour, then fold in the rest with the orange juice.

3 Spoon the mixture into the prepared tin, spreading evenly. Bake for 15-18 minutes, or until golden brown and firm to the touch.

4 Meanwhile, spread out a sheet of non-stick baking paper and sprinkle with caster sugar. Turn out the cake on to this and remove the lining paper. Roll up the sponge loosely from one short side, with the paper inside. Cool.

5 Unroll and remove the paper. Stir the strawberries into the fromage frais and spread over the sponge. Reroll and serve decorated with strawberries.

NUTRITION NOTES

Per portion:
Energy	154Kcals/646kJ
Fat	0.24g
Saturated fat	0.05g
Cholesterol	0.25mg
Fibre	0.6g

APRICOT AND ORANGE ROULADE

This elegant dessert is very good served with a spoonful of natural yogurt or crème fraîche.

INGREDIENTS

Serves 6
4 egg whites
115g/4oz/½ cup golden caster sugar
50g/2oz/½ cup plain flour
finely grated rind of 1 small orange
45ml/3 tbsp orange juice
10ml/2 tsp icing sugar and shreds of
    orange zest, to decorate

For the filling
115g/4oz/⅔ cup ready-to-eat dried
    apricots
150ml/¼ pint/⅔ cup orange juice

NUTRITION NOTES

Per portion:
Energy	203Kcals/853kJ
Fat	10.52g
Saturated fat	2.05g
Cholesterol	0
Fibre	2.53g

1 Preheat the oven to 200°C/400°F/ Gas 6. Grease a 23 x 33cm/9 x 13 in Swiss roll tin and line it with non-stick baking paper. Grease the paper.

2 For the roulade, place the egg whites in a large bowl and whisk them until they hold soft peaks. Gradually add the sugar, whisking hard between each addition.

3 Fold in the flour, orange rind and juice. Spoon the mixture into the prepared tin and spread it evenly.

4 Bake for about 15–18 minutes, or until the sponge is firm and light golden in colour. Turn out on to a sheet of non-stick baking paper and roll it up Swiss roll-style loosely from one short side. Leave to cool.

5 For the filling, roughly chop the apricots, and place them in a saucepan with the orange juice. Cover the pan and leave to simmer until most of the liquid has been absorbed. Purée the apricots in a food processor or blender.

6 Unroll the roulade and spread with the apricot mixture. Roll up, arrange strips of paper diagonally across the roll, sprinkle lightly with lines of icing sugar, remove the paper and scatter with orange zest to serve.

COOK'S TIP
Make and bake the sponge mixture a day in advance and keep it, rolled with the paper, in a cool place. Fill it with the fruit purée 2–3 hours before serving. The sponge can also be frozen for up to 2 months; thaw it at room temperature and fill it as above.

NECTARINE AMARETTO CAKE

Serves 8

3 eggs, separated
175g/6oz caster sugar
grated rind and juice of 1 lemon
50g/2oz semolina
40g/1oz ground almonds
25g/1oz plain flour
2 nectarines, halved and stoned
60ml/4 tbsp apricot glaze

For the syrup
75g/3oz caster sugar
90ml/6 tbsp water
30ml/2 tbsp Amaretto liqueur

1 Preheat the oven to 180°C/350°F/ Gas 4. Grease a 20cm/8in round, loose-bottomed cake tin. Whisk together the egg yolks, caster sugar, lemon rind and juice in a bowl until the mixture is thick, pale and creamy.

2 Fold in the semolina, almonds and flour until smooth.

3 Whisk the egg whites in a bowl until fairly stiff. Use a metal spoon to stir a generous spoonful of the whites into the semolina mixture, then fold in the remaining egg whites. Spoon the mixture into the cake tin.

4 Bake for 30–35 minutes until the centre of the cake springs back when pressed lightly. Remove from the oven and loosen around the edge with a palette knife. Prick the top with a skewer. Leave to cool in the tin.

5 To make the syrup, heat the sugar and water in a small pan, stirring until the sugar is dissolved. Boil without stirring for 2 minutes. Add the Amaretto liqueur and drizzle over the cake in the tin.

6 Remove the cake from the tin and transfer to a serving plate. Decorate with sliced nectarines. Brush with warm apricot glaze.

NUTRITION NOTES	
Per portion:	
Energy	264Kcals/1108kJ
Fat	5.70g
Saturated Fat	0.85g
Cholesterol	72.19mg
Fibre	1.08g

BANANA GINGER PARKIN

Parkin keeps well and really improves with keeping. Store it in a covered container for up to two months.

INGREDIENTS

Makes 1 cake
200g/7oz/1¼ cups plain flour
10ml/2 tsp bicarbonate of soda
10ml/2 tsp ground ginger
150g/5oz/1¼ cups medium oatmeal
60ml/4 tbsp dark muscovado sugar
75g/3oz/6 tbsp sunflower margarine
150g/5oz/⅔ cup golden syrup
1 egg, beaten
3 ripe bananas, mashed
75g/3oz/¼ cup icing sugar
stem ginger, to decorate

1 Preheat the oven to 160°C/325°F/ Gas 3. Grease and line an 18 x 28cm/7 x 11in cake tin.

2 Sift together the flour, bicarbonate of soda and ginger, then stir in the oatmeal. Melt the sugar, margarine and syrup in a saucepan, then stir into the flour mixture. Beat in the egg and mashed bananas.

3 Spoon into the tin and bake for about 1 hour, or until firm to the touch. Allow to cool in the tin, then turn out and cut into squares.

4 Sift the icing sugar into a bowl and stir in just enough water to make a smooth, runny icing. Drizzle the icing over each square and top with a piece of stem ginger, if you like.

COOK'S TIP
This is a nutritious, energy-giving cake that is a really good choice for packed lunches as it doesn't break up too easily.

NUTRITION NOTES

Per cake:
Energy	3320Kcals/13946kJ
Fat	83.65g
Saturated fat	16.34g
Cholesterol	197.75mg
Fibre	20.69g

SPICED DATE AND WALNUT CAKE

A classic flavour combination, which makes a very easy low fat, high-fibre cake.

INGREDIENTS

Makes 1 cake
300g/11oz/2½ cups wholemeal self-raising flour
10ml/2 tsp mixed spice
150g/5oz/¾ cup chopped dates
50g/2oz/½ cup chopped walnuts
60ml/4 tbsp sunflower oil
115g/4oz/½ cup dark muscovado sugar
300ml/½ pint/1¼ cups skimmed milk
walnut halves, to decorate

1 Preheat the oven to 180°C/350°F/Gas 4. Grease and line a 900g/2 lb loaf tin with greaseproof paper.

2 Sift together the flour and spice, adding back any bran from the sieve. Stir in the dates and walnuts.

3 Mix the oil, sugar and milk, then stir evenly into the dry ingredients. Spoon into the prepared tin and arrange the walnut halves on top.

4 Bake the cake in the oven for about 45–50 minutes, or until golden brown and firm. Turn out the cake, remove the lining paper and leave to cool on a wire rack.

NUTRITION NOTES

Per cake:
Energy	2654Kcals/11146kJ
Fat	92.78g
Saturated fat	11.44g
Cholesterol	6mg
Fibre	35.1g

COOK'S TIP
Pecan nuts can be used in place of the walnuts in this cake.

EGGLESS CHRISTMAS CAKE

INGREDIENTS

Makes 1 x 18cm / 7in square cake
75g / 3oz / ⅔ cup sultanas
75g / 3oz / ⅔ cup raisins
75g / 3oz / 1½ cup currants
75g / 3oz / ⅓ cup glacé cherries, halved
50g / 2oz / ¼ cup cut mixed peel
250ml / 8 fl oz / 1 cup apple juice
25g / 1oz / ¼ cup toasted hazelnuts
30ml / 2 tbsp pumpkin seeds
2 pieces stem ginger in syrup, chopped
finely grated rind of 1 lemon
120ml / 4 fl oz / ½ cup skimmed milk
50ml / 2 fl oz / ¼ cup sunflower oil
225g / 8oz / 1¼ cups wholemeal self-
 raising flour
10ml / 2 tsp mixed spice
45ml / 3 tbsp brandy or dark rum
apricot jam, for brushing
glacé fruits, to decorate

1 Place the sultanas, raisins, currants, cherries and peel in a bowl and stir in the apple juice. Cover and leave to soak overnight.

2 Preheat the oven to 150°C / 300°F / Gas 2. Grease and line an 18cm / 7in square cake tin.

3 Add the hazelnuts, pumpkin seeds, ginger and lemon rind to the soaked fruit. Stir in the milk and oil. Sift the flour and spice and stir into the mixture with the brandy or rum.

4 Spoon into the prepared tin and bake for about 1½ hours, or until the cake is golden brown and firm to the touch.

5 Turn out and cool on a wire rack. Brush with sieved apricot jam and decorate with glacé fruits.

NUTRITION NOTES

Per cake:
Energy	2702Kcals / 11352kJ
Fat	73.61g
Saturated fat	10.69g
Cholesterol	2.4mg
Fibre	29.46g

CRANBERRY AND APPLE RING

Tangy cranberries add an unusual flavour to this low fat cake. It is best eaten very fresh.

INGREDIENTS

Makes 1 ring cake
225g/8oz/2 cups self-raising flour
5ml/1 tsp ground cinnamon
75g/3oz/½ cup light muscovado sugar
1 crisp eating apple, cored and diced
75g/3oz/⅔ cup fresh or frozen
    cranberries
60ml/4 tbsp sunflower oil
150ml/¼ pint/⅔ cup apple juice
cranberry jelly and apple slices, to
    decorate

1 Preheat the oven to 180°C/350°F/ Gas 4. Lightly grease a 1 litre/1¼ pint/4 cup ring tin with oil.

2 Sift together the flour and ground cinnamon, then stir in the sugar.

3 Toss together the diced apple and cranberries. Stir into the dry ingredients, then add the oil and apple juice and beat well.

4 Spoon the mixture into the prepared ring tin and bake for about 35–40 minutes, or until the cake is firm to the touch. Turn out and leave to cool completely on a wire rack.

5 To serve, drizzle warmed cranberry jelly over the cake and decorate with apple slices.

COOK'S TIP
Fresh cranberries are available throughout the winter months and if you don't use them all at once, they can be frozen for up to a year.

NUTRITION NOTES

Per cake:

Energy	1616Kcals/6787kJ
Fat	47.34g
Saturated fat	6.14g
Cholesterol	0
Fibre	12.46g

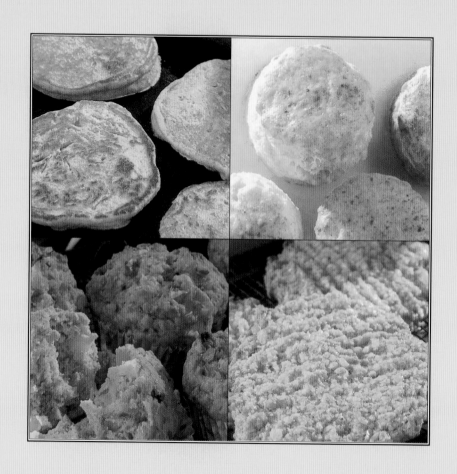

SCONES, MUFFINS, BUNS AND BISCUITS

Many scones, muffins, buns and biscuits are low in fat and make ideal snacks or treats at any time of day. Try serving them on their own or with a little low fat spread, honey or jam. They are delicious served warm for breakfast or brunch, cold for afternoon tea or packed up and taken away, to enjoy at your leisure. We include a selection of tempting scones, muffins, buns and biscuits, including Pineapple and Cinnamon Drop Scones, Date and Apple Muffins, Banana and Apricot Chelsea Buns and Oaty Crisps.

PINEAPPLE AND CINNAMON DROP SCONES

Making the batter with pineapple juice instead of milk cuts down on fat and adds to the taste.

INGREDIENTS

Makes 24

115g/4oz/1 cup self-raising wholemeal flour
115g/4oz/1 cup self-raising white flour
5ml/1 tsp ground cinnamon
15ml/1 tbsp caster sugar
1 egg
300ml/½ pint/1¼ cups pineapple juice
75g/3oz/½ cup semi-dried pineapple, chopped

NUTRITION NOTES

Per portion:	
Energy	15Kcals/215kJ
Fat	0.81g
Saturated Fat	0.14g
Cholesterol	8.02mg
Fibre	0.76g

1 Preheat a griddle, heavy-based frying pan or an electric frying pan. Put the wholemeal flour in a mixing bowl. Sift in the white flour, add the cinnamon and sugar and make a well in the centre.

COOK'S TIP
Drop scones do not keep well and are best eaten freshly cooked. Other semi-dried fruit, such as apricots or pears, can be used in place of the pineapple.

2 Add the egg with half the pineapple juice and gradually incorporate the surrounding flour to make a smooth batter. Beat in the remaining juice with the chopped pineapple.

3 Lightly grease the griddle or pan. Drop tablespoons of the batter on to the surface, leaving them until they bubble and the bubbles begin to burst.

4 Turn the drop scones with a palette knife and cook until the underside is golden brown. Keep the cooked scones warm and moist by wrapping them in a clean napkin while continuing to cook successive batches.

DROP SCONES

These little scones are delicious spread with jam.

──────── INGREDIENTS ────────

Makes 18
225g/8oz/2 cups self-raising flour
2.5ml/½ tsp salt
15ml/1 tbsp caster sugar
1 egg, beaten
300ml/½ pint/1¼ cups skimmed milk
oil, for frying

1 Preheat a griddle, heavy-based frying pan or an electric frying pan. Sift the flour and salt into a mixing bowl. Stir in the sugar and make a well in the centre.

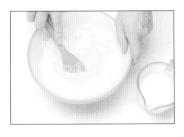

2 Add the egg and half the milk, then gradually incorporate the surrounding flour to make a smooth batter. Beat in the remaining milk.

3 Lightly oil the griddle or pan. Drop tablespoons of the batter on to the surface, leaving them until they bubble and the bubbles begin to burst.

4 Turn the drop scones over with a palette knife and cook until the underside is golden brown. Keep the cooked drop scones warm and moist by wrapping them in a clean napkin while cooking successive batches.

──── NUTRITION NOTES ────

Per portion:
Energy	64Kcals/270kJ
Fat	1.09g
Saturated Fat	0.2g
Cholesterol	11.03mg
Fibre	0.43g

COOK'S TIP
For savoury scones, add 2 chopped spring onions and 15ml/1 tbsp of freshly grated Parmesan cheese. Serve with cottage cheese.

CHIVE AND POTATO SCONES

These little scones should be fairly thin, soft and crisp on the outside. They're extremely quick to make, so serve them for breakfast or lunch.

INGREDIENTS

Makes 20
450g/1lb potatoes
115g/4oz/1 cup plain flour, sifted
30ml/2 tbsp olive oil
30ml/2 tbsp snipped chives
salt and black pepper
low fat spread, for topping (optional)

NUTRITION NOTES

Per portion:
Energy	50Kcals/211kJ
Fat	1.24g
Saturated Fat	0.17g
Cholesterol	0
Fibre	0.54g

1 Cook the potatoes in a saucepan of boiling salted water for 20 minutes, then drain thoroughly. Return the potatoes to the clean pan and mash them. Preheat a griddle or heavy-based frying pan over a low heat.

COOK'S TIP
Cook the scones over a low heat so that the outsides do not burn before the insides are cooked through.

2 Add the flour, olive oil and snipped chives with a little salt and pepper to the hot mashed potato in the pan. Mix to a soft dough.

3 Roll out the dough on a well-floured surface to a thickness of 5mm/¼in and stamp out rounds with a 5cm/2in plain pastry cutter.

4 Cook the scones, in batches, on the hot griddle or frying pan for about 10 minutes until they are golden brown on both sides. Keep the heat low. Top with a little low fat spread, if you like, and serve immediately.

CHEESE AND CHIVE SCONES

INGREDIENTS

Makes 9

115g/4oz/1 cup self-raising flour
150g/5oz/1 cup self-raising wholemeal
*   flour*
2.5ml/¹/₂ tsp salt
75g/3oz feta cheese
15ml/1 tbsp snipped fresh chives
150ml/¹/₄ pint/²/₃ cup skimmed milk,
*   plus extra for glazing*
1.25ml/¹/₄ tsp cayenne pepper

1 Preheat the oven to 200°C/400°F/ Gas 6. Sift the flours and salt into a mixing bowl, adding any bran left over from the flour in the sieve.

2 Crumble the feta cheese and rub into the dry ingredients. Stir in the chives, then add the milk and mix to a soft dough.

NUTRITION NOTES

Per portion:
Energy	121Kcals/507kJ
Fat	2.24g
Saturated Fat	1.13g
Fibre	1.92g

3 Turn out on to a floured surface and knead lightly until smooth. Roll out to 2cm/³/₄in thick and stamp out nine scones with a 6cm/2¹/₂in biscuit cutter.

4 Transfer the scones to a non-stick baking sheet. Brush with skimmed milk, then sprinkle over the cayenne pepper. Bake in the oven for 15 minutes, or until golden brown.

HAM AND TOMATO SCONES

These scones make an ideal accompaniment for soup. Choose a strongly flavoured ham, trimmed of fat, and chop it fairly finely, so that a little goes a long way. Use wholemeal flour or a mixture of wholemeal and white flour for extra flavour, texture and fibre.

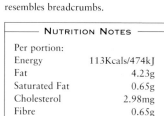

INGREDIENTS

Makes 12

225g/8oz/2 cups self-raising flour
5ml/1 tsp dry mustard
5ml/1 tsp paprika, plus extra for
    sprinkling
2.5ml/½ tsp salt
25g/1oz/2 tbsp soft margarine
15ml/1 tbsp snipped fresh basil
50g/2oz/1 cup drained sun-dried
    tomatoes in oil, chopped
50g/2oz cooked ham, chopped
90–120ml/3–4fl oz/6 tbsp–½ cup
    skimmed milk, plus extra for brushing

1 Preheat the oven to 200°C/ 400°F/Gas 6. Flour a large baking sheet. Sift the flour, mustard, paprika and salt into a bowl. Rub in the margarine until the mixture resembles breadcrumbs.

NUTRITION NOTES

Per portion:
Energy	113Kcals/474kJ
Fat	4.23g
Saturated Fat	0.65g
Cholesterol	2.98mg
Fibre	0.65g

2 Stir in the basil, sun-dried tomatoes and ham, and mix lightly. Pour in enough milk to mix to a soft dough.

3 Turn the dough out on to a lightly floured surface, knead briefly and roll out to a 20 x 15cm/8 x 6in rectangle. Cut into 5cm/2in squares and arrange on the baking sheet.

4 Brush lightly with milk, sprinkle with paprika and bake for about 12–15 minutes. Transfer to a wire rack to cool.

COOK'S TIP
To cut calories and fat, choose dry-packed sun-dried tomatoes and soak them in warm water.

DATE AND APPLE MUFFINS

You will only need one or two of these wholesome muffins per person, as they are very filling.

INGREDIENTS

Makes 12

150g/5oz/1¼ cups self-raising
   wholemeal flour
150g/5oz/1¼ cups self-raising
   white flour
5ml/1 tsp ground cinnamon
5ml/1 tsp baking powder
25g/1 oz/2 tbsp soft margarine
75g/3oz/½ cup light muscovado sugar
1 eating apple
250ml/8fl oz/1 cup apple juice
30ml/2 tbsp pear and apple spread
1 egg, lightly beaten
75g/3oz/½ cup chopped dates
15ml/1 tbsp chopped pecan nuts

1 Preheat the oven to 200°C/400°F/ Gas 6. Arrange 12 paper cake cases in a deep muffin tin. Put the wholemeal flour in a mixing bowl. Sift in the white flour with the cinnamon and baking powder. Rub in the margarine until the mixture resembles breadcrumbs, then stir in the muscovado sugar.

2 Quarter and core the apple, chop the flesh finely and set aside. Stir a little of the apple juice with the pear and apple spread until smooth. Mix in the remaining juice, then add to the rubbed-in mixture with the egg. Add the chopped apple to the bowl with the dates. Mix quickly until just combined.

3 Divide the mixture among the muffin cases.

4 Sprinkle with the chopped pecan nuts. Bake the muffins for 20–25 minutes until golden brown and firm in the middle. Remove to a wire rack and serve while still warm.

NUTRITION NOTES

Per muffin:	
Energy	163Kcals/686kJ
Fat	2.98g
Saturated Fat	0.47g
Cholesterol	16.04mg
Fibre	1.97g

COOK'S TIP
Use a pear in place of the eating apple and chopped ready-to-eat dried apricots in place of the dates. Ground mixed spice is a good alternative to cinnamon.

RASPBERRY MUFFINS

These American muffins are made using baking powder and low fat buttermilk, giving them a light and spongy texture. They are delicious to eat at any time of the day.

NUTRITION NOTES

Per muffin:

Energy	171Kcals/719kJ
Fat	4.55g
Saturated Fat	0.71g
Cholesterol	16.5mg
Fibre	1.02g

—————— INGREDIENTS ——————

Makes 10–12
275g/10oz/2½ cups plain flour
15ml/1 tbsp baking powder
115g/4oz/½ cup caster sugar
1 egg
250ml/8fl oz/1 cup buttermilk
60ml/4 tbsp sunflower oil
150g/5oz raspberries

1 Preheat the oven to 200°C/400°F/ Gas 6. Arrange 12 paper cake cases in a deep muffin tin. Sift the flour and baking powder into a mixing bowl, stir in the sugar, then make a well in the centre.

2 Mix the egg, buttermilk and sunflower oil together in a bowl, pour into the flour mixture and mix quickly.

3 Add the raspberries and lightly fold in with a metal spoon. Spoon the mixture into the paper cases.

4 Bake the muffins for 20–25 minutes until golden brown and firm in the middle. Transfer to a wire rack and serve warm or cold.

SPICED BANANA MUFFINS

These light and nutritious muffins include banana for added fibre, and make a tasty tea-time treat. If liked, slice off the tops and fill with jam.

INGREDIENTS

Makes 12

75g/3oz/⅔ cup plain wholemeal flour
50g/2oz/½ cup plain white flour
10ml/2 tsp baking powder
pinch of salt
5ml/1 tsp mixed spice
40g/1½oz/¼ cup soft light brown sugar
50g/2oz/¼ cup polyunsaturated margarine
1 egg, beaten
150ml/¼ pint/⅔ cup semi-skimmed milk
grated rind of 1 orange
1 ripe banana
20g/¾oz/¼ cup porridge oats
20g/¾oz/scant ¼ cup chopped hazelnuts

1 Preheat the oven to 200°C/400°F/ Gas 6. Line a muffin tin with 12 large paper cake cases. Sift together both flours, the baking powder, salt and mixed spice into a bowl, then tip the bran remaining in the sieve into the bowl. Stir in the sugar.

NUTRITION NOTES

Per muffin:

Energy	110Kcals/465kJ
Fat	5g
Saturated Fat	1g
Cholesterol	17.5mg

2 Melt the margarine and pour it into a mixing bowl. Cool slightly, then beat in the egg, milk and grated orange rind.

3 Gently fold in the dry ingredients. Mash the banana with a fork, then stir it gently into the mixture, being careful not to overmix.

4 Spoon the mixture into the paper cases. Combine the oats and hazelnuts and sprinkle a little of the mixture over each muffin.

5 Bake for 20 minutes until the muffins are well risen and golden, and a skewer inserted in the centre comes out clean. Transfer to a wire rack and serve warm or cold.

BANANA AND APRICOT CHELSEA BUNS

These buns are old favourites given a low fat twist with a delectable fruit filling.

INGREDIENTS

Serves 9
90ml/6 tbsp warm skimmed milk
5ml/1 tsp dried yeast
pinch of sugar
225g/8oz/2 cups strong plain flour
10ml/2 tsp mixed spice
2.5ml/¹/₂ tsp salt
50g/2oz/¹/₄ cup caster sugar
25g/1oz/2 tbsp soft margarine
1 egg

For the filling
1 large ripe banana
175g/6oz/1 cup ready-to-eat dried
  apricots
30ml/2 tbsp light muscovado sugar

For the glaze
30ml/2 tbsp caster sugar
30ml/2 tbsp water

COOK'S TIP
Do not leave the buns in the tins for too long, or the glaze will stick to the sides, making them very difficult to remove.

NUTRITION NOTES

Per bun:
Energy	214Kcals/901kJ
Fat	3.18g
Saturated Fat	0.63g
Cholesterol	21.59mg
Fibre	2.18g

1 Lightly grease an 18cm/7in square tin. Put the warm milk in a jug and sprinkle the yeast on top. Add a pinch of sugar to help activate the yeast, mix well and leave for 30 minutes.

2 Sift the flour, spice and salt into a mixing bowl. Stir in the caster sugar, rub in the margarine, then stir in the yeast mixture and the egg. Gradually mix in the flour to make a soft dough, adding extra milk if needed.

3 Turn out the dough on to a floured surface and knead for 5 minutes until smooth and elastic. Return the dough to the clean bowl, cover with a damp dish towel and leave in a warm place for about 2 hours, until doubled in bulk.

4 To prepare the filling, mash the banana in a bowl. Using scissors, snip the apricots into pieces, then stir into the banana with the sugar.

5 Knead the dough on a floured surface for 2 minutes, then roll out to a 30 x 23cm/12 x 9in rectangle. Spread the banana and apricot filling over the dough and roll up lengthways like a Swiss roll, with the join underneath.

6 Cut the roll into 9 buns. Place, cut side down, in the tin, cover and leave to rise for 30 minutes. Preheat the oven to 200°C/400°F/Gas 6 and bake for 20–25 minutes. Meanwhile, mix the caster sugar and water in a small saucepan. Heat, stirring, until dissolved, then boil for 2 minutes. Brush the glaze over the buns while still hot.

OATY CRISPS

These biscuits are very crisp and crunchy – ideal to serve with morning coffee.

INGREDIENTS

Makes 18

175g/6oz/1¾ cups rolled oats
75g/3oz/½ cup light muscovado
    sugar
1 egg
60ml/4 tbsp sunflower oil
30ml/2 tbsp malt extract

NUTRITION NOTES

Per portion:

Energy	86Kcals/360kJ
Fat	3.59g
Saturated Fat	0.57g
Cholesterol	10.7mg
Fibre	0.66g

1 Preheat the oven to 190°C/375°F/ Gas 5. Lightly grease two baking sheets. Mix the rolled oats and sugar in a bowl, breaking up any lumps in the sugar. Add the egg, sunflower oil and malt extract, mix well, then leave to soak for 15 minutes.

2 Using a teaspoon, place small heaps of the mixture well apart on the prepared baking sheets. Press the heaps into 7.5cm/3in rounds with the back of a dampened fork.

3 Bake the biscuits for 10–15 minutes until golden brown. Leave them to cool for 1 minute, then remove with a palette knife and cool on a wire rack.

COOK'S TIP
To give these biscuits a coarser texture, substitute jumbo oats for some or all of the rolled oats. Once cool, store the biscuits in an airtight container to keep them as crisp and fresh as possible.

OATCAKES

Try serving these oatcakes with reduced fat hard cheeses. They are delicious topped with thick honey for breakfast.

Makes 8
175g/6oz/1 cup medium oatmeal, plus
*   extra for sprinkling*
2.5ml/¹/₂ tsp salt
pinch of bicarbonate of soda
15g/¹/₂oz/1 tbsp butter
75ml/5 tbsp water

1 Preheat the oven to 150°C/300°F/ Gas 2. Mix the oatmeal with the salt and bicarbonate of soda in a bowl.

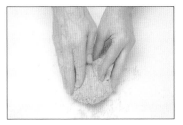

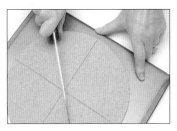

2 Melt the butter with the water in a small saucepan. Bring to the boil, then add to the oatmeal mixture and mix to a moist dough.

3 Turn the dough on to a surface sprinkled with oatmeal and knead to a smooth ball. Turn a large baking sheet upside-down, grease it, sprinkle it lightly with oatmeal and place the ball of dough on top. Sprinkle the dough with oatmeal, then roll out to a 25cm/10in round.

4 Cut the round into eight sections, ease them apart slightly and bake for about 50–60 minutes until crisp. Leave to cool on the baking sheet, then remove the oatcakes with a palette knife.

COOK'S TIP
To achieve a neat round, place a 25cm/10in cake board or plate on top of the oatcake. Cut away any excess dough with a palette knife.

NUTRITION NOTES	
Per portion:	
Energy	102Kcals/427kJ
Fat	3.43g
Saturated Fat	0.66g
Cholesterol	0.13mg
Fibre	1.49g

SUNFLOWER SULTANA SCONES

───── INGREDIENTS ─────

Makes 10–12
225g/8oz/2 cups self-raising flour
5ml/1 tsp baking powder
25g/1oz/2 tbsp soft sunflower
  margarine
30ml/2 tbsp golden caster sugar
50g/2oz/⅓ cup sultanas
30ml/2 tbsp sunflower seeds
150g/5oz/⅔ cup natural yogurt
about 30–45ml/2–3 tbsp skimmed milk

1 Preheat the oven to 230°C/450°F/
Gas 8. Lightly oil a baking sheet.
Sift the flour and baking powder into a
bowl and rub in the margarine evenly.

2 Stir in the sugar, sultanas and half
the sunflower seeds, then mix in the
yogurt, with just enough milk to make
a fairly soft, but not sticky dough.

3 Roll out on a lightly floured surface
to about 2cm/¾ in thickness. Cut
into 6cm/2½ in flower shapes or
rounds with a biscuit cutter and lift on
to the baking sheet.

4 Brush with milk and sprinkle with
the reserved sunflower seeds, then
bake for 10–12 minutes, until well
risen and golden brown.

5 Cool the scones on a wire rack.
Serve split and spread with jam or
low fat spread.

───── NUTRITION NOTES ─────	
Per portion:	
Energy	176Kcals/742kJ
Fat	5.32g
Saturated fat	0.81g
Cholesterol	0.84mg
Fibre	1.26g

PRUNE AND PEEL ROCK BUNS

───── INGREDIENTS ─────

Makes 12
225g/8oz/2 cups plain flour
10ml/2 tsp baking powder
75g/3oz/⅓ cup demerara sugar
50g/2oz/½ cup chopped ready-to-eat
  dried prunes
50g/2oz/⅓ cup chopped mixed peel
finely grated rind of 1 lemon
50ml/2 fl oz/¼ cup sunflower oil
75ml/5 tbsp skimmed milk

───── NUTRITION NOTES ─────	
Per portion:	
Energy	135Kcals/570kJ
Fat	3.35g
Saturated fat	0.44g
Cholesterol	0.13mg
Fibre	0.86g

1 Preheat the oven to 200°C/400°F/
Gas 6. Lightly oil a large baking
sheet. Sift together the flour and baking
powder, then stir in the sugar, prunes,
peel and lemon rind.

2 Mix the oil and milk, then stir into
the mixture, to make a dough
which just binds together.

3 Spoon into rocky heaps on the
baking sheet and bake for 20 minutes, until golden. Cool on a wire rack.

Blueberry Streusel Slice

Makes about 30 slices
225g/8oz shortcrust pastry
50g/2oz/½ cup plain flour
1.25ml/¼ tsp baking powder
40g/1½oz/3 tbsp butter or margarine
25g/1oz/2 tbsp fresh white breadcrumbs
50g/2oz/⅓ cup soft light brown sugar
1.25ml/¼ tsp salt
50g/2oz/4 tbsp flaked or chopped
  almonds
30ml/4 tbsp blackberry or bramble
  jelly
115g/4oz blueberries, fresh or frozen

1 Preheat the oven to 180°C/350°F/
Gas 4. Roll out the pastry on a
lightly floured surface to line an 18 x
28cm/7 x11in Swiss roll tin. Prick the
base with a fork evenly.

2 Rub together the flour, baking
powder, butter or margarine, breadcrumbs, sugar and salt until really
crumbly, then mix in the almonds.

Nutrition Notes	
Per slice:	
Energy	77Kcals/322kJ
Fat	4.16g
Saturated Fat	1.57g
Cholesterol	5.84mg

3 Spread the pastry with the jelly,
sprinkle with the blueberries, then
cover evenly with the streusel topping,
pressing down lightly. Bake for 30–40
minutes, reducing the temperature after
20 minutes to 170°C/325°F/Gas 3.

4 Remove from the oven when golden
on the top and the pastry is cooked
through. Cut into slices while still hot,
then allow to cool.

Sticky Date and Apple Bars

If possible allow this mixture to
mature for 1–2 days before
cutting – it will get stickier and
better!

Makes about 16 bars
115g/4oz/½ cup margarine
50g/2oz/4 tbsp soft dark brown sugar
50g/2oz/4 tbsp golden syrup
115g/4oz chopped dates
115g/4oz/1¼ cups rolled oats
115g/4oz/1 cup wholemeal self-raising
  flour
225g/8oz/2 eating apples, peeled,
  cored and grated
5–10 ml/1–2 tsp lemon juice
20–25 walnut halves

1 Preheat the oven to 190°C/375°F/
Gas 5. Line an 18–20cm/7–8in
square or rectangular loose-based cake
tin. In a large pan heat the margarine,
sugar, syrup and dates, stirring until the
dates soften completely.

2 Gradually work in the oats, flour,
apples and lemon juice until well
mixed. Spoon into the tin and spread
out evenly. Top with the walnut halves.

3 Bake for 30 minutes, then reduce
the temperature to 170°C/325°F/
Gas 3 and bake for 10–20 minutes
more, until firm to the touch and gold-
en. Cut into squares or bars while still
warm, or wrap in foil when nearly cold
and keep for 1–2 days before eating.

Nutrition Notes	
Per bar:	
Energy	183Kcals/763kJ
Fat	10.11g
Saturated Fat	1.64g
Cholesterol	0.14mg

BREADS AND TEABREADS

B reads and teabreads can be ideal low fat snacks at any
time of day. Bread is the perfect accompaniment to
many meals, and moist, flavourful teabread, served with a
warm beverage, is a delightful treat. Among the appetizing
selection of recipes presented here are Rosemary and Sea Salt
Focaccia, Parma Ham and Parmesan Bread, Pear and Sultana
Teabread and Banana and Cardamom Bread.

ROSEMARY AND SEA SALT FOCACCIA

Focaccia is an Italian flat bread made with olive oil. Here it is given added flavour with rosemary and coarse sea salt.

INGREDIENTS

Serves 8

350g/12oz/3 cups plain flour
2.5ml/½ tsp salt
10ml/2 tsp easy-blend dried yeast
about 250ml/8fl oz/1 cup
  lukewarm water
45ml/3 tbsp olive oil
1 small red onion
leaves from 1 large rosemary sprig
5ml/1 tsp coarse sea salt
oil, for greasing

1 Sift the flour and salt into a large mixing bowl. Stir in the yeast, then make a well in the middle of the dry ingredients. Pour in the water and 30ml/2 tbsp of the oil. Mix well, adding a little more water if the mixture seems too dry.

COOK'S TIP

Use flavoured olive oil, such as chilli or herb oil, for extra flavour. Wholemeal flour or a mixture of wholemeal and white flour works well with this recipe.

2 Turn the dough on to a lightly floured surface and knead for about 10 minutes until smooth and elastic.

3 Place the dough in a greased bowl, cover and leave in a warm place for about 1 hour until doubled in size. Knock back and knead the dough for 2–3 minutes.

4 Meanwhile, preheat the oven to 220°C/425°F/Gas 7. Roll out the dough to a large circle about 1cm/½in thick, and transfer to a greased baking sheet. Brush with the remaining oil.

5 Halve the onion and slice it into thin wedges. Sprinkle over the dough, with the rosemary and sea salt, pressing lightly.

6 Using a finger, make deep indentations in the dough. Cover the surface with greased clear film, then leave to rise in a warm place for 30 minutes. Remove the clear film and bake for 25–30 minutes until golden.

NUTRITION NOTES	
Per portion:	
Energy	191Kcals/807kJ
Fat	4.72g
Saturated Fat	0.68g
Cholesterol	0
Fibre	1.46g

OLIVE AND OREGANO BREAD

This is an excellent accompaniment to all salads and is particularly good served warm.

Serves 8–10
300ml/10fl oz/1¼ cups warm water
5ml/1 tsp dried yeast
pinch of sugar
15ml/1 tbsp olive oil
1 onion, chopped
450g/1lb/4 cups strong white flour
5ml/1 tsp salt
1.5ml/¼ tsp black pepper
*50g/2oz/⅓ cup stoned black olives,
  roughly chopped*
15ml/1 tbsp black olive paste
15ml/1 tbsp chopped fresh oregano
15ml/1 tbsp chopped fresh parsley

─────── NUTRITION NOTES ───────

Per portion:

Energy	202Kcals/847kJ
Fat	3.28g
Saturated Fat	0.46g
Cholesterol	0
Fibre	22.13g

1 Put half the warm water in a jug. Sprinkle the yeast on top. Add the sugar, mix well and leave to stand for 10 minutes.

2 Heat the olive oil in a small frying pan and fry the onion gently until golden brown.

3 Sift the flour into a mixing bowl with the salt and pepper. Make a well in the centre. Add the yeast mixture, the fried onion (with the oil), the olives, olive paste, herbs and remaining water. Gradually incorporate the flour and mix to a soft dough, adding a little extra water if necessary.

4 Turn the dough on to a floured surface and knead for 5 minutes until smooth and elastic. Place in a mixing bowl, cover with a damp dish towel and leave in a warm place to rise for about 2 hours until the dough has doubled in bulk. Lightly grease a baking sheet.

5 Turn the dough on to a floured surface and knead again for a few minutes. Shape into a 20cm/8in round and place on the prepared baking sheet. Using a large sharp knife, make criss-cross cuts over the top. Cover and leave in a warm place for 30 minutes until well risen. Preheat the oven to 220°C/425°F/Gas 7.

6 Dust the loaf with a little flour. Bake for 10 minutes, then lower the oven temperature to 200°C/400°F/Gas 6. Bake for 20 minutes more, or until the loaf sounds hollow when tapped underneath. Transfer to a wire rack and allow to cool slightly before serving.

COOK'S TIP
If fresh herbs are not available, use 5–10 ml/1–2 tsp dried herbs instead. Omit the olives and olive paste and use chopped sun-dried tomatoes and sun-dried tomato paste, for a tasty change.

RYE BREAD

Rye bread is popular in
northern Europe and makes
an excellent base for open
sandwiches – add a low fat
topping of your choice.

INGREDIENTS

Serves 16
350g/12oz/3 cups wholemeal flour
225g/8oz/2 cups rye flour
115g/4oz/1 cup strong white flour
7.5ml/1½ tsp salt
30ml/2 tbsp caraway seeds
475ml/16fl oz/2 cups warm water
10ml/2 tsp dried yeast
pinch of sugar
30ml/2 tbsp molasses

1 Put the flours and salt in a bowl. Set
aside 5ml/1 tsp of the caraway seeds
and add the rest to the bowl.

2 Put half the water in a jug. Sprinkle
the yeast on top. Add the sugar, mix
well and leave for 10 minutes.

3 Make a well in the flour mixture,
then add the yeast mixture with the
molasses and the remaining water.
Gradually incorporate the flour and
mix to a soft dough, adding a little
water if necessary.

4 Turn the dough on to a floured
surface and knead for 5 minutes
until smooth and elastic. Return to the
clean bowl, cover with a damp dish
towel and leave in a warm place for
about 2 hours until doubled in bulk.
Grease a baking sheet.

NUTRITION NOTES	
Per portion:	
Energy	156Kcals/655kJ
Fat	1.2g
Saturated Fat	0.05g
Cholesterol	0
Fibre	4.53g

5 Turn the dough on to a floured
surface and knead for 2 minutes.
Divide the dough in half, then shape
into two 23cm/9in long oval loaves.
Flatten the loaves slightly and place
them on a baking sheet.

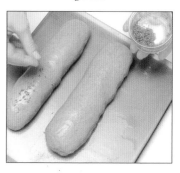

6 Brush the loaves with water and
sprinkle with the remaining
caraway seeds. Cover and leave in a
warm place for about 40 minutes until
well risen. Preheat the oven to 200°C/
400°F/Gas 6. Bake the loaves for
30 minutes or until they sound hollow
when tapped underneath. Cool on a
wire rack. Serve the bread plain, or
slice and add a low fat topping.

SODA BREAD

Finding the bread bin empty need never be a problem again when your repertoire includes a recipe for soda bread. It takes only a few minutes to make and needs no rising or proving. If possible, eat soda bread while still warm from the oven as it does not keep well.

───── INGREDIENTS ─────

Serves 8
450g/1lb/4 cups plain flour
5ml/1 tsp salt
5ml/1 tsp bicarbonate of soda
5ml/1 tsp cream of tartar
350ml/12fl oz/1½ cups buttermilk

1 Preheat the oven to 220°C/425°F/ Gas 7. Flour a baking sheet. Sift all the dry ingredients into a mixing bowl and make a small well in the centre.

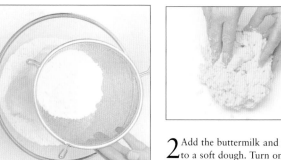

2 Add the buttermilk and mix quickly to a soft dough. Turn on to a floured surface and knead lightly. Shape into a round about 18cm/7in across and put on the baking sheet.

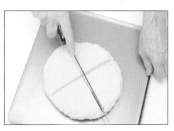

3 Cut a deep cross on top of the loaf and sprinkle with a little flour. Bake for 25–30 minutes, then transfer the soda bread to a wire rack to cool.

COOK'S TIP
Soda bread needs a light hand. The ingredients should be bound together quickly in the bowl and kneaded very briefly. The aim is to get rid of the largest cracks, as the dough will become tough if it is handled for too long.

───── NUTRITION NOTES ─────

Per portion:
Energy	230Kcals/967kJ
Fat	1.03g
Saturated Fat	0.24g
Cholesterol	0.88mg
Fibre	1.94g

PEAR AND SULTANA TEABREAD

This is an ideal teabread to make when pears are plentiful – an excellent use for windfalls.

INGREDIENTS

Serves 6–8

25g/1oz/¹⁄₄ cup rolled oats
50g/2oz/¹⁄₄ cup light muscovado sugar
30ml/2 tbsp pear or apple juice
30ml/2 tbsp sunflower oil
1 large or 2 small pears
115g/4oz/1 cup self-raising flour
115g/4oz/³⁄₄ cup sultanas
2.5ml/¹⁄₂ tsp baking powder
10ml/2 tsp mixed spice
1 egg

1 Preheat the oven to 180°C/350°F/ Gas 4. Grease and line a 450g/1lb loaf tin with non-stick baking paper. Put the oats in a bowl with the sugar, pour over the pear or apple juice and oil, mix well and leave to stand for 15 minutes.

2 Quarter, core and coarsely grate the pear(s). Add to the oat mixture with the flour, sultanas, baking powder, mixed spice and egg, then mix together thoroughly.

3 Spoon the mixture into the prepared loaf tin and level the top. Bake for 50–60 minutes or until a skewer inserted into the centre comes out clean.

COOK'S TIP
Health food shops sell concentrated pear and apple juice, ready for diluting as required.

4 Transfer the teabread on to a wire rack and peel off the lining paper. Leave to cool completely.

NUTRITION NOTES

Per portion:
Energy	200Kcals/814kJ
Fat	4.61g
Saturated Fat	0.79g
Cholesterol	27.50mg
Fibre	1.39g

PARMA HAM AND PARMESAN BREAD

This nourishing bread is almost a meal in itself.

1 Preheat the oven to 200°C/400°F/ Gas 6. Flour a baking sheet. Place the wholemeal flour in a bowl and sift in the white flour, baking powder and salt. Add the pepper and the ham. Set aside about 15ml/1 tbsp of the grated Parmesan and stir the rest into the flour mixture with the parsley. Make a well in the centre.

NUTRITION NOTES

Per portion:
Energy	250Kcals/1053kJ
Fat	3.65g
Saturated Fat	1.30g
Cholesterol	7.09mg
Fibre	3.81g

2 Mix the mustard and buttermilk, pour into the flour and quickly mix to a soft dough.

3 Turn the dough on to a floured surface and knead briefly. Shape into an oval loaf, brush with milk and sprinkle with the Parmesan cheese. Put the loaf on the prepared baking sheet.

4 Bake the loaf for 25–30 minutes. Allow to cool before serving.

CARAWAY BREAD STICKS

Ideal to nibble with drinks, these can be made with all sorts of other seeds – try cumin seeds, poppy seeds or celery seeds.

INGREDIENTS

Makes about 20
150ml/¼ pint/⅔ cup warm water
2.5ml/½ tsp dried yeast
pinch of sugar
225g/8oz/2 cups plain flour
2.5ml/½ tsp salt
10ml/2 tsp caraway seeds

3 Preheat the oven to 200°C/425°F/
Gas 7. Turn the dough on to a lightly floured surface and knead for 5 minutes until smooth. Divide the mixture into 20 pieces and roll each into a 30cm/12in stick.

4 Arrange the sticks on the baking sheets, leaving room to allow for rising.

5 Bake the bread sticks for about 10–12 minutes until golden brown. Cool on the baking sheets.

NUTRITION NOTES

Per portion:	
Energy	45Kcals/189kJ
Fat	0.24g
Saturated Fat	0.02g
Cholesterol	0
Fibre	0.3g

1 Grease two baking sheets. Put the warm water in a jug. Sprinkle the yeast on top. Add the sugar, mix well and leave for 10 minutes.

2 Sift the flour and salt into a mixing bowl, stir in the caraway seeds and make a well in the centre. Add the yeast mixture and gradually incorporate the flour to make a soft dough, adding a little water if necessary.

CHEESE AND ONION HERB STICKS

An extremely tasty bread which is very good with soups or salads. Use an extra-strong cheese to give plenty of flavour without piling on the fat.

INGREDIENTS

Makes 2 sticks, each serving 4–6
300ml/¹/2 pint/1¹/4 cups warm water
5ml/1 tsp dried yeast
pinch of sugar
15ml/1 tbsp sunflower oil
1 red onion, finely chopped
450g/1lb/4 cups strong white flour
5ml/1 tsp salt
5ml/1 tsp dry mustard
45ml/3 tbsp chopped fresh herbs, such
*   as thyme, parsley, marjoram or sage*
75g/3oz/³/4 cup grated reduced fat
*   Cheddar cheese*

NUTRITION NOTES

Per portion:
Energy	210Kcals/882kJ
Fat	3.16g
Saturated Fat	0.25g
Cholesterol	3.22mg
Fibre	1.79g

COOK'S TIP
To make Onion and Coriander Sticks, omit the cheese, herbs and mustard. Add 15ml/1 tbsp ground coriander and 45ml/3 tbsp chopped fresh coriander instead.

1 Put the water in a jug. Sprinkle the yeast on top. Add the sugar, mix well and leave for 10 minutes.

2 Heat the oil in a small frying pan and fry the onion until it is well coloured.

3 Stir the flour, salt and mustard into a mixing bowl, then add the herbs. Set aside 30ml/2 tbsp of the cheese. Stir the rest into the flour mixture and make a well in the centre. Add the yeast mixture with the fried onions and oil, then gradually incorporate the flour and mix to a soft dough, adding extra water if necessary.

4 Turn the dough on to a floured surface and knead for 5 minutes until smooth and elastic. Return to the clean bowl, cover with a damp dish towel and leave in a warm place to rise for about 2 hours until doubled in bulk. Lightly grease two baking sheets.

5 Turn the dough on to a floured surface, knead briefly, then divide the mixture in half and roll each piece into a 30cm/12in long stick. Place each stick on a baking sheet and make diagonal cuts along the top.

6 Sprinkle the sticks with the reserved cheese. Cover and leave for 30 minutes until well risen. Preheat the oven to 220°C/425°F/Gas 7. Bake the sticks for 25 minutes or until they sound hollow when tapped underneath.

GRANARY BAPS

These make excellent picnic fare, filled with cottage cheese, tuna, salad and low fat mayonnaise. They are also very good served warm with soup.

INGREDIENTS

Makes 8

300ml/¹/₂ pint/1¹/₄ cups warm water
5ml/1 tsp dried yeast
pinch of sugar
450g/1lb/4 cups malted brown flour
5ml/1 tsp salt
15ml/1 tbsp malt extract
15ml/1 tbsp rolled oats

NUTRITION NOTES

Per portion:

Energy	223Kcals/939kJ
Fat	1.14g
Saturated Fat	0.16g
Cholesterol	0
Fibre	3.10g

COOK'S TIP
To make a large loaf, shape the dough into a round, flatten it slightly and bake for 30–40 minutes. Test by tapping the base of the loaf – if it sounds hollow, it is cooked.

1 Put half the warm water in a jug. Sprinkle in the yeast. Add the sugar, mix well and leave for 10 minutes.

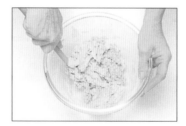

2 Put the malted brown flour and salt in a mixing bowl and make a well in the centre. Add the yeast mixture with the malt extract and the remaining water. Gradually incorporate the flour and mix to a soft dough.

3 Turn the dough on to a floured surface and knead for 5 minutes until smooth and elastic. Return to the clean bowl, cover with a damp dish towel and leave in a warm place to rise for about 2 hours until doubled in bulk.

4 Lightly grease a large baking sheet. Turn the dough on to a floured surface, knead for 2 minutes, then divide into eight pieces. Shape the pieces into balls and flatten them with the palm of your hand to make neat 10cm/4in rounds.

5 Place the rounds on the prepared baking sheet, cover loosely with a large plastic bag (ballooning it to trap the air inside), and leave to stand in a warm place until the baps are well risen. Preheat the oven to 220°C/425°F/Gas 7.

6 Brush the baps with water, sprinkle with the oats and bake for about 20–25 minutes or until they sound hollow when tapped underneath. Cool on a wire rack, then serve with the low fat filling of your choice.

POPPY SEED ROLLS

Pile these soft rolls in a basket and serve them for breakfast or with dinner.

INGREDIENTS

Makes 12

300ml/¹/₂ pint/1¹/₄ cups warm
  skimmed milk
5ml/1 tsp dried yeast
pinch of sugar
450g/1lb/4 cups strong white flour
5ml/1 tsp salt
1 egg, lightly beaten

For the topping
1 egg, beaten
poppy seeds

NUTRITION NOTES

Per portion:
Energy	160Kcals/674kJ
Fat	2.42g
Saturated Fat	0.46g
Cholesterol	32.58mg
Fibre	1.16g

1 Put half the warm milk in a small bowl. Sprinkle the yeast on top. Add the sugar, mix well and leave for 30 minutes.

2 Sift the flour and salt into a mixing bowl. Make a well in the centre and pour in the yeast mixture and the egg. Gradually incorporate the flour, adding enough of the remaining milk to mix to a soft dough.

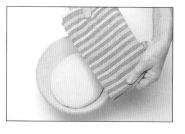

3 Turn the dough on to a floured surface and knead for 5 minutes until smooth and elastic. Return to the clean bowl, cover with a damp dish towel and leave in a warm place to rise for about 1 hour until doubled in bulk.

4 Lightly grease two baking sheets. Turn the dough on to a floured surface. Knead for 2 minutes, then cut into 12 pieces and shape into rolls.

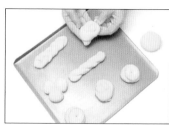

5 Place the rolls on the prepared baking sheets, cover loosely with a large plastic bag (ballooning it to trap the air inside) and leave to stand in a warm place until the rolls have risen well. Preheat the oven to 220°C/425°F/ Gas 7.

6 Glaze the rolls with beaten egg, sprinkle with poppy seeds and bake for 12–15 minutes until golden brown. Transfer to a wire rack to cool.

COOK'S TIP
Use easy-blend dried yeast if you prefer. Add it directly to the dry ingredients and mix with hand-hot milk. The rolls will only require one rising (see package instructions). Vary the toppings. Linseed, sesame seeds and car-away seeds are all good; try adding caraway seeds to the dough, too, for extra flavour.

BANANA AND CARDAMOM BREAD

The combination of banana and cardamom is delicious in this soft-textured moist loaf. It is perfect for tea time, served with low fat spread and jam. No fat is used or needed to make this delicious loaf, creating a healthy low fat bread for all to enjoy.

3 Sift the flour and salt into a mixing bowl and make a well in the centre. Add the yeast mixture with the malt extract, chopped cardamom seeds and bananas.

5 Grease a baking sheet. Turn the dough on to a floured surface, knead briefly, then divide into three and shape into a plait. Place the plait on the baking sheet and cover loosely with a plastic bag (ballooning it to trap the air). Leave until well risen. Preheat the oven to 220°C/425°F/Gas 7.

INGREDIENTS

Serves 6

150ml/¼ pint/²⁄₃ cup warm water
5ml/1 tsp dried yeast
pinch of sugar
10 cardamom pods
400g/14oz/3½ cups strong white flour
5ml/1 tsp salt
30ml/2 tbsp malt extract
2 ripe bananas, mashed
5ml/1 tsp sesame seeds

4 Gradually incorporate the flour and mix to a soft dough, adding a little extra water if necessary. Turn the dough on to a floured surface and knead for about 5 minutes until smooth and elastic. Return to the clean bowl, cover with a damp dish towel and leave to rise for about 2 hours until doubled in bulk.

1 Put the warm water in a small bowl. Sprinkle the yeast on top. Add the sugar, mix well and leave for 10 minutes.

NUTRITION NOTES

Per portion:

Energy	299Kcals/1254kJ
Fat	1.55g
Saturated Fat	0.23g
Cholesterol	0
Fibre	2.65g

6 Brush the plait lightly with water and sprinkle with the sesame seeds. Bake for 10 minutes, then lower the oven temperature to 200°C/400°F/Gas 6. Cook for 15 minutes more, or until the loaf sounds hollow when it is tapped underneath. Cool on a wire rack.

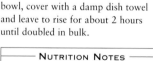

2 Split the cardamom pods. Remove the seeds and chop them finely.

COOK'S TIP
Make sure the bananas are really ripe, so that they impart maximum flavour to the bread. If you prefer, place the dough in one piece in a 450g/1lb loaf tin and bake for an extra 5 minutes. As well as being low in fat, bananas are a good source of potassium, therefore making an ideal nutritious, low fat snack.

SWEDISH SULTANA BREAD

A lightly sweetened fruit bread that is delicious served warm. It is also excellent toasted and topped with low fat spread.

INGREDIENTS

Serves 8–10
150ml/¼ pint/²/₃ cup warm water
5ml/1 tsp dried yeast
15ml/1 tbsp clear honey
225g/8oz/2 cups wholemeal flour
225g/8oz/2 cups strong white flour
5ml/1 tsp salt
115g/4oz/²/₃ cup sultanas
50g/2oz/½ cup walnuts, finely chopped
175ml/6fl oz/³/₄ cup warm skimmed milk, plus extra for glazing

NUTRITION NOTES

Per portion:
Energy	273Kcals/1145kJ
Fat	4.86g
Saturated Fat	0.57g
Cholesterol	0.39mg
Fibre	3.83g

1 Put the water in a small jug. Sprinkle the yeast on top. Add a few drops of the honey to help activate the yeast, mix well and leave to stand for 10 minutes.

2 Put the flours in a mixing bowl with the salt and sultanas. Set aside 15ml/1 tbsp of the walnuts and add the rest to the bowl. Mix together lightly and make a well in the centre.

3 Add the yeast mixture to the flour mixture with the milk and remaining honey. Gradually incorporate the flour, mixing to a soft dough; add a little extra water if you need to.

4 Turn the dough on to a floured surface and knead for 5 minutes until smooth and elastic. Return to the clean bowl, cover with a damp dish towel and leave in a warm place to rise for about 2 hours until doubled in bulk. Grease a baking sheet.

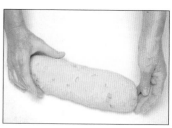

5 Turn the dough on to a floured surface and form into a 28cm/11in long sausage shape. Place on the baking sheet. Make some diagonal cuts down the whole length of the loaf.

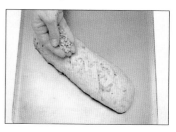

6 Brush the loaf with milk to glaze, sprinkle with the reserved walnuts and leave to rise for about 40 minutes. Preheat the oven to 220°C/425°F/ Gas 7. Bake the loaf for 10 minutes. Lower the oven temperature to 200°C/400°F/Gas 6 and bake for about 20 minutes more, or until the loaf sounds hollow when tapped underneath.

COOK'S TIP
To make Apple and Hazelnut Bread, replace the sultanas with two chopped eating apples and use chopped toasted hazelnuts instead of the walnuts. Add 5ml/1 tsp ground cinnamon with the flour.

Spiral Herb Bread

An attractive and delicious bread which is ideal for serving with a salad for a healthy lunch.

Ingredients

Makes 2 loaves
30ml/2 tbsp easy-blend dried yeast
600ml/1 pint/2½ cups lukewarm water
425g/15oz/3⅔ cups strong white flour
500g/1¼lb/5 cups wholemeal flour
7.5ml/3 tsp salt
25g/1oz/2 tbsp sunflower margarine
1 large bunch parsley, finely chopped
1 bunch spring onions, chopped
1 garlic clove, finely chopped
salt and black pepper
1 egg, lightly beaten
skimmed milk, for glazing

Nutrition Notes

Per loaf:

Energy	1698Kcals/7132kJ
Fat	24.55g
Saturated fat	9.87g
Cholesterol	144.33mg
Fibre	30.96g

1 Combine the yeast with approximately 50ml/2fl oz/¼ cup of the water, stir and leave to dissolve.

2 Mix together the flours and salt in a large bowl. Make a well in the centre and pour in the yeast mixture and the remaining water. With a wooden spoon, stir from the centre, working outwards to obtain a rough dough.

3 Transfer the dough to a floured surface and knead until smooth and elastic. Return to the bowl, cover with a plastic bag, and leave for about 2 hours until doubled in volume.

4 Meanwhile, combine the margarine, parsley, spring onions and garlic in a large frying pan. Cook over a low heat, stirring, until softened. Season and set aside.

5 Grease two 23 x 13cm/9 x 5 in loaf tins. When the dough has risen, cut in half and roll each half into a rectangle about 35 x 23cm/14 x 9 in.

6 Brush both with the beaten egg. Divide the herb mixture between the two, spreading just up to the edges.

7 Roll up to enclose the filling and pinch the short ends to seal. Place in the tins, seam-side down.

8 Cover the dough with a clean dish towel and leave undisturbed in a warm place until the dough rises above the rim of the tins.

9 Preheat the oven to 190°C/375°F/ Gas 5. Brush the loaves with milk and bake for about 55 minutes until the bottoms sound hollow when tapped. Cool on a wire rack.

WALNUT BREAD

Delicious at any time of day, this bread may be eaten plain or topped with some low fat cream cheese.

INGREDIENTS

Makes 1 loaf

425g/15oz/3¾ cups wholemeal flour
150g/5oz/1¼ cups strong white flour
12.5ml/2½ tsp salt
525ml/18fl oz/2¼ cups lukewarm water
15ml/1 tbsp clear honey
15ml/1 tbsp easy-blend dried yeast
150g/5oz/1¼ cups walnut pieces, plus
    more for decorating
1 egg, beaten, for glazing

NUTRITION NOTES

Per loaf:	
Energy	2852Kcals/11980kJ
Fat	109.34g
Saturated fat	12.04g
Cholesterol	77mg
Fibre	47.04g

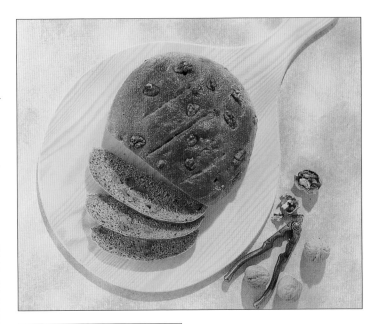

1 Mix together the flours and salt in a large bowl. Make a well in the centre and pour in 250ml/8fl oz/1 cup of the water, the honey and the yeast.

2 Set aside until the yeast dissolves and the mixture is frothy.

3 Add the remaining water. With a wooden spoon, stir from the centre, incorporating flour with each turn, to obtain a smooth dough. Add more flour if the dough is too sticky and use your hands if the dough becomes too stiff to stir.

4 Transfer to a floured board and knead, adding flour if necessary, until the dough is smooth and elastic. Place in a greased bowl and roll the dough around in the bowl to coat thoroughly all over.

5 Cover with a plastic bag and leave in a warm place until doubled in volume, about 1½ hours.

6 Punch down the dough very firmly and knead in the walnuts until they are evenly distributed.

7 Grease a baking sheet. Shape the dough into a round loaf and place on the baking sheet. Press in the walnut pieces to decorate the top. Cover the dough loosely with a damp dish towel and leave in a warm place for about 25–30 minutes until doubled in size.

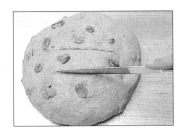

8 Preheat the oven to 220°C/425°F/Gas 7. With a sharp knife, score the top of the loaf and brush with the egg glaze. Bake for 15 minutes. Lower the temperature to 190°C/375°F/Gas 5 and bake until the bottom of the loaf sounds hollow when tapped, about 40 minutes. Leave to cool.

OATMEAL BREAD

A healthy bread, with a delightfully crumbly texture due to the inclusion of rolled oats.

INGREDIENTS

Makes 2 loaves

475ml/16fl oz/2 cups skimmed milk
25g/1oz/2 tbsp low fat margarine
50g/2oz/1¼ cups dark brown sugar
10ml/2 tsp salt
15ml/1 tbsp easy-blend dried yeast
50ml/2fl oz/¼ cup lukewarm water
400g/14oz/3½ cups rolled oats
450–675g/1–1½ lb/4–6 cups strong white flour

1 Scald the milk. Remove from the heat and stir in the margerine, sugar and salt. Leave until lukewarm.

2 Combine the yeast and lukewarm water in a large bowl and leave until the yeast is dissolved and the mixture is frothy. Stir in the milk mixture.

3 Add 275g/10oz/2½ cups of the oats and enough flour to obtain a soft pliable dough.

4 Transfer to a floured surface and knead until smooth and elastic.

5 Place the dough in a greased bowl, cover with a plastic bag, and leave it for about 2–3 hours, until doubled in volume. Grease a large baking sheet.

6 Transfer the dough to a lightly floured surface and divide in half.

7 Shape into rounds. Place on the baking sheet, cover with a damp dish towel and leave to rise for about 1 hour, until doubled in volume.

8 Preheat the oven to 200°C/400°F/Gas 6. Score the tops of the loaves and sprinkle with the remaining oats. Bake for about 45–50 minutes, until the bottoms sound hollow when tapped. Cool on wire racks.

NUTRITION NOTES

Per loaf:

Energy	2281Kcals/9581kJ
Fat	34.46g
Saturated fat	11.94g
Cholesterol	39mg
Fibre	24.11g

COURGETTE AND WALNUT LOAF

INGREDIENTS

Makes 1 loaf
3 eggs
75g/3oz/½ cup light brown sugar
50ml/2fl oz/¼ cup sunflower oil
225g/8oz/1½ cups wholemeal flour
5ml/1 tsp baking powder
5ml/1 tsp bicarbonate of soda
5ml/1 tsp ground cinnamon
2.5ml/½ tsp ground allspice
7.5ml/½ tbsp green cardamoms, seeds
  removed and crushed
150g/5oz/1 cup coarsely grated
  courgette
50g/2oz/¼ cup walnuts, chopped
50g/2oz/¼ cup sunflower seeds

NUTRITION NOTES

Per portion:

Energy	3073Kcals/12908kJ
Fat	201.98g
Saturated fat	26.43g
Cholesterol	654.5mg
Fibre	28.62g

1 Preheat the oven to 180°C/350°F/
Gas 4. Grease the base and sides of
a 900g/2 lb loaf tin and line with
greaseproof paper.

2 Beat the eggs and sugar together
and gradually add the oil.

3 Sift the flour into a bowl together
with the baking powder, bicarbon
ate of soda, cinnamon and allspice.

4 Mix into the egg mixture with the
rest of the ingredients, reserving
15ml/1 tbsp of the sunflower seeds for
the top.

5 Spoon into the loaf tin, level off the
top, and sprinkle with the reserved
sunflower seeds.

6 Bake for about 1 hour or until a
skewer inserted in the centre comes
out clean. Leave to cool slightly, then
turn out on to a wire cooling rack.

SAGE SODA BREAD

This wonderful loaf, quite unlike bread made with yeast, has a velvety texture and a powerful sage aroma.

INGREDIENTS

Makes 1 loaf
225g/8oz/1½ cups wholemeal flour
115g/4oz/1 cup strong white flour
2.5ml/½ tsp salt
5ml/1 tsp bicarbonate of soda
30ml/2 tbsp shredded fresh sage or
   10ml/2 tsp dried sage
300–450ml/½–¾ pint/1¼–1¾ cups
   buttermilk

VARIATION
As an alternative to the sage, try using either finely chopped rosemary or thyme.

NUTRITION NOTES

Per loaf:
Energy	1251Kcals/5255kJ
Fat	9.23g
Saturated fat	2g
Cholesterol	7mg
Fibre	23.81g

2 Stir in the sage and add enough buttermilk to make a soft dough.

1 Preheat the oven to 220°C/425°F/ Gas 7. Sift the dry ingredients into a mixing bowl.

3 Shape the dough into a round loaf with your hands and place on a lightly oiled baking sheet.

4 Cut a deep cross in the top. Bake in the oven for about 40 minutes until the loaf is well risen and sounds hollow when tapped on the bottom. Leave to cool on a wire rack.

ORANGE WHEAT LOAF

Perfect just with butter as a
breakfast or tea bread and lovely
for banana sandwiches.

INGREDIENTS

Makes one 450g/1lb loaf
275g/10oz/2¼ cups wholemeal plain
  flour
2.5ml/½ tsp salt
25g/1oz/2 tbsp butter
25g/1oz/2 tbsp soft light brown sugar
½ sachet easy-blend dried yeast
grated rind and juice of ½ orange

1 Sift the flour into a large bowl and
return any wheat flakes from the
sieve. Add the salt and rub in the butter
lightly with your fingertips.

2 Stir in the sugar, yeast and orange
rind. Pour the orange juice into a
measuring jug and make up to 200ml/
7fl oz/⅞ cup with hot water (the liquid
should not be more than hand hot).

3 Stir the liquid into the flour and
mix to a soft ball of dough. Knead
gently on a lightly floured surface until
quite smooth.

4 Place the dough in a greased
450g/1lb loaf tin and leave in a
warm place until nearly doubled in size.
Preheat the oven to 220°C/425°F/Gas 7.

5 Bake the bread for 30–35 minutes,
or until it sounds hollow when you
tap the underneath. Tip out of the tin
and cool on a wire rack.

NUTRITION NOTES

Per slice:	
Energy	144Kcals/607kJ
Fat	3.32g
Saturated Fat	1.82g
Cholesterol	7.19mg

SAFFRON FOCCACIA

A dazzling yellow bread with a distinctive flavour.

INGREDIENTS

Makes 1 loaf
pinch of saffron threads
150ml/¼ pint/⅔ cup boiling water
225g/8oz/2 cups plain flour
2.5ml/½ tsp salt
5ml/1 tsp easy-blend dried yeast
15ml/1 tbsp olive oil

For the topping
2 garlic cloves, sliced
1 red onion, cut into thin wedges
rosemary sprigs
12 black olives, stoned and coarsely
  chopped
15ml/1 tbsp olive oil

NUTRITION NOTES

Per loaf:
Energy	1047Kcals/4399kJ
Fat	29.15g
Saturated fat	4.06g
Cholesterol	0
Fibre	9.48g

1 Place the saffron in a heatproof jug and pour on the boiling water. Leave to infuse until the saffron mixture is lukewarm.

2 Place the flour, salt, yeast and olive oil in a food processor. Turn on and gradually add the saffron and its liquid until the dough forms a ball.

3 Turn out on to a floured board and knead for 10–15 minutes. Place in a bowl, cover and leave to rise for about 30–40 minutes, until doubled in size.

4 Punch down the risen dough on a lightly floured surface and roll out into an oval shape, 1cm/½ in thick. Place on a lightly greased baking sheet and leave to rise for 20–30 minutes.

5 Preheat the oven to 200°C/400°F/ Gas 6. Use your fingers to press small indentations in the dough.

6 Cover with the topping ingredients, brush lightly with olive oil, and bake for about 25 minutes or until the loaf sounds hollow when tapped on the bottom. Leave to cool.

TOMATO BREADSTICKS

Once you've tried this simple recipe you'll never buy manufactured breadsticks again. Serve as a snack, or with aperitifs and a dip at the beginning of a meal.

INGREDIENTS

Makes 16
225g/8oz/2 cups plain flour
2.5ml/½ tsp salt
2.5ml/½ tbsp easy-blend dry yeast
5ml/1 tsp honey
5ml/1 tsp olive oil
150ml/¼ pint/⅔ cup warm water
6 halves sun-dried tomatoes in olive oil, drained and chopped
15ml/1 tbsp skimmed milk
10ml/2 tsp poppy seeds

NUTRITION NOTES

Per portion:
Energy	82Kcals/346kJ
Fat	3.53g
Saturated fat	0.44g
Cholesterol	0
Fibre	0.44g

1 Place the flour, salt and yeast in a food processor. Add the honey and olive oil and, with the machine running, gradually pour in the water (you may not need it all as flours vary). Stop adding water as soon as the dough starts to cling together. Process for 1 minute more.

2 Turn out the dough on to a floured board and knead for 3–4 minutes until springy and smooth.

3 Knead in the chopped sun-dried tomatoes. Form into a ball and place in a lightly oiled bowl. Leave to rise for 5 minutes.

4 Preheat the oven to 150°C/300°F/ Gas 2. Divide the dough into sixteen pieces and roll each piece into a 28 x 1cm/11 x ½ in long stick. Place on a lightly oiled baking sheet and leave to rise in a warm place for 15 minutes.

5 Brush the sticks with milk and sprinkle with poppy seeds. Bake for 30 minutes. Leave to cool on a wire cooling rack.

VARIATION
Instead of sun-dried tomatoes, you could try making these breadsticks with reduced fat Cheddar cheese, sesame seeds or herbs.

APPLE, APRICOT AND WALNUT LOAF

─── INGREDIENTS ───

Makes 10–12 slices
225g/8oz/2 cups plain wholemeal flour
5ml/1 tsp baking powder
pinch of salt
115g/4oz/½ cup sunflower margarine
175g/6oz/1 cup soft light brown sugar
2 size 2 eggs, lightly beaten
grated rind and juice of 1 orange
50g/2oz/½ cup chopped walnuts
50g/2oz/⅓ cup ready-to-eat dried
    apricots, chopped
1 large cooking apple
oil, for greasing

1 Preheat the oven to 180°C/350°F/ Gas 4. Line and grease a 900g/2lb loaf tin.

2 Sift the flour, baking powder and salt into a large mixing bowl, then tip the bran remaining in the sieve into the mixture. Add the margarine, sugar, eggs, orange rind and juice. Stir, then beat with a hand-held electric beater until smooth.

3 Stir in the walnuts and apricots. Quarter, peel and core the apple, chop it roughly and add it to the mixture. Stir, then spoon the mixture into the prepared tin and level the top.

4 Bake for 1 hour, or until a skewer inserted into the centre of the loaf comes out clean. Cool in the tin for about 5 minutes, then turn the loaf out on to a wire rack and peel off the lining paper. When cold, store in an airtight tin.

NUTRITION NOTES	
Per portion:	
Energy	290Kcals/1220KJ
Fat	14.5g
Saturated Fat	2.5g
Cholesterol	43.5mg

DATE AND NUT MALTLOAF

INGREDIENTS

Makes 2 x 450g/1lb loaves

300g/11oz/2 cups strong plain flour
275g/10oz/2 cups strong plain whole-
    meal flour
5ml/1 tsp salt
75g/3oz/6 tbsp soft brown sugar
1 sachet easy-blend dried yeast
50g/2oz/4 tbsp butter or margarine
15ml/1 tbsp black treacle
60ml/4 tbsp malt extract
scant 250ml/8 floz/1 cup tepid milk
115g/4oz/½ cup chopped dates
50g/2oz/½ cup chopped nuts
75g/3oz/½ cup sultanas
75g/3oz/½ cup raisins
30ml/2 tbsp clear honey, to glaze

NUTRITION NOTES

Per slice:

Energy	261Kcals/1104kJ
Fat	5.57g
Saturated Fat	2.46g
Cholesterol	9.45mg

1 Sift the flours and salt into a large bowl, then tip in the wheat flakes that are caught in the sieve. Stir in the sugar and yeast.

2 Put the butter or margarine in a small pan with the treacle and malt extract. Stir over a low heat until melted. Leave to cool, then combine with the milk.

3 Stir the liquid into the dry ingredients and knead thoroughly for 15 minutes until the dough is elastic. (If you have a dough blade on your food processor, follow the manufacturers' instructions for timings.)

4 Knead in the fruits and nuts. Transfer the dough to an oiled bowl, cover with clear film and leave in a warm place for about 1½ hours, until the dough has doubled in size.

5 Grease two 450g/1lb loaf tins. Knock back the dough and knead lightly. Divide in half, form into loaves and place in the tins. Cover and leave in a warm place for about 30 minutes, until risen. Meanwhile, preheat the oven to 190°C/375°F/Gas 5.

6 Bake for 35–40 minutes, until well risen and sounding hollow when tapped underneath. Cool on a wire rack. Brush with honey while warm.

INDEX

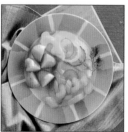